This book embodies the ﬁ... attempt to examine and an... composition of the Commo... ... . medieval parliament. It is the product of intensive research into the lives of the individual knights of the shire and parliamentary burgesses who sat in the first parliament of the reign of Henry VI and (for the most part) in many other parliaments of their day. The author has been able to show that the Lower House of parliament was already by that time far less abruptly divided in its social structure than has been hitherto supposed. He suggests that the "revolution" in the character of borough representation, which has for some time been recognised as mainly a feature of later fifteenth-century English political life, may be detected some time before the commotions of the Wars of the Roses complicated local politics and disturbed the parliamentary scene. He, therefore, regards its causes as being more social and economic than political. Although prefaced by a detailed inquiry into electoral processes in shire and borough, these important considerations form the kernel of the work. The author's findings are supported by evidence set out in alphabetically arranged biographical notes on all the knights of the shire and many of the burgesses elected in 1422, and these illuminate here and there some of the major political and military episodes of the Lancastrian period.

The constitutional and political crisis of 1422 and certain administrative difficulties, to which the untimely death of Henry V and the accession of the infant Henry VI gave rise, are specially treated, in particular where individual members of the Lower House were involved in them.

THE COMMONS IN THE
PARLIAMENT OF 1422

THE TAIT BEQUEST

The late James Tait, Professor of Ancient and Medieval History at the University of Manchester, 1902–1919, bequeathed one thousand pounds to be applied by the Manchester University Press to the publication of works of scholarship.

This is the first volume to be published under the terms of the Fund.

presented to

The International Commission for the History of Representative and Parliamentary Institutions.

(No. XIV)

THE COMMONS
IN THE PARLIAMENT OF
1422

English Society and Parliamentary Representation under the Lancastrians

by

J. S. ROSKELL

*Professor of Medieval History in
the University of Nottingham*

MANCHESTER UNIVERSITY PRESS

*Published by the
University of Manchester
at
The University Press
316–324, Oxford Road
Manchester 13
1954*

Made and Printed in Great Britain by Butler & Tanner Ltd., Frome and London

PREFACE

IN the early fifteenth century the Commons were occasionally described as being one single, the third, estate of the realm in parliament. Was their unity as an estate a political unity (suggested by the fact that they were the Lower House of parliament), or was it that and something more ? Was their social composition undergoing changes that further emphasised their unity as a political estate ? This is one of the most important questions, to which in this book I have tried to find some sort of answer. But the question of the social composition of the Lower House has a bearing on another important problem, as it seems to me. If the Commons, especially their still more significant element, the knights of the shire, were men of substance and influence, keen to sit in parliament as often as they could manage it, might this not simply suggest a capacity for some measure of independent collective action ? Might it not discourage at all events the notion that what such men were required to do in parliament was really of no very great importance there, or in the political life of the nation as a whole ? Were men of this type likely to have been generally content merely to sit ' as siphre doth in awgrym that noteth a place, and no thing availeth ', to use the words of a poem of 1399, *Mum and the Sothsegger*. The same passage here that derides those among the Commons who were such, suggests that there were some of their number who were by no means supine, or merely self-seeking, or in fear of their masters among the lords. As Professor J. G. Edwards has recently put one side of the case : ' That men of . . . [such] standing were prepared to be at the pains of repeatedly riding across England to serve as representatives in parliament is a notable fact, which scarcely supports the assumption that the part played by them at Westminster was a mere formality. Moreover, the payment of expenses to these representatives was evidently accepted by the local communities as an established and justified accessory of English government.'

It will be readily agreed that the historian of the medieval Commons works at a great disadvantage in comparison with him who treats of Tudor and later times. The rolls of the medieval parliaments disclose, directly, no details of proceedings outside the parliament house proper, and only refer to what was transacted even there if it was deemed to be worthy of record. Perhaps a Chancery clerk occasionally kept a journal of the Commons' doings. But even if so, none has survived. The Commons' own journals were not to begin until 1547. The veil is lifted somewhat by the account (based perhaps on a sort of journal) of some of the Commons' sessions during the Good Parliament of 1376 in the Anonimalle Chronicle of the abbey of St. Mary of York. But this is a unique contribution to our knowledge, the like of which is not supplied by any other medieval chronicle. Of all the Commons even the Anonimalle Chronicle only mentions their Speaker by name. The Paston correspondence gives merely glimpses of the Commons' doings from time to time and there is virtually nothing to put beside them from similar sources. In all this gloomy obscurity the individual knights of the shire and burgesses themselves are somewhat unsubstantial figures. Even what comes to light of the careers out of parliament of the more important of those who sat and stood in the chapter house or refectory of the abbey of Westminster is mainly derived from notices of them in the memoranda of one or another department of State or Household with which they came from time to time into contact in a variety of ways. Their lives can only be patchily described. Occasionally they show to our eyes, in the making of their wills, some aspects of their human personality ; but only here, at the point of death, are they ever likely to 'come alive'. John Michell, one of the citizens for London in 1422, was described in the records of the Brewers' Company as 'a good man and meke and softe to speke with'. Barring conventional remarks in monumental inscriptions, this is the only 'character' given anyone of the 1422 Commons that I have been able to discover. It is hardly a portrait.

I have tried to look steadily at the problem of parliamentary representation in the fifteenth century, and to see it whole, in its relation to the nature of later medieval English society. To achieve a systematic analysis of the Commons I have had, in the main, to limit my own original and detailed researches to a single parliament, the first parliament of Henry VI. There is, however, no particular reason to believe that the knights of the shire, citizens, and burgesses who represented their several communities on this and (in most cases) on many other occasions, were not typical of any nearly contemporary parliament. The parliament of 1422 is fortunately one for which all the names of the elected representatives are known (save those who came up from Dunwich). This was my main reason for choosing it, although I was influenced in making my choice by an awareness of the importance of some of the problems facing the parliament when it met, and of what it did in the course of its session. To study the parliamentary representation of a shire or group of shires over a period of years helps one to understand the short- and long-term effects, on local life especially, of family interests and of regional loyalties and tensions. But to use the 'horizontal' as distinct from the 'vertical' method, to take the county and borough returns across at one point, and analyse the composition of the Commons in a single parliament, perhaps produces results of greater interest; it admits of some sort of correlation of a knowledge of those who were elected, to the contemporary 'structure of politics', and to what is known of the doings of parliament during its session.

In an address given at the eighth Congrés Internationale des Sciences Historiques held at Zurich in 1938 Sir Maurice Powicke emphasised the need to study the history of the medieval English parliament in its relation to the nature of English society; and, because historians were being driven to consider the environment of parliament, he suggested that, 'the value of subsequent work on parliament lies not in explanation, but in description'. When this view was expressed much of my work of 'fact-finding' was completed; but I was heartened by it, as I had been by Sir Maurice Powicke's interest in my work when I went to Oxford and, as a research student, entered the Faculty of which he was then head. I had begun the work in my own university of Manchester under the direction of Professor E. F. Jacob, whose continuing help and advice it is beyond me to repay. I also owe great debts of gratitude to my former Oxford supervisor and tutor in Balliol College, Professor V. H. Galbraith, whose counsel was indispensable; to Mr. K. B. McFarlane and Miss M. McKisack, for the stimulus and help I have received from their published work relating to this subject, and for the personal assistance and guidance that they have both so generously given to me; to Professor J. G. Edwards for some important advice about particular aspects of the subject; and to Professor C. R. Cheney for being much interested in my work and encouraging me in it. To the custodians of libraries that I have worked in, I should like especially to thank Miss Hilda Lofthouse, Librarian of Chetham's Library in Manchester. I must thank Messrs. Longman for their permission to make full use of an article of mine in the *English Historical Review*, and the Editor of the *Bulletin of the Institute of Historical Research* for his permission to ' lift ' a few pieces from my two articles published in that periodical. I am most grateful to the Trustees of the Tait Memorial Fund of the University of Manchester for generously voting a subsidy to make the publication of this book possible. I am also grateful to Mr. T. L. Jones, the Secretary of the University Press, for his help. Lastly, but most importantly of all, I thank my mother and father, and my wife.

J. S. ROSKELL

THE UNIVERSITY OF NOTTINGHAM.

CONTENTS

TABLE OF ABBREVIATIONS USED IN REFERENCES

A. and N.H. Soc.	Archaeological and Natural History Society.
B.M.	British Museum.
C.C.R.	*Calendar of Close Rolls.*
C.Ch.R.	*Calendar of Charter Rolls.*
C.F.R.	*Calendar of Fine Rolls.*
Cal. Inq. p.m.	*Calendar of Inquisitions post mortem.*
C.P.R.	*Calendar of Patent Rolls.*
C. and W.A. and A.S.	Cumberland and Westmorland Antiquarian and Archaeological Society.
D.K.R.	*Reports of the Deputy Keeper of the Public Records.*
D.L. .	Duchy of Lancaster.
D.N.B.	*Dictionary of National Biography.*
E.E.T.S.	Early English Text Society.
E.H.R.	*English Historical Review.*
Hist. Mss. Comm.	Historical Manuscripts Commission.
K.R.	King's Remembrancer.
L.T.R.	Lord Treasurer's Remembrancer.
Miscell. Gen. et Herald	*Miscellanea Genealogica et Heraldica.*
N.S. .	New Series.
O.S. .	Old Series.
P.P.C.	*Proceedings and Ordinances of the Privy Council.*
P.R.O.	Public Record Office.
R.S. .	Rolls Series.
Rot. Parl. .	*Rotuli Parliamentorum.*
Statutes	Statutes of the Realm.
Test. Ebor.	*Testamenta Eboracensia.*
V.C.H.	*Victoria County History.*

PART ONE

CHAPTER I

THE SHIRE ELECTIONS

BY the time that Henry of Windsor came to the throne in 1422 parliament had been a distinct political and constitutional phenomenon for over a century and a half, in one form or another, and was by now something more than a realisation of the medieval doctrine of consent ; it had become a factor in government likely to stay in English constitutional life. It was the highest court of the realm and yet had features of which no inferior court could boast, for it was also a representative assembly. It was a court but a unique court, different and distinct from other courts, because— so common lawyers were thinking at the end of the fifteenth century—it represented all men, and, therefore, to it and to its acts every man was a party.

The parliament of conjoined estates in the form conceived by Edward I scarcely outlived the reign of his son. For soon after the deposition of Edward II the proctors of the inferior clergy virtually seceded from the parliamentary assembly, preferring to meet the financial demands of the Crown in their provincial convocations. By the beginning of Edward III's reign, however, the elected representatives of the secular communities of shire and borough had come to be considered an essential element in parliament's constitution. The contrast between them and those summoned by individual writs, the king's preference for dealing with them, especially in matters financial, as one group and not several groups, and the defection of the proctors of the lesser clergy, predetermined that the knights and burgesses should early realise a common political, and eventually constitutional, identity. The increasingly closer association with the Commons of the business of presenting petitions

Where references to the sources of biographical facts do not appear in the footnotes proper, they will be found in the biographical notes which, in the case of all the knights of the shire and many of the burgesses, have been supplied, alphabetically, in Part II.

I

of general import confirmed this tendency to consolidation : by 1363 they had already been allowed the services of a 'commun clerc' (*alias* ' *sub-clericus parliamenti* '). Edward III did occasionally resort to the device of separate negotiation with assemblies of merchants, but only for a time. By the end of the fourteenth century what came to be theoretically recognised in the fifteenth century was already implicit in the structure of parliament : parliament had come to be composed of but three estates of the realm, the lords spiritual, the lords temporal, and the elected commons. The last represented communities of different social importance and historical traditions, shires and boroughs ; they represented, in fact although not formally, different sectional interests in the nation, but, conscious of the need of corporate solidarity, they realised in parliament quite clearly their political identity as one estate of the realm. And yet, interestingly enough, the consciousness of the old ' gradus ' of knights of the shire, citizens, and burgesses inescapably persisted among the Commons themselves, even in that very institution which most clearly demonstrated (from 1376 onwards) the corporateness of the medieval Commons, their common speaker. He, until Tudor times, was invariably one of the knights of the shire.

One of the surest indications of the growing importance of the Commons as an integral part of the medieval English parliament is the increasing interest taken in the election of this more influential element of the Commons, the knights of the shire. The original Plantagenet intention to restrict the class from which the parliamentary knights were drawn to those who were ' milites gladio cincti ' had perforce, and for long, meant very little. It has been shrewdly observed by Sir Maurice Powicke that, in the term ' knight of the shire ', the word ' knight ' is sometimes not so important as the word ' shire '.[1] It is even doubtful, as Miss Kathleen Wood-Legh has said, whether more than a third of the county representatives in even the Model Parliament of 1295 had been belted knights. The demand for ' duo milites gladio cincti ' continued to appear irregularly down to 1377 in the summons to parliaments but regularly in those to parliaments in which the defence of the realm or the financial preliminaries of a foreign campaign were prominent on the agenda. Nevertheless, the pro-

---

[1] *Études présentées à la Commission Internationale pour l'Histoire des Assemblées d'États, L'Organisation corporative du Moyen Age à la fin de l'Ancien Régime*, III. 137.

vision for the payment of less than the normal daily allowance of parliamentary expenses in Edward II's reign to ' valetti ' elected as knights of the shire and the occasional concession, as for example in 1330 and 1372, specified in the writs of summons that representatives should be ' chivalers *ou serjeantz* ', is evidence of the official recognition that it was too much to expect members of the knightly class alone to bear the burden of representation.[1] By the end of Edward III's reign the main concern of the king had changed ; it had come to be that of attempting to insist that the Commons should collectively be primarily interested in the settlement of the king's business in parliament and in the discovery and expression there of the local attitude to governmental policy, and not individually in the exploitation of the opportunity a parliament afforded for the prosecution of their private concerns.

The end of a long period of comparative official indifference to the composition of the Commons came with a succession of formal measures designed to interfere in, or rather restrict, the choice of members. In 1372 statutory protest was made against the obstruction of the king's intentions in parliament resulting from the return of lawyers and against the occasional practice of sheriffs returning themselves. The protest against the return of sheriffs seems to have been framed with a view to ensuring the smooth running of local administration and not exclusively with the object of discovering the unbiased expression of the attitude of the communities of the shires to royal policy ; the ordinance of 1372 expressly insisted that the sheriffs should in the first place be regarded as ' communes Ministres au Poeple ' and in that capacity ' deivent demurer sur lour office pur droit faire a checuny '. This is not the first indication of a prejudice against the return of sheriffs ; as early as 1339 the Commons had asked that the writs of summons should specify that ' deux de mielx vauez chivalers des contez soient esluz et envoiez al preschein parlement pur la commune si qe nul de eux soit viscount ne oustre ministre ', and such a prohibition had henceforward been incorporated in the terms of the writ.[2]

---

[1] There is a full discussion of this and other related problems in Miss K. L. Wood-Legh, ' Sheriffs, Lawyers, and Belted Knights, in the Parliaments of Edward III ', *English Historical Review*, XLVI. 372 *et seq.* ; cf. W. Stubbs, *The Constitutional History of England* (Oxford, 1880), III, § 419, for variations of the form of the writs of summons requiring the return of elected representatives.

[2] *Rotuli Parliamentorum* (Record Commission), II. 104 ; *Statutes of the Realm*, I. 394 ; and cf. Stubbs, *loc. cit.*

Official prejudice against the return of interested lawyers had perhaps manifested itself, before it assumed statutory form in 1372, in the wording of the writs of summons of 1351, 1352, 1354, and 1355, which had declared against the return of *perlitatores, querelarum manutentores, aut ex huiusmodi questu viventes*. It would seem that Stubbs' observation on the ordinance of 1372 and its ruling that lawyers pursuing business in the king's courts were to be ineligible, is not a complete interpretation of the situation. The grounds for the request for their exclusion were that they ' procurent et font mettre plusours petitions en parlementz en nom des communes qe rien lour touche mes soulement les singulers persones ove queux ils sont demorez'. Stubbs insisted that the prejudice against lawyers was due to their preoccupation with their own business and failure to attend to that of parliament ; surely it is their appropriation of the device of the common petition for the rectification of private grievance that was being attacked.[1]

Such measures as these for the regulation of Commons' personnel were the legitimate concern of the Crown ; their object was to secure attention to what was parliament's proper business and function from the king's point of view. The instances of royal interference in the reign of Richard II were, however, less free from suspicion of unconstitutional action. The Lords Appellant of 1387 saw to it that the words which the king had inserted in the parliamentary writs of summons requiring the election of knights ' in debatis modernis magis indifferentes', perhaps in an effort to secure an unpacked parliament, should be withdrawn, and fresh writs were issued to the sheriffs.[2] One of the grounds for Richard's deposition was his interference with freedom of election to parliament two years before, in 1397.[3] Similarly Henry IV's exclusion of lawyers from the ' parliamentum indoctum ' of 1404 met with such serious objection as to preclude a repetition of the manoeuvre.[4] Henceforward the Lancastrian régime, if the absence of openly voiced grievance may be so interpreted, seems to have been characterised by a singular restraint from direct interference with, and undue influence on, the elections of knights of the shire. During the first half of the fifteenth century there was an increased interest being taken in the methods of election and the subject of electoral discipline,

---

[1] Noted by H. L. Gray in his book, *The Influence of the Commons on Early Legislation*, 344.   [2] *Lords' Report, On the Dignity of a Peer*, IV. 725–6.
[3] *Rot. Parl.*, III. 420a.   [4] *Lords' Report*, IV. 792.

but the Lancastrian statutes affecting the return of the knights of Parliament were designed to secure not the return of members from a particular section of the community of the shire or the exclusion of what in the king's eyes were undesirable elements, but freedom of election in accordance with its local interpretation. In the Good Parliament of 1376 a petition had demanded that representatives be elected in future from the better folk of the shires (*les meillours Gentz des ... Countees*) ; the official attitude, exemplified in the response to the petition, had been that knights of the shire should be elected by the common assent of the whole county.[1] To safeguard this common assent being elicited seems to have been the main concern of Lancastrian legislation and policy.

Lancastrian electoral legislation was dual in its intentions and effect ; it was increasingly directed towards determining and delimiting the constitution of electoral personnel, defining a ' plenus comitatus ', with a view to securing freedom of election by common assent, and eliminating more accidental influences, for example, corruption on the part of the sheriff in the conduct of elections in the shire court or in the actual process of making the return of the results. The statute of 1406 [2] was expressly meant to guard against ' affection ' on the part of the sheriff and any resultant undue election of knights of the shire ; as the complementary statute of 1410 pointed out, it had been passed ' en conservacion de les franchises et libertees de l'election des chivalers des countees usez parmy tout vostre Roialme '.[3] It provided that the time and place of parliament's assembling were to be proclaimed at the next shire court held after livery of the writ of summons, and that then the election was to be proceeded with ' en plein countee ', with the assistance of all those present ' si bien sueters duement summonez pour cell cause, come autres '. Subsequent parliamentary writs of summons laid similar emphasis on the requirement of free election in a full shire court with their stipulation that the choice of knights be made ' libere et indifferenter per illos qui proclamacioni huiusmodi interfuerint '.[4] What was new about the provisions of the 1406 statute was not the insistence on free election in a full county court, however, but the check on the validity of the sheriff's return

---

[1] *Rot. Parl.*, II. 355.
[2] *ibid.*, III. 601 ; *Statutes of the Realm*, II. 156 (Statute 7 Hen. IV, c. XV).
[3] *Rot. Parl.*, III. 641 ; *Statutes*, II. 162 (Statute 11 Hen. IV, c. 1).
[4] e.g. *Lords' Report*, IV. 802.

B

as arranged for in the indenture which was henceforward to be drawn up ' dessoutz les sealx de toutz ceux qi eux eslisent et tacchez au dit brief du parlement '.

Before 1406, the return of the writ of summons and the answer to it, consisting of no more than a simple brief endorsement of the writ itself, was made theoretically to the king in parliament. Afterwards the return was made to the Chancery, that is, in practice, to the clerk of the parliament or his deputy, both of them Chancery officials. Sometimes one or the other saw fit to record on either the writ or the indenture the name of the person responsible for their delivery. Occasionally the sheriff himself, or it might be his clerk, his under-sheriff, or his cursitor, handed in his return. Not infrequently one of the burgesses-elect might be entrusted with the job of tendering to the clerk of the parliament the return for his whole shire ; the 1422 returns for the joint bailiwicks of Nottinghamshire and Derbyshire, and of Somerset and Dorset, and for the single counties of Worcestershire, Hampshire, and Cumberland, were handed in respectively by one of the parliamentary burgesses for Nottingham, Bridport, Worcester (in this case the clerk of the peace for the county), Southampton, and Carlisle.[1] Now and then, one of the shire notables with professional connexions in London might make himself responsible for the delivery of the returns : the Cornish returns in 1419 were given in to the clerk of the parliament by William Richards ' de Furnyvalesyn ', not himself elected either as knight or burgess ;[2] those for Worcestershire, in the following year, by the then ' custos rotulorum ' for the county, John Wode, described in the note of delivery as ' commorans in medio templo ' ;[3] in 1427 the returns for Devon, Cornwall, Warwickshire, and Shropshire, were respectively submitted by four apprentices-at-law, only one of whom, as citizen-elect for Exeter, was himself returned.[4]

The method of return by indenture, as provided for in the statute of 1406, survived the Lancastrian dynasty, and the diplomatic form of the documents recording the electoral process did not after 1461 undergo fundamental alteration. The phraseology of the writ of summons, and consequently that of the indenture of return when it repeated it, might reiterate the terms of the provisions of statutes

---

[1] P.R.O., C.219/13/1.   [2] *ibid.*, 12/3.   [3] *ibid.*, 12/4.
[4] *ibid.*, 13/5 ; respectively by John Shapley, John Polrudan, William (or Robert) Welden, and Richard Blyke.

dealing with parliamentary personnel and the conduct of elections ; this was so, for example, with the franchisal statute passed in the parliament of 1429–30 or the statute of 1445 which insisted that, for the future, knights of the shire should be notable knights or else such notable squires or gentlemen of birth as could support the estate of knighthood, and not men of the degree of yeoman or beneath.[1] But, allowing for these alterations in verbal detail, the sheriffs' returns to the first of Henry VI's parliaments were typical of the Lancastrian period after 1406.

In 1422 the return made by a sheriff of the result of a county election had generally come to consist of two documents, the endorsed original writ of summons and the indenture certifying the correctness of the election. The sheriff's endorsement of the writ normally contained his name and a brief statement of the outcome of the election, along with a reference for details of the execution of the writ to the accompanying indenture of return. The endorsement might, however, merely run : ' Executio istius brevis patet in quibusdam indenturis huic brevi consutis.' The indenture stated the place and date of its composition, that is, where and when the county court making the election had met. In some cases the county court did not always meet in the customary place for its sessions, even for such an important event as a parliamentary election : the Buckinghamshire elections, normally held at Aylesbury, were made at Newport Pagnell in 1423 ; [2] usually made at Chelmsford, the Essex elections were held in the same year at Stratford Langthorn ; [3] in 1422 the Hertfordshire elections were made in a shire court which met at Cheshunt ; [4] the returns for Middlesex to Henry VI's first parliament were dated at Osilston,[5] to that of 1425 at Brentford,[6] in 1435 at Stony Cross,[7] and in 1437 again at Brentford ; [8] the Kentish elections, normally at Rochester, were in 1425 and 1429 held at Canterbury ; [9] the Berkshire county court, which usually met at Grandpont, just across the Thames from Oxford, for the parliamentary elections in 1432 was convened at Abingdon ; [10] the elections for the county palatine of Lancaster were most often held in the shire court at Lancaster, but in 1413 and 1427 the county court met at Wigan, in April 1421 and 1423 at Croston, and in 1426 at Preston.[11]

---

[1] *Lords' Report*, IV. 877, 913, 920, 924, etc.   [2] P.R.O., C.219/13/2.
[3] *ibid.*   [4] *ibid.*, 13/1.   [5] *ibid.*   [6] *ibid.*, 13/3.
[7] *ibid.*, 14/5.   [8] *ibid.*, 15/1.   [9] *ibid.*, 13/3 ; 14/1.   [10] *ibid.*, 14/3.
[11] *ibid.*, 11/1, 13/5 ; 12/5, 13/2, 13/4.

Drawn up as between the sheriff on the one hand and a number (not *all* as required by the terms of the 1406 statute) of those who had been present at the county court on the other, the indenture went on to state that the election of the shire-knights had been made in accordance with the writ of summons, usually in terms which echoed the formalised phraseology of the writ, certified the method of election as made ' libere et indifferenter ex unanimi assensu ', and affirmed the delegation to the knights-elect of the customary ' plena et sufficiens potestas ' to bind themselves and the community of their shire to what was ordained in parliament, again in accordance with the requirements of the writ of summons. The indenture usually ended with a statement to the effect that the parties to it had apposed their seals individually to testify to its validity.

If a brief summary of the results of the elections, both of the knights of the shire and the parliamentary burgesses from . the returning boroughs within the bailiwick, was not made on the dorse of the original writ of summons, a separate schedule comprising a simple list of names of the knights- and burgesses-elect might be sent in by the sheriff, along with the original writ and the indenture of return from the shire court and the borough authorities. This separate schedule of names might or might not contain the names of those who were prepared to act as ' manucaptores ' or sureties for the individual appearance in parliament of those elected. By the fifteenth century when attendance in parliament of elected representatives was no longer regarded as generally burdensome, these sureties may be regarded as a survival of little or no significance.[1] In the case of a joint bailiwick of two adjacent shires (eighteen of the

[1] In some instances it is certain that the names of sureties were not even the names of actual persons. The rhyming names of the ' manucaptores ' who went surety in couples for the individual knights of the shire and burgesses-elect of Staffordshire in 1422 (C.219/13/1) are obviously bogus : John Hunt and John Best, Robert Swan and Richard Rest, John Koo and John Roo, Thomas Short and William Stort, Henry Sprot and John Stot, Robert Brown and Gilbert Dun. The surnames of the sureties for the knights and burgesses returned for Wiltshire in 1433 are an even more striking comment upon the needlessness of returning the names of sureties at all ; strung together they make up the pious wish : ' God save alle this faire companye ande gyffe theym grace weel for to spede for ffayn wold they bee ryght mery. They been ryght mery thus too pray hyt hys nede [*sic*]. Godde thatte alle this worlde ganne make ande for usse dyed apon thee roode tree save usse alle ' (*ibid.*, 14/4). As Stubbs observes (*Constitutional History*, III, § 424), ' after the act of 1406 the importance of the manucaption was much diminished, the names of the electors marked on the indenture of return being a sufficient warrant for the responsibility of the persons elected '.

thirty-seven parliamentary shires were jointly administered) only one original writ of summons was directed to the sheriff. Though separate indentures were returned for each shire of his dual bailiwick, the bare result of the elections in both shires was communicated to the clerk of the parliament either on the dorse of the original writ or on one single schedule.[1]

There is no reason to believe that the determination as to who should attest and seal the indenture of return lay with any but the sheriff; and the number of shire-court suitors who figured as attestors seems to have been left very much to his discretion. The number of attestors varied from shire to shire, and in a single shire from election to election, but there is no more cause to think that the actual electoral body varied in number substantially from one election to another than there is to suppose that the named attestors were the only electors, much less that they were as a body deputed by the county court to make the election on behalf of the whole shire. The attestors may have been, and in all probability were, the more influential element of the ' communitas comitatus ', but neither theoretically nor in practice is it likely that they were themselves solely responsible for the election, the validity of which they were merely sponsoring. They may, of course, be presumed to have been participants in, and parties to, the act of election, but in the indenture of return their actual nomination is merely for the purpose of certifying the return and attesting the sheriff's correct administration of electoral procedure in accordance with statutory provisions. The point it is necessary to make is that the number of attestors need bear no relation to the numerical constitution of the electoral body as assembled in the county court for the purpose of making the return of the knights of the shire. There is no reason to doubt that the attestors were a minority selected by the sheriff, on the score of their local importance as the more influential magnates or notables of the shire, in order to ratify the election and satisfy Chancery of the bona fide nature of the return. They need not for obvious reasons be the same men from election to election, although in actual fact a great many of them were. The same men would not always find it convenient to attend, their influence on

---

[1] Early in Richard II's reign it was already customary·for the knights of the shire and burgesses to be called by name at the beginning of the parliamentary session, presumably by the clerk of the parliament, using the sheriffs' returns as the prototype of the later ' Crown Office Lists ' (*Rot. Parl.*, III. 55, 71, 98, 122, 149, 184).

the course of the election being perhaps exerted in their absence through friends and neighbours. A man's inclusion among the attestors may be taken as evidence of his presence at the election ; his failure to be included did not necessarily imply his absence. In other words, there is no reason to doubt that such phrases as often follow the list of names of attesting electors represent the facts and are not merely a concession to legal formality. The Northumbrian elections of 1407 were, for example, described as made by the attestors and ' alii sectatores et fideles domini regis comitatus ',[1] those of Warwickshire in the same year by the attestors and ' multi alii sectatores probi et legales homines de comitatu '.[2] In 1422 the Cornish shire court was attended by ' plures alii de dicto comitatu tunc ibidem presentes ' in addition to those who sealed the indenture of return ; [3] the attestors of the Kentish indenture of return to the same parliament were described as being ' ex illis qui in comitatu predicto presentes exstiterunt ' ; [4] the Surrey and Sussex elections were made by the attestors ' et plures alii de comitatu ' ; [5] the Nottinghamshire knights were chosen ' post consideracionem totius comitatus '.[6] The case of the Northumbrian elections to Henry VI's first parliament provides an interesting exception to the apparent general participation of the whole county court in the choice of the knights of the shire ; the description of the election as being made by the fourteen named attestors and by ' plures per totam communitatem eiusdem comitatus ad eligendum duos milites . . . nominati ex assensu eiusdem communitatis ',[7] points to something in the nature of a delegated electoral function, but this procedure does not seem to have been anything but abnormal even in Northumberland, assuming that this language may be taken at its face value.

Evidence that the attestors of the indenture of return were not a small body deputed for the sake of convenience by the county court to perform the actual function of election, in short that the shire election was not a sort of election ' per compromissionem ', is also afforded by those indentures which supply an unusually big list of named indenture-sealers and provide a safer indication of what constituted the real total electoral personnel. In the indenture recording the return of the Oxfordshire knights to the Gloucester parliament of 1407 the attestors numbered only 14 ; at the elections for the same county to the next parliament, there were, however,

[1] P.R.O., C.219/10/4.   [2] *ibid.*   [3] *ibid.*, 13/1.   [4] *ibid.*
[5] *ibid.*   [6] *ibid.*   [7] *ibid.*

in the neighbourhood of 200 attestors named.[1]   The Gloucestershire
sealers in 1422 were no more than 42 ; in the indenture of five
years later they numbered 188.[2]   The Norfolk and Suffolk elections
in 1435 were attested respectively by 124 and 100 suitors, but in
1422 the sealers of the indentures of return had been respectively
only 31 and 16.[3]   These numerical fluctuations speak loud against
any theory of the delegation or drastic restriction of the electoral
capacity of the freemen of the shire.   Even in the case of the Yorkshire elections, where the usual statement in the indenture of return
is that the choice of the shire-knights was made ' ex unanimi assensu
et consensu ' by the attorneys of those lords of the franchises who
were the ' sectatores communes ad comitatum Eboracensem de
sex septimanis in sex septimanas ' (in 1422 these were enumerated
as the archbishop of York, the earls of Northumberland and Westmorland and the Earl Marshal, the Barons Bromflete, Mellalieu,
and Graystoke, Sir Henry Percy, and Sir Robert Roos [4]), there is
no reason to think that they alone were responsible for the elections
to the exclusion of the more normal freeholding element in the
shire court.   The ordinary freeholders are not named as attestors
until 1432 when, in conformity with the requirements of the
franchisal statute passed in the 1429–30 parliament, eleven ' probi
et legales homines ', resident in the shire and worth 40 shillings
a year clear from free tenements in it, in addition to the attorneys of
the ' sectatores communes ' sealed the indenture of return.   In 1435
the Yorkshire indenture was attested by fifteen knights, including two
of the original ' sectatores communes ' themselves, and seventeen
esquires.   The returns to the next parliament of 1437 were again
attested by the attorneys of the lords of the franchises (in this instance
these were the archbishop of York, the earl of Northumberland,
the countesses of Westmorland and Cambridge, the Barons Graystoke and Hilton, the widows of the Lords Roos, Mellalieu, and
Scales, and of Sir John Etton, and Sir Thomas Metham and Sir
Robert Roos) but twelve free tenants worth 40 shillings and
more also attested.[5]   The next extant Yorkshire indenture of
election, that of 1442, is only distinctive in the number of its

---

[1] *ibid.*, 10/4, 10/5 ; Stubbs, admittedly basing his view on evidence from
Prynne's Register, is wrong in saying that ' the number of persons who seal the
indenture is in every case comparatively small . . .   The number of names rarely
if ever exceeds forty ' (*Constitutional History*, III, § 421).

[2] *ibid.*, 13/1 ; 13/5.   [3] *ibid.*, 14/5 ; 13/1.
[4] *ibid.*, 13/1.   [5] *ibid.*, 14/3 ; 14/5 ; 15/1.

attestors who were in the neighbourhood of 450 strong (no mention was made of the attorneys of the ' sectatores communes ', two of whom, Ralph Lord Graystoke and Sir Thomas Metham, head the list of attestors).[1]   This is a very unusual number of named attestors to find in an indenture.   It may be that the size of the county ought to be taken into account and Yorkshire figures regarded as exceptional ; in which case it might be conjectured that the number of actual electors in smaller shires would be proportionately less. It is interesting to note, however, that in a relatively small county like Huntingdonshire the freeholders who composed the electoral body could on occasion number as many as about 500.   This is the evidence of a petition presented to the king alleging certain irregularities at the elections held at Huntingdon before the meeting of parliament in November 1450 ;[2] 124 freeholders of the shire complained that though, along with ' a three hundred moo good comuners af the same shire ', they made their nomination and choice in ' pleyn shire ' of two ' gentilmen of youre honorable Houshold namyd in youre chekir [Exchequer] rolle ', another seventy ' freholders comoners ' appeared ' be labour of dyvers of gentilmen of other shires and of youre said shire of Huntingdon ' and named Henry Gimber to be one of the knights of the shire, although he was not ' of gentell berth accordyng to youre saide Wryt '.   Despite the fact that among these seventy, though they included ' receants ' (residents) as well as ' foreigners ', there were few who contributed to the knights' expenses, the under-sheriff suspended the scrutiny of voters as to their income from freehold in the county after only forty-seven supporters of Gimber had been examined.   Gimber's party then would not allow the petitioners ' to be examyned and to geve voys ', although there were some of them who possessed freehold worth 20 marks, and although together they made up a clear majority.   For ' dread of the . . . inconveniences that was likely to be done of manslaughter ' and out of respect for the king's peace, the petitioners had then departed but, being in doubt of the outcome, saw fit to complain.   It may be pleaded that these 494 electors in all made up a number in consideration of which the disturbed political atmosphere of the autumn of 1450 ought to be taken into account.   There is, however,

---

[1] P.R.O., C.219/15/2.

[2] W. Prynne, *A brief Register, Kalendar, and Survey of the several kinds of all parliamentary writs* (4 pts., London, 1659–64), III. 156–9, noted by Stubbs, *loc. cit.*

no gainsaying the fact that such instances as these go to prove that county elections were in practice not left by the whole assembly of the shire court to the select coterie who attested the indenture of return. The only conclusion is that the provision of the 1406 statute that the indenture certifying the election of knights be attested ' desoutz les sealx de toutz ceux qi eslisent ' was never literally observed.

It might be argued that this evidence for the view that the election of knights of parliament was normally accomplished in a formally-held, open, and full shire-court is, when not based on the variable phraseology of the indentures of return, merely circumstantial and fragmentary. The reasons, however, set out in the common petition of 1429,[1] which resulted in the restriction of the franchise, point to elections being conducted in shire courts that had become too full. So full, at any rate, as to upset formality and proper procedure. The danger of rioting had arisen because the shire elections ' en plusours countees d'Engleterre ' had been made ' par trop graunde et excessive nombre des gentz demurrantz deinz mesmes les countees, dount le greindre partie estoit par gentz sinoun de petit avoir ou de null value, dount chescun pretende d'avoir vois equivalent, quaunt au tielx elections fair, ov le pluis vaillantz chivalers ou esquiers demurrantz deinz mesmes les countees '. It was asked and granted that for the future elections should be made only by those who enjoyed a clear income of 40 shillings a year or more from freehold land, that these should be indwellers of the shire, and that the knights elected should be similarly resident there. This, the property qualification for electors apart, was after all only a reiteration of the provisions made in the electoral statute of 1413, which had insisted that knights of parliament should be ' receantz et demurrantz a temps de l'election es countees ou ils sont esluz ' and that they should be elected ' par chivalers, esquiers, et communes des countees ou ils sont issint esluz et nemy en autre manere '.[2] The important points made by the 1413 statute were that the elections were not to be influenced ' par voice, ne l'assent, ne maundement, de ceux qi sont absentz ', and that electors and elected were for the future to qualify by residence in the county on the day of the issue of the writ of summons ; in other words, there must be no ' moving-in ' just for an election,

---

[1] *Rot. Parl.*, IV. 350.
[2] *ibid.*, 8 ; *Statutes*, II. 170 (Statute 1 Hen. V, c. 1).

a likely manœuvre when elections were spaced out in time because county courts met each on its own appointed day. The vital innovations in actual electoral procedure made by the 1429 statute were partly the result of the imposition on voters of the property qualification of 40 shillings' income from freehold. The sheriff for the future was authorised to examine all electors on the Gospels as to their ability to fulfil this financial and tenurial condition. But the majority principle was also now recognised, explicitly for the first time in this connexion : nominees having the backing of the greater number of 40-shilling freeholders were to be returned.

Generally speaking, cases of infringement of existing statutory electoral regulations were few and far between, so far as is known. There were, for example, far fewer cases in the whole Lancastrian period of a sheriff being returned as a knight of the shire during his term of office, either by himself or by another sheriff in a different county, than in the reign of Richard II, when there were at least seventeen occurrences of the offence. Some notable exceptions were provided, however, by the Speakers of the parliaments of April and November 1414 and September 1427. The first of these was Sir Walter Hungerford, sheriff of Dorset and Somerset, returned as knight of the shire for Wilts ; [1] the Speaker in the next parliament was Thomas Chaucer, knight of the shire for Oxfordshire and sheriff of Hampshire ; [2] John Tyrell, who was Speaker in 1427, had then been returned for Herts when holding the joint shrievalty of Norfolk and Suffolk. [3] In 1420 we find the sheriff of Gloucester elected as one of the Herefordshire representatives. [4] To the same parliament Lewis John esquire was elected for Essex ; when the return was formally drafted he was sheriff of the county although his appointment to that office took place eleven days after the actual meeting of the shire court. [5] With this doubtful exception these few cases of election of a sheriff as knight of the shire took place outside his own bailiwick ; the phenomenon of the self-returning sheriff is no longer in evidence. A far more common offence against electoral statute law was the infringement of the requirements that both those elected and their electors should be

---

[1] P.R.O., *Lists and Indexes*, IX : *List of Sheriffs*, 123 ; *Official Return of Members of Parliament* (1878), I. 282.
[2] *List of Sheriffs*, 55 ; *Official Return*, 284.
[3] *List of Sheriffs*, 87 ; *Official Return*, 313.
[4] *List of Sheriffs*, 50 ; *Official Return*, 294.
[5] *List of Sheriffs*, 44 ; *Official Return*, 294 ; P.R.O., C.219/12/4.

resident in the shire when the writ of summons was issued. The stipulation regarding electors was in all probability not observed, for example, when the sheriff of Cambridge and Huntingdon, Robert Scot, was present at the Bedfordshire elections to the parliament of December 1421 ; [1] or when the sheriff of Hereford, Guy Whitington, assisted at the Gloucestershire elections in 1425 ; [2] or when Sir Thomas Gresley, sheriff of Nottingham and Derby, attended in 1427 the Staffordshire elections at which his own son was returned as one of the shire-knights. [3] One or the other of the two regulations as to residence of electors and elected was similarly not infrequently contravened and honoured in the breach. Cases in point were the elections for Bedfordshire and Huntingdon-shire in 1419 ; Sir Thomas Waweton and John Enderby were elected as knights of the shire for the former county and twelve days later attested the elections at Huntingdon when the first two men to seal the Bedfordshire indenture of return, Roger Hunt and Robert Scot, were themselves elected. [4]

Despite the lively political tempo throughout the whole of Henry VI's reign, there were very few disputed parliamentary elections in the shires that we are aware of. It is noteworthy, therefore, that in 1427 and 1429 there took place no less than four disputed elections and that three of them were made the subject of judicial inquiry ; and it is important to realise that in all probability the submission of the petition which resulted in the 1429 statute was conditioned by the knowledge of the facts which these inquiries disclosed, facts which in these instances pointed to flagrant contempt of the already existing electoral statutes, whose provisions this new statute was careful to reiterate. [5] The disputes over the four elections in question arose either as a result of undue influence on the part of the sheriff, or as a result of failure to conform to the existing statutory requirements touching the residence of both the electors and the knights of the shire elected, or as a result of a combination of both forms of illegality.

The first of these four disputed elections was in reality due to an improper return of an unconstitutional election. On 25 August 1427 Sir Thomas Gresley of Drakelowe in Derbyshire, acting in his capacity as sheriff of Nottingham, unduly returned Hugh Wyloughby and Ralph Makerell as knights of the shire, despite

---

[1] P.R.O., C.219/12/6.   [2] *ibid.*, 13/3.   [3] *ibid.*, 13/5.   [4] *ibid.*, 12/3.
[5] *Rot. Parl.*, IV. 350a ; *Statutes*, II. 243 (Statute 8 Hen. VI, c. VII).

the fact that the writ of summons authorising the election had not been delivered either to Gresley or his subordinates and that the suitors of the county court had not been summoned either on that occasion or in advance. The sheriff had then, moreover, ignored the usual procedure of return by indenture and had made the return to Chancery merely under his own seal 'in contempt of the King and to the manifest impediment of free election and against the form of the statutes'. In accordance with the statute of 1410, which provided that such cases of irregular election should be met with an inquiry by the justices of assize, the imposition of a fine of £100 on the sheriff where default was proved, and the loss of their wages by the unduly returned knights, writs were issued on 12 February 1428 to the justices of assize authorising an inquiry into the infringement of the statute of 1406. The inquest was taken at Nottingham on 27 February 1428 and a jury deposed to the effect that the return had been illegally made.[1] This was a full month after the beginning of the second session of the parliament. Sir Thomas Gresley's case must have prompted the common petition,[2] presented almost certainly in the course of this second session, asking that sheriffs and knights of the shire in such circumstances should not now or in future be 'forbarrez et oustez de lour response encountre tielx enquestes d'office prisez devaunt les ditz justices', but should be afforded opportunity to traverse the sworn verdict, and should not be 'endamaged' until convicted according to form of law. This request was granted, but not the demand that the findings of any inquests then proceeding before justices of assize and involving any sheriff or knights over the recent elections should be set aside. It may be conjectured that Sir Thomas Gresley's son, Sir John, then serving as knight of the shire for Staffordshire, worked to achieve this only partially successful result.

The three disputed elections which immediately preceded the assembling of the Westminster parliament on 22 September 1429 were those held in the counties of Cumberland, Buckingham, and Huntingdon. Originally summoned to meet on 13 October, the session had been later 'abbreviated' to begin three weeks earlier, and it was this alteration which made possible the falsified return for Cumberland. The shire court met at Carlisle on 30 August to obey the first writ of summons and Sir William Legh and Thomas de la More were elected. Then came along the second

---

[1] P.R.O., C.219/13/5.   [2] *Rot. Parl.*, IV. 331b.

writ summoning parliament to meet at the earlier date. The county court was not customarily bound to meet again during the period between the receipt of this second writ and the date of parliament's assembling, and the sheriff, Sir Christopher Moresby, took it upon himself to make out another return in response to the second writ without consulting the regularly constituted shire-court at all ; at another time and place he procured the substitution of one Thomas Parr for Sir William Legh and returned him along with De la More in an apparently normally attested indenture.[1] Parliament had only been in session six days when a royal letter patent was issued ordering an inquest in Cumberland into the breach of statute-law committed by the sheriff, accompanied by a demand for information touching the date and place of the first of the two elections, the names of those who attended, and the facts of the case generally. This prompt action was not, however, followed up and the justices of assize were being commissioned to hold further inquiry as late as 10 July 1430.[2]

It is not surprising that the act of 1429, in regulating the conduct of future parliamentary elections in the shires, imposed a deterrent to unlawful action on the part of the sheriff in the shape of a year's imprisonment without possibility of release on bail, in addition to the already existing provision for a £100 fine, because the disputed Buckinghamshire election was similarly the outcome of a false return on the part of the sheriff. The indenture of election, duly attested on 31 August 1429 by 83 names, was formally returned by the sheriff, Sir Thomas Waweton, as certifying the election of Sir John Cheyne and Walter Strickland.[3] Subsequently acting on a royal writ of 24 September[4] authorising an inquiry, the justices of assize found, by sworn inquest held promptly at Aylesbury before parliament was a week old, that the return had been made merely on the sheriff's authority. The depositions of the jurors disclosed that on 31 August 1429 the suitors to the shire court, 129 of whom are named in the finding of the inquest, had elected John Hampden of Hampden and Andrew Sperlyng. There can be little doubt that if not aristocratic unrest at least grave political discontents were behind these cases of illegality on the part of the sheriffs involved.[5]

---

[1] P.R.O., C.219/14/1.　　　　　　　[2] *C.P.R.*, *1429–36*, 40–1.
[3] P.R.O., C.219/14/1.　　　　　　　[4] *C.P.R.*, *1429–36*, 39, 41.
[5] Sir Thomas Waweton was appointed sheriff of Bedford and Buckingham on 4 November 1428. During the summer trouble had apparently been brewing between John Mowbray, duke of Norfolk, and John Holand, earl of Huntingdon. On 7 July 1428 they had been ordered by the Chancellor in a Council meeting

The Huntingdonshire disputed election raised different issues, but probably the same political influences had been at work at Huntingdon as at Aylesbury in view of the fact that Waweton, the sheriff of Bedford and Buckingham, was implicated in the Huntingdon affair too. On 20 August 1429, Sir Thomas had been present at the county court at Huntingdon and had been the first-named of those who attested the indenture, which falsely certified what was

not to sit on the commission of the peace in Bedfordshire, and the sessions there were postponed for a fortnight (*P.P.C.*, III. 302). On 22 August there had been public disturbances between the two lords, so much so that the duke of Gloucester hurried out from London, spent the night at St. Albans, and on the following day pushed on into Bedfordshire ' ut intelligeret finem et causam tantae indignationis et vindictae ' ; but Norfolk would not meet the Protector, who returned forthwith to London (J. Amundesham, *Annales Monasterii Sancti Albani*, ed. T. H. Riley [Rolls Series], I. 25). Apart from the fact that Bedfordshire, the scene of these particular troubles, was part of his joint-bailiwick, there is other evidence to suggest that Waweton was almost inevitably implicated in them. The earl of Huntingdon had married the widowed countess of March from whose dower-manor of Ryhall Waweton drew an annuity of 40 marks ; the earl's first cousin was wife to John Lord Tiptoft, a kinsman and connexion of Waweton's ; and the earl had strong personal links with some of the Bedfordshire magnates (Sir John Cornwall was his stepfather, and John, the son and heir of Reginald Lord Grey of Ruthyn, was his brother-in-law). It may have been in the Holand interest that Waweton had acted two days before the earl's dispute with Norfolk came to a head, when on 20 August he was present at the county court at Huntingdon along with many ' visitors ' from Bedfordshire, by whom the sheriff was there overborne into holding the parliamentary election which was four weeks later held again, on this occasion with different results. In the second election, one of the knights returned was a member of the duke of Norfolk's counsel, Roger Hunt. The Bedfordshire elections were held by Waweton on 5 September. In the meantime he had held the Buckinghamshire elections on 31 August. Two Lincoln's Inn lawyers, John Hampden and Andrew Sperling, were elected. But sometime between then and the beginning of parliament on 22 September, Waweton illegally substituted two others, solely on his own authority : Sir John Cheyne and Walter Strickland. The choice of Strickland again suggests the Holand interest being exercised, perhaps indirectly, for he was master forester to John Lord Arundel, who was first summoned to parliament in this year and was later to have his claim to the earldom of Arundel contested by the duke of Norfolk ; Lord Arundel had been the ward of Sir John Cornwall (stepfather to the earl of Huntingdon) and had become his son-in-law. Even more interesting is Waweton's substitution of Sir John Cheyne of Chesham, for this man was a notorious supporter of Lollards and Lollard notions. Both Sir John and his younger brother had been implicated in Oldcastle's rebellion in 1414. Two Buckinghamshire clergymen, both holding livings under Cheyne patronage, were examined before Convocation in July 1428 for heresy, and the vicar of Chesham was alleged to have been in touch with Ralph Mungyn who was also then arraigned for asserting the unrightfulness of the papal crusade against the Hussites and for holding communistic ideas. The recrudescence of Lollardy in these years was probably assisted by the repercussion on English opinion of the efforts to suppress the Bohemian heretics by force, and the diversion to Normandy in 1429 of the troops that Cardinal Beaufort had retained as papal legate later described as an irregular election to have been correctly made.[1] He had property in Huntingdonshire and had represented the county in no less than seven parliaments himself, but it is more than doubtful whether in view of his tenure of office as sheriff of Bedford and Buckingham he had now been able to comply strictly with the terms of the statute of 1413, which insisted on residence at the date of issue of the writ of summons as an electoral qualification.[2] In any case, it was not the first time he had contravened the letter of the statute : to take only three instances, when himself elected for Bedfordshire in 1413 and 1419, and when previously sheriff of Bedford and Buckinghamshire in 1416 he had been present at the Huntingdonshire elections.[3] But that is by the way. The objection made to the first Huntingdonshire return in 1429 was that the election had been made in a county court attended by intruders from Bedfordshire, one important exception being Sir William Malory, who was a Cambridgeshire knight ; in short, that the electors were not resident in Huntingdonshire, and that, moreover, the result of the election had been that one of the knights of the shire returned, William Waweton, was not a resident or even a possessor of estates in the county at all (Robert Stonham, the other knight, was a resident). There was no need for protest to be left until parliament assembled ; it could be and was registered locally at the next normal meeting of the shire court four weeks later, on 17 September, five days before parliament was summoned to meet : Sir Nicholas Stukeley and thirteen others, esquires and

may in part have been encouraged by the need for a gesture of conciliation, for political Lollardy was much astir. There is no doubt of Sir John Cheyne's religious sympathies. The family was undoubtedly suspected of complicity in the Lollard rising in the counties of the southern midlands in the spring of 1431, which had its headquarters seemingly in Abingdon where the bailiff was a ringleader. Because on 19 June 1431 Sir John's arrest was ordered and his manors of Grove in Chesham and Drayton Beauchamp were searched for hidden manuscripts and arms (*C.P.R.*, *1429–36*, 153), and both he and his brother were imprisoned in the Tower for nearly seven weeks (*C.C.R.*, *1429–35*, 89). If it be remembered that in 1425, when Waweton had been Speaker, there had been one or two petitions presented by the Commons that had a distinct Lollard flavour about them, it is hard to resist the thought that the Buckinghamshire false return of 1429 may have been at least complicated by Lollard activities. Waweton was a retainer of the late earl of March whose cousin, Sir John Mortimer, executed for treason in 1424, was tainted with heresy. In this connexion the pseudonym ' of Wigmoreland in Wales ' assumed by Jack Sharp, the Abingdon Lollard leader, is reminiscent of Mortimer associations with that part of the Welsh march.

[1] P.R.O., C.219/14/1.   [2] *Rot. Parl.*, IV. 8a ; *Statutes*, II. 170.
[3] P.R.O., C.219/11/4 ; 12/3 ; 11/8.

'homines generosi' resident in Huntingdonshire, then pressed on the sheriff, Sir Walter de la Pole, the need for a new and proper election. Along with the attorneys of the abbots of Ramsay and Thorney and other regular suitors to the shire court they proceeded to the election, in due and customary form, of Stukeley himself and Roger Hunt, a member of the duke of Norfolk's counsel, and the names of these two were ultimately returned on the dorse of the writ of summons with an appended explanation of the change. Apparently no process of inquiry by justices of assize was considered necessary.

The three disputed elections in Cumberland, Buckinghamshire, and Huntingdonshire, immediately preceding as they did the passage of the electoral franchise act of 1429, must in the nature of things have had some effect on the promotion of the bill which evoked it. They certainly seem to have affected the terms in which it was framed. For it is important to realise that the bill made a serious attempt to meet the old difficulties of raising safeguards against dishonest action on the part of the sheriff and of insisting on the residential qualification of both electors and elected. The significance of its corroboration of the terms of the statutes of 1410 and 1413 has tended to be passed over, being overshadowed by the interest of the new clause establishing an electoral franchise on the basis of a qualification which, incidentally, had governed jury service in the shire courts since 1293, namely, the possession of land freely held to the value of 40 shillings a year clear.[1] Stubbs asserted that it cannot be doubted that the resulting act, or rather this particular section of it, was designed to meet ' the disorderly condition of the county courts' generally, that is, in more than these three shires in which disputed elections actually took place ; and the evidence of the preamble of the petition itself is that the ' trop graunde et excessive nombre des gentz' present at elections was threatening the peace ' en plusours countees d'Engleterre'. On the other hand, it is going beyond the evidence to assert, as Stubbs does, that the complaint exemplifies the lack of governance common to the whole Lancastrian period. The very fact that exception was taken to elections not correctly conducted and that resentment was aroused by the disregard paid to the rights of resident freeholders is evidence of at least a will to legality and correctness in the matter of parliamentary election. Probably greater emphasis should be laid on the local insistence on the rights of the resident freeholders of the shire,

---

[1] Stubbs, *Constitutional History*, II, § 236.

and on the local demand that electoral privilege should be restricted to those on whom lay the burden of contributing to the wages of parliamentary representatives, than on the respect for law and order. Nevertheless, the actual fewness of elections disputed on the grounds of illegality, coupled with the readiness of the government to accede to remedial petitions (possibly officially-inspired), gives the lie to, rather than supports, the charge of lack of governance sometimes levelled against the Lancastrian régime.

On the other hand, there must be taken into account and weighed against this deduction from the fewness of disputed elections the fact that, on many previous occasions, the indentures of shire elections at Huntingdon, the scene of one of the recent disputes, and also at Bedford, disclose a disregard in these two adjacent counties for the statutory regulations regarding the residence of electors ; on such occasions no objections were raised and no disputed election resulted. Sir Thomas Waweton himself, who was one of the Bedfordshire intruders at Huntingdon complained against in 1429, was no stranger to parliamentary elections there, as has already been pointed out, and had himself served as shire-knight for Huntingdonshire in seven parliaments (twice in 1397 and in 1401, 1402, November 1414, 1420, and 1422), oftener in fact than he was ever to serve for Bedfordshire ; but it is perhaps significant that after the 1429 dispute he never again attested a Huntingdonshire indenture (or represented the county in parliament). Roger Hunt, one of the knights substituted in the second Huntingdonshire election of 1429, had himself often trespassed along the same lines as Waweton : although he had already sat in the Commons eleven times for Huntingdonshire he had also thrice represented Bedfordshire, and in 1419 and 1425 had attended the elections at Bedford to parliaments in which he sat for Huntingdonshire. Hunt, however, had landed interests in Bedfordshire and so had Waweton in Huntingdonshire : in this respect they were each qualified to attend both shire courts, if not by residence. The invasion by outsiders from Bedfordshire of the first, repudiated Huntingdonshire election in 1429 must have been on too big a scale and too flagrant a breach of local practice to be ignored. It is interesting to see William Waweton, whose election in 1429 was quashed on the grounds that he was neither a resident nor possessed of estates in the county, again representing Huntingdonshire less than four years later (1433).

C

Official policy towards parliamentary elections in the shires had been consistently that they should be conducted 'libere et indifferenter'. But the most that the Crown could do was to attempt to restrain the sheriff from making illegal returns and to secure—the difficulty was here much greater—the observance of the residential qualification of both electors and elected. The extent to which the shire elections were amenable to the influence, open or indirect, of local magnates, it could not hope to regulate or control. There is more circumstantial evidence of 'corruption' of this sort later on in the fifteenth century when the data provided by such collections of private correspondence as the Paston Letters can be drawn upon, although precious little of it even then. Three weeks before parliament assembled on 6 November 1450 the duke of Norfolk could instruct John Paston esquire not to 'labour' against the two persons whom he and his uncle, the duke of York, 'have fully appointed and agreed for to be knights of the shire of Norfolk'; and two days later the earl of Oxford, another party to this local compact, sent on a schedule which gave their names. In point of fact only one of these recommended candidates was, however, returned by the shire court. From another letter in the collection of Paston correspondence, written a month before the parliament of 9 July 1455 met, comes a further bit of evidence of the power which the Mowbrays possessed in East Anglia and of the influence which they could exert on the returns to the Lower House. The duchess of Norfolk wrote to John Paston from Framlingham castle pointing out how necessary it was that 'my lord have at this time in the parliament such persons as belong unto him and be of his menial servants'. Dictation, indeed; but now in 1455, in spite of the recent Yorkist triumph in the field at St. Albans, there was articulate opposition in Norfolk, just as in 1450 reluctance to conform may be deduced from the election result itself. In a letter which John Jenny wrote to John Paston before a fortnight had elapsed since the duchess disclosed the Mowbray policy, he pointed out that one of the candidates of the duke of Norfolk was likely to be accepted but not the other. The local grounds for objection were significant: public opinion in Norfolk was against the 'evil precedent for the shire that a strange man [John Howard, a non-resident] should be chosen', and men accounted it 'no worship to my lord of York nor to my lord of Norfolk to write for him'. The 'worship' of the shire was at stake, and its gentry were fully aware of the need to curb aristocratic direction too perfunctorily and glibly imposed. Official policy would seem only to have been abreast, and not ahead, of local sentiment. In 1455, however, the ducal candidates for Norfolk arrived at Westminster in due course, if perhaps not by duly free and indifferent election. It says much for the weight of the Mowbray pressure that they did so. But ducal authority in itself was not enough ; only electioneering and careful manipulation in the ducal interest could do the trick.

When the elections of 1455 took place the times were very much out of joint. But it is significant that the royal council, when writing, only four days before parliament was due to begin, to Sir John Cheyne, sheriff of Kent, in order to require him to see that the peace was kept at the elections for his bailiwick ' as ye wol answere unto us at your perill ', saw fit to couch its note in terms which acknowledged the right of free local election. The writ issuing by the royal authority drew attention to rumours that ' besy labour ' on the part of certain persons was afoot so that ' by liklyhood inconvenient [*sic*] might ensue of such partie as shall be at the said election . . . of the whiche labour we mervaylle greetly inso-muche as it is noothing to the honour of the laborers but ayenst their worship '. The note continued : ' it is also ayenst the lawes of this our Lande and Ordinaunces made in that behalf '. And the sheriff, who had been a supporter of Cade's revolt and probably was sympathetic to the Yorkists, was charged to declare it to be the king's will that ' the said shire have theire free election accordyng to oure said lawes and ordenaunces ', and that anyone who presumed to attempt the contrary ' shall renne in our grevous displesour '. There is no reason to believe that these sentiments were as bogus as they were pious. However either interested or impartial was the policy behind the writ, its terms reflected current notions of proper electoral practice locally as well as officially held.

Seventeen years after these events, that is, prior to the elections of 1472, Sir John Paston's younger brother wrote to him (they were the sons of the John Paston formerly mentioned) to the effect that he had better give up his intention of being elected as one of the knights of the shire for Norfolk, in view of the fact that a fortnight earlier the dukes of Norfolk and Suffolk had agreed as to who were to be the knights returned ; the letter went on to warn him to see to it that as few of his supporters as possible came to the elections ; it would be wise to clear himself of the danger of causing offence. Paston senior took the hint ; and, as it happened, the ducal candidates were returned.[1]

As Mr. McFarlane justly and judiciously has pointed out, the assent of the shire, however, had to be worked for and won over. Aristocratic control of the suffrage of the county was not automatic. There was perhaps always some element of predestination or predetermination about any medieval parliamentary election—the word ' election ' in political practice often bore something of its theological connotation—but influence over the electoral body was not the same thing as usurpation of its constitutional, customary privileges.   In any case, Norfolk, from which most of these examples of electoral ' labouring ' come, was a limited area especially amenable to the aristocratic influence and pressure of the Mowbrays and their friends, and the third quarter of the fifteenth century was a time of abnormal political dislocation, and therefore not a period from which it would be safe to generalise for the earlier half of the century. Even in the disturbed conditions of 1450 certain shires were still capable of expressing their resentment at attempts to interfere unduly with their electoral rights. The disputed return at the Huntingdonshire election in that year [2] is a case in point, but a clearer expression of such a grievance is that which formed (according to the Elizabethan antiquary John Stow) one of the articles of the complaint of the commons of Kent and was one of their reasons for participating in the Cade rising earlier in that same year, 1450. The complaint expressed in this article was that ' the people of the saide shire of Kent may not have their free elections in the choosing knights of the shire, but letters beene sent from divers estates to the great rulers of all the countrie, the which imbraceth their tenants and other people by force to choose other persons than the common will is '.[3]   One inference to be drawn from these cases of protest is that the subject of their complaint was not regarded as a normal condition of electoral practice.   The enjoyment of ' good-lordship ' was a *sine qua non* of success in fifteenth-century politics and society,

---

[1] *The Paston Letters*, ed. J. Gairdner (Library Edition, 1904), II. 184–5 ; III. 38–9 ; V. 149 ; K. B. McFarlane makes a detailed examination of the circumstances of those Norfolk elections in the third quarter of the fifteenth century where the Paston correspondence is most helpful (i.e. in 1450, 1455, 1461, 1470, and 1472) in *Transactions of the Royal Historical Society*, 4th Series, Vol. XXXVI. 56–64 ; for the 1455 writ to the sheriff of Kent, see *P.P.C.*, VI. 246–7.

[2] See above, p. 12.

[3] John Stow, *The Annales of England* (London, 1592), 632–3.

and to many a fifteenth-century esquire or gentleman to stand well in the conceit of his lord was the be-all and end-all of existence ; to John Paston in 1450 wrote an unknown correspondent of considerable perspicacity and savoir-faire : ' Spende sumwhat of your good now and gette you lordship and freendship ther, quia ibi pendet tota lex et prophetae.' [1] Sufficient indication of the quality of the political life of the period was the perennial inability of governments to cope effectively with that abuse of the revived practice of ' commendatory lordship ' and ' bastard feudalism ', the problem of livery and maintenance. But, even if we take into account these tendencies and the fact that earlier in the century such details of local political developments and events as the Paston correspondence reveals are withheld from us, such evidence as is accessible does not lead us to infer that local aristocratic influence on parliamentary elections was exerted with the same degree of pressure and interference and on the same scale earlier as later in the Lancastrian period. In any case, even if in the earlier part of the fifteenth century aristocratic influence on elections was as prevalent as later, it must have been just as indirectly brought to bear by ' labouring ' and by the use of those manipulative services which members of the gentry class, who themselves made up the more important suitors or attenders of the shire courts, were prepared to supply on their lords' behalf.

The electoral body in the county court usually did not include members of any class higher than that from which the knights of the shire themselves or the local administrative officials like sheriffs, escheators, or bailiffs were drawn. Attendance at the shire elections of members of the baronial class themselves was seemingly very rare. At the Cumberland elections in December 1421 Ralph Neville, the son of the earl of Westmorland, was the first to attest the indenture of return ; [2] Thomas Lord Dacre of Gilsland and his son headed the list of those who certified as valid the elections for the same county in 1433,[3] and Lord Dacre was again present at the 1442 Cumberland elections ; Ralph Lord Graystoke attended the Yorkshire elections to the same parliament.[4] It is possible that many of the lords who owed suit to the county court discharged their obligation, and so exercised a personal influence over the elections held there, in and through the persons of their bailiffs acting in the capacity of attorneys. Until 1432

[1] *Paston Letters, op. cit.,* II. 180.   [2] P.R.O., C.219/12/6.
[3] *ibid.,* 14/4.   [4] *ibid.,* 15/2.

the only attestors of the actual indenture of return at the Yorkshire elections were the attorneys of the 'sectatores communes ad comitatum', who were almost without exception the great aristocratic landowners of the shire.[1]   Similarly, in 1413, at the Devon elections to Henry V's first parliament there had been present the local stewards respectively of the king, the bishop of Exeter, the earls of Devon and Salisbury, and the abbots of Dunkeswill and Tavistock, doubtless acting as their lords' attorneys.[2]   But precisely the same reason was behind this magnate representation in the county court as may be detected in the presence at the Staffordshire elections in 1407 of the local bailiff of the duchy of Lancaster and the bailiff of the liberty of the bishop of Coventry and Lichfield,[3] in the attendance at the 1422 Norfolk elections of the receiver and bailiff of the duchy of Lancaster in the county,[4] or in the appearance of the attorneys of the abbots of Ramsay and Thorney at the repeated Huntingdonshire elections in 1429.[5]   Attendance at the shire court in these instances is not so much to be regarded as the representation of a special aristocratic interest in these particular elections as the spasmodic expression of an obligation and right inhering in landed estates from which suit to the county court was customarily due. In any event, these instances are exceptional.

The tenurial obligation of suit of service had long since gone by the board as a predominant factor in the constitution of county courts assembled for the purpose of making parliamentary elections. The electoral statute of 1406 clearly expected the attendance at elections of others than the duly summoned suitors proper.[6]   The phrases used in the indentures of return to cover those of the electors not actually named as attestors leave no doubt that the tenurial 'secta' must normally have formed only a small if not insignificant proportion of the electoral body ; this seems a safe deduction to make from the use of such expressions as 'alii liberi homines de comitatu' (1411), 'multi alii proceres comitatus', (1425), or 'multi alii probi et legales homines comitatus' (on many occasions), variously used, for example, to describe the individually unnamed Lancashire electors, or of such a phrase as 'les gentilles et les comunes du dit countee', used to describe the electors at the Sussex elections in 1413.[7]   The act of 1429 did not extend the franchisal right to

[1] See above, p. 11.   [2] P.R.O., C.219/11/1.   [3] *ibid.*, 10/4.
[4] *ibid.*, 13/1.   [5] *ibid.*, 14/1.   [6] *Rot. Parl.*, III. 601a ;   *Statutes*, II. 156.
[7] P.R.O., C.219/10/6 ;   14/3 ;   11/3.

those freeholders of the shire enjoying an income from freehold of £2 and more ; its operation was intended to restrict it merely to them ; for they did already possess it.

It is true that one of the reasons for presenting the 1429 petition, which sought to determine the right to vote in county elections on the basis of a property qualification, was to exclude ' gentz sinoun de petit avoir ou de null value ', who came to elections in great numbers and each of whom pretended to an equal voice with a knight or esquire.[1] But the property qualification then established, in terms of revenue from land or as a standard of livelihood, was not high. And what seems to have been especially significant about it was not so much the amount of income that was required of an elector as its being derived from *freehold* land : the community of the shire was re-defined as its freeholders. The fact that the property qualification imposed by the 1429 statute stood at no more than two-fifths of what Sir John Fortescue,[2] little more than a generation later, could describe as ' a feyre lyvynge for a yeoman ', suggests that the shire electorate under the new arrangement still remained fairly comprehensive. And whether shire courts of such still large proportions quickly and inevitably reacted to seigneurial influences exerted on individual, or groups of individual, electors is a matter for speculation. Direct intervention in, or open interference with, the actual process of election on the part of local magnates above and outside the class which normally composed the better sort of the county court (the class from which the shire-knights and sheriffs themselves came) is even more doubtful. We must remember, too, that though many of the knights of the shire had demonstrably close connexions with aristocratic patrons, which might at first sight suggest that their election would have naturally owed something to their influence, these aristocratic connexions were not necessarily, in fact, local connexions at all, although they might be and frequently were. The influence of local magnates on elections throughout the Lancastrian period must have been a factor of considerable importance, but it was only one of several factors each playing its part ; freedom of election in the shires would seem generally to have been more than an inadequately guarded local privilege or a well-intentioned governmental aspiration.

[1] *Rot. Parl.*, IV. 350a.
[2] Sir John Fortescue, *The Governance of England*, ed. Chas. Plummer (2nd impression, 1926), 151.

CHAPTER II

THE CITY AND BOROUGH ELECTIONS

THE returns of their elected representatives made by cities and boroughs were even more varied in form than those coming in from the shire courts. Two main categories may, however, be easily discerned. To a town which was itself a shire incorporate and in which the elections were made or eventually declared in its own county court, a separate parliamentary writ of summons authorising the election of representatives was sent direct, and the return to it was communicated direct to Chancery by the civic sheriff or sheriffs who had the return of writs. In 1422 the towns so constituted were the cities of London (since 1283 at latest), York (since 1397), Norwich (since 1404), and Lincoln (since 1413), and the boroughs of Bristol (since 1377) and Newcastle-on-Tyne (since 1402).[1] In the case of all other parliamentary cities and boroughs, the sheriff of the county in which they were situated was ordered by the parliamentary writ of summons to see that they elected representatives and the ultimate responsibility for forwarding their returns rested with him. Diversity in the manner and method of return was here inevitable; the sheriff's practice in even a single county was not always the same over a period of years.

The sheriff, as ultimate returning officer for the parliamentary boroughs of his bailiwick, might be content to make the returns of their elections in the indenture embodying the result of the shire election, and without supplying further details of the different

---

[1] Additions to this list of towns receiving a separate writ of summons direct were made later on in the century: Kingston-upon-Hull (1445), Southampton and Nottingham (1449), Coventry (1459), Canterbury (1463) (*Report on the Dignity of a Peer*, II. 671, 757, 783, 792, 815 ; *ibid.*, 909, 925, 943, 959). Riess demonstrated that boroughs not in possession of the privilege of ' returnum omnium brevium ', that is, boroughs not free from interference from the bailiffs of hundreds or boroughs within liberties, had lost their right to be summoned at all before the end of Edward II's reign, except in the case of the boroughs of Somerset, Dorset, Devon, Wiltshire, and Cornwall, where the sheriff had already adopted the more convenient practice of summoning them direct to make their returns to him, and had by-passed the bailiffs of the hundreds in which they were situated (L. Riess, *The History of the English Electoral Law in the Middle Ages*, trans. and ed. Miss K. L. Wood-Legh, 1940, 32–6).

borough elections than the names of the burgesses who tendered
to him in the shire court the result of the election in their particular
borough. He might, on the other hand, make a bare return of
the parliamentary burgesses-elect on the dorse of the original
Chancery writ of summons authorising the election, and enclose
with it the individual borough indentures of election (just as they
came in to him from the borough authorities) along with the
indenture certifying the election of the knights of the shire. The
methods of return of borough elections used by the sheriffs in
1422 were in fact, however, far more diverse than these.

In certain boroughs, where normally the county court of the
shire was held, it was the practice for some of the burgesses to
present themselves in the county court itself on the occasion of
the election of the knights of the shire, and there make formal
election of their own parliamentary representatives. This was so
at Cambridge, Huntingdon, Warwick, Leicester, Appleby, and
Carlisle. And, in 1422, in the case of Canterbury and Rochester,
the Hampshire boroughs of Winchester, Southampton, and Ports-
mouth, and at Nottingham, Derby, and Worcester, a common
indenture certified the election of both knights of the shire and
burgesses in terms suggesting a common election in the shire court.[1]
The presence of burgesses in the county court was, nevertheless, in
all probability occasioned merely for the purpose of reporting an
election already made. Apart from the fact that the established
Cambridge practice of electing its parliamentary burgesses is known
to have been on the basis of ' one for the bench by the mayor and
his assistants, and another by the commonalty' until 1452, when
an attempt was made to secure that henceforward the choice
should be made ' by the most part of the burgesses in the gildhall
at the election',[2] both the Cambridge and Huntingdon burgesses
attested indentures of return in 1422 altogether distinct from those
which certified the election of the shire-knights.[3] In the case of
Appleby, in that year, however, the mayor and seven burgesses
attested *separately* and together but in the same indenture which
certified the Westmorland county elections. And ten Warwick
and twelve Leicester burgesses were present in the shire courts of

[1] P.R.O., C.219/13/1.
[2] C. H. Cooper, *Annals of Cambridge*, I. 205, cited by Miss M. McKisack, *The
Parliamentary Representation of the English Boroughs during the Middle Ages* (1932), 34–5.
[3] P.R.O., C.219/13/1.

their respective counties when the indentures certifying the election there of both knights and burgesses were attested (in this case, as in others, the identity of practice is due to the two shires forming a joint-bailiwick under the same sheriff). But how dangerous it is to accept the phraseology of the indentures of return at its face value is brought out in the similar case of Nottingham and Derby (again boroughs in the two shires of a joint-bailiwick). The terms of the returns of 1422 [1] point to the election of their burgesses in the county courts held in those boroughs ; but, judging from the returns made to the parliament of 1411, the election must in each case have been actually made ' in plena curia burgi '.[2] Similarly from returns for other years we know that the elections in the cities of Canterbury and Rochester were made by the citizens apart. To the parliament of 1429 there was a disputed election at Canterbury : the bishop of Rochester, John Langdon, successfully persuaded the sheriff of Kent to override an election *already made* and to declare as elected one of his own servants, who had represented the city in 1426 and was himself a citizen, in the place of one of the civic representatives regularly chosen.[3] At Rochester itself the elections of 1410 had disclosed an interesting arrangement which places beyond doubt the fact that the citizens normally had complete, sole control over their own parliamentary returns : on that occasion the bailiff of the city pointed out that it was the custom for any stranger, ' non de eadem civitate natus ' but coming there to dwell as a free citizen, to go to the next parliament to be summoned after his admission to the freedom, and stay there for its duration at his own expense ; on this particular occasion it was noted that one of the citizens-elect had undertaken this duty, but that the other had been elected in accordance with the usual practice.[4]

There is no more reason to believe that, in these instances where a common indenture certified the election of both shire-knights and burgesses, the parliamentary burgesses were elected by the freeholders of the shire or by the freeholders of the shire and the

---

[1] P.R.O., C.219/13/1.　　　　　　　　　　[2] *ibid.*, 10/6.

[3] *Hist. Mss. Comm., IXth Report*, Part 1, App. 1, 138b, cited by M. McKisack, *op. cit.*, 64 ; Miss McKisack does not, however, say that John Bonyngton, the bishop's servant, was a citizen of Canterbury, which somewhat alters the complexion of the case. The disputed election belongs to 1429, and not 1430 (cf. *Official Return*, I. 316).

[4] P.R.O., C.219/10/5 ; cited by M. McKisack, *op. cit.*, 37 n.

burgesses together than there is to assume that the choice of the citizens of Exeter and the representatives of other Devon boroughs was made in the shire court held at Exeter from the fact that the election of both knights and burgesses alike was similarly certified in one comprehensive indenture of return.   Again, on the grounds that the separate indenture, made between the sheriff of Somerset and four delegates each from the city of Bath and the boroughs of Wells, Bridgwater, and Taunton, was drawn up on the same day and at the same place (Ilchester) as the shire elections were held, it might have been concluded that the election of their parliamentary burgesses took place in the shire court, were it not for the statement that the elections had been made with the assent of the whole community of each of their towns.   And so it was in the case of the boroughs of the other shire of the joint-bailiwick, the seven boroughs of Dorset.   The procedure demanded by the statute of 1445, in accordance with which a sheriff was to send to the several cities and boroughs in his bailiwick a precept for the election to be made by the citizens or burgesses, the result of which was to be returned in a separate indenture drawn up between them and himself, would have obviated such difficulties of interpretation.[1] But the statute did not change existing practice ; it merely provided for its proper regulation.[2]

There would have been no temptation to see an insoluble constitutional problem where none existed [3] if this device of a separate indenture, as stipulated in 1445, had been previously followed.   It was in fact already being used in 1422 in the case of Bedford, Wycombe, Northampton, and Leominster ; their return took the form of a completely separate indenture drawn up between the sheriff and a select number of attesting burgesses in the case of Bedford and Wycombe, between the sheriff of Hereford and the bailiff of the abbot of Reading's liberty and a

---

[1] *Rot. Parl.*, V. 116a ; *Statutes*, II. 340–2 (Stat. 23 Hen. VI, c. XIV).

[2] Miss McKisack generally came to the same conclusions, discussing the evidence of the sheriffs' indentures of return : M. McKisack, *op. cit.*, 54–57 ; 59–60.

[3] Stubbs (*Constitutional History*, III, § 422) was forced to leave it an open question whether there were not serious discrepancies between what the sheriffs' indentures between 1406 and 1445 appeared to show and what he himself called ' the legal method of proceeding '.   Miss McKisack's evidence, especially that adduced from the archives of boroughs, convinces me, as do my own findings, that when a borough election appears in the sheriff's comprehensive indenture of return to have taken place in the shire court, the literal terms of the indenture are more likely than not to be quite misleading in that respect.

number of burgesses in the case of Leominster, and between the sheriff of Northampton and the mayor and bailiffs of the borough in the case of Northampton. The returns made by the East Anglian boroughs of Bishop's Lynn, Great Yarmouth, Ipswich, and Dunwich, were similarly transmitted to the sheriff of Norfolk and Suffolk (a joint-bailiwick) by their respective town bailiffs (in the case of Lynn, of course, by the bishop's steward of the liberty) in the form of separate indentures drawn up, ' sub sigillo communi ville ', presumably between themselves and certain attesting burgesses. A similar method was followed at Hereford, Oxford, Wallingford, and Reading, a certificate of election being forwarded in each case to the sheriff and sent on by him to Chancery along with the indenture certifying the shire election ; in the case of Hereford and Reading this certificate was in the form of an indenture, but the Oxford return took the form of a letter patent issued in the name of the mayor, bailiffs, aldermen, ' et tota com- munitas burgensium ville Oxonie '.[1]

The 1422 returns for the remaining boroughs, with the exception of the coastal boroughs of Hull and Scarborough (Yorks) and Grimsby (Lincs), give little indication of the form in which the sheriff received his notification of the election of their parliamentary burgesses. In these three instances we have a simple notice on the dorse of the sheriff's writ of summons to the effect that a return of names had been made to his precept by the bailiffs of the boroughs. But in the case of the returns from the boroughs of Shrewsbury, Bridgnorth, Stafford, Newcastle-under-Lyme, Colchester, Maldon, and Gloucester, we have nothing more to rely on than a mere list of names of burgesses-elect on the dorse of the writ of summons ; and in the case of the boroughs of Cornwall, Wiltshire, Surrey, and Sussex (the two latter jointly administered under one sheriff), and the Cinque Ports, nothing more than simple, detached schedules of names.

On the basis of the returns to the parliament of 1422 it would be, then, dangerous to assume that any borough elections were made other than by the burgesses themselves, even in such cases where there must still remain a possibility that the elections were not ' home-made ' in the boroughs themselves. Where we know the election to have been either made or declared in the shire court, burgesses have been present and explicitly in their capacity as

[1] P.R.O., C.219/13/1.

burgesses, and not otherwise. And there is no more reason to believe that those enfranchised of a borough would continually surrender their electoral rights than that freeholders of the shire would agree to the shire court becoming a mixed assembly in the electoral activities of which burgesses would have an equal share with themselves. The norm in 1422 was for the elections to be made independently by the body of burgesses in individual boroughs in accordance with their own peculiar constitution or practice, then in boroughs that were not incorporated as shires for the return of the accomplished election to be made to the sheriff, and finally for him to pass on to Chancery either the return itself or its import.

There was no more uniformity in the methods by which borough elections were conducted than in the ways utilised by the borough authorities and the sheriffs for submitting the results of elections to Chancery. The constitution of the electoral body might and did vary as much as the form of return. Moreover, from one borough to another there was no uniformity of procedure. In some cases there is little doubt but that the electorate was oligarchical in character and that the electoral function was discharged by a select body of burgesses acting more or less as the delegates of the rest. A clear case in point was the city of Hereford, where the election in 1422 was made by a small number of citizens who acted 'per assensum aliorum concivium suorum'. Other similar instances were supplied by the borough of Wallingford, where the mayor and two aldermen elected 'cum consensu et assensu ceterorum comburgensium'; by the borough of Leominster where in 1422, for example, the abbot of Reading's bailiff and twenty-six burgesses chose their parliamentary representatives 'ex assensu communitatis burgi'; and by the borough of Great Yarmouth where the four bailiffs caused its members to be elected by the burgesses, no more than four of whom are ever named. In these instances the actual election seems to have rested with a small, compact, exclusive, oligarchical group, acting in the name of the whole community.

In some of those cities and boroughs which had been incorporated as shires in themselves the practice was for elections to be similarly close; in others they seem to have been freer, more open, and more popular. The London writs of summons were published by the sheriffs in the Court of Husting and normally the elections took place there. They did so in 1422, but, on occasion, might still be held in smaller assemblies. Unlike all other towns, which returned two burgesses each, London had come to elect four citizens, two aldermen and two commoners, to represent it in parliament. In 1378 the election of the two aldermen had made ' per aldermannos ' and that of the two commoners ' per communitatem ', that is, by representatives of the wards. This practice had superseded the theoretically more correct procedure of election in the Court of Husting, perhaps by the end of the thirteenth century. In 1383, however, the election of all four took place in the old Common Assembly, then lately resuscitated as the Common Council and comprising representatives of misteries, not wards. The statute of 1406, demanding formal proclamation of parliamentary writs of summons in county courts, necessitated, so far as London was concerned, a return to the practice of election in the Husting Court as the county court of the city. But at least occasional evasion is evidenced : in 1419 both aldermen and commoners were nominated in the Court of Aldermen ; in 1420 ' in pleno hustengo et communi concilio ', in 1422 simply and more properly ' in hustengo ', but later in Henry VI's reign and afterwards, with less orthodoxy, in either the Court of Aldermen and Common Council (as in 1445 and 1450) or in Common Council (as in 1439, 1450, 1460, 1462, 1463), formality being satisfied with proclamation, and probably approval, in the Court of Husting.[1]

As Miss McKisack points out, when elections took place in the Hustings, the result was recorded in the Letter-books whereas the unorthodox elections in the Court of Aldermen and Common Council were only entered up in the Journals. At York there does not seem to have been the same internal constitutional uncertainty. Here the returns seem to have been made consistently in the full county court of the city by a small electoral body composed of the mayor, aldermen and leading citizens ;[2] in 1422 they numbered no more than a dozen.[3]

The elections at Norwich had formerly been restricted in much the same sort of way, from 1380 onwards until 1404, when the city was incorporated as a shire, being generally left to the four bailiffs and the twenty-four leading citizens. Probably after this date the ' burgesses for knights of the shire ' (as they were called)

[1] M. McKisack, *op. cit.*, 30–2, 48–51.   [2] *ibid.*, 52.
[3] P.R.O., C.219/13/1.

were chosen in the Common Assembly, their names being declared to the mayor, sheriffs, and aldermen ' in pleyn shire ' in the Gild-hall ; this was certainly the practice agreed on in a ' composition ' of 1415, which proved a failure as far as electing a mayor and other annual officers was involved but apparently not in the case of the city's representatives in parliaments.[1] According to the indenture of 1422,[2] the election then took place simply ' in pleno comitatu civitatis . . . tento in Gilda aula civitatis ', the mayor, the two coroners, and only twelve other citizens attesting ; but there is no reason to believe that the real election had not been made before-hand in the Common Assembly. The Lincoln elections were similarly conducted in the full county court of the city in the Gildhall, but not on the principle of a double election : in 1422 the indenture of return, drawn up between the sheriffs and the mayor and twenty-seven citizens (in 1411 the attestors numbered forty-five), certified that ' in plena communi congregatione civitatis ' they had made the election ' in propriis personis suis tunc ibidem existentibus, eorum unanimi assensu et aliorum fidedignorum tunc ibidem existentium '.[3] At Bristol the constitutional sanction for parliamentary elections seems to have been similarly wider. There, in 1422, according to the sheriff's endorsement of his writ of summons,[4] the election was made ' coadunatis discretioribus et magis sufficientibus burgensibus ville ex assensu maioris ville pre-dicte ac aliorum plurimorum ibidem existentium ', and the inden-ture of return was attested by the mayor, bailiffs, and twenty-six leading burgesses to the effect that they and ' alii probi homines ville ' had performed the electoral function. Bristol was to be unique among the urban counties in its adherence to the county franchise statute of 1429, from 1432 onwards restricting the right to participate in elections to its 40-shilling freeholders.[5]

In all other borough elections, whether the electoral function was an oligarchical privilege or whether it was less restricted, the general usage was for the procedure of election to be direct and go through only one stage. At the beginning of the sixteenth century it was the usage at Cambridge for the elections of parliamentary burgesses to proceed by an indirect method : the mayor and his assistants (the aldermen ?) nominated one person, the commonalty

---

[1] Hudson and Tingey, *Norwich Records*, I. 107 ; M. McKisack, *op. cit.*, 52.
[2] P.R.O., C.219/13/1.   [3] *ibid.*
[4] *ibid.*   [5] M. McKisack, *op. cit.*, 51.

of the borough another ; these two chose a select body of eight ; and the eight elected the burgesses of parliament. This was not the method in employment there as late as 1452, when an ordinance provided for the election of the burgesses of parliament by a majority of their co-burgesses in the Gildhall, and certainly it was not the practice used before that date, for the mayor and his assistants had formerly elected one representative and the commonalty of the borough, the other.[1] Early in the fifteenth century such a practice of indirect election seems to have been confined to Bishop's Lynn. But this is an argument from the silence or absence of the records of other boroughs, and if more of these collections were extant or available we might find that the device was more prevalent. From the domestic records of Lynn it is clear that by 1373 it was already the practice for the choice of parliamentary representatives to be made there by a jury appointed *ad hoc* with the sanction of the commonalty, and the practice becomes more clearly discernible in the fifteenth century when more details are available. The mayor with the assent of the whole congregation assembled in the Gildhall, where the parliamentary writ was proclaimed, selected the first four jurors, two from among the twenty-four Jurati and two from the members of the Common Council ; these four nominees chose another four, again two from each body ; these eight co-opted two more and then all ten nominated another two, so making up a complete jury of twelve, who were then sworn according to custom to preserve the liberty of the borough and proceed to election ; the outcome of these proceedings was ratified later by the whole congregation. This was the procedure demonstrably in operation in 1413. A protest in 1419 that, in view of the fact that the assessment and levy of the parliamentary burgesses' expenses fell on the commonalty of the borough, the elections ought to be made by the commonalty openly in the Gildhall, was rejected by the mayor who said that he would proceed according to the terms of the exemplification of their charter as enrolled in the chancery of their lord, the bishop of Norwich. And the method in current use continued to be applied, as available details of the electoral procedure used in 1425, 1426, 1433, and 1437 disclose.[2]

[1] Cooper, *op. cit.*, I. 173, 205, 272, cited by Stubbs, *op. cit.*, III § 422.

[2] H. Ingleby, *The Red Register of King's Lynn*, II. 113 (cited by M. McKisack, *op. cit.*, 33) ; H. Harrod, *Report on the Deeds and Records of the Borough of King's Lynn*, 95 *et seq.* ; *Hist. Mss. Comm., Report XI*, App. 3, 158–9 ; *Archæologia*, XXIV. 320.

We owe to the borough's own records our knowledge of the employment at Lynn of this indirect method of election by a constitutionally selected jury. The possibility of the use of similar methods in other boroughs is not precluded merely by the fact that such documentary evidence is not there available or even because no reference to the method of election by jury is made in the writs or in the indentures of return. Despite the fact that the jury method had long been operative at Lynn, its 1422 indenture of return (to which William Paston as the bishop's steward of the liberty of the town was party) merely certified that the elections there had been made by the mayor, three named attestors, and ' alii burgenses '.[1] As a guide to the details of domestic procedure employed in borough elections the indentures of return are often similarly unreliable, and at best they are inadequate.

[1] P.R.O., C.219/13/1.

D

CHAPTER III

THE PROBLEM OF PARLIAMENTARY EXPERIENCE

ANY appreciation of the growth of something approaching an esprit de corps in the Lower House must take into account the problem of the parliamentary experience of its individual members. In view of the fact that medieval parliaments were frequently convened but of short duration—prorogations were by 1422 still exceptional—repeated election rather than re-election, which is to be interpreted in the strict sense of election to consecutive parliaments, must be adopted as the criterion on which the continuity of Commons' personnel is judged.[1]

In the Lancastrian period continuous re-election over even a short space of time was still, if not a rare thing, at least unusual ; and in the period of Henry VI's minority (1422–37) never more than roughly a quarter of the knights of the shire and burgesses together sitting in one parliament were re-elected to sit in its successor. The most noteworthy instance of an ' overlap ' of Commons' personnel in the whole of Henry VI's reign is that afforded by the returns of election to the parliament of October 1423 when no fewer than 65 out of 258 knights and burgesses who had sat in the first parliament of the reign, nearly exactly a quarter, were re-elected. In September 1427 no more than an eighth of those who had sat far away from Westminster in the Leicester parliament of the previous year were again returned as re-elected members ; and this was at a time of immense political activity when lack of interest and apathy towards parliamentary affairs and parliamentary representation are inconceivable. In the parliaments of Henry VI's minority the ' overlap ' of personnel (knights and burgesses together) from one assembly to another was no more on the average than a fifth. Moreover, it should be borne in mind that the greater proportionate contribution to this meagre continuity of personnel from one parliament to the next came from the less important and influential element among the Commons,

---

[1] For an important controversy on this point, see *History*, Vol. XI (1926) : ' History, English and Statistics ', by A. F. Pollard, and ' Re-Election and the Medieval Parliament ', by J. G. Edwards. I prefer Mr. Edwards's point of view.

the representatives from the parliamentary cities and boroughs. The number of knights of the shire who were re-elected from one to another of the eleven parliaments, for instance, which sat between 1422 and 1437, averaged no more than eleven ; in other words, since the number of shire representatives stood at seventy-four throughout this period, on an average no more than one out of seven (roughly) of the knights sitting in any one parliament was chosen to sit in its successor. The highest number of re-elected knights in these years was that of the session of April 1425 when as many as fifteen knights were returned who had sat in the parliament of October 1423. In the whole of Henry VI's reign the highest number of knights re-elected did not exceed twenty-one ; this figure was reached in the assembly which followed the 1447 meeting at Bury St. Edmunds, namely, the Westminster parliament of February 1449. In the first ten years of the reign, however, the numerical fluctuation was comparatively slight—the extremes between which it oscillated were eleven and fifteen cases of re-election—but in the last two parliaments of the minority period the variation of personnel at the level of the county representatives was more considerable. Of the seventy-four knights returned in 1433 no more than seven were returned to the next parliament of 1435 and in 1437 there was the same number of cases of re-election of shire-knights. The continuity of personnel between Henry V's last and Henry VI's first parliament was slightly under average ; the names of only ten knights are common to both lists of returns ; the relative unimportance of the parliament of December 1421 should, however, be borne in mind. No less that twenty-three of the fifty-five experienced knights of 1422 had sat in the important parliament of May 1421, the only one of the last five parliaments of his reign that Henry V himself was permitted by his military preoccupations to attend.

It should, of course, be realised that this analysis does not take account of the fact that it might and did happen that a few of the knights sitting in one parliament were appointed as sheriffs before its successor was summoned and so were statutorily disqualified from re-election ; but even if such appointments had not been made and if the men so concerned had all been re-elected the generalisation that re-election was comparatively not usual would still be largely unaffected. For example, either during the actual assembly of 1422 or early in the following year there were appointed as sheriffs five men who sat as knights of the shire in the first parliament of the reign of Henry VI ; by reason of their appointment they were statutorily barred from re-election to the parliament which met in the following October. But even if all five had been re-eligible and had been again returned the number of shire-knights re-elected in 1423 would not have exceeded sixteen, considerably less than a quarter of those who had sat in the previous year.

These figures relating to service in the Commons in successive parliaments compare rather unfavourably with those which Professor Neale has supplied for one or two of the later Elizabethan parliaments : over half of those who sat as knights and burgesses in the parliament of 1584, for example, were re-elected in 1586, and over a third of the Commons in 1593 were returned again in 1597.[1] Continuity of personnel from parliament to parliament, although by no means negligible, cannot, however, in view of the greater frequency with which parliament was summoned in the Lancastrian period, be accepted as a safe guide to the corporate experience to be found in any one parliament among the Commons. The parliamentary experience of individual knights and burgesses and the occasions of their *repeated* election give a better idea of the extent to which the continuity of Commons' personnel may well have been an important factor contributing to the formation of political and procedural traditions in the Lower House. It is interesting again to make a comparison between this Lancastrian parliament of 1422 and Elizabethan parliaments in order to bring out the significance of some statistics derived from an examination of the experience of the men elected to it. In the Lancastrian period parliament sat roughly three times as frequently as it was to sit in Elizabeth's reign and, as a result, it is not surprising to find that Lancastrian knights and burgesses sat oftener than did their Elizabethan successors : whereas, Neale estimates, two out of every three Elizabethan members sat more than one (' a high proportion ', as he says), roughly only one out of every five of the Commons in 1422 did not sit in some other parliament before or after that date. Although the number of cases of re-election to a Lancastrian parliament was nothing like so great as in an Elizabethan one, because of the comparatively greater frequency of parliaments in the earlier period, for the selfsame reason the number of newcomers to any Elizabethan parliament was considerably greater than was the case in

[1] J. E. Neale, *The Elizabethan House of Commons* (London, 1949), 309.

a Lancastrian session : whereas in 1584 the proportion of 'novices' in the Lower House was as high as 70 per cent (in 1571 it stood at 62 per cent and in 1593 at 48 per cent),[1] in 1422 it was no more than 33 per cent and proportionately more of these were burgesses than knights of the shire. As keen an anxiety to serve in parliament would seem to have motivated the Lancastrian gentry, and even the burgess class in certain towns, as was to be evident in the case of their successors something like a century and a half later. Reluctance on their part to serve just did not exist. And competition would seem to have been every bit as acute in the shires among the gentry of the fifteenth century as it was to be in the later sixteenth century ; so acute, in fact, that it constitutes perhaps the main single reason for the changing character of borough representation in the fifteenth century, a subject that we shall examine later.

On the point of general parliamentary experience, the record of the members of the Commons of November 1422 is illuminating in other ways. Let us take first the case of the shire-knights of 1422. It certainly suggests that there was nothing unusual about the description given by the father of Thomas Chaucer, knight of the shire for Oxfordshire in 1422, of the franklin in his company of late fourteenth-century Canterbury pilgrims as one who 'ful ofte tyme' had been knight of the shire. The passage of little more than a generation separated Geoffrey Chaucer's observation from the meeting of Henry VI's first parliament, and the careers of the knights of the shire who assembled there bore out the truthfulness of the poet's chance reference to the fact of repeated election. His own son's, for example : in 1422 Thomas Chaucer of Ewelme had already represented Oxfordshire in nine parliaments and was to sit another four times. And the average previous attendance in parliament of the fifty-five knights (out of the seventy-four returned) who are definitely known to have sat in the Commons before 1422 —the nineteen knights presumed to be 'novices' would almost certainly be reduced in numbers if there were not such wide gaps in our knowledge of the returns to some of the parliaments of Henry V's reign—was roughly four times each. If we deduct from

[1] J. E. Neale, *loc. cit.* Whereas of the elected members of parliament in 1584 the number of those who sat only once or twice formed as high a proportion as 46 per cent, those of 1422 who sat so infrequently were only 33 per cent ; of those who sat in 1584 only one out of ten (9 per cent) sat oftener than on half a dozen occasions, whereas among the 1422 Commons nearly one out of every three (30 per cent) sat so frequently as that.

the number of shire-knights who certainly had previously sat in parliament the six who had not been elected (so far as is known) since Henry IV's reign, we are faced with a more significant conclusion : two-thirds of the knights in Henry VI's first parliament had attended on an average no fewer than three of his father's eleven parliaments ; moreover, on an average three out of every four of the already experienced knights had sat in one or another of the last five parliaments which had met between 1417 and Henry V's death. It is also worth pointing out that, from the point of view of length of parliamentary experience on the part of individual knights, no less than ten out of the seventy-four sitting in 1422 had represented their shires in the reign of Richard II and no less than half of the number of already experienced knights had sat in one or more (on an average, over two) of Henry IV's parliaments. Occasionally a fair number of the shire-knights and burgesses of 1422 can be shown to have been assembled together in some previous parliament. The further back one goes the smaller naturally becomes the figure, until it dwindles to a single individual and then finally peters out altogether. But the collective memory of the Commons in 1422, indeed of the knights alone, could range back through every single one of the twenty-three parliaments that had met since 1395. Five of the knights had sat in Richard II's last parliament at Shrewsbury in 1398, and another four had witnessed his deposition and the accession of the first Lancastrian. Forty-three members of the Lower House of 1422, one out of every six, had sat when Henry of Monmouth met his first parliament nearly ten years before, in 1413 ; and nearly twice as many of them in the last parliament he was destined to open in person, the spring session of 1421.

The 1422 member with the longest, if not the most intensive or continuous, parliamentary experience was the Cumberland knight, Sir Peter Tilliol. In the 1370's the ward of Alice Perrers, Edward III's mistress, as a young man just out of his nonage he had sat in so remote a session as that of the Gloucester parliament of the autumn of 1378 and had since then sat in no fewer than ten parliaments, admittedly at well-spaced intervals. At the time of his thirteenth and last return to the parliament of Bats in 1426 he must have been about seventy years of age. In the 1422 parliament along with Tilliol there sat for Shropshire a young apprentice-at-law, William Burley of Bromcroft, who was to become the father-in-law of the great common lawyer and legal writer, Justice Littleton. In 1422 he had already sat for his county in four out of the last five of Henry V's parliaments, was to become Speaker in 1437 and 1445, and was to sit as a prominent supporter of the Yorkist faction in 1455, when he was making his last and nineteenth appearance as a knight of the shire at Westminster. On that occasion he sat there alone of all those, knights and burgesses alike, who had sat in Henry VI's first parliament. None of them was to sit as late as he, although as many as twenty-two members of the Lower House in 1422 had been returned to one or other of the parliaments of the 1440's. More than three-quarters of a century separated Tilliol's first return and Burley's last appearance as knight of the shire.

Judging from the returns to the 1422 parliament, it seems safe to conclude that knights of the shire with substantial parliamentary experience far outnumbered those with none at all or even those who had but slender acquaintance with Westminster as representative agents. Instances of shire-knights being elected to no more than one parliament were, in fact, considerably rarer than cases of straightforward re-election. Of the knights who sat in Henry VI's first parliament only seven of the nineteen ' novices ' or newcomers were never to sit again,[1] and the average number of parliaments which the rest went on to attend in due course was over six. As many, in fact, as sixteen of the shire-knights had sat or were to sit in all no fewer than ten times each [2] and, of these, men like Roger Hunt, who attended fifteen parliaments for Huntingdonshire and three for Bedfordshire between 1407 and 1433, or William Burley of Bromcroft, who represented Shropshire (as we have seen) in nineteen parliaments between 1417 and 1455, had almost an

[1] John Gerard (Lancs), Sir Robert Moton (Leics), Sir John Gray and Sir Robert Roos (Lincs), Henry Mulsho (Northants), Sir William Palton (Somerset), and Thomas Stanley (Staffs).

[2] Sir John Arundell (12 times, 1397–1423, Cornwall) ; Robert Cary (12 times, 1407–26, Devon) ; Thomas Chaucer (14 times, 1401–31, Oxfordshire) ; Sir John Cockayne (9 times for Derbyshire, twice for Warwickshire, 1395–1433) ; Sir William Coggeshall (10 times, 1391–1422, Essex) ; John Enderby (11 times, 1414–45, Bedfordshire) ; Roger Flore (12 times, 1397–1422, Rutland) ; John Golafre (once for Oxfordshire, 12 times for Berkshire, 1397–1429) ; John Russell (13 times, 1414–33, Herefordshire) ; Sir Humphrey Stafford (once for Staffs, 10 times for Dorset, 1406–32) ; Sir William Sturmy (twice for Hants, 8 times for Wilts, twice for Devon, 1384–1422) ; Sir Peter Tilliol (13 times, 1378–1426, Cumberland) ; John Tyrell (12 times Essex, once for Herts, 1411–37) ; Sir Thomas Waweton (7 times for Huntingdonshire, 5 times for Bedfordshire, 1397–1432) ; and Roger Hunt and William Burley (the dates in each case are of their first and last parliaments).

uninterrupted, and certainly an habitual, parliamentary connexion. The former only once missed being elected from the beginning of Henry V's reign until his last appearance at Westminster twenty years later (this observation does not take into account the three parliaments of 1415–16 for which the Huntingdonshire returns are not known); Burley was elected to all but six of the twenty-five parliaments which sat between his first return in 1417 and his last in 1455. To use an expression of a later age, such became ' old parliament men ' indeed.

Of nearly equal importance with these instances of almost uninterrupted parliamentary service over a long period are the cases of completely uninterrupted service over shorter periods. It is interesting to note that the Speaker for the Commons in the second parliament of Henry VI's reign (1423), John Russell, had then served as knight of the shire for the county of Hereford in each of the previous six parliaments. Roger Flore, Speaker in 1422, had sat for Rutland in no less than seven consecutive parliaments between April 1414 and October 1419, serving as Speaker in each of the three last of these sessions and so equalling the previous record of Thomas Chaucer of Ewelme who had acted in that capacity in Henry IV's last three parliaments (Chaucer was Speaker again in November 1414 and May 1421, five times in all). There was not to be such another instance as Flore's of uninterrupted occupation of the Speaker's office from parliament to parliament until the end of Charles II's reign.

The force of these examples among the shire-knights of repeated or continuous election to the Commons is all the more striking if it is remembered that, in the main, they are furnished by men filled with a keen professional appreciation of the value of business-like procedure and of the significance of precedent, and doubtless with a consciousness of the need to create established traditions for the conduct of affairs in the Lower House. Many of these men, whom it is not going too far to describe as habitual parliamentary figures, were lawyers, either at some time or another in Crown employment, like John Tyrell, Roger Hunt, John Throckmorton, Robert Darcy, or like Roger Flore the Speaker himself, or for the most part engaged in private practice like John Enderby, John Russell, or William Burley.

At a rough estimation, continued parliamentary attendance among the citizens and burgesses who sat in the 1422 parliament was of the same order as that obtaining among the shire-knights. More than one-eighth of their number were to have the experience of sitting in as many as ten or more parliaments ; [1] two out of every five sat in at least six parliaments in the course of their life ; and the average number of parliaments attended by all the parliamentary burgesses of 1422 was in the neighbourhood of five each. In 1422 slightly more than a third of the burgesses in the Commons were sitting for the first time, so far as we know ; certainly not more than 67 of the 188 citizens and burgesses were ' novices ', for, as in the case of the shire-knights, their numbers would certainly be fewer if the returns to some of Henry V's parliaments had not been lost. Another 31 had perhaps only sat once before, but the remaining 90 had sat already on an average in nearer four than three parliaments, and nearly a third of these had attended one parliament or more before Henry V's accession in 1413.

[1] Nicholas Ayssheton (10 times, Liskeard, Helston, Launceston, and Cornwall, 1421–39) ; Henry Boteler (10 times, Horsham, 1386–1427) ; Richard Clitheroe (14 times, Romney, 1414–47) ; Thomas Coventry (16 times, Oxford, 1404–35) ; Robert Darcy (once, Newcastle-on-Tyne, 9 times, Essex, once, Maldon, 1402–45) ; Richard Duffield (13 times, Grimsby, 1413–49) ; John Fitlyng (11 times, Hull, 1406–31) ; Simon atte Ford (11 times, Bridport, 1402–26) ; William Forster (10 times, Scarborough, 1419–42) ; William Gascoigne (12 times, Bridgewater, 1406–22) ; Thomas Godstone (13 times, Colchester, 1399–1427) ; John Harleston (9 times, Wilton, once, Old Sarum, 1414–23) ; John Hawley (12 times, Dartmouth, 1410–32) ; John Hill (3 times, Arundel, 7 times, Chichester, 1419–53) ; Richard Horde (10 times, Bridgnorth, 1414–32) ; Thomas Kempston (11 times, Bedford, 1421–50) ; Thomas Lavington (12 times, Reading, 1416–42) ; Robert Pekke (12 times, Huntingdon, 1411–29) ; Walter Portman (10 times, Taunton, 1417–35) ; Walter Reson (9 times, Wareham, once, Melcombe, 1416–32) ; Walter Shirley (13 times, Salisbury, once, Old Sarum, 1411–23) ; Hamond Sutton (7 times, Lincoln, 3 times, Lincolnshire, 1416–39) ; Robert Walsh (10 times, Lincoln, 1417–35) ; Robert Whitgreve (17 times, Stafford, twice, Staffordshire, 1411–49) ; John Whithorne (11 times, Wilton, 1414–33).

CHAPTER IV

THE PARLIAMENTARY BURGESSES OF 1422

THE preponderance of the professional lawyers among the more continuously sitting members of the Commons was strengthened by the fact that many of the more influential burgesses as well as many of the knights were lawyers with considerable parliamentary experience. It is possible to *identify* as lawyers no fewer than thirty-seven of the burgesses elected to Henry VI's first parliament (possibly another six were lawyers) and their total, life-long, parliamentary experience was to result in an average attendance at as many as between six and seven parliaments. These lawyers among the 1422 burgesses included such men as Robert Whitgreve, one of the tellers of the Exchequer, who represented the borough of Stafford in every parliament sitting between 1420 and 1442, and his fellow-burgess, John Harpour, who went up to every Westminster parliament with one exception between 1419 and 1429 ; the clerks of the peace in Surrey, Wiltshire, Worcestershire, and the parts of Lindsey in Lincolnshire—John Hipperon, John Giles, John Forthey, and Richard Duffield—who were returned in 1422 respectively from Guildford, Calne, Worcester, and Grimsby ; Edward Burnby, John Whithorne, William Kyrton, and John Exton, who filled the office of coroner in their shires, elected respectively at Launceston, Wilton, Southwark, and Chichester, John Trewint, returned from Lostwithiel, and Thomas Cricklade, from Cricklade, who had until recently occupied the office of coroner, and John Warfeld of Wallingford, who was later to be one of the coroners in Berkshire. Winchester sent up to Westminster a former recorder of the city in the person of William Wood, who was sharing with the then mayor the right of farming at the Exchequer the subsidy and alnage of cloth in Hampshire ; he came up in company with John Bye, its then recorder. The borough of Southampton elected its town-clerk as one of its representatives, Thomas Marlborough. No less than seven of the burgesses may be identified as members of the society of Lincoln's Inn, the only one of the inns of court to have records of its members extant from so early a date : Nicholas Wotton of Ramsbury, returned for Marlborough, one of the parliamentary proxies, too, of the abbot of Malmesbury and a lawyer with considerable employment at this time as attorney in both the courts of King's Bench and Common Pleas ; Robert Gilbert, a member of the quorum of the commission of the peace for Gloucestershire, whom his own borough of Gloucester elected ; Richard Wynnesley of Winslow, who, as bailiff to the abbot of Reading in his liberty of Leominster, returned himself as one of its burgesses ; Robert Karlell or Carlisle the younger and Richard Drax, both elected as representatives from Carlisle ; and the burgesses for the neighbouring borough of Appleby in Westmorland, Nicholas Stanshawe (the brother of another member of the Inn, Robert Stanshawe, knight of the shire for Gloucestershire) and John Forester or Forster were both probably members of Lincoln's Inn.[1]   Even at such an early date in their careers, probably of greater prominence were such lawyers as Nicholas Ayssheton and John Hody.   The former attended all but four of the parliaments between 1421 and 1435 as member for one or another of the three Cornish boroughs of Liskeard, Helston, and Launceston, to within only a few years of his appointment as a justice of the Common Bench (he sat for Cornwall in 1437 and 1439) ; Hody sat for Shaftesbury in all but one of the parliaments from 1421 to 1427, after which he attended all but two parliaments as knight of the shire for either Dorset or Somerset to within less than three years of his promotion to the Chief Justiceship of the King's Bench in 1440.[2]   Men of this calibre, it is true, were rather exceptional among the burgesses.

Quite a good number of these lawyers among the 1422 parliamentary burgesses owed their return to their vocation, to their professional ability to serve and watch over the interests of the boroughs they represented, and possibly to their willingness to

[1] What makes this identification of the Appleby burgesses as members of Lincoln's Inn more convincing is that Robert Crakanthorpe, under-sheriff of Westmorland, February 1421–October 1423, who made the electoral return in 1422, was himself a member of the Inn (*Admission Book*, p. 1).

[2] To this list of lawyers elected from boroughs must be added the following : Robert Squibbe (Shaftesbury), William Gascoigne (Bridgewater), Nicholas Clopton (Wycombe), Robert Darcy (Maldon), Robert de Whelpyngton (Newcastle-on-Tyne), William Fenyngham (East Grinstead), Walter Portman (Taunton), John Langley (Chippenham), John Ludwell (Chippenham), John Shelley (Rye), John Cork (Liskeard).   The six possible burgess-lawyers who sat in the Commons in 1422 were Thomas Lavington (Reading), John But (Truro), John Ford (Dorchester), William Gerard (Wareham), Richard Galon (Maldon), and Robert Walsh (Lincoln).

accept wages either at a compounded fee or at a reduced rate. This would be especially likely in the case of the mere handful of those non-residents who do not seem to have had any tie at all with the boroughs they represented, not even any influential personal connexion or property qualification. Richard Drax, one of the Carlisle representatives, may have owed his one and only return for the city in 1422 to his connexion with Robert Karlell the younger through their common membership of Lincoln's Inn, but no such link, or known possession of property in the borough, explains the return of Nicholas Clopton, who was either resident at Langley Marsh or Eton, as burgess for Wycombe, although it may explain that of Nicholas Stanshawe, who was almost certainly a Gloucestershire man, as the representative for the county town of Westmorland, where the returning officer (the sheriff) and the parliamentary burgesses, were all three, members of Lincoln's Inn. Most of the 1422 burgesses who failed to come up to the requirements of the 1413 statute as being disqualified by non-residence were men who lived in the near neighbourhood of the borough they represented and/or had property in it which would justify their designation as foreign- or out-burgesses. Such were the two Shaftesbury nominees ; both John Hody and Robert Squibbe had town-houses in the borough, their main seats being outside it although within easy reach.

For the most part, however, the burgesses elected to Henry VI's first parliament were resident in the boroughs returning them and as a result statutorily fully-qualified. Moreover, the exceptions to the observance of the 1413 stature in this respect were in 1422 even less considerable if we exclude the representatives of the Cornish boroughs, all twelve of whom, except one,[1] were non-residents, plus the eight Dorset and nine Wiltshire non-resident burgesses ; only one out of every ten representatives returned from cities and boroughs in other parts of the country was a non-resident burgess. Even if we include the returns for the twenty-four boroughs of these three heavily-represented counties we may still say that only

---

[1] John Cory, six times parliamentary burgess for Launceston only 1410–23, controller of customs and subsidies at Plymouth and Fowey from April 1419 to November 1423 when he was made collector, was a resident of Launceston where he had been mayor in 1397 and 1405 (R. and O. B. Peters, *History of Launceston and Dunheved*, 111–13, 119, 400 ; W. Page and J. Dallas, *Notes and Gleanings for Devon and Cornwall*, V. 98 ; *C.F.R., 1413–22*, 293 ; *1422–30*, 52, 55, 61, 89, 90, 98, 108).

one out of every four burgesses returned to the parliament of 1422 was, according to the letter of the 1413 statute, a non-resident. A parliamentary burgess might have property in the borough, be entered on the roll of out-burgesses, and live near the borough, and yet be a non-resident ; even in this strict sense no more than 43 out of the 188 citizens and burgesses elected to Henry VI's first parliament were non-resident.

There were but few instances in 1422 of a tendency to that whole-sale ' invasion ' of the parliamentary boroughs by outsiders which later fifteenth-century conditions were to accelerate, or of the practice of ' carpet-bagging '. Although there were no less than twenty-six [1] of the 1422 burgesses who at some time or other were returned for more than one borough, only five of these ever sat for boroughs outside their own counties : John But, burgess for Truro in 1422, had represented Barnstaple early in the reign of Henry IV when he was occupying the office of duchy of Lancaster feodar in Devon ; Robert Halsewell, one of the Lyme representa-tives in 1422, was returned from Bridgwater in 1433 and Taunton in 1437 ; John Langley, one of the Chippenham burgesses in 1422, lived at Siddington in Gloucestershire and was a justice of the peace of the quorum in that county at the time ; Hugh Stanford, elected as one of the Newcastle-under-Lyme burgesses in 1422, had sat for the Salopian borough of Bridgnorth in 1411 and 1413 ; and Robert Darcy of Maldon had in 1402 been returned for Newcastle-on-Tyne when he was controller of tunnage and poundage there and along the coast between Berwick-on-Tweed and Scarborough. In the instances of parliamentary borough ' colonisation ' afforded by an

---

[1] Fifteen of the twenty-six sat for only two boroughs, and then sometimes only once for the second of these. Eight in all sat for three boroughs (Nicholas Ayssheton, once for Liskeard, five times for Helston, twice for Launceston, twice for Cornwall ; John Cork, once for Helston, twice for Liskeard, once for Bodmin ; John Trewint, twice for Liskeard, once for Truro, five times for Lostwithiel ; John Ford, once for Melcombe Regis, seven times for Dorchester, once for Shaftesbury ; Robert Halsewell, twice for Lyme, once for Bridgwater, once for Taunton ; William Fenyngham, three times for East Grinstead, once each for Midhurst and Arundel ; John Ludwell, twice for Old Sarum, once each for Chippenham and Cricklade ; John Sturmy, once each for Ludgershall, Marlborough and Bedwin). Two in all sat for four boroughs (John But, once each for Barnstaple and Liskeard and twice each for Bodmin and Truro ; John Giles, once each for Old Sarum and Wilton, twice for Calne, and thrice for Devizes).

Robert Treage between 1413 and 1425 represented five Cornish boroughs at one time or another (Bodmin, Helston, Lostwithiel, Truro, twice each ; Liskeard once).

examination of the returns of the burgesses to the 1422 parliament there is nothing like the conditions obtaining, for example, in Sussex between 1449 and 1478 when the four sons of Sir Thomas Lewkenore (knight of the shire in 1422) at one time or another were elected to parliament for the shire and each of its five parliamentary boroughs.

Most of the parliamentary burgesses returned to the parliament of 1422 were resident in-burgesses of the boroughs which they represented and many of them were members of the class which supplied the administration elements in the cities and boroughs themselves ; they filled the local offices of mayor, sheriff (in the case of a city or borough constituted by royal charter as a county *in se*), bailiff, and minor administrative positions.   At the time of their election to, and throughout the course of, Henry VI's first parliament one of the representatives of the boroughs of Wareham and Hull and the Cinque Port of Winchelsea was holding the office of mayor of his town (Walter Reson,[1] John Fitlyng,[2] and John Tamworth [3]), and as many as six more burgesses had been mayors until either just before or just after their return to parliament, that is, during the previous administrative year, 1421-2, namely, John Cook of Exeter,[4] Ralph Hunt of Bath,[5] John Mascall of Southampton,[6] John Shelley of Rye, Richard Russell [7] of York, and Thomas Poge [8] of Nottingham.   No sheriff of a city or borough which by charter-right was a shire-incorporate contravened in 1422 the prohibition of the writ of summons by returning himself, but of the twelve representatives returned by the towns which were shires in themselves seven had previously acted as one of the two annually appointed sheriffs.   Again, to the parliament of 1422 came one of the two bailiffs of Dartmouth (Thomas Ayssheldon [9]), Colchester (John Sumpter [10]) Ipswich (Thomas Astylle [11]), Huntingdon (John

[1] J. Hutchins, *History and Antiquities of Dorset*, I. 82 ; see below, p. 54.
[2] Exchequer L.T.R. Memoranda Roll, 1 Henry VI, P.R.O., E.368/195.
[3] See below, p. 54.
[4] R. and S. Izacke, *Remarkable Antiquities of the city of Exeter* (1724), 73 ; see below, p. 53.
[5] P.R.O., C.219/12/6.   [6] J. S. Davies, *History of Southampton*, 173.
[7] Surtees Society, CXXV, *York Memoranda Book*, Vol. II, 103 ; C.C.R., *1419-22*, 236.
[8] W. H. Stevenson, *Records of the Borough of Nottingham*, II. 428.
[9] *Hist. Mss. Comm., Fifth Report*, 602b.
[10] W. Gurney Benham, *Colchester Oath Book*, 102.
[11] Nicholas Bacon, *Annals of Ipswich*, ed. W. H. Richardson, 92.

Colles [1]), Scarborough (Hugh Rasyn [2]), and Shrewsbury (John Perle [3]), and one of the four bailiffs of Great Yarmouth (Robert Ellis [4]) ; Henry Frowyk,[5] one of the two commoners returned by London, was one of the auditors of the city, and one of the Cambridge burgesses, Simon Rankyn [6] had just been made one of the two new treasurers for the town.   Oligarchical elements, dominant in many of the cities and boroughs, naturally secured their representation by local election in the national assembly of parliament.

The trading and mercantile interests of the country were fairly well represented among the burgess members of the Lower House in 1422 by some forty parliamentary burgesses whom it is possible to identify as concerned in the conduct of some form of commercial activity ; of these fully half were involved in overseas trade mainly as either exporters or importers, but in some cases they were engaged in both branches of this trade.   The still all-important export trade in wool was represented by six of the most influential members of the Calais staple.   Thomas Fauconer,[7] who, after starting life as a draper, belonged to the London Mercers' Company (he was master of the gild in 1406, 1412, 1418, and 1424), was keenly interested in the Flanders wool trade, and had long-established connexions with the big Italian exporting firms, was one of the two aldermen returned by the city of London.   The activities of one of the two commoners of London, Thomas Mayneld the grocer (master of his company in 1401, 1408, 1420, and 1421),[8] may also have been partly in this direction, for he too had relations with the Albertini of Florence, who were large-scale wool exporters as well as the financial agents of the Roman Curia in England, and also with firms from Genoa.   The other five known Calais staplers elected to parliament in 1422 were, however, returned from towns in the basins of the Trent, Humber, and Ouse, towns whose main lines of communication with the continent lay through the ports of Hull

[1] *C.C.R.*, *1422–9*, 73.

[2] Exchequer L.T.R. Memoranda Roll 1 Henry VI, P.R.O., E.368/195.

[3] *Transactions of the Shropshire Archaeological and Natural History Society*, Vol. 3 243.

[4] F. Blomefield, *Topographical History of Norfolk*, XI. 324.

[5] R. R. Sharpe, *op. cit.*, *Letter Book K*, 1 ; A. B. Beaven, *Aldermen of the City of London*, II. 7.

[6] C. H. Cooper, *Annals of Cambridge*, I. 170.

[7] A. B. Beaven, *op. cit.*, II. 2 ; *C.C.R.*, *1399–1402*, 149 ; *1405–9*, 478 ; *1413–19*, 36 ; *C.P.R.*, *1401–5*, 214 ; *1413–16*, 277.

[8] *C.C.R.*, *1402–5*, 345, 375 ; *C.P.R.*, *1401–5*, 132.

and Boston and whose main sources of supply were the Yorkshire and Lincolnshire Wolds and the moorland sheep-runs of the West Riding. Both the York citizens returned in 1422 were Calais staplers ; William Bowes [1] had been a member of the fellowship for at least fifteen years and his co-representative, Richard Russell,[2] at the time of his next election to parliament in the spring of 1425 was to be mayor of the Calais staple, a position twice to be occupied later on by Hamond Sutton, one of the Lincoln representatives. Both Sutton and Russell were to be closely involved in the negotiation of the loans made to the Crown by the staplers in May 1433. Another merchant-stapler came from the port of Hull itself in the person of Robert Holme, and from Nottingham was returned another prominent wool-exporter, Thomas Poge, who had business connexions with Calais, York, and Hull, and with London too. It is not improbable that Thomas Stevens, mercer of Gloucester and London, whom Gloucester returned as one of its representatives in 1422, was also involved in the Calais wool-trade, and it is possible that Henry Frowyk, another but a more influential member of the London company of mercers, had interests in that direction as well ; John Colles,[3] one of the Huntingdon burgesses, was described as a ' wolman ', but he may have been merely a non-exporting entrepreneur.

Thomas Stevens of Gloucester was not the only provincial trader elected to parliament in 1422 to have connexions with the London merchant companies. Robert Trenerth,[4] a Cornish tin merchant returned as one of the Truro burgesses, was free of the City and a member of the Mercers' Company ; Richard Peny,[5] a ' clothier ', burgess for Melcombe Regis, was also a citizen of London ; and John Michell, one of the aldermen returned by the City, had a fellow-member of the London Fishmongers' Company among the

---

[1] *C.P.R., 1405–8*, 321, 414.

[2] *ibid.*, 321, 414 ; *1422–9*, 349 ; *Rot. Parl.*, IV. 474b ; Surtees Society, CXXV, *York Memoranda Book*, II. 157, 159 ; Surtees Society, XXX, *Testamenta Eboracensia*, II. 52, for his will (dated 1 December 1435), in which there were bequests of £20 and £10 to be divided respectively ' inter yconomos de Yorkes Walde de quibus emi lanam ' and among those of the parts of Lindsey, Lincolnshire. He had been sheriff of the city in 1412–13, and mayor in 1420–2 and 1429–30 (Surtees Society, XCVI, *op. cit.*, 130, 143 ; *C.C.R., 1419–22*, 148, 236).

[3] *C.P.R., 1436–41*, 113, 498.

[4] M.p. for Liskeard in December 1421 and for Truro in 1422 (*C.C.R., 1405–9, 275* ; *C.P.R., 1429–36*, 170 ; *C.F.R., 1413–22*, 237 ; R. R. Sharpe, *Letter Book* I ; 140).

[5] *Rot. Parl.*, IV. 111.

Commons in Robert Vessy of Exeter, then at the end of his year of office both as senior bailiff of Exeter and as constable of the staple there. Another representative of the distributive side of this section of the victualling trade was William Ufford, one of the Oxford burgesses, and at least one important part of the trade at its source was represented in the two burgesses of Great Yarmouth, Robert Ellis and John Hasting, both of whom were engaged in the town's main industry, the herring-fishery. Generally, however, such other merchant burgesses whose callings are identifiable, and who are not merely described vaguely as 'merchant', seem to have belonged to the distributive trades, some of them importers, others just internal middlemen; men like the Northampton mercer, John Bray, the Hereford grocer, Henry Chippenham, John Cook, the Exeter draper, and Cook's fellow-citizen, Robert Vessy, who was a 'chapman' as well as a member of the London Fishmongers' Company.

One other well-represented mercantile interest among the Commons of 1422 was that of the shipowners. Both the London aldermen, John Michell and Thomas Fauconer,[1] exported and imported in their own vessels; so did John Bourton, the great Bristol merchant, who retained his share in the town's interest in the importation of Gascon wines even when like his son-in-law, William Canynges, he later began to dabble in the Icelandic trade. It is probable that more of the barons returned by the Cinque Ports had shipping interests than John Green of Sandwich, whom we know to have had a share in the possession of coasting-vessels, or John Tamworth of Winchelsea, who earlier in the very same year (1422) had been engaged in freighting across the Channel both reinforcements of men and livestock provisions for Henry V's army in France.

Tamworth was at this time one of the two collectors of customs and subsidies in the customs area which had its centre in the port of Chichester. He was only one of several of the 1422 parliamentary burgesses who were occupied in this sphere of administrative activity, indicative of the government's interest in, and surveillance of, the import and export trade from English ports, men in close touch with most branches of commercial operation on the one hand and on the other with the Exchequer (as accounting officials). The port-officials of one sort or another returned to Henry VI's

[1] Rymer, *Foedera*, VIII. 727.

first parliament, drawn with one exception from the ports of the south and the south-west coasts of England, numbered no fewer than thirteen. John Exton, elected at Chichester, was Tamworth's fellow-customer there and shared with him and James Knottesford, then in 1422 filling the post of sheriff in Sussex and Surrey, the office of controller of tronage and pesage of wool and other staple commodities in the same port ; and Tamworth within six weeks of the parliamentary dissolution was to be appointed, in addition, to the office of deputy-butler at Winchelsea. Wareham returned in 1422 as one of its representatives Walter Reson, one of the customers in the Melcombe area and deputy-butler both there and at Weymouth. From Dartmouth came John Hawley, collector of customs and subsidies there and at Exeter also, and before the end of the parliamentary session to be appointed deputy-butler in the port of Dartmouth. John Gonne, one of the two customers and also joint-controller of tronage and pesage at Bridgwater, was elected in that borough. Melcombe returned William Balsham, the controller of customs there (that is, along the coast between Poole and Weymouth) and in the customs areas of Bridgwater, Dartmouth, and Exeter too. Robert Treage, a collector of customs and subsidies at Plymouth and Fowey, and John Cory, the controller of customs in the same districts, were respectively elected by the Cornish boroughs of Lostwithiel and Launceston. John But, the deputy-butler in the ports of Tawmouth and Barnstaple, was elected as one of the parliamentary burgesses of yet another of the Cornish towns, Truro. The two representatives from Exeter, John Cook and Robert Vessy, who a year later was to be appointed a collector of customs there and at Dartmouth, were respectively newly-appointed mayor and resigning constable of the staple in their own town, offices held by annual royal appointment and accountable in the Exchequer. Within the week before parliament met, to the office of troner of wools in the port of Southampton was appointed one of the burgesses-elect of Old Sarum, John Fruysthorp. All these instances of the return of port-officials accountable to the Exchequer are furnished by the ports of the south coast and the west country or from not-far-distant boroughs. The only port-official from the east coast came in the person of a lawyer and burgess of Newcastle-on-Tyne, Robert Whelpington, who was controller of customs in that port ; both the Hull burgesses (John Fitlyng and Robert Holme) had, however, been respectively searcher and searcher's overseer in the Humber only five years before 1422, and as late as 1419 Robert Ellis of Great Yarmouth had been one of the customers in the customs area which centred on that port. None of the customs-officials of the west coast, either at Bristol or in the ports giving on to the Irish Sea, were returned, but towards the close of the 1422 parliamentary session one of the Lancashire shire-knights, Thomas Urswyk, since 1417 receiver of the duchy of Lancaster estates in the county palatine and in the adjacent palatinate of Chester, was appointed as deputy to the Chief Butler of England (Thomas Chaucer) in the port of Liverpool. Such men as these, appointed either by the Treasurer or, in the case of the deputy-butlers, responsible to the King's Butler with his surveillance of the royal rights of prisage of wines, were officials by the King's commission and in the King's fee, and though aware of, and conversant with, the state and condition of trade were doubtless more interested in its possibilities as a source of revenue to the Crown ; they may have acted as a useful counterpoise to the inevitably self-considering and self-preservative ideas of the purely mercantile elements in the capitalist class, still adequately represented among the parliamentary burgesses.

A division of the analysis of the parliamentary experience and character of the Commons in the first assembly convened after Henry V's death into an examination of knights of the shires on the one hand and citizens and burgesses on the other, is partly one dictated by considerations of convenience, but it also rests on a recognition of the fact that the citizens and burgesses were as a class traditionally a less politically important element in the Commons than the knights of the shire. It was possible as late as 1439 for the knights to be distinguished from the burgesses in parliamentary petitions destined for the prior consideration of the Commons ;[1] in 1475 it was possible for Justice Littleton to speak as though the legislative capacity of the Commons was still monopolised by the shire-knights : 'Sir, en le Parliament si le greindre partie des Chivaliers des Countys assentent al feasans d'un acte du Parliament, et le meindre partie ne voillent my agreer a cel act, uncore ce sera bon statute a durer en perpetuity' ;[2] and even in

[1] A. R. Myers, ' Observations on the Procedure of the Commons in dealing with Bills in the Lancastrian Period ', *University of Toronto Law Journal*, III, No. 1, p. 62.

[2] S. B. Chrimes, *English Constitutional Ideas in the Fifteenth Century*, Appendix of Extracts from Year Book Cases, 373.

1523 it was not out of the question for the Lower House to separate out into its component estates and for knights and burgesses to divide as such on a motion for an increased supply, after the knights and gentlemen had already agreed on a grant to be taken from their landed income.[1]   The different rates of wages at which the knights of the shire and citizens and burgesses served, during the time of their journeying to the meeting-place of parliament and returning home as well as during the time of parliament itself, reflect the different social status to which it was expected they should belong. By the fifteenth century the knights had for long enjoyed a daily allowance double what was the accepted wage for a citizen or burgess, 4 as against 2 shillings.   As Mr. Richardson and Professor Sayles in a consideration of the position of parliament in Edward III's reign have suggested the corporateness of the Commons was, in its beginnings at any rate, likely to have been something imposed from above and not generated internally, the principal factors in its achievement being the privileged position of the Lords, the contrast between the representatives of communities and those who represented themselves, and the administrative convenience of the King's government.   For purposes of taxation especially, it had been found easier in the fourteenth century to treat with the knights and burgesses as one body and not two.[2]   It is interesting to observe those reminders of the fact that the constitutional integration of the Commons in parliament into a ' house ' whose members came to be regarded as representing the commonalty of the realm and not simply its different communities of shire, city, and borough, was an historical process, which requires chronological punctuation fully two centuries after the Commons became virtually an integral and necessary part of parliament.

The fifteenth-century Commons were not a completely homogeneous assembly either socially or politically.   The knights occupied a clearly leading position—there was a *Common* Speaker but he was always drawn from their ranks [3] and so was the personnel of any extraordinary deputation either to King or Lords.   Though

[1] Edward Hall, *Chronicle* [Henry IV–Henry VIII], ed. Henry Ellis, London, 1809, p. 657.

[2] H. G. Richardson and G. O. Sayles, ' The Parliaments of Edward III ', *The Bulletin of the Institute of Historical Research*, IX. 13.

[3] John Say, chosen as Speaker for the first time in February 1449, had, however, represented Cambridge borough in the preceding parliament, that which had met at Bury St. Edmunds two years earlier.

for normal purposes it is probable that they had ceased to act independently of the burgesses, the knights were still a social class apart ; but they were by no means as exclusively so as in times past. However wide apart were the social extremities of those who composed the Commons, the frontiers of demarcation were becoming so blurred as to make unreasonable any thought of a continued absence of identity of political or social interests between the knights and the burgesses as such. No fewer than 35 of the 188 parliamentary burgesses of 1422 twelve years later found their way into that fifteenth-century ' Who's Who ', the returns made by the shire-knights of 1433 in the following year of those local gentry and notables of their county whom they considered of sufficient standing and influence to be sworn not to maintain breakers of the King's peace.[1]

Occasionally a parliamentary burgess might be found to be holding some local position of royal appointment other than that of a mere Exchequer port-official, a position which was after all one for which he was well fitted by training and circumstance : John Hawley of Dartmouth, besides his office as customer at Dartmouth and Exeter, had at the time of his election in 1422 been holding for nineteen years the position of feodar of the duchy of Cornwall property in Devon and Cornwall ; Thomas Godstone of Colchester was then high bailiff of Guînes in Picardy ; John Forester, returned for Appleby, probably he of the same name who was a member of Lincoln's Inn, was the forester of Penrith-ward in the royal forest of Inglewood ; Walter Shirle, merchant of Salisbury, held the office of verderer in the forest of Clarendon ; [2] and John Mynors, one of the burgesses of Newcastle-under-Lyme, was a member of the royal Household and forester in the duchy of Lancaster honour of Tutbury.[3] At the time of their return in 1422 two of the parliamentary burgesses were justices of the peace in Cornwall (John Cork and John Hawley, the former being of the quorum,) and two in Gloucestershire (John Langley and Robert Gilbert, both being of the quorum), and later on an additional fifteen [4] were to serve on the same kind of royal commission in

---

[1] *C.P.R., 1429–36*, 370 *et seq.*   [2] *C.C.R., 1422–9*, 91.
[3] Duchy of Lancaster Accounts, P.R.O., D.L.29. 402. 6451.
[4] Robert Carlisle junior (m.p. Carlisle, for the first time j.p. 1423), Robert Elys (m.p. Great Yarmouth, j.p. 1423), Robert Whelpington (m.p. Newcastle-on-Tyne, j.p. 1424), John Hody (m.p. Shaftesbury, j.p. 1430), John Harpour (m.p. Stafford, j.p. 1430), Nicholas Ayssheton (m.p. Helston, j.p. 1431), Hamond Sutton (m.p.

their own counties. Eight of these nineteen and five others [1] were at some time or another to serve as escheators. At the outset of Henry VI's reign four burgesses were coroners in their shires, Edward Burneby (Launceston), John Whithorne (Wilton), William Kyrton (Southwark), and John Exton (Chichester), and three others [2] held the office either earlier or later than that date. Hugh Stanford,[3] parliamentary burgess for Newcastle-under-Lyme, Thomas Kempston [4] of Bedford, and Richard Wynnesley [5] of Leominster, had only just, that is, in the previous year, occupied the position of under-sheriff in their respective counties ; five of the 1422 burgesses [6] were even qualified by their ' sufficiency ' to fill the office of sheriff itself at some time in their lives, an office, which as one of the Stonore correspondents was to point out towards the end of the century, was still a ' presentable office ' and one which was sure to gain much ' acquaintance ' for its occupier, for which reason, he was able to add, ' the worcheppefollyst yn the scher have been schervys and yet theye hope to be '.[7] Almost without exception these men holding such Crown appointments and commissions

Lincoln, j.p. 1433), Robert Walsh (m.p. Lincoln, j.p. 1435), John Seymour (m.p. Ludgershall, j.p. 1438), Robert Whitgreve (m.p. Stafford, j.p. 1439), Walter Portman (m.p. Taunton, j.p. 1442), Henry Frowick (m.p. London, j.p. Middlesex 1445), William Gascoigne (m.p. Bridgwater, j.p. 1449), Richard Drax (m.p. Carlisle, j.p. Surrey 1452), Thomas Lavington (m.p. Reading, j.p. 1453). For the commissions of the peace, see *C.P.R., passim.*

[1] John Cork (escheator, Devon and Cornwall, 1426-7), John Langley (Gloucs, 1436-7), Robert Gilbert (Gloucs, 1412-13, 1416-17, 1428-30), Robert Whelpyngton (Northumberland, 1432-3), John Hody (Somerset and Dorset, 1431-2), John Harpour (Staffs, 1428-30, 1432-3, 1439-40), Hamond Sutton (Lincolnshire, 1423-4,) Robert Whitgreve (Staffs, 1427-8) ; Hugh Stanford (m.p. Newcastle-under-Lyme, escheator Staffs, 1403-5, 1407-8), Richard Hord (m.p. Bridgnorth, escheator Shropshire 1419-20), John Wise (m.p. Bodmin, escheator Devon and Cornwall, Feb.-Nov. 1430), John Forthey (m.p. Worcester, escheator Worcs 1432-3), John Whithorne (m.p. Wilton, escheator Hants and Wilts 1435-6) (see P.R.O., typescript *List of Escheators, passim*).

[2] Thomas Cricklade (m.p. Cricklade, coroner in Wilts before July 1419 ; *C.C.R., 1419-22,* 2. 141) ; John Trewint (m.p. Lostwithiel, coroner in Cornwall before July 1421 ; *C.C.R., 1419-22,* 168) ; John Warfield (m.p. Wallingford, coroner in Berks by December 1430 ; P.R.O., C.219, Bundle 14).

[3] P.R.O., C.219, Bundle 12, No. 6.   [4] *ibid.,* No. 5.   [5] *ibid.,* No. 5.

[6] John Polmorna (m.p. Liskeard, executive sheriff Cornwall 1406-7), John Hawley (m.p. Dartmouth, executive-sheriff Cornwall 1411-12), Hamond Sutton (m.p. Lincoln, sheriff of Lincolnshire 1428-9), John Seymour (m.p. Ludgershall, sheriff of Hants 1430-1 ; Wilts 1431-2 ; Somerset and Dorset 1433-4 ; Hants 1436-7), Nicholas Rody (m.p. Warwick, executive sheriff Worcs 1437-8).

[7] *Stonor Letters and Papers, 1290-1483* (The Royal Historical Society, Camden Series, XXX), 134.

were members of the armigerous class or at least men whom a Chancery clerk would not have scrupled to describe as ' gentilmen '.

Many of the parliamentary burgesses of 1422, both lawyers and others, show by their connexion or acquaintance with members of the local governing caste that they were essentially of the same stratum of society, men at least likely to be in active sympathy with the squirearchy if not country gentlemen themselves. John Warfeld of Wallingford, for example, was receiver to the prominent Buckinghamshire family of Stonore ; Nicholas Clopton, a Buckinghamshire lawyer, returned by the borough of Wycombe, was a great friend of Richard Wyot and his fellow administrator in the manorial courts of the college of St. George's Windsor (Wyot was seven times knight of the shire for Buckinghamshire between 1407 and 1426, and once for Middlesex, and in Henry IV's reign was steward to Bishop Beaufort of Winchester) ; John Marchaunt of Taunton [1] was a friend and feoffee of Sir Hugh Luttrell of Dunster, who had been seneschal of Normandy from October 1420 until the summer of 1422, and his fellow parliamentary burgess, Walter Portman, acted as legal counsel to the same local magnate ; incidentally, John Hody of Shaftesbury was Luttrell's former receiver-general's son ; [2] Richard Secheville, parliamentary burgess of Tavistock in 1422, was a friend of Henry V's Chief Justice of King's Bench, Sir William Hankford ; [3] John Hawley of Dartmouth was a grandson of Richard II's unhappily-fated Chief Justice, Sir Robert Tresilian, and father-in-law to John Coplestone junior, one of the two men who, at the beginning of Henry VI's reign, were together holding the offices of receiver and steward of the duchy of Cornwall ; [4] John Allestry of Nottingham, at the time of his return in 1422, had recently appointed the then sheriff of Nottingham and Derby, Ralph Makerell, as the overseer of his will.[5] A few of the burgesses had even ' acquaintance '

[1] M.P. Taunton, April and November 1414, 1422, 1425, 1426 (H. C. Maxwell-Lyte, *Dunster and its Lords*, 122 ; *C.P.R.*, *1429–36*, 99 ; *C.C.R.*, *1429–35*, 73, 76).

[2] H. C. Maxwell-Lyte, *op. cit.*, 120.

[3] E. F. Jacob, *Chichele Register*, II. 291.

[4] *Reports and Trans. Devon Assocn.*, Vol. 43 (1911), 138 ; Wedgwood, *op. cit.*, 220 (Coplestone junior, m.p. for Devon in December 1421, 1435, and 1439, was joint receiver-general and steward of the duchy of Cornwall 28 May 1422–10 February 1423).

[5] Surtees Society, Vol. 53, *Testamenta Eboracensia*, IV. 63a ; the will was dated 20 April 1422 ; Allestry died between January and 6 April 1431 when probate was granted at York (the monetary provisions of the will totalled some £486).

among the titular nobility : both the Bedford burgesses, later on
at any rate, had connexions with Sir John Cornwall, the new king's
great-uncle by marriage, the later Lord Fanhope ; [1] Nicholas Rody
of Warwick was afterwards to be executor and feoffee to Richard
Beauchamp, earl of Warwick ; [2] John Harpour,[3] parliamentary
burgess for Stafford, was in close touch shortly before his election
in 1422 with Joan Beauchamp dame Abergavenny and her agent,
Brokesby (in 1422 shire-knight for Leicestershire), as a result of his
lifelong intimate connexion with the family of Humphrey, earl of
Stafford, then a minor in royal wardship ; William Warnecamp,[4]
one of the Arundel burgesses, was a member of a family who were
tenants of the FitzAlans at nearby Houghton and had other connexions with the earls of Arundel ; Henry Boteler of Horsham
was closely enough attached to the lords of the borough, the great
family of Mowbray, to provide for their inclusion on the bede-roll
of his chantry ; [5] John Bye, the recorder of Winchester and the
city's representative in the 1422 parliament, had been appointed
only three days before the opening of the session as one of the
receivers in the city to Henry IV's queen, Joan of Navarre ; and
Thomas Marlborough, town-clerk of Southampton and parliamentary burgess, was one of her attorneys in the royal courts.

Quite a number of the 1422 burgesses were connected too either
by blood or interest with members of the ecclesiastical hierarchy or
with clerks favourably placed in the administrative system of the
Church : Thomas Lavyngton ' gentilman ' of Reading was a cousin

---

Ironmonger and merchant of Nottingham, Allestry had been bailiff of the borough
in 1402–3 ; mayor in 1409–10, 1414–15, 1420–1, 1426–7, 1430–1 ; and m.p. March
1416, May 1421, 1422, 1425. His eldest son, Thomas, became one of the foremost
members of the Calais staple (*Hist. Mss. Comm., Report on Mss. of Lord Middleton at
Wollaton Hall, Notts.,* 100 ; W. H. Stevenson, *Records of the borough of Nottingham,*
I. 284 ; II. 426–7.

[1] Thomas Kempston (*C.P.R., 1436–41,* 246) ; John Ferrour (*ibid.,* 246 ;
H. Gibbons, *Early Lincoln Wills,* 166).

[2] Nicholas Rody, m.p. Warwick 1413, November 1414, 1419, May and December
1421, 1422, 1423, 1425, 1437 ; he was under-sheriff of Worcestershire November
1437–8 (the shrievalty was held in fee by the earls of Warwick) ; he was feoffee
and executor to Richard Beauchamp, earl of Warwick (ob. 1439) (*William Salt
Arch. Society Trans.,* N.S., VII. 251 ; Blomefield, *Norfolk,* VI. 53–4 ; VII. 294 ;
C.P.R., 1436–41, 429).

[3] *C.F.R., 1413–22,* 440.

[4] *C.P.R., 1452–61,* 203 ; *Hist. Mss. Comm., Various I, Report on the muniments
of the bishop of Chichester,* 184.

[5] Henry Boteler, m.p. Horsham 1413, March 1416, December 1421, 1422, 1437
(*C.P.R., 1441–6,* 278 ; D. E. Hurst, *History and Antiquities of Horsham,* 2).

and ' servant ' (and later an executor and legatee) of Thomas Polton, who, at the time of the former's election to parliament in 1422, had been recently translated from the see of Hereford to that of Chichester ; Robert Halsewell ' gentilman ', returned to parliament in 1422 from Lyme Regis, was a cousin (and later receiver and executor) to Simon Sydenham, then dean of Salisbury but promoted in 1431 to the see of Chichester where he died in 1438 ; John Hody of Shaftesbury,[1] later Chief Justice, was a nephew of the precentor of Wells, Master John Hody, who had been in the summer of 1422 one of the farmers of the temporalities of the then vacant see of Chichester ; and John Hill of Chichester, parliamentary burgess for Arundel in 1422, had been one of their sureties in the Exchequer. It is a singular coincidence that yet another of the 1422 burgesses should have had connexions with the see of Chichester, namely, Richard Clitheroe of Romney, the brother of John Clitheroe, clerk of the Apostolic Camera in the Roman Curia, who in 1422 was canon of Chichester and three years later was to be preferred to the see of Bangor in North Wales.

Connexions were not entirely wanting between one or two of the lawyer burgesses and neighbouring monastic houses and sometimes in a way particularly interesting from the point of view of the relations between parliament and convocation : Nicholas Wotton of Ramsbury, parliamentary burgess for Marlborough, was parliamentary proxy in 1422 for the abbot of Malmesbury ; Robert Gilbert, burgess for Gloucester, had once previously acted in a similar capacity for the abbot of Gloucester ; and Richard Duffeld, clerk of the peace in the parts of Lindsey in Lincolnshire and burgess for Grimsby, had formerly been and was to be again parliamentary proxy for the abbot of Bardney. It has already been noticed that Richard Wynnesley, returned from Leominster, was the abbot of Reading's bailiff in the liberty of the borough.

While these seigneurial and ecclesiastical relationships are indicative of a considerably high social or professional standing and were probably productive of a certain amount of influence and reputation, perhaps of more immediate concern were the connexions between individual burgesses and knights of the shire returned to parliament alongside of them in 1422. It is interesting to note, for example, that the brother and half-brother of Henry Frowyk, one

---

[1] E. F. Jacob, *op. cit.*, II. 244 ; J. Hutchins, *History and Antiquities of Dorset*, II. 233 ; *C.F.R.*, *1413–22*, 439.

of the London representatives, namely, Sir Thomas Charleton and
Thomas Frowyk, were returned for Middlesex. Sir William
Sturmy, the Wiltshire shire-knight, numbered quite a few kinsmen
or friends from the Wiltshire burgesses among his acquaintance in
the Commons : his bastard son, John Sturmy, and his grandson
and heir, John Seymour, together represented the borough of
Ludgershall ; his kinsman and close friend, feoffee to uses, and
executor, Robert Erle, was one of the Bedwin burgesses ; and his
near neighbour, Nicholas Wotton of Ramsbury, who had attested
some of his private deeds,[1] was returned by the borough of Marlborough. John Warfeld of Wallingford [2] was a feoffee of the
estates of his neighbour, Thomas Chaucer of Ewelme, one of the
Oxfordshire knights, and was in close touch with John Golafre,
knight of the shire for Berkshire ; both of these knights of parliament were Warfeld's co-feoffees in the Stonore property, of which
he was receiver and steward. William Gascoyne of Bridgwater
numbered among his feoffees the knight of the shire for Dorset,
Sir Humphrey Stafford, a big west-country landed proprietor.[3]
John Sumpter, one of the Colchester burgesses, must have had
contacts with John Leventhorpe, receiver-general of the duchy of
Lancaster and knight of the shire for Hertfordshire, and he was one
of the trustees of the property of Sir William Coggeshall, knight
of the shire for Essex. The Ipswich burgess, Thomas Astley, stood
in the same relationship to one of the Norfolk representatives,
Edmund Wynter. Richard Clitheroe, one of the ' barons ' returned by Romney, and the Kentish shire-knight, Geoffrey Lowther,
lieutenant-warden of the Cinque Ports, had recently been associated
as executors to the former's kinsman and namesake, Richard
Clitheroe of Goldstanton, admiral in the south and west in 1406,
who then and in the parliament of 1407 had been himself knight of
the shire for Kent. David Urban, returned in 1422 as burgess for
Helston, had been in 1418 lieutenant to Sir John Arundell, one of
the Cornish knights of the shire, when the latter was vice-admiral
in the west to the duke of Exeter. With a considerable proportion
of burgesses thus influentially and officially connected, it is no longer
possible to hold the view, in the case of fifteenth-century parliaments at any rate, that borough members were ' men of business
reluctantly diverted from their private affairs for occasional public

---

[1] *C.C.R., 1413–19*, 458.   [2] *C.P.R., 1429–36*, 448 ; *C.F.R., 1413–22*, 338.
[3] *Hist. Mss. Comm., Reports on Wells Mss.*, II. 664–5.

service ', as Pollard thought they were. The social connexions between the two formally differentiated sections, shire-knights and burgesses, probably did more than counterbalance the adverse effects of the continued brevity of sessions and the relative instability of personnel on the development of a corporate consciousness in the Lower House.

There is yet another indication of the way in which the old distinctions between ' town ' and ' country ', between ' landlordism ' and ' trade ', were breaking down in parliamentary representation as they had been doing in other directions for long enough. This is yielded by an examination of the extent to which the boroughs were in many cases returning men to parliament who were (in the sheriff's eyes) of sufficient standing to attest the indentures of return at the elections of the shire-knights in the county courts. No fewer than sixty-three of the 1422 parliamentary burgesses at some time or other sealed a sheriff's indenture of election, twenty-nine of them prior to their own return in 1422. In the case of the shire-elections to the 1422 parliament itself, fourteen of the parliamentary burgesses had attested the indentures of return of the knights of their shire : John Polmorna, John Cory, Edward Burneby, and John But, were present at the Cornish elections ; the Chichester member, John Exton, sealed the electoral indenture for Sussex ; John Bye, returned for Winchester, sealed that embodying the return for Hampshire ; Nicholas Stokes of Worcester apposed his seal to the Worcestershire return ; and seven of the Wiltshire burgesses-elect had assisted at the election of the knights of the shire for that county.[1]

[1] P.R.O., C.219, Bundle 13, File 1.

CHAPTER V

THE KNIGHTS OF THE SHIRE OF 1422

NO single element in the Commons contributed more to the shading off of the higher non-noble landed class into the lower professional and mercantile classes than the lawyers who were common to both groups and who might seek to appear in parliament as the representatives of either shire or borough. Of the nine borough members of the 1422 parliament who had already sat or were to sit later on as knights of the shire, six were lawyers ; two of them, Robert Darcy, steward of the Bohun estates that were then in slow process of being conjoined with the hereditary property of the King in the duchy of Lancaster, and soon to be confirmed in his former office of *Custos Brevium* in the Court of Common Pleas, and John Langley, a justice of the peace in Gloucestershire, were in 1422 merely using a borough return as a temporary expedient. In contravention of the statute of 1413 with its insistence on residential qualification, John Langley secured his election for the Wiltshire borough of Chippenham ; when later he sat four times in the 'thirties as knight of the shire it was from his own, the neighbouring, county of Gloucestershire that he was returned. Darcy, who had before 1422 already served as shire-knight for Essex on three occasions and was to sit for the same county in six later parliaments, was, however, a resident burgess of Maldon which returned him to Henry VI's first parliament.

The fourteenth-century official prejudice against the return of lawyers as parliamentary representatives had been mainly a protest against the way in which they had put the petitioning function and method of the Commons in danger of subservience to the private requirements of their clients, and against the unconscious tendency of their manœuvres to obstruct the consideration of the *negotia regni* which in the king's eyes it was parliament's real purpose and function to secure. For all that, lawyers continued to form a considerable element in the Commons, and the importance of their presence, with its indefinite but undoubtedly none the less real effect on the development of procedures and on the formation of the constitutional traditions of the Commons, cannot be overestimated. Their professional conservatism, born of a veneration for the past and its precedents, was later, in Elizabethan and Stuart England, to determine that their main task should be that of challenging administrative practice not warranted in existing statute law, and signs are not wanting in the early fifteenth century that the lawyers in parliament were already aware that this watch and ward over the law and practice of the constitution was to be their peculiar contribution to its work. The Commons' insistence on the correct and precise enactment and engrossment of statutes in 1401 and again in 1406, their circumvented attempt in 1414 to secure that the intent of their bills should not be altered when enacted without their assent being given to any amendments, their effort in the parliament of 1422 itself to shackle the growing judicial activities of the Council and Chancery by a restriction of the operation of privy seal writs of *subpena*, are only random selections from a mass of evidence pointing to the jealous vigilance of the *jurisperiti* in the Commons on matters affecting procedure and the *pratique* of legislation.

The lawyers, sitting in the Commons as parliamentary burgesses or as knights of the shire (some of them sitting indifferently in either rôle as opportunity and circumstance afforded), tended to obliterate the effects of the social distinction between these two still formally distinct, component elements in the Lower House. To bring about a great degree of homogeneity in the Commons was a useful function in itself. But an estimate of what their numerical strength in the House might on occasion attain to, conditions any appreciation of the inevitability of their effect on parliamentary procedure and practice.

In Henry VI's first parliament the men of law constituted roughly no less than between a fifth and a quarter of the Commons who at this time numbered altogether about 262 members. This is a remarkably high proportion : a century and a half or so later, in Elizabeth's reign, the numbers of practising lawyers were usually no greater in a House of Commons which, however, was well on the way to having doubled its mid-Lancastrian size. According to Professor Neale's figures for the parliament of 1584, for example, the practising lawyers returned to it numbered 53 out of a total membership of some 460.[1] In 1422 at least 37 lawyers were

[1] J. E. Neale, *op. cit.*, 302 ; Professor Neale is, however, able to say that in 1593 ' forty-three per cent of the members possessed a legal education ' (*ibid.*, 307). The

returned as burgesses [1] and no fewer than 20 as shire-knights ; [2] of these 57 lawyers elected in 1422 probably as many as 12 were fellow-members of the society of Lincoln's Inn, the only one of the several inns of court of which the records have come down to us from so early a date. [3] Perhaps the most interesting fact about these statistics for 1422 is, however, the high proportion of lawyers (twenty out of seventy-four) among the knights of the shire who, as a class, still carried more weight than the borough representatives, thanks to their generally superior social standing, to their greater political and administrative experience, and to the fact that they were the representatives of counties and of the socially superior elements in the population. Two out of every seven of the shire-knights were lawyers.

Some of the more important of these shire-knights learned in the law were in Crown employment either at the time of their return in 1422 or later. John Wodehouse and John Throckmorton, respectively returned from Suffolk and Worcestershire, were the then two chamberlains of the Exchequer, that is, in charge, under the treasurer, of the Lower Exchequer of receipt and issue as distinct from the Exchequer court of audit and pleas. The former held, in addition, the appointment of chancellor of the duchy of Lancaster, and was chancellor to Henry V's queen, Catherine of Valois. This last appointment Wodehouse doubtless owed to the fact that Catherine's dower-income was largely forthcoming from the revenues of the duchy of Lancaster. Other ex-officio members of the council of the duchy of Lancaster to be elected in 1422 were its chief steward north of Trent, Roger Flore, whom the Commons

records of Lincoln's Inn are unfortunately the only records of an Inn of Court to have survived from so early a date as 1420, when its Register of Admissions begins.

[1] See above, pp. 46–7.

[2] Roger Flore (m.p. Rutland), John Enderby (Beds), John Russell (Herefords), Thomas Urswick (Lancs), William Burley (Salop), Hugh Burgh (Salop), John Barton junior (Bucks), Robert Stanshawe (Glos), John Leventhorpe (Herts), John Hotoft (Herts), Geoffrey Lowther (Kent), Bartholomew Brokesby (Leics), Edmund Winter (Norfolk), John Wodehouse (Suffolk), Robert Skerne (Surrey), Robert Andrew (Wilts), John Tyrell (Essex), Roger Hunt (Huntingdonshire), John Throckmorton (Worcs), John Vampage (Worcs). It will be noticed that only three counties returned men of law for both their knights : Shropshire, Herts, and Worcestershire.

[3] For the seven probable members of Lincoln's Inn who sat in 1422 as parliamentary burgesses, see above pp. 46–7 ; the five probable members who sat as knights of the shire were Roger Hunt, John Barton junior, Robert Stanshawe, John Hotoft, and Geoffrey Lowther.

elected as speaker for the fourth time, and its receiver- and attorney-general since 1399, John Leventhorpe. The latter's fellow-knight of the shire for Hertfordshire was John Hotoft, formerly controller of Household to Henry V before his accession in 1413, and since then keeper of the writs of the Court of Common Pleas, an office he was soon (in February 1423) to relinquish in favour of the parliamentary burgess for Maldon, Robert Darcy (Darcy had held it under Henry IV), just when he himself assumed the office of treasurer of the royal Household ; later on, in 1431, Hotoft was to succeed Wodehouse as chamberlain of the Exchequer. John Tyrell, knight of the shire for Essex in Henry VI's first parliament, who was in 1431 to follow Hotoft as treasurer of the Household, had then since December 1427 been occupying the office of chief steward of the duchy of Lancaster south of Trent ; he retained both these offices until his death in 1437. Incidentally, it is interesting to notice that, perhaps because immediately after Henry VI's accession the royal Household was in process of re-organisation, members of the Household staff proper were almost completely absent from the Lower House of 1422. Certainly the only minor accounting official of the Household to find a place there was an old retainer of the late king, Robert Castell esquire, knight of the shire for Warwickshire, who was serving Henry V at the time of his death as serjeant of the ' avenerie ' of the Household and as such was in charge of its supply of oats.

There were others among the lawyer knights of the shire who later on received official preferment in the royal service. Roger Hunt, one of the Huntingdonshire knights, was in 1428 to be appointed to the stewardship of the Household and ten years later to be made a Baron of the Exchequer. Geoffrey Lowther, one of the Kentish representatives, was at the time of his return in 1422 the duke of Gloucester's lieutenant-warden of the Cinque ports and early in the following year was to be receiver-general and attorney-general in those estates of the duchy of Lancaster not vested in Henry V's feoffees for the administration of his will. John Vampage, knight of the shire for Worcestershire, was appointed as the king's attorney-general in 1429. By this time Vampage was one of the lawyers retained as counsel by Richard Beauchamp, earl of Warwick. In fact, all the lawyers returned as shire-knights in 1422 and not at that time employed in the service of the Crown were either then or later in the fee of one or even more than one of the great baronial families, acting as legal counsel or in some other advisory or administrative capacity. Vampage's fellow-knight of the shire for Worcestershire, John Throckmorton, enjoyed a long family connexion with the Beauchamps (his father before him had been constable of the Beauchamp castle of Elmley) ; he had served as a member of Warwick's retinue in Normandy in the 1417 expedition ; he was feoffee in the earl's estates and was later to act as his executor ; since 1419 he had held his Exchequer office of Warwick chamberlain by the earl's appointment ; and he married the daughter of another of the Beauchamp tenantry. Soon after if not already by 1422 Robert Stanshawe (of Gloucestershire) and Robert Andrewe (of Wiltshire) were to be retained as legal counsel by the earl, and John Barton junior (of Buckinghamshire), who before the end of Henry IV's reign had been eminent enough in his profession to be offered promotion to the position of royal serjeant-at-law and to be serving the office of steward to the abbey of St. Albans, had acted as legal counsel to Warwick in 1417. He had acted in a similar capacity for a kinswoman of Warwick's, Joan Beauchamp dame Abergavenny, whose foremost land agent and principal executor, Bartholomew Brokesby, represented Leicestershire in the 1422 parliament. John Russell, knight of the shire for Herefordshire, an apprentice-at-law who had been retained as counsel to the duchy of Lancaster continuously from 1403 until early in 1421, was, like Brokesby and Barton, another of Dame Abergavenny's feoffees to uses.

The lawyers of 1422 were by no means the only shire-knights to have connexions with the parliamentary aristocracy. In fact, those of the shire-knights who were without such seigneurial attachments, either of interest or of kinship, were few and far between. In a period when the baronage was hopelessly divided within itself such a representation and reflection of its varied affections and antipathies could only tend to divide the knights into cliques representing sectional interests, and to influence adversely any movement towards corporate solidarity in the Commons even when the interests of their own class demanded it. But at a time when aristocratic aims and public opinion coincided, the policy binding together the generality of the lords spiritual and temporal would result in a corresponding solidarity in the more influential element in the Lower House, simply because a great number of the knights of the shire there were already aware of, and to a certain extent likely to be in sympathy with, the political outlook and attitude of individual magnates.

It is only necessary to look at the personal connexions among the knights of the shire possessed by the four lords prominent in the resistance to Gloucester's claim in 1422 to have the governance of the land as well by right of birth as by the will of Henry V— Henry Beaufort, bishop of Winchester, his brother, Thomas, duke of Exeter, and the earls of March (Edmund Mortimer) and Warwick (Richard Beauchamp)—to realise the nature of the opportunities for sympathetic contact between the Lords and Commons in 1422. One of the most influential of the shire-knights, Thomas Chaucer of Ewelme (Oxon), Chief Butler of England almost continuously since 1402, steward since 1399 of the associated duchy of Cornwall honours of Wallingford and St. Valery, Speaker for the Commons in no fewer than five parliaments, was a man possessed of many friends in the Lower House of 1422—John Golafre (Berkshire), John Warfeld of Wallingford, Robert James (Buckinghamshire), John Arundell the younger of Bideford, Chaucer's brother-in-law, who was returned from Cornwall with his father, and others who would include such of the deputy-butlers as were returned to or appointed during this parliament, John But, returned from Bodmin, John Hawley, from Dartmouth, Walter Reson, from Wareham, and Thomas Urswyk, knight of the shire for Lancashire. As the putative son of Geoffrey Chaucer by Philippa Roet (sister of Catherine Swinford, John of Gaunt's mistress and then his third duchess), Chaucer was Bishop Henry Beaufort's cousin and in 1422 had long been overseer of the estates of the diocese of Winchester in Somerset ; their relationship, now that Henry V was dead, was doubtless much less complicated than it had been since 1417 when Beaufort's ecclesiastical ambitions had outrun his judgement of his royal nephew's character. John Tamworth of Winchelsea was before the end of January 1423 to be appointed as Chaucer's deputy-butler there. From Chichester, where Tamworth was already collector of customs, was returned John Exton, his fellow-customer, Bishop Beaufort's own nominee to the office in accordance with the arrangements made for the repayment of the bishop's loans to the Crown. The bishop's brother, the duke of Exeter, was similarly not without his known connexions in the Lower House. Sir John Arundell, elected knight of the shire for Cornwall along with his son, had recently been the duke's vice-admiral in the West ; David

F

Urban, parliamentary burgess for Helston, had been Arundell's deputy in this office ; and Sir William Palton (Somerset), cousin german of William Lord Botreaux and a relative by marriage of Sir John Tiptoft (a commoner member of the new Council), had been in 1418 and 1419 a member of the duke's military retinue. Sir Thomas Waweton (Bedfordshire) at the time of his Speakership in 1425 (and probably already) was a retainer of the earl of March, perhaps as a result of his kinship with Sir John Tiptoft, who was the earl's brother-in-law ; and Sir John Pelham (Sussex), treasurer of England in the last fifteen months of Henry IV's reign and still in 1422 acting as executor to that king, was one of Mortimer's feoffees. Pelham was, of course, a great landed magnate in his own right.

The most powerful single seigneurial bloc in the Commons seems, however, to have been that of the earl of Warwick. Five lawyers likely to have had Beauchamp interests in mind, Throckmorton (Worcestershire), Vampage (Worcestershire), Stanshawe (Gloucestershire), Andrewe (Wiltshire), and Barton (Buckinghamshire), have already been referred to, but they were not the only Beauchamp adherents in the Lower House. Sir William Montfort, knight of the shire for Warwickshire, a grandson of John Lord Clinton of Maxstoke and a distant kinsman of the earl, was his steward of household and chief of council. One of the Staffordshire knights, Thomas Stanley, had been a member of Warwick's retinue in 1414 when the earl was occupying the captaincy of Calais, and Joan Astley, the sister of Stanley's fellow knight of the shire, Sir John Gresley, had married a kinsman of the earl of Warwick and probably owed her appointment as one of the nurses to the young Henry of Windsor to this connexion. One of the Warwick burgesses, Nicholas Rody, may be presumed to have been attached already to the Beauchamp interest in view of the fact that later he was so closely in touch with the earl as to be appointed one of his executors and a member of his committee of feoffees.

Henry V's two surviving brothers, John, duke of Bedford, and Humphrey, duke of Gloucester, the determination of whose constitutional position in England was the chief item of business in Henry VI's first parliament, were not without their recognisable supporters among the Commons. John Greville esquire, Bedford's receiver-general in England since (at the latest) May 1420, came up to Westminster as knight of the shire for his own county of

Gloucestershire. Geoffrey Lowther, duke Humphrey's lieutenant-warden of the Cinque Ports and one of his feoffees, was one of the Kentish representatives, and the son of his fellow-knight, Reginald Pympe, had served in the Agincourt campaign as a member of Gloucester's retinue and had still been his retainer when the duke left England with Henry V in June 1421. John Tyrell, one of the Essex knights, had served with Gloucester on Henry V's first expedition, was one of his feoffees, and had been steward of his estates in Essex in 1416, and probably still was. Certainly he was one of the duke's closest and steadiest partisans ; Sir William Coggeshall, Tyrell's father-in-law, was his fellow-representative for Essex. Whether the influential lawyer and parliamentary burgess of Maldon, Robert Darcy, was already nearly connected with Tyrell also, is not known, but two of his sons, including his heir, Robert, and two of his daughters were eventually at any rate to marry into the Tyrell family. Another shire-knight who had in 1415 indentured to serve as a member of Gloucester's retinue and who maintained this connexion, was Sir Robert Roos, returned from Lincolnshire in 1422. There is no evidence that one of the Northants knights, Henry Mulsho esquire, was in 1422 connected with the duke of Gloucester ; but, probably by 2 July 1423, certainly by the following October, Mulsho was acting as the treasurer of the ducal household, an office which he continued to serve for at least a year and probably until shortly before his death in the spring of 1425 ; the importance of the office suggests a confidence of some long standing on Gloucester's part. Another connexion of Gloucester's—he was at any rate retained by the duke in September 1423 with the substantial fee of £20 a year—was John Skelton esquire, son of the Cumberland knight of the shire of the same name, Sir John Skelton of Armathwaite, one of whose other sons (Richard) had served in Gloucester's retinue in Normandy in 1417–18. Both the Dorset knights of the shire also had close ties with the duke : Sir Humphrey Stafford of Southwick (Wiltshire) and Hooke (Dorset) and Robert Lovell. Little more than a year before Henry VI's first parliament assembled, Gloucester, then *Custos Anglie*, had been largely instrumental (at a price) in securing for Sir Humphrey Stafford's young son-in-law, James Lord Berkeley, the requisite royal licence to sue out livery of the castle and lordship of Berkeley and pay his baronial relief. All this in face of the opposition of the earl of Warwick whose wife was excluded (so Berkeley maintained) by the entail, although she was the only daughter and heir of the last Lord Berkeley.   Seven years later (in 1429) Sir Humphrey and his half-brother, Dr. John Stafford, who two days before the dissolution of the parliament of 1422 surrendered the keepership of the privy seal to take up the office of treasurer of England (he resigned this office in the crisis of 1426), were to amortise land to Abbotsbury abbey in return for spiritual offices expressly designed to benefit Gloucester as well as themselves and others, who included each of the Lancastrian kings : an act of devotion to the dynasty and the Protector in particular.   Stafford's fellow shire-knight, Robert Lovell, had formerly been the duke of Gloucester's receiver (probably in Wiltshire) and, though sued for debt as such, still retained sufficient influence with the duke as late as 1427 to secure his support for a petition he then presented to the King and Lords asking for the repayment of Henry V's debts to him, debts amounting to £2,330. In any case, Stafford and Lovell were closely enough related to warrant an assumption that ways and means were ready to make the latter disposed to sympathise with Gloucester's political aims : Stafford's son had married Lovell's daughter, and Stafford himself had served Lovell as feoffee.

Besides the dukes of Bedford, Gloucester, and Exeter, the earls of Warwick and March, and the bishop of Winchester, quite a few of the other members of the Council appointed in December 1422 had their 'acquaintance' in the Common House. The Earl Marshal, John Mowbray, soon to be recognised (in 1425) by the greater dignity of duke of Norfolk, was represented in the persons of both the Norfolk knights and was related by ties of kinship with one of the Suffolk members.   John Lancastre, who had been in the service of the Mowbrays for at least thirty years as a counsellor to the present Earl Marshal, and to his father and elder brother before him, and was now steward of their castle of Framlingham, was elected in Norfolk ; Edmund Wynter, a mesne-tenant of the Mowbrays, whom the duke was to appoint in 1429 as one of his executors and attorneys-general, was Lancastre's fellow-knight of the shire. The son of the Suffolk knight of the shire, Sir John Howard, had married the Earl Marshal's sister and Sir John's grandson was ultimately, for want of heirs in the direct Mowbray male line, to succeed to the dukedom.

The Nevilles, with their Beaufort connexion, also had men of their own attached to their interest sitting in the Commons.   One

of the Cumberland shire-knights, Sir Peter Tilliol, before two years
had elapsed after the meeting of Henry VI's first parliament was
to be appointed an executor of the will of Ralph Neville earl of
Westmorland, father-in-law to the Earl Marshal and the young earl
of Northumberland, and brother-in-law to Bishop Henry Beaufort
and Thomas Beaufort duke of Exeter who, with Bishop Langley
of Durham, were together overseers of the will.   Tilliol held his
manor of Torpenhow as tenant of one of the Neville honours and
could presumably be relied on to support the Neville political
interest.   Probably the same could be said of Sir Edmund Hastings,
one of the knights returned from Yorkshire, where the earl of
Westmorland was one of the most influential of the great lords of
the franchises whose attorneys still played such an important part
in the shire elections.   Hastings had long had close connexions with
the Neville family and at the time of his return to parliament in
1422 was acting as feoffee, for the fulfilment of her will, to the earl
of Westmorland's daughter-in-law, the wife of Sir John Neville ;
Westmorland's eighth son, William, had, moreover, married the
niece of Hastings's wife.

Hastings's fellow-representative for Yorkshire was Sir William
Eure, now returned for the first time, a young man of twenty-six
who, with his name still to make in the political world, had just
succeeded to the family estates in the North Riding of Yorkshire,
the county palatine of Durham, and Northumberland.   Eure was
son-in-law to one of the foremost of the northern peerage, no less
a magnate than Henry Lord FitzHugh of Ravensworth, the head of
a baronial family powerful in lands and influence between Swale
and Tees and of considerable consequence at the Lancastrian court
(FitzHugh had been chamberlain to Henry V, treasurer of England
from 1417 to 1421, was the only one of the late king's operative
executors of baronial rank, and now was to be appointed a member
of the new Council).   Another knight of the shire likely to be of
Lord FitzHugh's acquaintance, although probably with no close
attachment like Eure's, was Sir John Bertram, one of the Northumbrian representatives, whose brother was related to the FitzHughs
through his marriage into the family of Grey of Heton.   Another
member of the new Council with a clear connexion in the Lower
House was Sir Ralph Cromwell, now summoned for the first time
to sit among the lords temporal : his brother-in-law, Sir Richard
Stanhope of Rampton, was sitting for the sixth time as knight of

the shire for Nottinghamshire. The ninth of the dozen lay members of the Council with friends among the Commons was Sir John Tiptoft, himself a former Speaker who was not to have to wait long for his individual writ of summons as a peer to parliament (he was summoned in 1425). His kinsman and feoffee to uses, Sir Thomas Waweton, who was also attached to the earl of March, Tiptoft's brother-in-law, was shire-knight in 1422 for Huntingdon-shire ; Sir William Palton, one of the Somerset representatives, a first cousin of William Lord Botreaux, was a relative of Tiptoft's by marriage ; and Roger Hunt, the second Huntingdonshire knight, was certainly closely, and had been for long, connected with Tiptoft as his feoffee and as his main financial agent.

The temporal magnates on the new Council were therefore well represented by either relatives, retainers, counsellors, or political associates, among the knights of the shire, and of the five spiritual peers who made up the Council, Bishop Beaufort was not alone in being represented in the Lower House. Certainly John Kemp, bishop of London, who had recently resigned office as chancellor of the duchy of Normandy to attend to his conciliar responsibilities in England, had a kinsman among the Commons in Sir Thomas Lewkenore, one of the Sussex shire-knights. He was the bishop's first cousin. Lewkenore's Middlesex property made him a near neighbour of one of the Middlesex shire-knights, Thomas Frowyke, whose heir was to marry Lewkenore's daughter. There was no particular discernible tie of interest between Bishop John Wakering of Norwich and John Wodehouse, chamberlain of the Exchequer, chancellor of the duchy of Lancaster, and chancellor to the Queen-mother, one of the Suffolk shire-knights in 1422, but they were well acquainted and probably good friends : Wakering at some time or another gave Wodehouse a gold tablet of the Trinity, which the latter was able to bequeath to Wakering's successor at Norwich, William Alnwick (Alnwick was to be one of the overseers of Wodehouse's will). It is difficult to conceive of Archbishop Chichele having no friends in the Commons but, in fact, none are clearly traceable, although Geoffrey Lowther, one of the repre-sentatives for Kent and Gloucester's lieutenant-warden of the Cinque Ports, had certainly indirect if no other connexions with the primate ; Lowther was a friend of the archbishop's nephew-in-law and steward, John Darell, who as sheriff of Kent at this time had acted as returning officer at the shire elections.

The three most important administrative officials of state, the chancellor, the treasurer, and the keeper of the privy seal, were by letters patent issued on 16 November 1422 confirmed in their offices. Thomas Langley, bishop of Durham, was re-nominated to the custody of the great seal, an office he was to hold until July 1424 ; William Kynwolmarsh, the treasurer, died within a week of his reappointment, and the newly-confirmed keeper of the privy seal, John Stafford, archdeacon of Salisbury, moved up into his place, to be succeeded at the office of privy seal by William Alnwick, the late king's secretary. These three officials became automatically members of the new Council. Stafford had his connexion among the Commons in the person of his half-brother, Sir Humphrey Stafford, knight for Dorset ; and his nephew, Sir Humphrey's eldest son, had married the daughter of the other shire-knight, Robert Lovell. The bishop of Durham too was by no means without acquaintance among the knights of the shire. The senior of the two Northumbrian representatives, Sir John Bertram, justice of the peace in the episcopal franchises of Norham-shire and Elandshire (in Northumberland) where his eldest brother, Sir Robert Ogle, was steward, sheriff, and escheater, was a close friend of the bishop's steward, Thomas Holden ; the other knight of the shire, Sir William Elmeden, constable of the royal castle and receiver-general of the lordship of Bamburgh, was one of the episcopal tenants in his Durham estates ; the son-in-law of Lord FitzHugh, Sir William Eure, knight of the shire for Yorkshire, was the son of Langley's former steward, was lessee (like his father) of the episcopal coal and iron workings in south Durham, and was justice of the peace, of gaol delivery, and of assize in this great northern palatinate. Chancellor (for a second term, his first being from February 1405 to January 1407) since the summer of 1417, Langley's personal and official attachments in the Commons must have ranged through a much wider arc than this small segment of local connexions from his northern diocese would suggest.

Apart from these lords of the Council, not a few of the other lords spiritual and temporal of Parliament had their friends, either through kinship or by political affiliation, in the Lower House. The great Benedictine abbots of St. Albans and St. Edmundsbury were unofficially represented in the persons of their respective stewards, John Barton junior (Buckinghamshire) and John Wode-house (Suffolk) ; John Russell (Herefordshire) had his connexions with the abbot of St. Peter's, Gloucester; so had the Speaker, Roger Flore, with the abbot of Croyland; Robert Andrewe (Wiltshire) and Nicholas Wotton (Malmesbury), with the abbot of Malmesbury; and Richard Duffeld (Grimsby), with the head of the Lincolnshire house of Bardney. During their not uncommon absence from parliament, however, the abbots, and for that matter absent bishops, tended to rely for the representation of their interests in parliament on proxies drawn from the more highly-placed officials in the royal civil service, mainly from the masters in Chancery. The obligations in parliament of bishops and abbots as spiritual peers would seem often to have been discharged by letters of excusation and the appointment of proxies, but the presence of friendly parties in the Lower House must frequently have proved of value when their particular interests were involved in legislation originating with, or assented to by, the Commons.

Of the lords temporal in parliament those who were appointed to membership of the new Council were not alone in having their connexions in the Lower House. Reginald Lord Grey of Ruthin, with his extensive estates in Bedfordshire, may well have had much to do with the frequent return for that county during these years of John Enderby, a member of his council and a lawyer whose services were always at his disposal. Enderby's fellow shire-knight, Sir Thomas Wenlock, was just as firmly attached to another important Bedfordshire magnate, who had, in fact, attended his election: Sir John Cornwall of Ampthill, Henry V's uncle through his marriage with Henry IV's sister Elizabeth, the dowager countess of Huntingdon; but Cornwall was not to be summoned to parliament as Lord Fanhope until 1432, although he was a man of influence and ability (he was, for instance, a member of the delegation sent by the Council to mediate between the duke of Gloucester and Bishop Beaufort in January 1426 at a time when there was considerable danger of open warfare between their factions); Cornwall's stepson, John Holland, earl of Huntingdon, had of course been captured at the disaster which had befallen English arms in March 1421 at Baugé and was not destined to be released until 1425; in the meantime Cornwall looked after his interests. Often during the minority years of Henry VI's reign these two influential local magnates in Bedfordshire, Grey of Ruthin and Cornwall, would seem virtually to have shared the representation of the county between them in the persons of the adherents. Lord Grey of Ruthin had at least one other connexion in the Commons besides his retained adviser, Enderby ; for the thirty-year-old Sir William Bonville, the senior knight of the shire for Devon, was his son-in-law. Others of the lords temporal, who attended the 1422 parliament but were outside the newly-constructed Council, and who had kinsmen in the Lower House, were James Lord Berkeley, whose father-in-law, Sir Humphrey Stafford, was elected for Dorset, and William Lord Botreaux, whose first cousin, Sir William Palton, was returned for Somerset ; the son of one of the Hampshire knights of the shire, John Lisle esquire, was married to one of Lord Botreaux's nieces. Sir Robert Moton, returned for Leicestershire, was uncle by marriage to John Lord Grey of Codnor with whose father he had had continuous and close associations. Sir John Zouche, senior knight for Nottinghamshire, was uncle to Lord Zouche. A few of the lords temporal, who were not summoned to parliament in 1422 because they were out of the country on military service in France, had their connexions in the Commons, either through kinsmen or through men likely to have their interests at heart : Thomas Chaucer of Ewelme, who sat for Oxfordshire, was father-in-law of Thomas Montacute, earl of Salisbury, then Lieutenant-general of Normandy and governor of Champagne and Brie ; one of the Cambridgeshire knights, Sir Walter de la Pole, was first cousin to William de la Pole, earl of Suffolk, who was to succeed to the command of the English forces in France on Salisbury's death in 1428 ; John Lord Talbot, who was also in France at this time, could probably rely upon one of the knights of the shire for Shropshire, Hugh Burgh esquire, a retainer of his who had been treasurer of Ireland during his lieutenancy, to keep a watching brief for his concerns.

There were other reasons for the attenuation of the ranks of the lords temporal in the parliament of 1422 than simply military pre-occupations across the Channel. No fewer than six representatives of baronial families were then still in their minority and had not yet been summoned to parliament, but their interests too did not go unrepresented in the Lower House. Humphrey earl of Stafford, then still a minor in the king's ward, would naturally be concerned over the petition presented during the session to the King and Lords in parliament by the Commons on behalf of his mother, the dowager countess, touching the partition of the Bohun inheritance between herself and the late king. Almost certainly the earl's interests would be watched over by the two parliamentary burgesses for Stafford, Robert Whitgreve and John Harpour, both of whom were closely connected with him certainly not long afterwards. Reginald Pympe esquire, knight of the shire for Kent, was a mesne-tenant of the Staffords (as his forebears had been of their ancestors, the Clares, as lords of this parcel of the earldom of Gloucester) in his holding at Nettlestead, one of his most important manors, and he had married into the family of Frenyngham of East Farleigh who were also Stafford tenants and devoted to the house of Stafford.[1] Despite the fact that tenurial connexion no longer necessarily involved political attachment, Pympe may well have been prepared to back the Stafford interest if necessary (his descendants incurred attainder and forfeiture for assisting the revolt of Henry Stafford, duke of Buckingham, the first duke's grandson, against Richard III). Some time during the parliamentary session of 1422 the young Earl Humphrey received livery of his estates, with the assent of the lords spiritual and temporal in parliament, in accordance with a grant made by word of mouth only by the king's father.[2] Among the shire-knights were two of the feoffees of another minor, Walter Lord FitzWalter, a prisoner in France since Clarence's defeat at Baugé in March 1421, namely, Sir John Howard (Suffolk) and John Tyrell (Essex). In the following July (1423), like FitzWalter, another of the younger lords sued out livery of his hereditary lands, namely, William Lord Lovell of Titchmarsh; Robert Lovell, knight of the shire for Dorset, was his uncle. Thomas Blenkinsop, one of the Westmorland representatives, was almost certainly a nominee or elected by the influence of the Clifford family, who as heirs of the Viponts had come into the lordship of Westmorland, the hereditary shrievalty of the county, and large estates in the valley of the Eden, notably the castles and lordships of Brough and Brougham and Appleby, the shire-town. Thomas Lord Clifford, who had recently succeeded to his father's estates although he was not eight years old at the time, was a minor in the ward of his mother and grandmother and was not to be summoned to parlia-

---

[1] For the Frenyngham chantry founded in 1411 in East Farleigh church by John Frenyngham of Loose, on whose bede-roll were numbered Hugh and Thomas, respectively 2nd and 3rd earls of Stafford, and Ralph, Hugh's son, murdered near Beverley in 1385 by John Holland, Richard II's younger half-brother, see *Archaeologia Cantiana, Kent Records*, Vol. XII (*Kent Chantries*, ed. A. Hussey), 125–6.

[2] *Rot. Parl.*, IV. 195.

ment until 1437 ; the Blenkinsops were tenants of the Cliffords and hereditary constables of their castle at Brough.

These links between members of the Commons and the parliamentary aristocracy need not be taken as evidence to suggest that the Lower House would be subservient to the Lords or automatically predisposed to adopt the attitude of the magnates to the political and constitutional problems of the moment.[1] Mr. McFarlane has warned us of the dangers of attributing an uncomplicated and exclusive loyalty to those members of the gentry who took fees of retainer from their aristocratic connexions or who served them in some administrative capacity. We must also be aware of the dangers of under-rating the contribution such men must have made by way of counsel to the formulation of the policy, in and out of time of parliament, of the lord by whom they were engaged. The ties between many of the parliamentary knights and members of the nobility were only the natural outcome of the fact that, socially, the knights as a class were far more closely in touch and sympathy with the aristocracy than they were with the class from which still preponderantly came their fellow-members of the Common House, the parliamentary burgesses. Even from the point of view of territorial standing the class of the knights in its upper limits was hardly distinguishable from the lower ranks of the titular nobility ; and it was, of course, members of this class of quasi-baronial proprietors that from time to time, particularly following the crises of dynastic revolution, the king ennobled by making them the recipients of individual writs of summons to the Upper House of parliament or the beneficiaries of patents of creation. We need only recall at random the Tiptofts, the Hungerfords, the Stourtons, the Wenlocks, the Stanleys, the Staffords of Southwick, and the Bonvilles, who one after another slowly made their way upwards into the parliamentary aristocracy in the course of the fifteenth century, to realise the absence of any social gulf between the most important of the class which furnished the knights of the shire and the titular nobility. Quite a number of the shire-knights of 1422, who did not themselves or in their descendants achieve the distinction of an individual writ

---

[1] On this large problem *vide* J. E. Neale, ' The Commons' Privilege of Free Speech in Parliament ', *Tudor Studies presented to A. F. Pollard,* ed. R. W. Seton-Watson, p. 259 *et seq.* But, for contrariant views, *vide* K. B. McFarlane, ' Parliament and " Bastard Feudalism " ', *Trans. Royal Hist. Soc.* ; 4th Ser., XXVI, and the present writer's ' The Medieval Speakers for the Commons in Parliament ', *Bulletin Inst. Hist. Research,* XXIII. 31 *et seq.*

of parliamentary summons, could have supported elevation into the ranks of the peerage if only the changes and chances of that world of 'bastard feudalism' had been more favourable to them. For some of them surpassed and more of them could vie with at least the lesser magnates of the Upper House of parliament in the extent and value of their holding in landed estate. The estates of Sir John Pelham, one of the Sussex representatives, in that county and in Cambridgeshire were worth £540 a year according to an assessment made at the end of Henry IV's reign, and the sum did not include the duchy of Lancaster revenues from the rape of Pevensey and the honour of the Eagle (which themselves were worth half that sum at least) that he enjoyed by the king's favour along with other annuities. The annual income from the property of Sir Humphrey Stafford,[1] two-fifths of it in Dorset, the rest in Staffordshire, Warwickshire, Wiltshire, and Somerset, amounted according to the official return of the same 1412 assessors to some £570. Sir John Howard's manors in Essex and Cambridgeshire alone yielded upwards of £400 a year [2] and he held the considerable hereditary estates of his family in Norfolk and Suffolk apart from these. Property in Oxfordshire, Hampshire, Berkshire, and Somerset, as inherited from his great-uncle Bishop Wykeham of Winchester, alone brought in £400 a year to Sir Thomas Wykeham, the Oxfordshire knight, and he made considerable purchases himself from among the St. Amand estates in North Oxfordshire besides. Landed estate in Essex, Hertfordshire, Cambridgeshire, and Hampshire, and royal annuities in lieu of land were worth almost as much in 1436 to John Tyrell esquire, one of the Essex shire-knights.[3] The once forfeited property of Robert Cary esquire, one of the Devon representatives, was worth £230 a year. Sir John Cockayne, with his £200 a year income from lands in Derbyshire, Staffordshire, and Warwickshire, was the second largest non-baronial proprietor in Derbyshire according to the assessors' returns in 1436.

---

[1] These lands were held at the time of the assessment in 1412 by Sir Humphrey's father, Sir Humphrey Stafford senior, but they descended at his death in the following year to our Sir Humphrey (*Feudal Aids*, VI. 428 ; *C.C.R.*, *1413–19*, 42, 126–7, 338, 410 ; *C.F.R.*, *1413–22*, 47–8, 52).

[2] For these figures of assessment see *Cambridge Antiquarian Society Communications*, XV (*Cambridgeshire Subsidy Rolls*, 1250–1695), 115, 124 ; *Feudal Aids*, III. 581–2, 615, 643 ; VI. 408, 438–9.

[3] For Tyrell's estates, see Morant, *Essex*, I. 261 ; *Feudal Aids*, I. 190 ; II. 216, 350, 373, 451 ; III. 558 ; VI. 445, 523 ; *E.H.R.*, XLIX. 633.

In that year Sir Robert Roos of Gedney, one of the Lincolnshire knights of the shire, was similarly all but pre-eminent of those below baronial rank in *that* county with £165 of landed income. His fellow-knight of the shire in 1422, Sir John Graa, possessed (for the time being at any rate) estates in the counties of Lincoln, Suffolk, Leicester, Nottingham, Derby, and York, worth £186 a year.[1] Another eight of the 1422 parliamentary knights are *known* to have been in possession of landed property worth between £100 and £200 a year ; and men like Sir William Bonville with his thirty-five manors in Devon, Somerset, Dorset, Wiltshire, Leicestershire, and Sussex ; Sir John Arundell, with his twenty-four manors in Cornwall and ten in Devon ; Sir William Palton, with his twenty-one manors in the west country and Oxfordshire, Warwickshire, and Hampshire ; Sir Edmund Hastings, with his lands in the North and East Ridings of Yorkshire, in north Durham, and Northumberland ; his fellow-knight of the shire, Sir William Eure, with his extensive estates in Durham, Yorkshire, and Northumberland, and coal-mine leases on the south Durham field, must have been worth considerably more than many of those already enumerated. The significance of these income-figures will be better understood if it

---

[1] Most of these estates and certainly the more valuable (they were worth £164 a year clear) were held by Graa in jointure with his wife, Margaret, daughter and eventual heir of Sir Roger Swillington. By October 1423 he was estranged from her and she was living apart with her aunt, the wife of Sir William Haryngton of Hornby (Lancs). On her death in 1429 (without issue so that her husband had no rights by courtesy) he was heavily involved in difficulties arising out of his efforts to secure a life interest in her property, particularly with Ralph Lord Cromwell who was heir-general of her ancestors, Swillington and De Heriz. After the death of Lord Cromwell in 1456 Graa renewed his suit over the Swillington estates with the former's executors and negotiations were still proceeding in 1459, soon after which year he probably died (certainly before 1475) (*C.P.R.*, *1413–16*, 55 ; *1429–36*, 10, 99, 290 ; *1446–52*, 457–60 ; *C.C.R.*, *1422–9*, 189 ; *1429–36*, 10, 124, 304–5 ; *C.F.R.*, *1413–22*, 263, 375 ; *1422–30*, 205, 275, 280–1, 287, 310–19 ; *Hist. Mss. Comm. Report, De Lisle and Dudley Mss.*, I. 208, 211 ; Thoroton, *Notts.*, III. 51). For Graa's own estates, see *Feudal Aids*, VI. 481, 550, 612. Graa seems to have attached himself to the duke of Norfolk who became one of his feoffees in 1424 (*D.K.R.*, XLVIII. 271), and he probably found his second wife's father useful in his troubles : *he* was none other than Thomas Fauconer, mercer and alderman of London, one of the city's representatives in the parliament of 1422, on which unique occasion Graa himself had sat for Lincolnshire. Graa's recoverable history is almost entirely one of his difficulties with his first wife and her estates, but he did serve with Henry V in the Agincourt campaign and in the later expeditions of the reign, and from July 1423 for a short time he served as j.p. in the parts of Lindsey in Lincolnshire (N. H. Nicolas, *Agincourt*, 379 ; *D.K.R.*, XLIV. 571, 592, 594, 607, 614, 621).

is realised that the total number of English landowners assessed (for tax on incomes from land and Crown annuities) at over £100 was probably little more than 250 at this time. If territorial standing and good family connexions counted for anything in fifteenth-century England—and many of the parliamentary knights of 1422 were ' weel ykynde and of gret allyaunce ',[1]—their local position and influence must have differed little from that of many of the lesser temporal magnates in the upper chamber of parliament, the ' parliament house ' proper.

Sympathy with aristocratic opinion on the part of the more influential knights and some of the more important burgesses can be assumed, but not necessarily subservience to it. In some respects the connexions existing between individual representatives and individual magnates might help to bind together (as well as to divide) the members of the Lower House. As a result of their aristocractic ties, their interest in aristocratic concerns, their common membership of aristocratic councils, and their association in committees of feoffees in the property of the great landowning families, which was more usually scattered over the broad shires of England than concentrated in any particular county, the mutual ' acquaintance ' of individual representatives in the Commons was artificially but inevitably enlarged. Representatives from one part of the country already had points of social contact with representatives from another. In some ways and in certain circumstances the seigneurial attachments of individuals and small groups of members might mean a sectionalised Lower House, but they must at the same time be recognised to be a factor in facilitating contacts between individual representatives which might not otherwise have come about. As a factor in the process by which individuals established personal links with one another the aristocratic connexions of members of the Lower House must not, however, be exaggerated.

There were other factors, probably more important factors, in the process by which individual knights and burgesses would come to know and recognise one another and which must have made easier that informal discussion without which common opinion could not be effectively elucidated or common policy achieved. The numerous close family relationships and ties of friendship between members might conceivably have had a considerable effect

---

[1] An expression used of Sir John Howard, knight of the shire for Suffolk in 1422 (*P.P.C.*, II. 272–4).

on the development of political opinions and attitudes in the Lower House of 1422. Richard Tyrell, knight of the shire for Surrey, was a younger brother of John Tyrell, the Essex knight; Sir William Coggeshall, the other and senior Essex knight, was the latter's father-in-law. The two Cornish shire-knights were father and son; the latter, John Arundell esquire of Bideford, was husband to Thomas Chaucer's sister-in-law. Both Robert James, one of the Buckinghamshire knights, and John Golafre, one of the Berkshire representatives, were Chaucer's friends, and both were brothers-in-law to Sir Walter de la Pole, knight of the shire for Cambridgeshire. Sir Walter's fellow representative, Sir William Asenhill, an usher of the Chamber to Henry IV and Henry V, was another kinsman of his by marriage; de la Pole's daughter had married into Asenhill's wife's family. The Nottinghamshire shire-knight, Sir John Zouche, was Asenhill's brother-in-law.[1] Sir Thomas Wykeham, knight of the shire for Oxfordshire, and John Barton junior, the Buckinghamshire knight of the shire, were married to sisters, two of the many daughters of William Willicotes of North Leigh and Chastleton (Oxfordshire).[2] Speaker Roger Flore's son-in-law, Sir Henry Plesyngton, was his fellow-representative for Rutland. Flore, whose position as chief steward of the duchy of Lancaster north of Trent would make him a useful adjunct to any committee of feoffees to uses, was such a trustee to John Harpour, the lawyer returned by the borough of Stafford, to the father (recently deceased) of Sir William Eure, the young knight returned for Yorkshire, and to Edmund Wynter, one of the Norfolk representatives. The latter was a close friend of John Wodehouse, chancellor of the duchy of Lancaster, chancellor to Catherine of Valois, and chamberlain of the Exchequer, who was returned in 1422 for Suffolk; Wynter was later on to marry Wodehouse's widow. Roger Flore and Bartholomew Brokesby, one of the Leicestershire knights, had recently been in touch with each other as co-overseers of the will of James Bellers of Melton Mowbray, knight of the shire two years before.[3] Brokesby, as the land-agent of Joan dame Beauchamp of Abergavenny, would be in close

---

[1] Zouche had married Margaret, daughter and coheir of Sir John Burgh of Burgh Green and sister of Joan, Sir William Asenhill's wife (Blomefield, *op. cit.*, VII. 126–7).

[2] For information about the relationship by marriage between Wykeham and Barton junior I am indebted to Mr. K. B. McFarlane.

[3] For Bellers' will, see A. Gibbons, *Early Lincoln Wills*, 147.

contact with her other feoffees to uses who included John Barton the younger and John Russell, respectively shire-knights for Buckinghamshire and Herefordshire. Sir Thomas Charleton, and his fellow-knight for Middlesex, Thomas Frowyke, and Henry Frowyke, one of the four London representatives, were uterine brothers ; and along with Robert Skerne, the Kingston-on-Thames lawyer elected as one of the Surrey knights of the shire, both the Frowykes were Charleton's feoffees to uses. Thomas Frowyke was doubtless well acquainted with Sir Thomas Lewkenore, one of the Sussex representatives, for the latter held property in the same Middlesex parish and his daughter later on married Frowyke's son and heir. A compact little group of kinsmen came up from Wiltshire, headed by Sir William Sturmy of Wolfhall, a quondam Speaker and former expert in Anglo-Hanseatic and Anglo-German diplomacy : accompanying him, returned as the parliamentary burgesses of Ludgershall, where Sir William farmed the manor under an Exchequer grant, were his bastard son, John Sturmy, and his grandson and coheir, John Seymour, while from Bedwin came Sir William's nephew, feoffee, and later on his executor, Robert Erle.[1] The knight of the shire for Gloucestershire, Robert Stanshawe, had a younger brother, Nicholas, returned for Appleby as parliamentary burgess. Other families probably already on friendly terms, represented in the 1422 parliament, were to be later more directly connected by marriage, for example, the Skeltons and the Tilliols of Cumberland, (Sir John Skelton was to marry Sir Peter Tilliol's brother's widow), and the Stanleys and Gresleys of Staffordshire (Sir John Gresley's son was to wed Thomas Stanley's daughter). The Lovells and Staffords of Dorset were already allied through the marriage of Sir Humphrey Stafford's son with Robert Lovell's daughter. The representatives of the neighbouring county of Somerset, Sir William Palton and Sir Thomas Brooke, were close friends although not related.

Some of the knights and more influential burgesses by reason of their official employment would inevitably be well known to most of their fellows. The two chamberlains of the Exchequer, Wodehouse and Throckmorton, and Robert Whitgreve, the Stafford parliamentary burgess who was a teller in the Lower Exchequer, would be personally known to those members of the Common

---

[1] For Sturmy's kinship, see *Wilts. Arch. and Nat. Hist. Magazine*, LI. 271 *et seq.*, 500 *et seq.*, and Somerset House, Register Luffenham, fo. 7 (Sturmy's will).

House who held office as port officials,[1] and to men like Sir John Arundell, steward of the duchy of Cornwall in the counties of Devon and Cornwall ; Sir William Elmeden, the receiver-general of the castle and lordship of Bamburgh ; his fellow Northumberland representative, Sir John Bertram, until March 1421 warden of Roxburgh castle ; John Golafre, controller and overseer of the royal manor and park of Woodstock ; men who not only took the king's fees but accounted for their office in the Exchequer. They would be known, too, to all those who had recently held the office of sheriff, escheator, mayor, or bailiff, or any of the other local offices of royal appointment similarly accountable in the Exchequer but more limited in length of occupation. We can certainly be sure of one thing : the Lower House was filled by men, very many of whom were by no means complete strangers to one another. And this was doubtless generally the case and always had been so, for certainly men of that class which supplied the knights of the shire quite often held land in several counties, a fact which must in the nature of things have enriched their ' acquaintance '. Many of the knights and burgesses of 1422 had sat and stood together in the chapter-house of the abbey of Westminster on previous occasions and were to do so again ; but, this apart, many of them, particularly the shire-knights, were in frequent and close communication both in and between the times of parliamentary session on matters of their lord's concern and their own, and, as we have seen, not a few of them were related by close family alliances of blood.

Territorial standing and local office by royal appointment were not the only qualification which the shire-knights of 1422, or of any other parliament, possessed to sit for the communities of the counties from which they came. The class to which they belonged and whose interests they generally represented was the bedrock of English political and local administrative life. In 1422 for something like two centuries it had continuously supplied that element in local government whose employment had become, and was to remain, so characteristic of the English method, providing, as it did, a balance between the needs of the central administrative machine and the claims of the locality to sympathetic consideration. If they had shown no interest in political life beyond a concern to take the opportunities of local administrative and judicial service which the

---

[1] See above, pp. 53–5

Crown afforded, most of the knights of the shire of 1422 would still have been qualified to represent the communities of their counties if only because, by virtue of the amount of time and energy which they had devoted to local governmental activity, they were men who knew the needs and were aware of the temper of the areas from which they were returned. Exactly half of the seventy-four knights of the shire returned to Henry VI's first parliament had already occupied the office of sheriff, and thirty out of these thirty-seven had served in that capacity during the previous reign. A few at different times had discharged a sheriff's functions in more than one bailiwick : Sir John Arundell had been sheriff of Devon in 1414–15 and of Cornwall in 1418–19 ; Sir Thomas Wykeham was sheriff of Oxfordshire and Berkshire in 1413–14, of Hampshire in 1416–17, and then in the following year, 1417–18, was sheriff of Oxfordshire and Berkshire again ; Sir Edmund Hastings had been sheriff of Northumberland in the years 1414–15 and 1418–19, in the meantime serving the office in Yorkshire in 1416–17. Five of the 1422 shire-knights were appointed to the shrievalty of their counties either during or soon after this parliamentary session for the current Exchequer year. Nine of the thirty knights who had acted as sheriff during the previous reign had also served the office of escheator, again sometimes in different shires. For instance, William Fynderne, knight of the shire for Berkshire, had passed in the autumn of 1417 from the administration of the escheatorship of Essex and Hertfordshire to the shrievalty of Wiltshire ; Robert James, knight of the shire for Buckinghamshire, had been escheator in Oxfordshire and Berkshire in 1413–14, in Bedfordshire and Buckinghamshire in 1415–16, and then in the following year was sheriff of Oxfordshire and Berkshire. Thirteen other knights of the shire had previously exercised the office of escheator alone. Of these, John Vampage esquire, shire-knight for Worcestershire, was escheator in his county at the very time of his return in 1422 and during the parliamentary session ; Edmund Wynter esquire, one of the Norfolk representatives, was escheator in Norfolk and Suffolk at the same time too.

The sense of administrative responsibility of the class which furnished the county representatives is, however, even more clearly brought out by the way in which most of the 1422 shire-knights filled at some time or other the all-important local office of justice of the peace. Only ten of the seventy-four shire-knights never occupied the position. Two out of every three of the parliamentary knights of 1422 were at that time justices of the peace in the county they were representing, forty-nine knights in all ; of these, five were justices of some other county besides, and there were, moreover, three knights of the shire who were justices in a single county other than the one from which they were returned. Altogether fifty-two of the seventy-four knights of the shire were, at the time of their actual return to parliament in 1422, serving somewhere or other as justices of the peace, and, of these, nine were members of the quorum of their commissions ; [1] William Fynderne (shire-knight for Berkshire) was of the quorum in both the Oxfordshire and Berkshire commissions, and Roger Hunt, (elected for Huntingdonshire) sat as a member of the quorum on both the Huntingdonshire and Bedfordshire benches. Most, if not all, of the 1422 knights of the shire had served on local commissions of array, inquest, oyer and terminer, or other such royally-inspired enterprises of limited scope and duration. To these men a return to parliament was but one stage in the ' cursus honorum ' of the country gentleman.

In the case of many of the knights of the shire in Henry VI's first parliament, as in others, administrative experience was the natural accompaniment and consequence of a keen interest in and concern with political events and developments. Parliamentary experience and service was itself as much a result of a general preoccupation with politics on the part of the country gentry as, by virtue of the operation of royal and seigneurial patronage and of something like a ' spoils-system ', was their interest in ' engrossing ' local administrative positions. Far too many of them had connexions with the great lords of the land and with the Court for it to have been otherwise. A return to parliament had ceased to be the penalty of social position, if indeed it had ever been that ; it was one of the forms that a recognition of social prestige and local influence took. But election for the shire to parliament might mean much more : it was frequently the result of a local test of the local strength or

---

[1] *C.P.R., 1416–22*, 449–63 ; Patent Roll, 9 Henry V : P.R.O., C.66. 404, Mems. 20d–16d (commissions of the peace dated 12 February 1422). The nine knights of the shire who were members of the quorum of their commissions of the peace were Roger Hunt (Huntingdonshire and Beds), John Barton junior (Bucks), John Tyrell (Essex), Robert Skerne (Surrey), John Russell (Herefordshire), William Burley (Shropshire), John Throckmorton and John Vampage (Worcestershire), and William Fynderne (Oxfordshire and Berks). Three parliamentary burgesses in 1422 were also j.p.s. of the quorum : Robert Gilbert (m.p. Gloucester) and John Langley (m.p. Chippenham, Wilts) in Gloucestershire, and John Cork (m.p. Liskeard) in Cornwall.

weakness of aristocratic party affiliations and combinations that were capable, however tenuously and casually organised, of influencing large questions of national policy in parliament and in the royal Council.

At many points the careers of some of the more influential of the parliamentary knights of 1422 become a commentary on the political history of the late fourteenth century and the reigns of the first two Lancastrian kings ; their biographies cannot be written without reference to the major incidents and important political trends of this period, which their very names sometimes recall. The names of Burley, Cary, and Plesyngton, for example, recall the troubles of the reign of Richard of Bordeaux. William Burley, the rising young lawyer returned for the fifth time in 1422 as knight of the shire for Shropshire, was the great-grand-nephew of Sir Simon Burley whose impeachment by the Commons in the Merciless Parliament of 1388 the Lords Appellant had engineered ; Robert Cary, one of the two Devon representatives, was the son of the Chief Baron of the Exchequer who had incurred exile and forfeiture at the same time for being party to the judges' declaration that the parliamentary commission of 1386 had been a treasonable concoction. Sir Henry Plesyngton, the young son-in-law of Speaker Flore, was the grandson of another of the dispossessed of Richard's reign. The Mowbray connexions of John Lancastre, knight of the shire for Norfolk, had led to his being closely involved in the murder at Calais of the foremost of the Lords Appellant, Thomas of Woodstock, during Richard's coup of September 1397. John Golafre, returned for Berkshire in 1422, had been one of the six commoners on the commission to which Richard had provided, during what Stubbs mistakenly called the ' suicidal ' session at Shrewsbury early in 1398, that parliamentary powers should be delegated ; the reasons prompting his arrest by Henry of Bolingbroke at Berkeley castle in July 1399 had long been forgiven and forgotten in the slow but steady application of a policy of oblivion and indemnity and of political reconciliation by the first two Lancastrians. Golafre was not alone among those who had worn the livery and white-hart badge of the deposed Richard or taken his fees to be utilised in the Lancastrian service. His brother-in-law, Sir Walter de la Pole (of Cambridgeshire), Sir Peter Tilliol (of Cumberland), Sir William Coggeshall (of Essex) Sir William Sturmy (of Wiltshire), Sir John Howard (of Suffolk), and Robert

Lovell esquire (of Dorset) had all been members of Richard II's Household, recipients of royal annuities, and close enough to the king to accompany him on his fateful second expedition to Ireland in the spring of 1399. All these men had lived to serve the usurping dynasty, some as administrative agents of the Crown in their shires or on local commissions of array, of inquest, or of oyer and terminer, or as members of the more permanent commission of the peace. Sturmy, in fact, was frequently used by Henry IV on really important diplomatic undertakings and commercial missions and was an acceptable Speaker in one of his early parliaments. De la Pole's skill in negotiation had, too, been put to the test by Henry V in the last three years of his reign in embassies to central Europe and western Germany; in fact, at the time of his election to the parliament of 1422, he had only just got back from a six months' diplomatic mission to the Emperor Sigismund, the Wittelsbachs, and the Rhenish prince-bishops. The case of William Brocas, knight of the shire for Hampshire, affords another example of the early rehabilitation of a family which might have been politically and socially extinguished permanently by its previous intimate connexion with the person and Household of Richard of Bordeaux and by ' treason ' on his behalf between his deposition and death; Brocas's grandfather had been chamberlain to Anne of Bohemia, and his father had been executed in London for complicity in the anti-Lancastrian rising of January 1400. The forfeited family estates, however, had been restored by the end of the year, and the young heir recovered also the hereditary mastership of the royal buckhounds with its customary fees. But Brocas's career was never more than one of plain and unspectacular employment in local administration; he enjoyed no brilliant renewal of court favour at the high levels achieved by his grandfather. Perhaps he had just not got it in him. But he held aloof from one of the surest ways to quick returns : service in the French wars under Henry V when things were still going well. To vegetate was fatal in such circumstances.

The accession of Henry of Bolingbroke had involved considerable disturbance and discomfort for some other of the families represented in the first parliament of his grandson, and some took time to recover a sense of balance and attain stability. But in 1399 there were those who had ' cashed in ' on their old connexions with the new king (or with his supporters among the magnates) like the Erpinghams, the Tiptofts, and the Hungerfords, or who had purposefully taken the risk of backing the house of Lancaster in the initial uncertainties of its new position, like the Stanleys of Lancashire. Ideas of constitutional reform and moderate governance, of a ' new deal' in domestic policy, there may have been in some hopeful minds in 1399, but there would be few who were unaware of the fact that with the revolution the control of ' good lordship' had quickly changed hands from one sovereign to another, from one branch of the Plantagenet family to another, and from one group of great lords close to the king's person to another, or who were unaware, in this age of litigiousness and graft, of the significance of this fact. On the other hand, the ' loyalties' of those less committed than the Lancastrian retainers proper were in a state of flux and, as in most times of political crisis in this period of ' bastard feudalism', where ' loyalties' were for sale it was only at a price and in more of a sellers' than a buyers' market. Although both sides stood to gain by the transaction, it was the new dynasty that more anxiously sought re-insurance and its supporters, both firm and vacillating, who took the premiums. And there were some who came up to sit among the Commons in the parliament of 1422 for whom the revolution of 1399 had meant political and social elevation and the prospect of success. Three of the 1422 shire-knights—Sir John Pelham, Sir John Arundell, and Sir Richard Stanhope—had been among the forty-six esquires created knights of the bath on the eve of Henry IV's coronation, and two more, Sir John Gresley and John Lisle esquire, were the sons of pro-Lancastrian esquires similarly honoured in the Tower at the same ceremony. Service in Lancastrian retinues with, and the receipt of Lancastrian annuities and pensions from, either John of Gaunt, Henry of Bolingbroke when earl of Derby, or the young prince Henry of Monmouth, had meant political and administrative advancement for more than a few of the 1422 shire-knights either at Henry IV's accession or later on. Sir John Pelham had been constable of the duke of Lancaster's castle of Pevensey and his wife had held it for Henry of Bolingbroke when Sir John had joined him in the north soon after his landing at Ravenspur ; Henry made him a knight of his Chamber, in March 1405 appointed him keeper of the New Forest for life, in the following December chief steward of the duchy of Lancaster south of Trent, and from December 1411 to the end of the reign Pelham was treasurer of England as well.

Sir John Arundell, another of the new knights of the bath at Henry IV's coronation, was appointed for life in February 1402 steward of the duchy of Cornwall in Cornwall. Thomas Chaucer esquire of Ewelme, Catherine Swynford's nephew, had been, like his father Geoffrey, in John of Gaunt's *familia* and had been his constable of the castle and chief forester on the ducal estates at Knaresborough; Henry IV in the first month of his reign appointed him for life constable of Wallingford castle and steward of the honours of Wallingford and St. Valery and three years later made him chief butler of England, also for life. John Leventhorpe esquire automatically graduated from his office of receiver to Henry of Bolingbroke as earl of Derby and duke of Hereford to the receiver-ship-general of the hereditary estates of the duchy of Lancaster and accepted, in addition, the position of steward of the duchy property in the home counties; Leventhorpe was so indispensable as to be kept on in 1413 in his duchy offices by Henry V, the only member of the higher duchy administrative staff and of the duchy council to emerge still in office from the new king's first regnal year. One of the new duchy officials then appointed was another of the 1422 knights of the shire who had long been in the Lancastrian service—John Wodehouse esquire, a lawyer retained by Henry of Monmouth since (at the latest) 1402 when he had made him his steward at Castle Rising (Norfolk). Henry V at the outset of his reign made him chancellor of the duchy of Lancaster and two years later one of the two chamberlains of the Exchequer. Henry V's accession had meant promotion, too, for another lawyer, the new king's former controller of Household, John Hotoft of Knebworth (Herts), who replaced Robert Darcy esquire of Maldon in the clerkship of the Common Bench. The younger son of a former knight of John of Gaunt's entourage (Sir Robert Urswyk of Upper Rawcliffe [Lancashire], who had represented the county palatine of Lancaster in thirteen parliaments between 1379 and 1401) and member of a family long attached to the Lancastrian interest, Thomas Urswyk esquire had been holding the office of receiver of the income from the hereditary Lancastrian estates in Lancashire and Cheshire for five years at the time of his return to Henry VI's first parliament.

The assumption by the Lancastrian house of the *culmen dignitatis regiae* had meant official advancement and promotion for some of the families represented in the parliament of 1422; for others it had involved expenditure of energy and devotion, and sometimes of life, especially in the unquiet time of Henry IV and later in the period of the re-assertion of the old Plantagenet claims to rights and territories across the Channel in Normandy and France.   The Cumberland knight of the shire, Sir John Skelton, had fought at the battle of Homildon Hill in the late summer of 1402, when a Scottish army under Earl Douglas was met by the Percies at the foot of the Cheviots on its way back from Durham, and had won distinction in the engagement by taking as prisoners Murdoch earl of Fife, who was the son and heir of the duke of Albany, the Scottish regent, and William Lord Graham.   The father of Sir William Eure, one of the Yorkshire representatives, had also been at Homildon Hill ; in the following year he had helped the earl of Westmorland to prevent the earl of Northumberland from join-ing his son, Hotspur, in the rising which ended at Shrewsbury ; and two years later (1405) Sir Ralph Eure had again been with Westmorland at Shipton Moor facing the rebel forces of the Earl Marshal and the northern primate, Archbishop Scrope of York. The father of one of the Derbyshire knights, Sir John Cockayne of Ashbourne, had fallen at the field of Shrewsbury and Sir Richard Stanhope, shire-knight for Nottinghamshire, had survived it.   Both the father and uncle of Sir Robert Whitney, knight of the shire for Herefordshire, had been killed fighting in the early stages of the conflict with Owen Glendower, and their family estates in the Wye valley had later suffered heavy devastation at the hands of the Welsh rebels.

It is true that by 1422 for at least half a century, and probably for much longer, the term ' knight of the shire ' had been employed as a technical term bearing no necessary relation to, or correspon-dence with, the rank of those who belonged to the ' ordo militaris '. Few of those who served as knights of the shire in 1422 would have been free from a liability to distraint for knighthood, being qualified by their substance to assume it ; but it is interesting to find that as great a fraction of them as a half was, in fact, comprised of knights by rank, many of whom, moreover, lived up to their title and followed the profession of arms.   Only the co-operation, either direct or indirect, of the class of knights and the class of esquires, who in this period of military service by contract had attained (for all practical purposes) equality with the knights, had made possible the resumption of the French wars in 1415 on an effective scale.

No fewer than fourteen [1] of the 1422 knights of the shire and the sons of two others [2] had indentured for service in Henry V's first expedition of 1415 which resulted in the siege and capture of Harfleur and culminated in the victory of Agincourt. Five of these fourteen and another fifteen [3] made their contribution to the later military activities of the reign, some of them securing either administrative posts in the conquered territories or military commands of importance (albeit sometimes in the back-areas). Sir John Arundell of Cornwall was vice-admiral to the duke of Exeter in 1418 and served at sea in the course of the next two years also. John Golafre esquire, knight of the shire for Berkshire, had been appointed in the spring of 1418 to the office of receiver-general for Normandy and had held the position until May in the following year. Sir John Bertram, one of the Northumberland representatives, had been made custodian of the castle of Fronsac near Bordeaux in August 1419. In the following year Sir Robert Whitney, shire-knight for Herefordshire, had been appointed captain of the town of Vire in the Côtentin. In May 1421 the lieutenancy of Harfleur had been given to Henry Mulsho esquire, one of the Northamptonshire knights, and in the following July Thomas Chambre esquire, who was to be his fellow-knight of the shire in the 1422 parliament, had been appointed captain of the town of Guînes in the march of Picardy.

Far more than these must have been fairly well conversant with the state of English affairs across the Channel from their family and business connexions with magnates and others charged with

[1] Sir Thomas Wenlock (Beds), Sir William Asenhill (Cambs), Sir Robert Moton (Leics), Sir Robert Roos (Lincs), Sir John Graa (Lincs), Sir Thomas Gresley (Staffs), Sir Thomas Lewkenore (Sussex), Sir William Eure (Yorks), Robert Lovell esquire (Dorset), John Tyrell esquire (Essex), Geoffrey Lowther esquire (Kent), Bartholomew Brokesley esquire (Leics), Thomas Chaucer esquire (Oxon), Robert Castell esquire (Warwickshire).

[2] John, son of Sir John Cockayne (Derbyshire) ; John, son of Reginald Pympe (Kent).

[3] Sir Thomas Wenlock, Sir John Graa, Sir Thomas Gresley, Robert Lovell, and Thomas Chaucer ; the additional fifteen were Sir John Arundell (Cornwall), Sir Richard Vernon (Derbyshire), Sir William Bonville (Devon), Sir Robert Whitney (Herefordshire), Sir Thomas Charleton (Middlesex), Sir John Bertram (Northumberland), Sir William Elmeden (Northumberland), Sir Henry Pleasington (Rutland), Sir Thomas Brooke (Somerset), Sir William Palton (Somerset), Sir William Montfort (Warwickshire), John Golafre esquire (Berks), Thomas Chambre esquire (Northants), Henry Mulsho esquire (Northants), John Throckmorton (Worcs).

the furtherance of policy at the highest military and administrative levels. We need only to recall the connexions, among the parliamentary knights, of such lords as Exeter, Warwick, the Earl Marshal, and Lord FitzHugh, to realise this fact. And we could add to their numbers by including Sir William Sturmy of Wiltshire, whose son-in-law by marriage and feoffee, Sir Hugh Luttrell of Dunster, was seneschal of Normandy in the last two years of Henry V's reign, and by including the handful of county representatives who in recent years had been entrusted with such important diplomatic negotiations as required a working knowledge of the trends of English policy abroad. Like Sturmy himself, who had treated (unsuccessfully) in 1418 for the marriage of the duke of Bedford to Jacqueline of Hainault ; or Thomas Chaucer, who in the summer of 1420 had proceeded as a member of an embassy to Brittany to elucidate the terms of the treaty of Troyes to the prelates and barons of the duchy and to secure its acceptance by the duke himself; or Sir Walter de la Pole, who between 1419 and Henry V's death (as we have already seen) had participated in a series of missions to Wladislaus II of Poland, the High Master of the Order of Teutonic Knights, and the Emperor Sigismund, the Rhenish prince-bishops, the elector and the duke of Bavaria, all of which enterprises hinged on Henry V's need to secure Sigismund's fulfilment of the defensive and offensive alliance concluded in the treaty of Canterbury (1416).

Nearly half of the 1422 shire-knights had been personally involved in the conduct of the English war activities in France at some time or other since 1415. Only a few of the younger ones of these retained a first-hand interest in English affairs overseas after Henry V's death. Henry Mulsho evidently joined Humphrey of Gloucester's expeditionary force to Hainault in 1424, when the duke attempted to recover his wife's inheritance. In the summer of 1426 and later we find Thomas Chambre crossing to Calais as a member of the retinue of its treasurer and victualler. Sir John Gresley, knight of the shire for Staffordshire in 1422, more or less continuously served in France with Bedford until the duke's death in 1435, by which time he had become lieutenant-general to the vicomte of Rouen. The son of Sir John Skelton, one of the Cumberland representatives in 1422, had property, acquired in the previous reign, at Harfleur and in the *bailliages* of Caen and the Côtentin. Sir William Bonville, shire-knight for Devon, held the important position of seneschal

f Aquitaine for three years from November 1442, and he again
vent out in the same capacity in the summer of 1449. Between
445 and 1451 the treasurership of Calais was occupied by Sir
Richard Vernon, who had been knight of the shire for Derbyshire
n 1422 and Speaker in the parliament of 1426.

National dislike of a foreign policy which aimed at eventually
chieving some peaceful modus vivendi with France had been an
mportant factor in the undoing of Richard of Bordeaux ; the
bject failure of Henry VI to consolidate and retain the earlier
.ancastrian conquest in France was one of the reasons for the change
f dynasty in 1461. An even more important factor was his
nability to satisfy the clamouring need for strong monarchical
:ontrol in England. The class which supplied the most influential
:lements in the Lower House of parliament was unable to prevent
ts traditional willingness to participate in local administration and
)rovincial government from degenerating into a pre-occupation
with the ' engrossing ' of local offices, and it failed to abstain from
:he pursuit of individual selfish aims and ambitions to the detriment
)f orderly government ; it allowed the loyalty inspiring its early
:espect for the house of Lancaster to be overlaid by less generous,
.f more immediately politically self-satisfying, sentiments. The
.ater history of some of the 1422 shire-knights, or of the families
from which they came, was sometimes characteristic of that political
malaise, that conflict and uncertainty of loyalties, which afflicted the
middle-class, as well as the higher aristocratic, elements in English
landed society in the middle decades of the fifteenth century. Sir
William Bonville's continued quarrel with the earl of Devon, his
nephew by marriage, who ousted him in May 1441 from the duchy
of Cornwall stewardship in Cornwall, a post Bonville had held
since November 1437, was to have serious repercussions on the
whole problem of the duke of York's proposed second Protectorship
in November 1455. Foremost among the members of the Commons who then pressed for York's reappointment as Protector was
the lawyer, William Burley, who at the time of his return for Salop
in 1422 was only on the threshold of his interesting career. Others
of the Commons of 1422 or their descendants participated in the
drawn-out civil wars which these events helped to precipitate.
Edmund, the son of the Warwickshire knight and former steward
of the Beauchamp household, Sir William Montfort of Coleshill,
had served Henry VI as *councellor and kerver* and, after fighting at

Towton in March 1461, staunchly went into exile with Margaret of Anjou and her entourage. The son of Sir William Eure, shire-knight for Yorkshire in the first parliament of the reign, died as a loyal Lancastrian on the same field. Sir William (now Baron) Bonville of Chewton lived to hear of the death of his son and grandson (the latter was the brother-in-law of the Kingmaker) fighting as rebels in the temporary disaster which befell the Yorkist cause at Wakefield in December 1460, and was himself executed after the Lancastrian victory at St. Albans seven weeks later. The earl of Oxford, the great-grandson of Sir John Howard, one of the Suffolk representatives in 1422, landed with Henry Tudor at Milford Haven and fought at Bosworth ; on the defeated side fell Howard's grandson of another line of descendants, the duke of Norfolk. The two members of the great Lancashire family of Stanley whose tardy support, postponed until the battle itself, decided the day in favour of the Tudor competitor, Thomas second Baron Stanley and his brother, Sir William Stanley, were the sons of the nephew of Thomas Stanley esquire of Elford, one of the Staffordshire representatives in 1422, whose own son had fought as a Lancastrian at Bloreheath in 1459 and was made a knight banneret as a Yorkist at Tewkesbury in 1471. Only the active co-operation of the knightly and armigerous class, from which the knights of parliament were continually and for the most part drawn, with that cause and effect of the later medieval ' bastard feudalism ', the over-mighty subject of higher rank, made possible the political disquiet and then open civil conflict, in the atmosphere of which the reigns of the ill-fated Henry of Windsor and Richard of Fotheringay came to their respective ends.

CHAPTER VI

THE ACTS OF THE PARLIAMENT OF 1422

HENRY V died in France, and with comparative suddenness, on 31 August 1422. He left to succeed him as king of England and heir of France Henry of Windsor, a baby of nearly nine months old, whom he had never seen. With the death of Charles VI of France on 21 October the child became king of both realms in accordance with the treaty of Troyes of 1420.

England was unprepared for the catastrophe of the death of Henry V. Moreover, the news of it came so tardily across the Channel that it does not seem to have been generally known in England before 10 September.[1] But this was no great matter. For comparatively little of constitutional or political moment could be decided forthwith in England, because some of the leading magnates of the realm were still in France.[2] The great seal had been, however, made available for authenticating certain acts of royal authority at a meeting of such magnates as were at hand, held at Windsor on 28 September.[3] There and then parliamentary approval and sanction for whatever constitutional form government was to assume under the infant king were evidently considered necessary. And on Michaelmas day the parliamentary writs of individual summons and the writs authorising the elections of knights of the shire, citizens, and burgesses, were dated at Windsor.[4] They were 'tested' by the king and not by the 'custos Anglie', as had been the case in the late reign at such times as Henry V was absent from the realm. Humphrey, duke of Gloucester, the younger of the infant king's two uncles, himself now received a summons although, as 'custos', neither he nor his elder brother, John, duke of Bedford, had done so. Gloucester's

---

[1] *Rot. Parl.*, IV. 194a.
[2] What follows relating to the actions of the lords between the coming of the news of Henry V's death and the meeting of parliament, and to the ultimate emergence, during the session, of a Protectorship to be vested in either the duke of Bedford or the duke of Gloucester, Henry VI's two uncles, is a précis of the greater part of an article by the present writer : 'The Office and Dignity of Protector of England, with special reference to its Origins', *E.H.R.*, LXVIII, pp. 193–233.
[3] *C.C.R.*, *1422–9*, 46.
[4] *Lords' Reports, touching the Dignity of a Peer of the Realm* (1829), IV. 855–6.

recent 'custody', exercised since May 1422 when Bedford re
joined Henry V in France, was clearly considered to have ende
with Henry V's demise. With the king present in the realm ther
could legally be no 'custos' or royal 'locum tenens'.

In the constitutional theory of the time it seems likely that th
legally valid existence of the royal continual council came to a
end with the death of the king to whose special service its mem
bers were sworn, just as did the commissions held on oath by th
great officials.[1] But the summoning of Henry VI's first parliamen
was advised by 'the council' and the writs were jointly warrante
'by king and council'; so, or with the advice or assent of th
council, within the next few days, were issued the letters paten
renewing the appointments of certain major and minor officials o
the state and of the Household.[2]

The royal authority, as the available lords spiritual and tem
poral seem to have assumed, had devolved upon them by reaso
of Henry V's death and the tender youth of his heir. Being, a
one of their minutes of 1 October alleged, the 'major et sanio
pars omnium dominorum et procerum regni', it was they wh
must act, pending the appointment of a sworn continual counc
of the regular kind, not only as the king's advisers but as virtuall
constituting the executive. After all, this was only in accordanc
with what had happened at the very beginning of Richard II'
reign, the last previous occasion to this of a royal minority, an
with the doctrine to be explicitly enunciated in 1427 that the gener
ality of the lords of the kingdom might be regarded in such
circumstance as invested with the royal authority when they wer
met together in a parliament or great council, even if (as was, c
course, by then the case) a normal sworn council was in being
Nevertheless, this council of magnates and principal officials, whic
met in the course of the seven weeks preceding Henry VI's firs
parliament, enjoyed only a provisional status and was only a
interim body acting to tide over government until a new counc
was properly appointed in parliament. For the lords who ha
exercised the functions of government evidently saw fit to see
and secure from the parliament of 1422 its ratification and approv
of the most significant of their acts, including the summoning c
this parliament itself.[3]

[1] J. F. Baldwin, *The King's Council*, p. 169.   [2] *C.P.R.*, *1422-9*, 1-4.
[3] *Rot. Parl.*, IV. 170b.

The final arrangements for the meeting of parliament on 9 November were made four days before that date at a fairly representative meeting of certain lords spiritual and temporal in the council chamber next the chamber of parliament at Westminster.[1] For the first time, so far as surviving records show, there then came to the surface the problem of the duke of Gloucester's future status in the form of government to be devised for the period of Henry VI's minority. For here was definitively decided the form of the duke's commission to begin and end the parliament that was pending and to supply the king's place in it as the royal commissary. For this position, as the highest of the blood royal and premier peer then in England, Gloucester was the obvious choice. His commission to open, conduct, and dissolve parliament was, however, limited by the stipulation that he was so to act only ' de assensu concilii '. To this Gloucester objected, on the grounds that it would be ' in prejudicium status sui ' and that, in any case, such terms of qualification had not been employed in those commissions by which, as ' custos ', he had previously presided over parliament in Henry V's name ; were the phrase ' de assensu concilii ' to be included, the lords, so he asserted, could keep parliament in being for a year on end if they so wished, which would be ' contra libertatem suam '. But the lords stood firm and refused to change the terms of the commission, so that Gloucester had to fall into line. Dated 6 November his commission passed the great seal.[2] The hedged-in power it granted Gloucester was all that the lords would allow him of a distinctive position in the state before parliament met.

This feat of aristocratic solidarity had in all probability been largely achieved as a result of the sustained opposition to Gloucester's ambition of his uncle, Henry Beaufort, bishop of Winchester, although he was not alone prominent among the lords who did not share Gloucester's estimate of his own abilities and rights.[3] The tactical weakness of the position of Gloucester face to face with the problem of his authority in the new régime was, of course, that over a month before, at the end of September, he had accepted, without any known objection, his obligation to receive and obey a summons to parliament simply as duke of Gloucester. His failure

[1] *P.P.C.*, III. 6–7.   [2] *Rot. Parl.*, IV. 169.
[3] *The Chronicle of John Hardyng*, ed. Henry Ellis (London, 1812), pp. 390–1 ; *Rot. Parl.*, IV. 326b.

to challenge this implied denial of any vestigial power and authority that he may well have hoped to salvage from his late position as 'custos Anglie', was fatal. Merely imprudent was Gloucester's attitude in the council meeting of 5 November. Moderation would then, on the eve of parliament's assembly, have been his better course. But Gloucester was not a moderate man. Accordingly, it was in an atmosphere of disquiet that Henry VI's first parliament met at Westminster on 9 November 1422, two days after the late king's entombment by the Confessor's chapel in the adjacent abbey church. Gloucester's hopes of a 'regency' during his young nephew's minority and in his elder brother Bedford's absence must, when parliament assembled, have now rested mainly on the possibility of the generality of the lords in parliament falling in with the requirements of the testament of Henry V. For the late king had decided on his death-bed that the governance of Normandy and France should fall upon the shoulders of his elder surviving brother, the duke of Bedford, and in his written will that the governance of the realm of England should remain with Gloucester, the guardianship of the infant Henry of Windsor devolving upon a select group of nobles at the head of which stood Thomas Beaufort, duke of Exeter. The knowledge that Henry V had by his written will declared that Gloucester was to enjoy the 'regency' of England during his heir's minority—'tutelam et defensionem principales'[1] —perhaps sustained the duke in the interval between the arrival of the news of Henry V's death and the meeting of the first parliament of the new reign, and his confidence in the value of his political stock may well have been revived after the setbacks of the council meeting of 5 November by the reading of Henry V's will immediately following the late king's burial on 7 November. He could hardly have been more sanguine of his prospects, however, by Archbishop Chichele's sermon or 'pronunciatio' at the ceremonial opening of parliament in the Painted Chamber in the palace of Westminster two days later again.[2]

After the reading of Gloucester's patent of commission as the king's lieutenant in parliament, the primate preached on 9 November to the assembled Lords and Commons on the words 'Principes populorum congregati sunt cum Deo', a text taken from a psalm of

[1] S. B. Chrimes, 'The Pretensions of the Duke of Gloucester in 1422', *E.H.R.*, XLV. 102.
[2] *Rot. Parl.*, IV. 169.

rejoicing in God as the King of His people.[1] In his discourse Chichele recommended the new king as the son of his father. God had perfected His creation in six days, and thus was perfection associated with the number six. The infant king was the sixth of his name to occupy the English throne. Syllogistically, the perfection of his father's work was to be expected of him. But the king was now of tender age and parliament had been summoned to provide for 'la bone governance des tres excellent persone du Roi', for the maintenance of the peace and the administration of the law, and for the defence of the realm. Arrangements must therefore be made, so the sermon as reported in the parliament-roll went on, for government to be undertaken by 'honurables et discretes persones . . . et ceo de chescun estate de ceste Roialme'. What the archbishop clearly had in mind was provision for the exercise of the royal authority by the appointment during the session of parliament of a council representatively constituted on the basis of 'estate'.

All this, as Chichele is reported to have stated, finding his analogy in the Old Testament story of the Exodus, was the stuff of the wise counsel given by Jethro to his kinsman, Moses, 'Duc des gents de Israel'.[2] Whether the archbishop expatiated or not in his discourse upon other aspects of Jethro's advice is not to be deduced from the brief notes of the sermon in the parliament-roll. But the moral of the story and its appositeness to the then crisis in English affairs, in any case, would not be lost upon all of his hearers. Moses had been found by Jethro to be overworked in fulfilling the obligations of government. And Jethro had told him that this was no good thing : 'stulto labore consumeris et tu et populus iste qui tecum est ; ultra vires tuas est negotium, solus illud non poteris sustinere'. When Jethro had advised the appointment of continuing assistants from among the powerful and worthy, Moses fell in with the advice given him : 'et electis viris strenuis de cuncto Israel, constituit eos principes populi'. Gloucester was Chichele's Moses, his own was the part of Jethro, the priest of Midian. If he held to the whole of his script, the primate must have referred to the inferior and subordinate powers of Moses's helpers in government : 'quicquid autem majus fuerit, referant ad te [Moysen] et ipsi minora tantummodo judicent'. It is, however, doubtful whether he was disposed so to prejudice the issue before parliament.

<hr />

[1] *Biblia Sacra Vulgata*, Psalmus xlvi. 10.   [2] *ibid.*, Exodus xviii. 12–27.

H

And the emphasis of his discourse, if we may judge from the abbreviated report of it on the parliament-roll, was simply on the need for co-operation in government on the part of the magnates of the realm, of whom Gloucester was foremost among those present. This was as far as Chichele seemingly would go. Whether executive control was to be either monarchical in character, vested in view of Bedford's absence in the person of Gloucester, or oligarchical, resting in the hands of the lords of the continual council, was a matter for parliament to decide. It is improbable that scriptural analogies played any further part in the ensuing discussions.

After this formal opening of parliament the four committees normally set up to receive and try respectively the petitions from England, Ireland, Wales, and Scotland, and those from Gascony and overseas, were then appointed, the last day for the presentation of petitions being fixed as the following Saturday, 14 November ; and the knights, citizens, and burgesses were ordered to proceed immediately to the election of their common Speaker and to present him on the following day. It was not until Thursday, 12 November, however, that Roger Flore esquire, knight of the shire for Rutland, was presented and, after his customary protestation, accepted by Gloucester.[1] The arrangements for the administration of Henry V's will out of the revenues of those estates of the duchy of Lancaster specially enfeoffed for that purpose, were bound to be of parliamentary concern. Flore's position as chief steward of the duchy property north of Trent (he was to be reappointed on 1 December), his membership of the duchy council, and the fact that the late king had put him on a list of men on whom the duchy feoffees had been instructed to draw in event of their own numbers suffering attenuation, made him a wise choice for the Speaker's office. He had, moreover, already three times served the Commons in that capacity : in fact, on each of the three last previous occasions on which he had been elected to parliament.

Almost certainly to the first week of the session belongs the undated affirmation and authorisation by parliament of certain important commissions already issued under the great seal and of the parliamentary writs of summons ;[2] the grant by the duke of Gloucester and all the lords that the testification in parliament of the bishop of Durham's surrender of the great seal at Windsor on 28 September should be enrolled among the acts of the parliament ;

[1] *Rot. Parl.*, IV. 170.   [2] *ibid.*, 170.

the shewing of Bishop Kemp of London, late chancellor of the duchy of Normandy, that he had delivered the seal of the duchy after Henry V's death to the duke of Bedford at Rouen and a replica of the great seal of England to the king at Windsor on his arrival from overseas ; and the arrangements for the alteration of the present king's seals in accordance with the changes in his title necessitated by the death on 21 October of his grandfather, Charles VI of France, and by the consequential application of the terms of the treaty concluded at Troyes in 1420.[1]

Either on, as was more probable, or before Monday, 16 November, a deputation of knights was sent by the Speaker and their fellows to ask the duke of Gloucester that, with the advice of the lords spiritual and temporal, he would disclose to the Commons ' ad eorum majorem consolationem ' the names of those who were to be appointed to the offices of Chancellor, Treasurer, and Keeper of the Privy Seal.   After the appointment to these offices of Thomas Langley, bishop of Durham, William Kynwolmersh clerk, and Master John Stafford, respectively, a delegation of lords comprising Archbishop Chichele, the bishops of Winchester and Worcester, the duke of Exeter, the earl of Warwick, Lord Ferrers, and Lord Talbot, went across to the Common House to make the requested announcement.[2]   After this incident precisely what business was being considered by parliament is not known from the record of the parliament-roll itself until it gives the information that after nearly another three weeks, on the twenty-seventh day of the session, 5 December, it was decided with the assent and advice of the lords present in parliament and with the assent of the Commons that the duke of Bedford, or in his absence overseas, the duke of Gloucester, should be ' Protector et Defensor ' of the realm and of the English Church, and ' Consiliarius Principalis ' of the king.[3]

It must have been, however, early in the session that the Commons requested in parliament to know who should have ' the gouernance of this Reme undre our souverain lord [the King] bi his high auctorite '.[4]   According to the Lords' answer to a request which Gloucester was to make on 3 March 1428 when he asked to be furnished with a definition of his authority and power as

[1] *ibid.*, 170–1.   [2] *ibid.*, 171–2.   [3] *ibid.*, 174–5.
[4] S. B. Chrimes, *loc. cit.* ; the request of the Commons, here referred to, does not appear on the parliament-roll and was perhaps made by word of the Speaker's mouth only.

' protectour and defendour of this Lond ', Gloucester in 1422 had first made a twofold claim in parliament to the ' governaunce ' of England : it was his right, ' as wel be the mene of . . . birth, as be the laste wylle of the Kyng that was '. The Lords in 1422 had, however, rejected this claim as being not ' grounded in precident, nor in the lawe of the land ', the objection to the provision of Henry V's will being that ' the Kyng that ded ys, in his lyf ne migzt by his last will nor otherwyse altre, change nor abroge [abrogate] with oute thassent of the thre Estates, nor committe or graunte to any persone, governaunce or rule of this land lenger thanne he lyved '.[1] The Lords had simply harked back to the precedent of 1377 when neither had any regency been established for Richard II's minority nor any distinctive position been allowed to the foremost of the king's uncles, John of Gaunt ; and the Lords had accordingly granted Gloucester the title of ' Defensor of this Reme and chief Counseiller of the kyng '. The granting of this title, Gloucester pretended in a memorandum [2] he submitted to the Lords, did not properly meet the request of the Commons which could only be satisfied, he insisted, if he were given the title of ' Governour undre the Kyng ' or another equivalent name. But why should he not take, he then suggested, following the precedent of 1216, when there occurred the earliest minority after the Conquest (that of Henry III), the title of ' Rector regni ' which had been granted on that occasion to William Marshal, earl of Pembroke ? He would accept this charge with the assent of the council ; the word ' defensor ' could be added to meet the already expressed ' desire and appointment ' of the Lords.

As Mr. Chrimes has pointed out, there is no other evidence than this memorandum of Gloucester's supplies that the Commons, to satisfy whose petition Gloucester pretended was here his motive, thought insufficient the title of ' protector and defender of the realm and church in England and principal councillor of the King ', which Gloucester was ultimately granted in this parliament : its conferment, in fact, was formally to be made by the advice and assent of the Lords in parliament ' et auxi de la Commune d'Engleterre assemblez en la mesme '.[3] But whether the Commons were dissatisfied, as Gloucester speciously pretended, or not (and he was not without his friends in the Lower House), the Lords apparently clamped down on the duke's historical subtleties and his researches

[1] *Rot. Parl.*, IV. 326.   [2] S. B. Chrimes, *loc. cit.*   [3] *Rot. Parl.*, IV. 175b.

proved fruitless : the Lords had decided by 5 December, the twenty-seventh day of the parliamentary session, that Bedford, when in England, should be ' Regni Anglie et Ecclesie Anglicane Protector et Defensor ac Consiliarius Principalis domini Regis,' and that during Bedford's absence Gloucester should occupy that same and no higher position. The appointment was not made for the duration of the king's minority, but was to last expressly during his pleasure.[1] This limitation perhaps depended on the fact that the current form of the settlement was subject to Bedford's acceptance. But what it seems to have meant in effect, and what it may well have been intended to mean, was that the duration of the Protectorship, and the capacity to revoke it, rested with the magnates collectively : this would certainly seem to be implied from the statement made in council on 28 January 1427 by the chancellor (Archbishop Kemp of York) that the royal authority was vested in the lords in parliament or in great council or, if neither such assembly were in session, in the continual council.[2] In the end the Lords had been brought, seemingly, to the view that in the matter of Bedford's or Gloucester's title it would be better for its terms to reflect simply such of those vaguely worded functions, undertaken by a king in his coronation oath, as were compatible with the circumstances of the moment : the preservation of peace for the Church and for clergy and people. This is made reasonably clear by the fact that when Henry VI, still in his minority, was crowned on 5 November 1429, the Protectorship came by the Lords' determination to its logical end, although the chief councillorship remained in force.

The notice of the Lords' decision of 5 December 1422 is followed on the parliament-roll by a grant of certain rights of official and ecclesiastical patronage to whichever of the two royal dukes was occupying the office of Protector.[3] But these rights were simply grants by royal favour and in consideration of the Protector's future labours in his office, and were not intrinsically related to it or essential to its exercise. All other patronage was to be at the disposal of the whole council, except the chancellor's and treasurer's traditional ex officio patronage.

There next follows on the parliament-roll a memorandum referring to the nomination (probably on 9 December) of seventeen ' conseillers assistentz a la governance '. This act, prompted by a request of the Commons, was performed ' by the advice and assent '

---

[1] *ibid.*, 174–5.   [2] *P.P.C.*, III. 233.   [3] *Rot. Parl.*, IV. 175.

of all the lords and the names of the members of the new council were read openly in parliament. That there was no peculiar restrictive significance attached to the word 'assistentz' is clear from the fact that Gloucester's name headed the list. The only other peer in England of ducal status, the duke of Exeter, as the foremost of the king's personal guardians was naturally included. Apart from these two, and except for its ex-officio members, the construction of the council was framed on something like the now time-honoured basis of representation by estates : five prelates (the archbishop of Canterbury and the bishops of London, Winchester, Norwich, and Worcester), five earls (March, Warwick, the Earl Marshal, Northumberland, and Westmorland), and five others of varying status but all knights (the Barons FitzHugh and Cromwell, both peers of parliament, and three commoners, Sir Walter Hungerford, Sir John Tiptoft, and Sir Walter Beauchamp). These collectively submitted the conditions on which they took office in a paper schedule of five articles written in English ; [1] this schedule, after the Lords had approved its contents, was carried down to the Commons for their perusal by a delegation from the Upper House. The Lords would have their views ('lour entent').

The Commons scrutinised the whole schedule, apparently with care, and suggested an amendment to the first article which the Lords later accepted. This article stipulated that the choice of justices of the peace, sheriffs, escheators, and port officials should lie with the council, except those appointments left with the acting Protector and those customs appointments already resigned by Henry V to Bishop Beaufort as part of the security which the latter had demanded for the repayment of his loans to the Crown. The Commons now pointed out that a proviso of non-prejudice should be inserted on behalf of those who had the authority (either by inheritance or by grant for life) to appoint to certain of these offices as of right. The other articles of the schedule were not changed. One of them reserved to the council the control of the exercise of the feudal rights of the Crown, the bestowal of wardships and marriages and other 'casueltees', 'and that indifferently atte the derrest with oute favour or eny maner parcialtee or fraude'. Another provided for the custody of the royal treasury and the keeping of secrecy about its contents. Among the knights of the shire, John Wodehouse and John Throckmorton would be especially

[1] *Rot. Parl.*, IV. 176a.

interested in this article because it provided for them, as chamberlains of the Exchequer, being entrusted along with the treasurer with keys to the office of Receipt so long as they swore before Gloucester and the other lords of the council ' that for no frendship they schul make no man privee but the Lordis of the Counseill what the Kyng hath withynne his Tresour'. Another article was a device of administration : the clerk of the council was to be required on oath to write day by day the names of all the lords present at its sessions, ' to see what, howe, and by whom, eny thyng passeth'. The remaining one of the five articles was related to the important point of procedure within the council itself : the council was not to proceed to business unless six or four at the least were present, not counting the ex-officio members ; but if ' grete maters ' were to be discussed, then the attendance of all or of a majority was necessary. The appointment of a Protector made a difference to previously established rules of conciliar procedure : where it had been usual for the council to consult the king, the Protector's advice must be taken. On the point of procedure this arrangement was by no means all that Gloucester had wished, but the councillors-designate ignored or passed over his desires. Even so, it was far short of what was required to be defined of their procedures, and in 1423 and 1426 more specific rules regarding the council's passage of bills and other matters had to be devised. Nevertheless, in the years between 1422 and 1426 it had been worked out that the council should have control of government and that its consent was necessary before its chief member could act in even his capacity of Protector in any important issue.

The determination of the nature of the ' regency ' during Henry VI's minority and the limitation of the Protector's powers, once it had been decided to create this novel office, were matters depending on the implicit acceptance in 1422 of the doctrine (which became explicit only in January 1427) that the royal authority was vested in the lords of parliament, or in the lords met together in great council, or in the lords of the continual council if neither a parliament nor a great council were in session. We cannot say for sure what position it was that the Commons in parliament took up in this crisis of 1422. Seemingly they observed from the background, but watchfully and perhaps with great and sustained interest. It was from the Lower House that there emerged the petition for knowledge of ' who shuld haue the gouernance of this

Reme undre our soverain lord bi his high auctorite ', which moved
Gloucester to submit his subtly worded ' memorandum ' ; the
appointments to the offices of chancellor, treasurer, and keeper of
the privy seal, were made known to the Commons, at the instance
of ' certi milites ' acting on behalf of their fellows in the Lower
House, by a select delegation of the Lords who went to the Commons for that special purpose ; the new ' counseillers assistentz a
la governance ' were nominated at the Commons' request. Moreover, the articles which the newly chosen councillors submitted to
the Lords as the conditions on which they agreed to assume appointment, after being assented to by the Lords, were conveyed, as we
have seen, to the Lower House and were there amended and
accepted. That the Commons of 1422 did not insist, as the Commons of 1406 had done, that this new council should be answerable
for its conduct to parliament, and that ' the Lower House did not
grasp so obvious a moment for asserting its rights ',[1] was due, I
think, to the fact that the baronage was able to carry the Commons
with it in its policies rather than to the fact that it needed, or desired
and was able, to ignore them. The willingness of the Commons
to accept a position in which the council dictated to parliament
its own terms of service may well have been prompted by the
re-assuring inclusion in its numbers of three of their own former
Speakers, Sir John Tiptoft (1406), Sir Walter Hungerford (April
1414), and Sir Walter Beauchamp (March 1416). And Thomas
Chaucer, now knight of the shire for Oxfordshire, formerly Speaker
in 1407, 1410, 1411, November 1414, and May 1421, was to
join them on the council in the second parliament of the reign
(1423).

It is difficult to imagine the Commons of 1422 as a subservient
body. Among them was foregathered as fine an array of political
talent and experience as perhaps any Lancastrian parliament was to
witness : among their numbers were four knights of the shire who
had formerly occupied, and five more who were later to occupy,
the Speaker's office, and who together filled that position in no less
than half of the parliaments of the three Lancastrian reigns.[2]   The

[1] K. B. McFarlane, ' England : The Lancastrian Kings ', *Cambridge Medieval
History*, VIII. 388–90.

[2] Sir William Sturmy, now m.p. for Wilts, Speaker in October 1404 ; Thomas
Chaucer, for Oxfordshire, Speaker in 1407, 1410, 1411, November 1414, May 1421 ;
Roger Flore, for Rutland, Speaker in October 1416, 1417, 1419, 1422 ; Roger
Hunt, for Huntingdonshire, Speaker in 1420, 1433 ; John Russell, for Herefordshire,

personal composition of the Commons in 1422 reflects the national (or their own) sense of the gravity of the political situation : they were mostly men tried out in previous parliaments and were otherwise experienced in political and administrative life. A House of Commons of this calibre was not likely to have acquiesced out of mere subservience to any, even veiled, aristocratic dictation. The support of a majority, at least of the knights, was essential to the Lords, and must have been obtained. It may well be argued that the Commons in this critical year failed to appreciate the dangers of oligarchical government and the need for a formal recognition of their own right to a constitutional share in its future control. It may be suggested, on the other hand, that even if they did realise the risks involved in an aristocratic régime, the political circumstances of the moment would have made their criticisms seem unpatriotic ; and that, moreover, the absence of any request for a vote of direct taxation weakened their powers of making effective criticism. But the evidence seems to suggest that the Commons were quite prepared to fall into line behind the Lords and were genuinely more appreciative of their policy than blind to its defects. In view of the social and political ties which bound most of the more important members of the Lower House to one or another of the parliamentary aristocracy, it is not surprising that the Commons in 1422 acquiesced in its aims and saw eye to eye with its successful efforts to realise them. Even so, the opportunity of 1422, so far as was concerned any constitutionally recognised right of the Commons to control the main instrument of government at this time (the council), was an opportunity lost. How remote a possibility a continuing parliamentary nomination of the royal council soon became is clearly shown by the fact that less than eight years were to elapse before (on 16 April 1430) the council was able to assume that it had itself a right to add to, or remove from, its own membership.[1] The large measure of political initiative held by the Commons in the Good Parliament of 1376, during the early years of Richard II's reign, and again in the first part of Henry IV's, was lost by default in 1422 for more than two centuries.

After the notices of the appointment of a Protector and a Council

Speaker in 1423, 1432 ; Sir Thomas Waweton, for Bedfordshire, Speaker in 1425 ; Sir Richard Vernon, for Derbyshire, Speaker in 1426 ; John Tyrell, for Essex, Speaker in 1427, 1431, 1437 ; William Burley, for Shropshire, Speaker in 1437, 1445.

[1] *P.P.C.*, IV., 38.

and of the definition of their respective capacities, no further dated memorandum occurs in the parliament-roll until there appears a statement of the acts of the last day of the session, 18 December.[1] On that day the Speaker announced the terms and conditions of a grant of the subsidies on native and alien exports of wool and of a grant of tonnage and poundage. In the popular enthusiasm that followed the successful siege of Harfleur and the victory of Agincourt the Commons, in November 1415, had granted the subsidy on wool and other staple exports and the subsidy of tonnage and poundage to Henry V for life. These grants had now, of course, lapsed. The terms of their renewal were nothing like so favourable to the Crown as had been the generous grants of seven years earlier. The subsidy on native exports of wool was now to stand at 33 shillings and 4 pence per sack instead of at the earlier rate which was 10 shillings higher. The reduction of the subsidy on alien exports was not quite so considerable, but a reduction, nevertheless, took place here also ; from £3 to 53 shillings and 4 pence per sack. So far as native merchants were concerned a grant of tonnage and poundage was not forthcoming at all and, though this subsidy was levied on alien merchants and at the former rate, it was only for a very limited period : as from the commencement of the reign until two years from the beginning of the parliamentary session, that is, as from 1 September 1422 to 9 November 1424. The wool subsidy was granted for the same restricted period. Whether or not a parliamentary subsidy of a tenth and a fifteenth on movables was asked for by the new Council is not known. Certainly none was granted. It may be that in this parsimony, if parsimony it was, the Commons in 1422 lost an important opportunity to help secure an articulated financial responsibility on the part of the new government to parliament. A revival of the device of Richard II's reign, renewed for a time under Henry IV, of appointing Treasurers for the War answerable to parliament, might have been tied as a condition to a grant of a lay subsidy.

Coming between these notices and statements that petitions not already answered in parliament (including some preferred by the Commons) should be determined later by the Council, and that the duke of Gloucester should be confirmed in his offices of chamberlain of England and constable of Gloucester castle,[2] a request by the Commons, orally communicated to the Lords by the bishop

---

[1] *Rot. Parl.*, IV. 173.   [2] *ibid.*, 174.

of London, was made, possibly on the last day of the session.[1] This petition may have excited a more than casual interest on the part of one of the Somerset shire-knights, Sir Thomas Brooke, who had married the step-daughter of Sir John Oldcastle, had been imprisoned in the Tower after the Lollard rising of January 1414, had been bound over in the summer of 1417 to avoid all contact with his outlawed father-in-law, and may still have been perhaps doctrinally suspect. The petition asked that those imprisoned in London and elsewhere for heresy should be delivered to the ordinaries for judgement in accordance with the canon law ; Gloucester and the Lords partially acceded to the request, limiting its application simply to those imprisoned in the Tower or elsewhere in London.

Certain other petitions, either prompted in the first place, adopted, or assented to by the Commons, appear on the parliament-roll before those enrolled under the caption ' Petitiones Communitatis ' proper. All of these were connected with or involved Crown estates or grants. Among them was a request by Bartholomew Goldbeter, citizen of London, for an enlargement of his commission as master of the royal mints in the Tower and at Calais by a grant of the office of keeper of the exchange in the city, and this was allowed until the next parliament.[2] A petition, made by those lords and captains who had indentured to serve the late king in his wars, and by the executors of those who had died since so doing, for a settlement of their claims to wages and of Henry V's rights against them on the score of prisoners' ransoms and booty, was granted ; with the additional concession that, if claims were not met within a year, those royal jewels pledged in earnest of payment were to be retained on payment to the Exchequer of the difference between their value and the sums for which they had been pledged.[3] The Augustinian priory of Ivychurch successfully petitioned through the mediation of Henry V's secretary, Master William Alnwick (the new keeper of the privy seal), for the ratification and execution of a grant made by the late king of the alien priory of Uphaven (Wilts) in return for certain surrendered rights.[4] So that her letters patent might be backed by the authority of parliament the queen-mother petitioned for the assignment of her dower in accordance with the terms of the treaty of Troyes as ratified by parliament in 1421.[5] This petition would be of interest to those officials of the duchy of

---

[1] *ibid.*   [2] *ibid.*, 177–8.   [3] *ibid.*, 178.
[4] *ibid.*, 179–83.   [5] *ibid.*, 183–9.

Lancaster sitting in the Lower House, especially John Wodehouse who was the queen's own chancellor. Again of interest to some of the Commons would be the chancellor of England's verbal presentation before the Lords of their recommendation of Thomas Chaucer, knight of the shire for Oxfordshire, for confirmation in the office of chief butler, which he had held almost continuously for the past twenty years; the Lords granted that his patent of appointment should be ratified under the great seal without fine.[1]

Another petition [2] in which some individual members of the Lower House would be interested was that presented to the king and Lords by the Commons on behalf of Anne countess of Stafford touching certain difficulties which had arisen over the partition of the Bohun inheritance between herself and her coheir, Henry V (they were the children of the two daughters and coheirs of Humphrey de Bohun, that earl of Hereford, Essex, and Northampton who had died without male issue in 1372). The division into two equal halves had been arranged in the parliament of May 1421 with the exception of certain fees and advowsons 'en groos'. These latter, it had been decided, were to remain in the king's hands until their partition should be legally completed within the next two years at the discretion of the chancellor and the lords of the Council in consultation with the king's justices.[3] At the time of Henry V's death legal negotiations were still in progress, but a dispute had arisen over the four Welsh lordships of Penkelly, Bronllys, Llangoed, and Cantriff. These, the countess claimed, belonged to her purparty as members of the castle and manor of Brecknock, which had been assigned to her in May 1421. But the council of the duchy of Lancaster (the King's share of the Bohun estates were to be incorporated in the rest of the 'heritage de Lancastre') denied her claim and pretended that they were consequently 'en groos' and that their division was still to be arranged. The countess pointed to the fact that she had, on her side, been so reasonable as to allow manors and property worth £100 a year, the rights to which had descended to her alone by reversion—on the death (in April 1419) of her own and the king's maternal grandmother, Joan de Bohun, dowager countess of Hereford—to be subject to division between herself and the late king along with the rest of the inheritance. In this petition would be especially concerned among the Commons those three members of the duchy council who had been

---

[1] *Rot. Parl.*, IV. 178.   [2] *ibid.*, 176–7.   [3] *ibid.*, 135 *et seq.*

returned as knights of the shire (Speaker Roger Flore, John Wode-house, the chancellor of the duchy, and John Leventhorpe, its receiver- and attorney-general) and also Robert Darcy, parliamentary burgess for Maldon, who was receiver of the Essex estates of the late dowager countess of Hereford and since her death had been retained by the late king as legal counsel to the duchy of Lancaster, doubtless with a view to securing his co-operation in the work of partitioning the Bohun inheritance. Leventhorpe, by virtue of his office as keeper of the muniments of the duchy, was personally involved in another subsidiary complaint made by the countess in her petition, namely, that he would not surrender to her certain charters and evidences touching both parts of the partitioned estates without the sanction of the king's Council. It was decided in parliament that the petition should be enrolled on the parliament-roll and then entrusted for their determination to the lords of the Great Council.

Another petition [1] which nearly affected John Wodehouse and John Leventhorpe was one presented by them and their fellow-executors of Henry V's will. It requested parliamentary authority for them to proceed to act as such by royal letters patent to be drawn up in accordance with the form and content of a schedule which they now submitted to parliament.

Henry V had made his first will at Southampton on 24 July 1415 before setting out on his first expedition to Normandy.[2] In it he had provided *inter alia* for the conveyance to his executors of all his movable wealth for the payment of such of his father's debts as were still outstanding, the debts of his own Household, Wardrobe, and Chamber, and unpaid expenses incurred during his reign on the Scottish marches, at Calais, and in Ireland. If his movable property proved inadequate to meet this accumulation of debt, and Henry V had realised that it would be insufficient, the executors were to approach for assistance a committee of feoffees on whom were then settled, to enable them to meet the liability, certain estates of the duchy of Lancaster—they comprised most of the originally Lacy and Ferrers lands—and the whole of the king's moiety of the Bohun inheritance.[3] The revenues from these

---

[1] *ibid.*, 172–3. The following remarks about the administration of the wills of Henry IV and Henry V, owe much to some unpublished work on the subject by Mr. K. B. McFarlane of Magdalen College, Oxford, who kindly allowed me to use it.

[2] *Foedera*, IX. 289–93.   [3] *C.P.R., 1413–16*, 356–7.

properties were together expected to be in the region of £6,000 a
year.   All the executors appointed in the 1415 will with one exception (Sir John Rothenale) were also members of the committee of
feoffees ; they were, in fact, a majority of it.   On the last day of
November 1416, the duchy feoffees re-conveyed their estates, except
the Bohun property of the old earldom of Hereford, demising them
to the king and his assigns (*not* his heirs) for a period of twelve
years with reversion to themselves.[1]

And then just before embarking on his second expedition to
France, on 21 July 1417, Henry V made a second will, or rather a
declaration to his feoffees, providing for the settlement of all the
enfeoffed portions of the duchy after his death and the completion
of the administration of his will.[2]   The heir of his body, if he
should have one, was to inherit the whole of the duchy estates
enfeoffed.   Failing a direct heir, however, the castle and manor of
Higham Ferrers and other estates mainly in southern England, comprising one section of the enfeoffment, were to go to his heirs
general ;   but the northern portions [3] of the other section of
enfeoffed estates, which were composed in the main of the old
De Lacy fiefs dependent on the castles of Clitheroe (Lancs) and
Halton (Cheshire), were to be settled in tail male on the duke of
Bedford, and the southern portions of the same part of the enfeoffment similarly on the duke of Gloucester ;   in each case, if there
was no male issue, their estates were to remain to the king's heirs
occupying the throne and were to be annexed to the Crown.
Since the first will was drafted in the summer of 1415, two years
earlier, seven of the original feoffees had died : the surviving
members of the committee were now in 1417 authorised, should
they dwindle to three or less before the will was performed, to
enlarge their numbers by introducing to the trust those who were
then still living from another group of persons nominated on this
occasion by Henry V.   This group of reserve-feoffees included
Roger Flore, already chief steward of the duchy north of Trent
and Speaker-to-be of the Commons in 1422 ;   but it was destined
never to be resorted to.

At the end of a brief visit to England from overseas, by which
time he was expecting to have a direct heir, Henry V drew up,

---

[1] *C.P.R. 1422-9*, 472.   [2] J. Nichols, *Royal Wills*, 236-43.
[3] Presumably the duchy administrative boundary of the Trent was to mark the
line of division between north and south.

at Dover on 10 June 1421, a third will.[1]   On the previous day, 9 June, the king had himself composed a codicil addressed primarily to his feoffees.   We are ignorant of its terms because it has not survived, but in all probability it supplemented in some way the instructions already drawn up for the feoffees' guidance in 1417. The instrument of 10 June 1421 has also been lost and we are ignorant of its specifications too.   But, though it seems to have superseded the 1415 will, it doubtless included the still relevant terms of that will and confirmed, with certain amendments and additions, its provisions and bequests.[2]   One important difference between the 1415 and the 1421 wills was in the persons charged with their execution.   In 1415 the overseers nominated were the royal brothers (the dukes of Clarence, Bedford, and Gloucester), Archbishop Chichele, and Robert Hallum, bishop of Salisbury ; the executors were then the bishops of Winchester, Durham, and Norwich, the earls of Westmorland and Dorset (later duke of Exeter), Henry Lord FitzHugh, Sir Walter Hungerford, Sir John Rothenale, John Wodehouse, and John Leventhorpe, of whom Lord FitzHugh, Rothenale, and Wodehouse were to be the actual day-to-day administrators, being required to consult with the others over difficulties.[3]   By June 1421, of the five original overseers, Clarence and the bishop of Salisbury were dead, and of the original executors, the bishop of Norwich and Sir John Rothenale.   It seems doubtful whether Henry V added to the surviving overseers in 1421, except to include among them his queen, Catherine of Valois ; in fact, it would appear that he even withdrew the duke of Gloucester from this function and put him at the head of a much

---

[1] *Rot. Parl.*, IV. 299–300.

[2] The 1421 will probably, indeed almost certainly, superseded the 1415 will and was probably drawn up because the royal style of the 1415 will was out-of-date and had been so since the conclusion of the treaty of Troyes in 1420 (the earlier will described Henry V as ' Rex Anglie et Francie ', the later one as ' Rex Anglie, Heres et Regens Regni Francie ').   The 1421 will must inevitably have included new provisions, perhaps, for instance, Henry V's known bequests to certain French churches (*Foedera*, X. 346).   Moreover, it was the later will, and not the former as well, that Bishop Langley of Durham produced on 7 November 1422, immediately after Henry V's burial, along with the 1421 codicil.   Langley was to retain both these instruments until he surrendered them to the keeper of the privy seal on 29 January 1426 (*Rot. Parl.*, IV. 299b) ; the declaration to the Lancastrian feoffees of 1417 he retained until he gave it up to his surviving co-feoffees on 8 November 1435 (*ibid.*, 488b).   Langley, from the first an executor and feoffee, had been chancellor of England when the will of 1421 was drawn up.

[3] *Foedera, op. cit.*, IX. 293.

expanded body of executors. The original membership of *this* body, depleted by the loss of only two members, was now in 1421 more than doubled : to the eight survivors of the first board of executors were added the duke of Gloucester, the earls of Warwick, Northumberland, and Worcester, Lords Willoughby and Clifford, Sir William Porter, Sir Robert Babthorpe, Sir Walter Beauchamp, Sir Lewis Robessart, and John Wilcotes esquire. But those of the newly-constituted board who had held Household or other administrative positions were now distinguished from their fellow-executors of prelatical or aristocratic rank : Lord FitzHugh, Henry V's chamberlain, Sir Walter Hungerford, steward of the royal Household, Sir Walter Beauchamp (each of these three was to be a member of Henry VI's council as established during the 1422 parliament), Sir Lewis Robessart, Sir William Porter, Sir Robert Babthorpe, controller of the royal Household, John Wodehouse and John Leventhorpe, chancellor and receiver-general respectively of the duchy of Lancaster, and probably John Wilcotes, receiver-general of the duchy of Cornwall, were those ' les queux il [Henry V] volloit continuelment entendre et solliciter a l'execution de la volunte suisdite '.[1] These special administrators of the will were to report on their work twice a year, until the will should be fully administered, to the dukes of Gloucester and Exeter and the bishops of Winchester and Durham. What functions their other fellow-executors of high rank—the earls of Westmorland, Warwick, Northumberland, and Worcester, and the Lords Willoughby and Clifford—were intended to perform is not at all clear. Presumably they retained a general responsibility but were to be little more than sleeping partners. They might be (and were) convened, however, when and as often as the controlling committee of executors, the two dukes and the two bishops, found it expedient to consult them.

The earl of Worcester, Lord Clifford, and John Wilcotes predeceased Henry V. But otherwise the arrangements made in 1421 were still intact at the king's death on 31 August 1422. Preparations for the administration of the will would appear to have been temporarily in abeyance, although the committee of feoffees, one part of the dual organisation for fulfilling the will, was considered to have been in possession of the enfeoffed Lancastrian estates as from Henry V's death (by virtue of the reversionary clause in the settlement of November 1416). Immediately after Henry V's

[1] *Rot. Parl.*, IV. 399a ; 172–3.

funeral on 7 November 1422, however, the bishop of Durham produced the will and codicil of June 1421 for inspection by the overseer, Archbishop Chichele, in the presence of those other executors
who had been given like himself a special controlling position over
the administrative executors, that is, in the presence of Bishop
Beaufort and the dukes of Gloucester and Exeter.[1]   The next stage
was reached when parliamentary authority was sought by petition
for the measures which the executors proposed to take.

   Following Henry V's policy after his father's death in 1413, the
government in 1422 set aside that stipulation of the late king's will
which gave his executors all his movables and, instead, reserved
them for his successor's use.[2]   The authorisation by the first parliament of the new reign of the contents of the petition presented
for its approval put the seal on the government's compensatory
measures.[3]   The royal letters patent, which were to be issued according to the form and content of the schedule submitted to parliament,
provided that Henry V's administrative executors should receive
from the treasurer of England the sum of 40,000 marks in jewels,
goods, and money, for the fulfilment of the will.   Of these 40,000
marks, 19,000 marks were to be expended on discharging the debts
of Henry IV, towards which only 6,000 marks (out of the 25,000
promised in 1413) had been paid to his executors in the course of
Henry V's reign (in 1413 it had been thought that four years would
prove long enough to pay off what was due).   All Henry IV's
executors were still living in 1422.   They were Henry Bowet,
archbishop of York, Thomas Langley, bishop of Durham, Sir John
Pelham, knight of the shire for Sussex in the 1422 parliament, Sir
Robert Waterton, and John Leventhorpe, who, as we have seen,
sat for Hertfordshire.   Leventhorpe's almost unique position as
executor to both Henry IV and Henry V (he shared this distinction
with the bishop of Durham but was the only intermediary link
between the executors administrating the will of the first Lancastrian
king and the operative section of the executors of the second) and
his position as one of Henry V's duchy of Lancaster feoffees were
immediately recognised by his co-feoffees when they appointed him
(at a fee of £100 a year) to be overseer of the property under their
control and his son, John Leventhorpe the younger, to succeed him

[1] *ibid.*, 299 ; the duke of Bedford, Chichele's co-overseer, was, of course, in
France.
[2] *ibid.*, 399–400 ; cf. *C.P.R.*, *1413–16*, 54.   [3] *ibid.*, IV. 172–3.

as receiver-general of the same estates. Leventhorpe senior continued to hold his office of keeper of the records of the duchy.[1]

The sums, granted in the 1422 parliament for the administration of Henry V's and his father's wills in accordance with the petition then presented, were to have been applied to their fulfilment before the next parliament met. When Henry VI's second parliament met on 20 October 1423, therefore, Henry V's executors ought to have been able to render their final account to their controlling committee and the overseers, so that after the parliament they could seek further and final exoneration from Chichele, exercising his ecclesiastical prerogative rights over probate as archbishop. It had taken until 26 August 1423, however, for goods and chattels, jewels, and cash, together worth only £18,404 4s. 10d.—roughly seven-tenths of the agreed total sum of 40,000 marks—to be handed over to Henry V's executors by the treasurer, John Stafford.[2] And when the second parliament of the reign met, nothing further had been done. Though both groups of royal executors then submitted to parliament petitions [3] for the approval of fresh letters patent which embodied the terms of those of the year before, it was not until 18 December 1423, the day after the close of the first session of this parliament, that provision was made for raising the balance.[4] The various sources of revenue then laid under contribution were largely inaccessible and not likely to be fruitful, but if the assignments proved deficient the treasurer was to meet his liabilities to Henry V's executors before the next parliament.

The concurrent administration of the two wills was proving a slow business. Henry IV's executors were, of course, dependent upon the ability and readiness of Henry V's to make the necessary moves. In view of the fact that the latter had only recently (on 26 August 1423) arrived at a partial and interim settlement with the treasurer, it is not at all surprising to find that when the 1423 parliament met, Henry IV's executors had received nothing of what was due to them. During this second parliament of the reign, it is true, certain steps were taken to enable them to act more effectively : by this time Archbishop Chichele and (nominally) the king were acting as their 'overseers', and sometime during the session the treasurer, the keeper of the privy seal, the keeper of the Great Wardrobe, and Robert Chichele (the archbishop's brother) were

---

[1] Duchy of Lancaster, Accounts Various, P.R.O., D.L.28/4/11 ; 5/1.
[2] *Rot. Parl.*, IV. 213–42.   [3] *ibid.*, 206–8.   [4] *C.P.R., 1422–9,* 176.

appointed to act as the king's deputy-overseers along with the arch-bishop.[1]   But when nearly yet another year had passed Henry IV's executors had received only 10,000 out of the 19,000 marks assigned them in 1422.   Perhaps Henry V's operative executors were not finding it easy to dispose of, or convert into more negotiable form, the wealth of movables turned over to them by the treasurer ; and then their obligation to Henry IV's executors was only one, even if the chief single, item on their list of liabilities.   However this may be, Henry IV's executors found funds to meet their obligations so difficult to come by that they eventually had recourse to the duchy of Lancaster feoffees.   On 30 September 1424 the feoffees granted them 3,000 marks a year from the issues of the enfeoffed estates until 9,000 marks outstanding should be paid off (this arrangement was ratified in the third parliament of the reign, the parliament of April 1425).[2]   From this time forward until the administration of Henry IV's will was completed and Chichele on 5 October 1429 ordered Leventhorpe's account to be audited and determined,[3] the executors of this will accounted with the feoffees and *not* either with their own overseers (Chichele and the royal deputies) or with the over-seers of Henry V's will.[4]   On 4 December 1429 the archbishop exonerated and acquitted Henry IV's executors.[5]   Over seven years had elapsed since Henry V's death and nearly another ten more since the testator's.

By December 1429 Henry V's executors were still unpaid some £2,050 of the £14,000 granted them (their share of the 40,000 marks assigned in 1422 for the administration of both royal wills), and when, by May 1432, these deficits had been made up, they then pointed out in a petition to the Commons that their liabilities to the late king's creditors and servitors still amounted to £8,000. The triple organisation of feoffees, executors, and their supervisors, as set up in Henry V's will, now lapsed ; because, in undertaking to supply the deficiency of funds, the feoffees insisted that the sums

---

[1] E. F. Jacob, *Chichele Register*, II. 430 ; the original overseers of Henry IV's will had been Henry V and Archbishop Arundel of Canterbury.   The latter, how-ever, died on 19 February 1414 and on 16 June 1414 Henry V delegated his own supervisory functions to Arundel's successor as primate (Chichele) and Henry Beaufort, bishop of Winchester (*ibid.*, 423).   Their commission seemingly lapsed with Henry V's death, but a year later Chichele was acting as full overseer along with Henry VI's deputy-overseers.

[2] *Rot. Parl.*, IV. 280–2.   [3] Jacob, *op. cit.*, II. 426
[4] Exchequer Warrants, P.R.O., E.404/43, from information received from Mr. McFarlane.   [5] Jacob, *op. cit.*, II. 430–1.

they were prepared to grant to complete the will should be administered by *their* nominees responsible to them alone.[1] The feoffees stated on this occasion that they had expended all the issues of the enfeoffed estates on the execution of the will, except £9,232 14s. 9½d. (which had been loaned to Henry VI) and those revenues still in the hands of their local receivers and other officials. Another nine years were to elapse before the feoffees were able (or could be induced) to surrender their trust.

Being doubtless preoccupied with constitutional and administrative business, Henry VI's first parliament is not noteworthy for any considerable legislative output. Only one of the six ' communes petitiones '[2] was granted as it stood and without modification. This was a petition for the confirmation of grants of offices, held for life or in fee, made by Henry IV and by Henry V as prince of Wales and as king. Presented by the Commons but doubtless inspired by the representatives of the communities of the counties of Oxfordshire, Berkshire, Wiltshire, and Buckinghamshire, another petition demanded that, in view of the outrages perpetrated by Irish clerks frequenting the University of Oxford, all Irishmen should be compelled to leave the country before Candlemas following, except assured graduates in the schools, clerks beneficed in England, men with landed property here, or honest resident merchants, and that the ordinance resulting from this petition should be proclaimed in the counties affected. This petition was granted and later issued as a statute but with qualifications : Irish scholars, not yet graduates but of the king's obedience, might enter or stay on in England if they found surety for their good behaviour and letters under the seal of the lieutenant or justice of Ireland attesting their loyalty. Another petition presented by the Commons as their own but probably emanating from the group of merchant-staplers in the Lower House—Fauconer (London), Poge (Nottingham), Sutton (Lincoln), Holme (Hull), Bowes, and Russell (York),—asked for the confirmation of the privileges of the Staple. This was granted, but a request for non-interference by writs of privy seal in the conduct of pleas before, or execution of judgements by, the mayor and constables of the staples (the Exeter parliamentary representatives, Cook and Vessey, were respectively mayor and constable of the Exeter staple) was refused. A petition presented

---

[1] *Rot. Parl.*, IV. 393–4, 399–400 ; *C.P.R., 1429–36,* 349–50.
[2] *Rot. Parl.*, IV. 189–191.

by the Commons asking for the full application of the existing statutes and ordinances touching royal purveyance was, on the whole, not unsympathetically received. Instead of the relevant statutes and ordinances being proclaimed by the sheriff each year where necessary, as the petition requested, the official response was to the effect that, if in obedience to a royal mandate he did not either proclaim them *four* times a year or deliver the mandate to his successor, he was to be amerced by a £5 fine ; the second demand on this score contained in the petition, that the bailiff or constable of a town or hamlet where an infringement of the regulations took place should prefer a bill of particulars before the next session of the local justices of the peace, so that an inquiry might be held, and that the justices should then have power of oyer and terminer, was ignored in the response and the resultant statute. A similar attitude on the part of the government was adopted over the Commons' petition for the enforcement of the statutes of 14 and 28 Edward III and 1 Richard II, limiting a sheriff's term of office to a year, insisting on the lapse of three years before a sheriff could be reappointed, and providing for the possession by both sheriffs and escheators of a sufficiency of property in their bailiwicks ; the petition asked also for the annulment of the statute of 1421, which had allowed the late king the right to keep sheriffs and escheators in office for the ensuing four years. In reply, the government insisted on the continuance of the recent statute, but the Council promised to address itself to the problem of revision and undertook for the future to see that all appointees were ' sufficient '. It refused to admit the request that sheriffs, escheators, mayors, and bailiffs should be enabled to make their proffers in the Exchequer by attorney. The complaint that sheriffs were not allowed there any relief for sums which they found impossible to raise (the Commons instanced the sum of £200 annually charged on the shrievalty of Essex and Hertfordshire) was met by an undertaking that allowance should be made, albeit from year to year, and pardons issued if the Council thought them justified. This petition and its answer would naturally arouse great interest in the Commons particularly among the knights of the shire, a majority of whom had already occupied the offices chiefly in question, and especially in Edmund Wynter (Norfolk) and John Vampage (Worcestershire), who were at the time escheators in their counties, in Sir Thomas Waweton (Huntingdonshire) already appointed sheriff of Bedford and

Buckingham for the current year, and possibly in Sir John Cockayne, Sir William Bonville, Sir John Bertram, and John Tyrell, who were soon to be nominated as sheriffs and whose appointments were perhaps already under discussion. Among the parliamentary burgesses especially and immediately interested in the request for the option of indirect proffer in the Exchequer by attorney on the part of mayors and bailiffs, would be Walter Reson, John Tamworth, Thomas Poge, and John Fitlyng, respectively mayors of Wareham, Winchelsea, Nottingham, and Hull, and Thomas Ayssheldon, John Sumpter, Thomas Astley, Robert Elys, John Colles, John Perle, and Hugh Rasyn, respectively bailiffs at Dartmouth, Colchester, Ipswich, Great Yarmouth, Huntingdon, and Scarborough, all of whose offices were accountable at the Exchequer. The only common petition to meet with an unqualified negative was the request for a statute to stop pleas actionable at common law from being entertained by the Council or Chancery : it had asked that writs of *subpena*, issued by the keeper of the privy seal, should be withheld until the pleas concerned had been found by two of the common law judges to be outside the competence of the two Benches. The official response referred the petitioners to the statute of 17 Richard II which had merely empowered the chancellor to award damages to those compelled to appear before the Council or in Chancery in virtue of writs grounded upon untrue suggestion.

Of the six private petitions unenrolled but printed in the *Rotuli Parliamentorum* as having been presented in this parliament,[1] three were addressed to the king, one to the king and Lords, one to Gloucester and the Lords, and one to the Commons. The only one of these likely to interest personally any members of the Lower House was the petition addressed to the king by his ward, Humphrey, the son and heir of the earl of Stafford who had been killed at Shrewsbury nearly twenty years before. It pointed out that on his death-bed the late king had granted ' par bouche ' that the petitioner should have possession of his lands despite the fact that he was still under age. After the duke of Exeter and Lord FitzHugh and several other knights had testified in parliament to Henry V's verbal declaration, it was ordered that the grant should be put into operation with the proviso that livery should be sued out in the customary form when the young earl properly came of age. Both the parliamentary burgesses for Stafford, Harpour and

[1] *Rot. Parl.*, IV. 192–6.

Whitgreve, had close connexions with the Stafford lords of the
borough, and Reginald Pympe, knight of the shire for Kent, was
a Stafford tenant.

Three group-petitions were presented in the 1422 parliament.
The bill addressed to the king and Lords by the Hanseatic merchants
in England, asking for a determination by the judges of the King's
Bench and the Common Bench on the subject of certain customs
exacted by the sheriffs of London during the last two years, would
probably be of no more than casual interest to all but the London
representatives. Probably none of the Commons was directly
interested in the petition preferred by the Dominicans of London,
Cambridge, and Oxford, and the Franciscans of Cambridge and
Oxford, who together successfully asked for the continuance, and
the payment of arrears, of the annuities accorded them by Henry V.
But many of the merchants and others in the Lower House would
be in support of the petition of anonymous origin which asked the
Commons to request the king and Lords to ordain by statute that
no alien broker should ask for recognition at the Exchequer, and
that all local officials should be ordered annually to make search in
order to enforce the regulation. Among the alleged reasons behind
the bill's promotion were the time-honoured and hoary complaints
that alien brokers were inclined to favour alien merchants and,
moreover, ' desclosent a eux tout le privite du Roialme ' so that
they could regulate their buying and selling prices accordingly.
John Cook, the Exeter draper, Richard Peny, the Dorset clothier
with his London connexions, Ralph Hunt [1] of Bath with his
interests in the cloth trade, and doubtless William Wood, the
Winchester representative, then alnager of cloth in Hampshire,
would be able to bear out the truth of the information in the bill
that the price of ' Western cloth ' had recently dropped by a third,
although they were probably aware that alien brokerage was not
the only reason. Adopted by the Commons and sent up to the
Lords, where it apparently passed, the bill was, however, officially
turned down.

Most of the knights of the shire in the first parliament of
Henry VI's reign were of more than local importance and were
well-connected by kinship and political attachment ; and many
of the parliamentary burgesses were ' gentilmen ', many of them

---

[1] For Ralph Hunt's interest in the manufacture of cloth and probably in wool-
growing, see his will in E. F. Jacob, *Chichele Register*, II. 462–5.

lawyers, many well-to-do merchants, and but few of them nonentities even outside their borough communities.   Together their solidarity and good-sense probably contributed much to the work of a parliament which was above all unspectacular in its political results especially where the Commons were concerned, but constitutionally and administratively of great importance for the new reign. But a parliamentary session was more than a recognition of a constitutional, legislative, and representative principle.   It was a great opportunity, political, administrative, and social.   Sometimes, especially when parliament met at Westminster, the judicial and administrative centre of the realm, being returned as a representative could be, and in many cases undoubtedly was, of considerable, immediately personal advantage.   It is a noteworthy fact, to cite only one instance of this, that, at the time the parliament of 1422 was in session, three out of every ten members of the Lower House were impleading or being impleaded, mainly in debt and trespass actions, in the Court of Common Pleas alone.[1]

[1] Common Pleas, Michs. term 1 Henry VI, P.R.O., C.P.40/647.

CHAPTER VII

THE CHANGING CHARACTER OF BOROUGH REPRESENTATION IN THE FIFTEENTH CENTURY

IN our earlier analysis of the parliamentary burgesses returned to parliament in 1422 we were able to state that only some forty could be positively identified as merchants. The direct representation of the mercantile and trading interest in parliament by men who were themselves merchants seems to have remained fairly constant round and about this figure throughout the fifteenth century. As many identifiable merchants were sitting in the Commons at the end of the century as were at the beginning of Henry VI's reign, and throughout the century there was invariably a solid bloc of merchants of greater or lesser importance in the Lower House of parliament. Now it is true that in the last century or so of the medieval period the more well-to-do of the mercantile class were less averse than ever to investing the profits of trade in landed estate to help them secure social advancement and perhaps to promote health and stability of economic interest and investment—this is especially true of the leaders of the commercial life of the capital—and some of them were coming to regard themselves and to be accounted as ' gentilmen ' even when they did not go on to dissociate themselves completely from ' trade '. But the burgess element proper was not enlarging—or was perhaps not being allowed to enlarge—its outlook and aspirations in the field of parliamentary representation. Of the 1422 knights of the shire those who had been demonstrably occupied in merchantry at any time or who came of a merchant family formed only a tiny group. The Speaker, Roger Flore of Oakham, was the son-in-law of a local member of the Calais staple and himself in 1394 had been partner in an export of wool lost in transit from Lynn to Calais. But there is no record of his continued connexion with trade. John Greville of Chipping Campden, knight of the shire for Gloucestershire, was a younger son of a very important Cotswold wool factor and in 1395 had himself been involved in this branch of English export-trade. But there is no knowing whether or not he maintained this early mercantile interest, although it is unlikely that he did so on any scale of importance.   The family of Sir Richard Stanhope (Nottingham-shire) had been wool merchants operating from the Tyne in Edward III's reign, and the Frowykes kept one foot in London after their rustication to South Mimms which was handy for the city. But that is about all.   Nine of the parliamentary burgesses of 1422 at one time or another also sat as knights of the shire.[1]   Only one of them was a merchant : the sometime mayor of the Calais staple, Hamond Sutton of Lincoln, later represented his shire in three parliaments in the 1430's.   The others were lawyers and/or country gentlemen.   Between 1439 and the end of Henry VII's reign [2] there are known for sure to have been over a hundred cases of men who sat at one time or another as parliamentary burgesses and as knights of the shire, but only two of these men were ever merchants : John Prout of Reading and Streatley,[3] a merchant stapler, who represented Reading in 1453, 1460, and 1472, but sat as knight of the shire for Berkshire in 1467 ; and Thomas Fowler, sometime stock-fishmonger of London, who, a younger brother of Richard Fowler chancellor of the duchy of Lancaster, came as a yeoman of the crown to represent Wycombe in 1472 and as a royal esquire of the body to sit for Buckinghamshire in 1478 and 1495.[4]

In some senses the merchant class in the fifteenth century was achieving greater social recognition, but in the sphere of parliamentary representation it was clearly not forging ahead.   Even in

[1] (a) Nicholas Ayssheton, m.p. Liskeard, May 1421 ; Helston, 1422, 1423, 1425, 1427, 1435 ; Launceston, 1431, 1432 ; Cornwall, 1437, 1439 ;

(b) John Hody, m.p. Shaftesbury (Dorset), December 1421, 1422, 1423, 1425, 1427 ; Dorset, 1431 ; Somerset, 1433, 1435, 1437 ;

(c) Robert Darcy, m.p. Newcastle-on-Tyne, 1402 ; Essex, March 1416, 1419, May 1421, 1423, 1425, 1426, 1432, 1439, 1445 ; Maldon (Essex), 1422 ;

(d) John Langley, m.p. Chippenham (Wilts), 1422 ; Gloucestershire, 1429, 1432, 1435, 1437, 1442 ;

(e) Robert Whitgreve, m.p. Stafford, 1411, March 1416, 1420, May and December 1421, 1422, 1423, 1425, 1426, 1427, 1429, 1431, 1432, 1433, 1435, 1437, 1442 ; Staffordshire, 1445, November 1449 ;

(f) John Harpour, m.p. Stafford, 1419, 1420, May 1421, 1422, 1423, 1425, 1427, 1429 ; Staffordshire, 1431 ;

(g) John Mynors, m.p. Newcastle-under-Lyme, 1419, 1422 ; Staffordshire, 1420, 1431, 1437 ;

(h) Hamond Sutton, m.p. Lincoln March 1416, 1420, May 1421, 1422, 1423, 1425, 1426 ; Lincolnshire, 1431, 1435, 1439 ;

(i) John Seymour, m.p. Ludgershall, 1422 ; Wiltshire, 1435, 1439, 1445. The first six of these nine were lawyers.

[2] J. C. Wedgwood, *History of Parliament, Biographies of the Members of the Commons House 1439–1509, passim.*

[3] *ibid.,* 700.   [4] *ibid.,* 352.

borough representation it had already lost ground by the beginning of Henry VI's reign and was never to recover that rôle and place in the medieval parliament which it had occupied in the fourteenth century, when the breakdown of Edward III's intention to negotiate in separate assemblies with the ' estate of merchants ' was largely due to the fact that they were fully represented in the Commons in parliament. We have stated that there was invariably a solid bloc of merchants of greater or lesser importance in the Lower House of parliament throughout the fifteenth century and that from the beginning of Henry VI's reign it is unlikely that the representation of mercantile interests in parliament by the merchants themselves suffered any further attenuation. But it is important to recognise the fact that this constancy of merchant representation was due to the way in which the bigger centres only of mercantile activity and enterprise held on (successfully, for the most part) to their traditions of representation by members of their own merchant oligarchies, cities and towns like London, Bristol, Norwich, York, Hull, Southampton, Exeter, Colchester, Nottingham, and (to a lesser degree) Salisbury. Very many of the smaller boroughs, especially those far distant from Westminster, were not even by the beginning of Henry VI's reign returning to parliament merchants or members of the burgess class proper. Of the twelve parliamentary burgesses elected by the Cornish boroughs in 1422, for instance, seemingly only one was a merchant.[1] The approximation in the fifteenth century of the type of man returned to parliament from the boroughs to the type of man returned from the shires was due mainly to the fact that the country gentry and the professional élite of the country were, at a progressively quicker tempo, coming to realise that the *sole* approach to the privilege of a return to parliament did not lie through election in the county court. And it is quite clear that the movement which resulted in a certain degree of interpenetration of county and borough representative personnel was one of the landowning and professional classes and those classes of retainers, royal and seigneurial, down into borough representation rather than one of the mercantile elements up into a social position from which they could seek election to parliament for the counties.

It is interesting to observe towards the middle of the fifteenth century a few members of the merchant class taking a leaf out of the gentry's book and seeking election to parliament in small and

[1] Robert Trenerth, m.p. Truro.

unimportant boroughs not their own. John Willy, draper and merchant of Salisbury, for instance, understandably got himself returned as burgess for Old Sarum in 1437 and in the two parliaments of 1449, but in the meantime he was returned for the other Wiltshire boroughs of Wilton (1439) and Marlborough (1447).[1] On two of these occasions (1439 and January 1449) his own city of Salisbury returned one and two outsiders respectively and presumably passed him over : in the first case, William Ludlow, king's serjeant and parker of Ludgershall ;[2] on the second occasion, John Whittokesmede of Benacre,[3] the bailiff of the bishop of Salisbury and a royal serjeant-at-arms, together with a lawyer, Philip Morgan esquire.[4]   This return of two outsiders by Salisbury in January 1449 made it necessary for another Salisbury merchant, Thomas Freeman,[5] mercer, to seek election, like Willy, in another borough of his county.   In 1447 Freeman had resorted to Calne and this time he managed it at Westbury ; for the next parliament (November 1449) and again in 1453 and 1455, he had no need, however, to go farther afield than Old Sarum.   Although Thomas Freeman sat in every one of the six parliaments between 1447 and 1455, he only once in these years secured his election for his own city of Salisbury (in 1450).   His fellow parliamentary burgess from Old Sarum in 1453 was a London grocer, Richard Joiner [6] (*alias* Vern) who had sat in 1450 for Heytesbury, another Wiltshire borough.   Another London grocer, John Tyngelden, represented Reigate in November 1449.[7]   Almost all these few instances of merchants intruding themselves into the parliamentary representation of boroughs of inferior status to their own cities are confined to Wiltshire.   Moreover, these are all the examples of this phenomenon that I have been able to discover round about the middle of the century ; and for a clear repetition of such incidents we must wait until early in Henry VII's reign when, in 1491, two mercers and staplers of London (Richard Copley and John Holgrave) are to be found returned from Gatton (Surrey) and Old Sarum respectively.[8]   But that is all.   It is true that for this parliament and for certain parliaments in the intervening period the returns of elections for cities and boroughs are far from complete, but it is doubtful whether this mere handful of cases of merchants joining in the scramble of outsiders for borough seats

[1] J. C. Wedgwood, *op. cit.*, *Biographies*, 953.   [2] *ibid.*, 561.
[3] *ibid.*, 944–5.   [4] *ibid.*, 611–12.   [5] *ibid.*, 355–6.
[6] *ibid.*, 504.   [7] *ibid.*, 857.   [8] *ibid.*, 221, 464.

would be substantially added to if the returns were complete. Wealthy merchants, certainly in any significant numbers, were clearly either not prepared or were unable to compete with the gentry, lawyers, or members of the official or retainer classes, in the process whereby in the course of the fifteenth century the parliamentary representation of boroughs generally took on a different complexion.

Considering some of the parliaments of Edward IV's reign (especially those of 1467, 1472–5, and 1478) in her book on *The Parliamentary Representation of the English Boroughs during the Middle Ages*, Miss McKisack was of the opinion (and the official *History of Parliament* bears her out) that, as a result of a ' great influx of the country gentry ', ' at least one-half of the borough representatives were not true burgesses ', and she claimed that in consequence there had been something of a ' revolution ' in the composition of the Lower House of parliament.[1] The social balance among the Commons had been tilted over in favour of the gentry who may be said, of course, to include all the seventy-four knights of the shire who represented the counties electing to parliament at this time. The Tudor creation of parliamentary boroughs, very largely the answer to demands from magnates desirous of extending their control of parliamentary patronage, did nothing to stem or hold back this revolution in the composition of the Commons in parliament—it did in fact promote it. And Professor Neale has shown us that by the end of the sixteenth century the statutorily-qualified resident burgesses elected to parliament (recorders, gentlemen holding borough offices, and resident gentlemen generously included in his estimate) tended to be no more than a quarter of those returned by the parliamentary boroughs. As a result, ' instead of one gentleman to four townsmen [which would have been the proportion if the statutes relating to the residential qualification of parliamentary burgesses had been observed] Elizabeth's later parliaments contained four gentlemen to every townsman '.[2] In the Yorkist parliaments. for which something like full returns have survived (those of 1467–8, 1472–5, and 1478) there were among the Commons two gentlemen to every one townsman, whereas, by that time (if statutes had been given their full legal force), the townsmen should have outnumbered the gentry by three to one. The earlier actual, and still legally

---

[1] M. McKisack, *op. cit.*, 106–12.
[2] J. E. Neale, *The Elizabethan House of Commons*, London, 1949, 147.

required, preponderance of burgesses over gentry quite clearly by the middle of Edward IV's reign had ended. This 'revolution' in the class structure of the Lower House of parliament Miss McKisack regarded as the product of the political disturbances of the mid-fifteenth century, as coincidental with the beginnings of civil strife in England, although she thought that the substitution of country gentlemen or officials for burgesses was noticeable as a tendency at least from the beginning of Henry VI's reign. My own feeling is that her more detailed examination of the burgess personnel of the Yorkist parliaments led her to post-date developments that were already well in progress by the time of the accession of Henry of Windsor, and to lay too much emphasis on the share of the commotions of the middle years of the century in their generation. In Henry VI's first parliament the townsmen, again in the comprehensive sense of residents, still outnumbered the gentry among the parliamentary Commons by something like five to four. For, as we have seen, in 1422 less than a quarter (not a half, as fifty years later) of the parliamentary burgesses were non-residents. But we should bear in mind the fact that the remaining resident three-quarters of the parliamentary burgesses of 1422 were by no means necessarily members of the 'burgess-class' proper in the occupational sense of that term, that is, men interested in the production or distribution of merchandise of one sort or another. And if we include in our estimate of the 'gentry' who sat as parliamentary burgesses in 1422 all those who had attained the rank of esquire, those unconnected with trade who could be described in official documents as 'gentilmen', those who were justices of the peace in their shires, those who were lawyers or acted as administrative agents of estates, those who from time to time attended *shire* elections to parliament and attested their validity in the sheriff's indentures, and, for example, those who were included in 1434 among the notables of their shire as being of sufficient standing to take the oath (provided for by act of parliament) not to maintain or support breakers of the peace, we shall arrive at a figure (between eighty and ninety) enabling us to say that something like half of the parliamentary burgesses were already, at the beginning of Henry VI's reign, not burgesses in the usually accepted 'class' sense of that term, although fully three out of four were still burgesses in the sense that they lived in the towns returning them. The 'revolution' in the class structure of the Lower House of parliament was clearly already past the stage of being a mere tendency. In the 1422 parliament the gentry in the Commons outnumbered the members of the burgess class proper by something like four to three.

Many a town which succumbed in the course of Henry VI's and the Yorkist reigns to the practice of resorting to outsiders was one which, in 1422, was ceasing to look for its representatives in parliament among its merchant and trading elements but had not yet begun to look for them outside its own limits or its burgess-roll. Cases in point which spring to mind are those of Robert Darcy of Maldon, a lawyer in Crown employment, John Warfeld of Wallingford, the receiver of the Buckinghamshire family of Stonore, Robert Carlisle junior of Carlisle, a member of Lincoln's Inn, Robert Gilbert of Gloucester, another member of Lincoln's Inn, Richard Duffield of Grimsby, clerk of the peace for the parts of Lindsey in Lincolnshire, John Forthey of Worcester, clerk of the peace for Worcestershire, William Wood and John Bye, the ex-recorder and recorder respectively of Winchester, to instance some of the resident burgesses of the legal profession only. From the point of view of a departure from the statutory residential qualification of borough representatives, the change from representation by a lawyer or ' gentilman ' resident in the borough to representation by one who was not so resident was perhaps an important step for the individual borough to take. From the point of view of its contribution to a transformation of the social character of the Commons in parliament its effect was negligible.

Let us, however, re-examine the problem of the change in the character of borough representation during the fifteenth century from the narrower (and perhaps safer) point of view of the fulfilment of the qualification of residence imposed on parliamentary burgesses by the statute of 1413. We shall not only ask ourselves the straightforward and obvious question as to what was the ratio among the parliamentary burgesses of residents to non-residents in one and another parliament and how this ratio changed in the course of the period under review, but also such questions as these that follow : What was the rate of the change in the proportion of boroughs partially breaking the statutory requirement by returning to parliament at least one ' outsider ' or non-resident ? What was the rate of change in the number of boroughs breaking it completely by returning no residents at all ? Conversely, what was the rate of change in the proportion of boroughs faithfully observing the statute and properly represented by two of their resident burgesses ?

A large decline in the number of resident burgesses elected to parliament took place in the course of the reign of Henry VI and Edward IV : from 77 per cent in 1422 to 43 per cent in 1478. There was, however, a bigger drop in the twenty years between 1422 and 1442 (from 77 per cent to 58 per cent) than came about in the forty years that followed. By the middle of the century the non-resident were as numerous as the resident burgesses and there-after until 1478 (the last date for which there are something like full returns until the 'Reformation' Parliament of 1529) such decline as there was in the percentage of resident burgesses was comparatively not very appreciable.[1]

The direct representation in parliament of the interests of indivi-dual boroughs by at least one of their own burgesses suffered an almost parallel lapse in this period : in 1422 some 85 per cent of the boroughs were represented by at least one resident burgess, whereas we shall not be far wrong if we put the average figure for Edward IV's reign at only 56 per cent. Here, however, the most sudden and rapid decline occurred in the 1440's.

The number of boroughs returning one or two 'outsiders' and so infringing statutory requirements, either partially or completely, was by the end of Edward IV's reign nearly double what it had been in the first parliament of his predecessor's reign : 70 per cent as against 36 per cent (in 1422). But here again the intensification of the practice of resorting either partially or wholly to non-residents is far more striking in the first half of Henry VI's reign than in its second half or under Edward IV ; there were almost as many boroughs returning either one or two non-residents to the parliaments of the 1440's as there were to those of twenty and thirty years later.

If we look at the figures of boroughs that were prepared to allow both their parliamentary burgesses to be 'outsiders' we find that in Yorkist times there were nearly three times as many as had been the case in 1422 (44 per cent as against 15 per cent). But once again it is the decade before 1450 which produced the steepest part of the upward trend of the curve. The numbers of boroughs returning to any one parliament no resident burgess at all rapidly

---

[1] For these and subsequent figures illustrating the changes in the character of borough representation in this period, see the table of percentages in the Appendix.

increased in the 1440's from 23 per cent in 1442 to 39 per cent in November 1449.

The most important phase of the decline of the number of towns completely conforming to the statute of 1413 and returning two in-burgesses to parliament seems clearly to belong to the first half of Henry VI's reign : in 1422 the proportion of such boroughs wholly adhering to the statutory requirement of residence was 64 per cent ; twenty years later it was 39 per cent and from then on until the end of Edward IV's reign or thereabouts the proportion moved up and down between 40 per cent and 30 per cent, standing (at 30 per cent) as low in January 1449 as it was to stand in 1478. It is interesting to observe that whereas in the parliament of 1422 there were just over four times as many boroughs electing two resident burgesses as there were returning two non-residents, in those parliaments of Edward IV's reign for which something like full returns have survived, there were four boroughs returning two ' outsiders ' (and so completely disregarding the statutory rule) to every three returning two of their own resident burgesses.

Whether we look at the problem of the change in the character of borough representation during the fifteenth century from the point of view of the partial or complete failure of boroughs to adhere to the statutes restricting their choice of representatives to their own resident burgesses, or from the point of view of the effect of this failure on the general composition of the nominally burgess element in the Lower House of parliament, it is clear from this statistical analysis that the transformation had really taken place before the middle of the century, that is, before the time when the government of Henry VI was submitted to those strains and stresses which brought him ultimately to deposition. The civil wars and commotions of that time do not seem to have been even responsible for a catalytic quickening of the process. The curve, so to say, shows a tendency to ' flatten out ' after 1450. The revolution in the character of borough representation was already a fact by the middle of the fifteenth century. Already one half of the borough representatives were not true burgesses in the sense of being residents.

Was there any change, as time moved on, in the character of these non-residential parliamentary burgesses and of those residential burgesses who did not belong to the ' burgess-class ' proper, using the term in its usual occupational sense ? Something of a change there does seem to have taken place. It was not, however, simply

K

that neighbouring or resident gentry and resident or local lawyers began to come in for a large share of borough representation (they already enjoyed a considerable share of it), but rather that before the middle of the fifteenth century a different sort of gentry was making its way into borough representation in far greater numbers than before : the busy administrators, retainers, and hangers-on of nobles and men of influence, and officials and servants of the royal Household and members of the royal civil service, careerists with more clearly marked political affiliations and attachments. Of these types there was no more than a handful among the parliamentary burgesses of 1422 ; towards the middle of the century they were becoming very numerous. The reign of Henry VI witnessed an upward trend in the numbers of such men seeking and finding a place in the Lower House. Among them royal officials, men occupied in tending the administrative and legal machinery of the Crown and especially those holding positions of greater or lesser authority in the royal Household and frequently about the very person of the sovereign, were especially conspicuous. It is, of course, important to recognise that this adulteration of the personnel of the Commons by the ' Westminster crowd ' was not achieved solely through the exploitation of opportunities that borough representation more easily allowed. It was from boroughs that Exchequer officials and other civil servants—they were generally of no very great importance and usually made up only a small group—more often than not secured election. So it was also with those yeomen of the royal Chamber and other miscellaneous small fry of the Household entourage of the king who regarded a seat in the Commons as worth the getting. But when highly-placed Household officials like its treasurer or controller or when knights or esquires of the body royal sat in the Lower House they were almost invariably returned as knights of their shires. Even the members of the little fragmentary groups of ushers of the Chamber who got themselves elected to parliament were for the most part returned by their county courts. In fact, members of the royal Household and civil servants almost invariably formed a much bigger proportion of the knights of the shire than they did of the parliamentary burgesses. The return of Sir John Fogge, privy councillor and treasurer of the Household, by the citizens of Canterbury in 1467 was then something of a remarkable occurrence.[1]

---

[1] Wedgwood, *Biographies, op. cit.*, 339.

But not only because he was a Household official of importance. The only knights by rank who had previously been elected for a city or borough had been merchant-princes of London, and they had been few and far between.[1]   Fogge's example was followed by Sir John Scott and Sir John Say : [2] in 1472, when he was still a privy councillor although no longer controller of the Household, as he had been when returned for Kent in 1467, Scott sat for Appleby, along with the keeper of the Great Wardrobe, Piers Curteys ; Say sat for Tavistock.   Sir George Browne [3] during this same long-drawn-out parliament represented Gatton (Surrey), and in the next parliament (1478), Sir John Paston [4] and Sir William Knyvet [5] secured election for Yarmouth and Bletchingley respectively. These were obviously still exceptional cases, but they illustrate clearly that the breakdown of the earlier distinction in the Commons between the ' gradus ' of those who represented shires and the ' gradus ' of those who represented boroughs was far advanced by the end of the medieval period.   If we may still describe the Lower House in the fifteenth century as a *communitas communitatum* it must be with some reservations in mind.   Its composition was becoming more homogeneous.

An examination of the composition of the Commons in those parliaments of the second half of Henry VI's and the whole of Edward IV's reign for which the electoral returns are as good as complete,[6] shows, taking an over-all view, that the ' Westminster ' element was on the increase until in 1478, when it comprised no less than 17 per cent of the whole House, it had attained to as high a proportion as it was to have reached a century later by the middle of Elizabeth's reign.[7]

It must be realised, of course, that this representation of ' Westminster ' interests was subject to very considerable fluctuations. These seem to have been the direct result of the political influences of the moment.   At the Bury St. Edmunds parliament of 1447 where the planned attack on ' the good duke Humphrey ' of

[1] The only exception to this generalisation, so far as I know, was the election of Henry Evelcombe, ' miles ', as burgess for Lostwithiel to the parliament of September 1402.

[2] Wedgwood, *Biographies, op. cit.*, 750.   [3] *ibid.*, 121.   [4] *ibid.*, 666.   [5] *ibid.*, 520.

[6] The parliaments of 1442, 1447, January and November 1449, 1450, 1453, 1467, 1472, and 1478.

[7] Neale, *op. cit.*, 302 : in 1584 there were 75 ' royal officials—men in the political or legal service of the Crown or attached to the Royal Household ' out of a House which then numbered 460.

Gloucester succeeded all too well (but not by his impeachment as evidently intended), the Household contingent of elected representatives moved into this town, ' where Suffolk's influence was strong ', to the number of no fewer than twenty-six parliamentary burgesses, among whom were seven yeomen of the Chamber, and seventeen knights of the shire, among whom were the controller of the Household (Sir Thomas Stanley of Lancashire), three knights of the body, two esquires of the body, and five ushers of the royal Chamber, making up at least some 16 per cent of the Lower House.[1] How low and inexorably in the country at large had fallen the credit of the government by the autumn of 1450 we could guess, if there were a shortage of other evidence, from the fact that in the three parliaments of 1449 and 1450 the number of seats commanded by the royal Household declined steadily until in November 1450 the elections yielded no more than three knights of the shire and fourteen parliamentary burgesses who were members of its staff, a mere 6 per cent of the Commons.[2]   But the Lancastrians, as we may now begin to call them, recovered some measure of poise after the 1450–1 crisis and when parliament next assembled (at Reading in March 1453) the representation of the Household interest seemingly reached the highest point (some 17 per cent) it ever achieved (so far as gaps from time to time in the returns to later parliaments will allow us to say) before 1478.[3]   No fewer than one knight and eight esquires of the body, and two ushers of the Chamber, with nine others, secured election on this occasion as knights of the shire, the controller of the Household, Sir Thomas Stanley, sitting as usual, of course, for Lancashire.   And at least another twenty-four Household retainers, among whom ushers and yeomen of the Chamber and yeomen of the Crown predominated, together with three minor employees of the Exchequer, were returned from boroughs (mainly in Surrey, Sussex, and Wiltshire, although one or more boroughs in as many as twelve shires returned

---

[1] Wedgwood, *op. cit.*, *Register*, 76–87 ;   cf. *Biographies* volume, *passim*.

[2] To the parliament of January 1449, 39 members of the royal Household were returned, 16 as knights of the shire, 23 as burgesses ; in November 1449, those of the Household elected numbered only 26, 10 as knights, 16 as burgesses ;   see Wedgwood, *Register*, 103–14, and 133–44 ; cf. *Biographies* volume, *passim*.   For the 1450 Commons, see *Register*, 161–73, and *Biographies* volume, *passim*.

[3] *ibid.*, 197–210 : in the 1453 parliament 20 knights of the shire were members of the Household, and 27 parliamentary burgesses.   In 1478, 23 knights of the shire were of the Household, and 27 burgesses, 50 in all but the proportion was as in 1453, the Common House being a little bigger at the later date.

a member of the Household). Among these parliamentary burgesses helping to make up the Household quota in the Commons in 1453 all but three were non-resident in the boroughs for which they were returned, and two out of every three of the non-residents did not even live in the same counties where their boroughs were located. More than half these Household men sitting as parliamentary burgesses in 1453 were being returned for the first time.

In these consecutive parliaments of the middle years of the century (1447, January and November 1449, 1450, 1453) for which the returns are almost wholly complete, it is, in fact, by no means unusual to find ' Westminster ' men being elected once and (so far as we know) never again, with the result that not many of them became practised ' carpet-baggers ' ; very few assiduously and persistently courted the favours of the authorities of any one borough unless they happened to reside there. And this was very seldom. The impression one actually gets, especially from a scrutiny of the borough returns for such heavily represented counties as Dorset, Surrey, Sussex, and Wiltshire, is that many of the returns to parliament of minor Household retainers and civil servants were negotiated, not directly between would-be burgess and borough, but indirectly through the sheriff who finally made the election returns for the boroughs in his bailiwick. It may well be that in these particular counties, and possibly in others, a list of recommended names was sent down to the sheriff along with the writ of summons, and that, acting on instructions from Westminster, the sheriff proceeded to make suggestions to those small boroughs which were indifferent to that direct representation by their own resident burgesses which the statute of 1413 had (even then necessarily) been passed to prescribe, and which the statute of 1445 also enjoined. The preamble of this latter act had noticed that sheriffs, after their receipt of the writ of summons, sometimes high-handedly omitted to send to borough authorities the requisite precept to elect, and later returned as burgesses men not locally chosen by due process. The practice, common to the shires of Surrey and Sussex, Hampshire, Wiltshire, Dorset and Somerset, Devon, and Cornwall, whereby the sheriff normally received the several reports of the numerous borough elections at the county court when the shire-knights were chosen and incorporated them into one common comprehensive indenture, may especially in these counties have encouraged him to interfere and put in either his own nominees or persons recommended to him from above.   The act of 1445 forbade this practice of the common indenture made up in the county court and required a separate indenture between the sheriff and the authorities of each borough.   Most sheriffs did conform, it is true, but in those counties of the comprehensive indenture, where borough representation was heavy, conformity was reluctant and spasmodic, sometimes altogether absent, and often only partial.[1] Devon seems never to have come into line.

After 1445 there were many cases of borough returns being tampered with in some way or another, usually by the erasure of the name of a burgess-elect and the substitution of another in its place.[2]   And by far the greater number of these alterations appear in the returns of the small boroughs of Surrey, Sussex, Wiltshire, Dorset, and Cornwall.   It looks as though, in these counties at any rate, the statute of 1445 was not only cavalierly treated so far as the form of the electoral returns from boroughs was concerned, but substantially failed in its intention.   I do not mean in the vain hope its promoters may have entertained of restoring the qualification of residence to borough representation, but in their aim of ensuring that boroughs were freely responsible for the choice of their parliamentary representatives, whether these were resident or not.   There is sometimes no means of knowing whether these instances of electoral returns being tampered with were the result of the action of the sheriff or of some other agency between him and the Chancery (whither the writs were returned) or of the Chancery itself.   But that the last contingency was not utterly remote from possibility is suggested by the Bodmin and Liskeard indentures of return of 1467 : [3]   in each case the latter half of the indenture, which included the name of one of the burgesses (John, the heir of Justice Sir Walter Moyle) and left a space for a second name, was written in advance in what would appear to be a Chancery hand ; the first half of the indenture, including the name of the

[1] In Surrey the statute of 1445 was adhered to completely in 1453, not at all in 1459, partially in 1460, not at all in 1467, partially in 1472, and not completely in 1478 ; in Sussex, completely in 1453, partially in 1459 and 1460, not at all in 1467, completely in 1472, but only partially in 1478 ; in Wiltshire, completely in 1453, partially in 1460, not at all in 1467, 1472, and 1478 ; in Dorset and Somerset, not at all until 1472, but then and in 1478 completely ; in Cornwall, not until 1467 seemingly, and in 1478 only in the case of one borough (see Wedgwood, *Register*, *op. cit.*, *passim*).

[2] Wedgwood, *Register*, *op. cit.*, footnotes, *passim* ; *ibid.*, Introduction, CXI–CXIV.

[3] *ibid.*, 350 n. 2, and facsimile opposite.

locally-chosen burgess, was written in afterwards in a rather crude hand. That this is a case of direct interference by Chancery would seem more probable because this was (so far as is known) the first time that indentures between the sheriff and the Cornish boroughs embodied their electoral returns. If Chancery interference it is, Chancery's disregard of the tenor of its own writs of summons is a clear sign (if one were needed) of the failure of the 1445 statute to stem the revolution that was taking place in the character of borough representation. Not that this kind of interference was very different from the ' labouring ' of borough officers such as took place (unsuccessfully) at Norwich in 1450 and 1455 on behalf of one or other of those eloquent East Anglian lawyers, the Jenneys,[1] or is to be distinguished in its nature from the earl of Westmorland's advice and request to the burgesses of Grimsby (undated but perhaps written in 1460) ' to send unto my hondes youre wrytte directed for the electioune of the seid Burgessis wheche I shall cause to be substauncially retourned and appoynt ij of my Counsale to be Burgessis for youre seid towne '.[2] Some cases of tampering with electoral returns must have been occasioned, as Wedgwood suggests,[3] by the opportunity afforded by the failure of a burgess-elect to agree to his election, or (as is more likely) to appear at the beginning of a parliamentary session. The 1467 Bodmin and Liskeard cases were none such. On the other hand, these two Cornish boroughs could have ignored the Chancery recommendation and made out an indenture that was entirely their own. We may not deny them this option any more than the Chancery-fashioned indenture did. The Chancery had made, however, only one nomination ; it was doubtless deemed the wiser course to fall in with this modest request.

If we had any doubts about the ineffectiveness of the 1445 statute so far as it was designed to halt the current and continuing transformation of borough representation in parliament, an examination of the electoral returns for 1453 in Wiltshire, Surrey, and Sussex, would remove them.[4] These were the counties of the system of the common comprehensive indenture of return (forbidden by the 1445 act). In 1453 for the first known time they abandoned it and conformed to the statute (if but temporarily).

---

[1] *Paston Letters, op. cit.,* I. 152 ; 340 (quoted in Wedgwood, *Register, op. cit.,* CXX).
[2] *Hist. Mss. Comm., 14th Report,* App. 8, 252 (quoted in Wedgwood, *Register, op. cit.,* CXIX).
[3] Wedgwood, *Register, op. cit.,* CXVI. [4] *ibid.,* 206–7, 208–9.

Elections in the thirty parliamentary boroughs of these three shires were represented as having taken place on stated days and the results were embodied in separate indentures drawn up as between the sheriff and each local borough officer or officers (usually mayor, bailiff or bailiffs, constable or constables of the borough). The statute had aimed at restoring observance of the residential qualification and a proper local responsibility for borough elections. But only eight of the sixty parliamentary burgesses returned from these three shires in 1453 were resident in the boroughs they represented. The Surrey and Sussex returns were drawn up in proper statutory form and seem to have been made in good faith except at Gatton, where the lordship belonged to the duke of Norfolk; here the names of the parliamentary burgesses-elect would appear to have been 'squeezed' into the indenture after it had been drafted and not included in the normal course of its composition. One of the Gatton burgesses-elect, John Framlingham of Suffolk, was a man whose very name suggests his known tenurial connexions with the house of Mowbray; the other, John Dauntsey, a yeoman of the royal Chamber, was of Trowbridge in Wiltshire. In the indentured returns of 1453 from the Wiltshire boroughs there are twelve names of burgesses-elect which have suffered erasure and substitution; the returns of eight, half the county's, parliamentary boroughs were in this way doctored or otherwise altered. All the new names substituted were those of 'foreigners' even to the shire, except one, William Ludlow of Hill Deverell, yeoman of the royal cellar, parker of Ludgershall, where he was now returned for at least the fifth time. Among the four other royal servants who profited by these amended returns was Richard Baron, one of the two ushers of the parliament chamber at this time. In these three counties of Surrey, Sussex, and Wiltshire the temporary adherence to the form of return prescribed by the 1445 statute in order to safeguard the principle of local responsibility for borough elections, had then little or no effect on the burgess personnel returned: the burgesses remained, as before, by a large majority non-resident, and in Wiltshire many of them were, in spite of formal appearances to the contrary, only nominally elected by the boroughs they nominally represented. Incidentally, members of the royal Household were especially conspicuous among the profiteers of these practices: in 1453 the Surrey boroughs returned seven, those of Sussex three, and those of Wiltshire five: in the aggregate one out of every four burgesses returned from these three counties in 1453 was a member of the staff of the royal Household. Clearly the statute of 1445 had not even papered over the cracks in the walls of the old system. The charter of incorporation granted to the burgesses of Ludlow in 1462, with its concession of a right to be represented in parliaments by two burgesses chosen ' of themselves *or others* ', suggests that the statutory rule requiring parliamentary burgesses to be resident was no longer (even officially) regarded as of much significance.[1]

Any sure and certain reasons for the changes that took place in the character of the burgess element in the Commons during the fifteenth century are difficult to discern. The towns were the first to feel the effects of the contraction in external and internal trade and upper-class prosperity which in this period affected most aspects of the nation's economic life. We are told by Professor Postan,[2] almost axiomatically, that the fifteenth century was ' an age of recession, arrested economic development and declining national income ', and that one of the most impressive symptoms of this economic trend was the decline of the corporate towns and of those forms of productive and commercial organisation (the craft and merchants' gilds) which, often enough, were part of their institutional fabric. Certainly the increasing tendency in borough parliamentary representation for the resident burgess to yield place to the ' outsider '—especially one with influence at court or in the households of powerful personages—suggests the reality of this decline. Was this tendency the result of a feeling on the part of the authorities of the less wealthy towns that they must make all possible provision for the exertion of influence on their behalf when parliamentary bills, in which they were directly or indirectly interested, required promotion or resistance ? Or was it that the expense of parliamentary representation by their own burgesses was becoming a luxury that boroughs on the margin of economic stability could ill afford, especially when there was the seductive option of seemingly more influential service, free or at merely nominal rates ? It is difficult to say.

Certainly there were few boroughs or even cities that by the middle of the fifteenth century were paying their parliamentary representatives the old official minimum expenses of 2 shillings a

---

[1] C.Ch.R., VI. 160. [2] *Economic History Review*, Vol. 9, 161.

day each.   York [1] and London [2] remained generous in their payments, but from time to time found them something of an embarrassment.   Norwich [3] paid well but not consistently so, and Bishop's Lynn,[4] although fairly free-handed, clearly went sometimes beyond its means.   Exeter [5] always seems to have inclined towards economy.   Canterbury [6] scaled down its vote in 1445, and from about the same time Salisbury [7] ' showed no tendency to over-pay '.   Some boroughs reduced their burgesses' wages by ordinance :   Cambridge in 1427 to a shilling a day each ; [8] Lynn in 1442 from half a noble a day (3s./4d.) to 2 shillings ; [9] in 1437 Nottingham decided that 16 pence a day was enough.[10]   Other boroughs were seemingly in favour of a lump-sum payment for the whole term of a parliament, whatever its duration, in order to safeguard themselves against the incurring of heavy liabilities : as early as 1423 Bridport [11] was paying £2 ' pro parliamento ' and within a year or two had lopped this fee to 2 marks (26s./8d.) ;   in 1432 Launceston [12] was getting away with a single mark for the service of each of its burgesses, and in 1459 this modest fee was halved ;   in 1478 Barnstaple [13] also paid no more than a noble ;   in 1487 Plymouth [14] paid its mayor 2 marks for his parliamentary wages and in 1495 no more than £2 for both its burgesses.   Wilton [15] in 1485 had compromised with fees of £1 a month.   Most boroughs were unsystematic in the measures they took to deal with the problem of parliamentary wages and chopped and changed, doing the best they could do for themselves as election times came round, and sometimes the price was down, sometimes up, as the bargains with their prospective parliamentary burgesses were more or less successfully wagered.   Some boroughs concluded special, separate agreements with each or only one of their burgesses of parliament : Canterbury in January 1449 arranged to pay Thomas Walter, yeoman of the Crown, a shilling a day ' with his own permission ', his fellow-burgess receiving the same wage willy-nilly, plus £1 for his special

[1] M. McKisack, *op. cit.*, 86–7.   [2] *ibid.*, 85–6.   [3] *ibid.*, 87–9.
[4] *ibid.*, 89–90   [5] *ibid.*, 91–3.   [6] *ibid.*, 93–4.   [7] *ibid.*, 94–6.
[8] C. H. Cooper, *Annals of Cambridge*, I. 177.
[9] Wedgwood, *Register, op. cit.*, 37.
[10] Stevenson, *Records of the Borough of Nottingham*, II. 423.
[11] *H.M.C.*, *6th Report*, 494a ; Hutchins, *History of Dorset*, II. 13.
[12] R. and O. B. Peters, *History of Launceston and Dunheved*, 124, 137.
[13] Wedgwood, *Register, op. cit.*, 435.
[14] *ibid.*, 522, 576.   [15] *ibid.*, 509.

services ; [1] in 1467 Sir John Fogge gave up all the wages due to him, and in 1483 Sir George Browne renounced his fee likewise ; [2] in 1491–2 one of the citizens was to receive 2 shillings a day, the other half as much and then only for his days of attendance.[3] In 1453 the Cinque port of Rye paid one of its barons 1 shilling and 8 pence a day and the other 2 pence less.[4] In 1455 a Southampton merchant representing his borough took ' but half wages accordyng to his promys '.[5] In 1463 an alderman of Norwich sat for the city at 2 shillings a day, while his fellow, a resident ' gentleman ', secured half a noble a day.[6] In the same parliament one of the Ipswich burgesses was to serve for a shilling a day ; his fellow-burgess was to serve for the same wage if the parliament sat at Westminster but for 20 pence if it sat at York and for 16 pence if nearer.[7] In 1469 one of the Ipswich representatives undertook to serve for nothing if he were admitted to the freedom of the borough, the other for 8 pence a day.[8] Three years later one burgess was prepared to sit for 5 shillings a week, the other for 3 shillings and 4 pence.[9] And this kind of hand-to-mouth and unequal arrangement persisted at Ipswich as in other boroughs. Sometimes such agreements might miscarry and come to grief as happened—so Miss McKisack discovered—at Salisbury in 1478 : though it had been undertaken on behalf of Edward Hardgill esquire, usher of the Chamber and the then sheriff of Hampshire, that he would ask no more than £2 no matter how long parliament should last, he later presented a writ claiming wages at the rate of 2 shillings a day, and amounting to £4 14s.[10] Contravening the century-old and oft-confirmed statute against the election of sheriffs to parliament though he was, Hardwick was bent on extorting his rights. Others were generally more accommodating. Payments were reduced or waived and sometimes even commuted for renders in kind : prior to the parliament of 1463 John Sackville esquire undertook to sit for Weymouth for a barrel of mackerel to be delivered for the following Christmas,[11] and for his services for Dunwich in the same parliament one of its members took his wages in herrings.[12]

---

[1] *ibid.*, 107. [2] M. McKisack, *op. cit.*, 93–4. [3] *ibid.*, 93.
[4] Wedgwood, *Register, op. cit.*, 210. [5] M. McKisack, *op. cit.*, 97.
[6] Wedgwood, *Register, op. cit.*, 330.
[7] Nicholas Bacon, *Annals of Ipswich*, ed. W. H. Richardson, 105.
[8] *ibid.*, 129. [9] *ibid.*
[10] M. McKisack, *op. cit.*, 96. [11] Hutchins, *op. cit.*, II. 433.
[12] Wedgwood, *Register, op. cit.*, 331.

But these are variations on one common theme : economy. A borough with a tradition of independence in its parliamentary elections might seek to safeguard it.   So Nottingham did in 1437 [1] when an ordinance passed to the effect that no burgess should be elected for parliament except he were of the mayor's livery ; and so Cambridge did in 1459 [2] when it was there decided that only resident burgesses should be returned to parliament, on pain of a £5 fine.   But, as Miss McKisack says, canvassing for seats by country gentlemen, lawyers, and others who were prepared to accept reduced or nominal rates of pay, or no pay at all, must have become more and more difficult to resist.   Certainly as the fifteenth century wore on the results become clearer and more positive in the composition of the Lower House : the burgess element proper became much diluted.   The shrivelling interest in the less important and some of even the more important boroughs in direct representation in parliament provided opportunities for the courtiers, the members of the legal and professional administrative class, and those members of the landed gentry, who, like the townsmen, were undergoing an economic crisis, albeit of a different, though related, kind.

[1] Stevenson, *Records of Nottingham, op. cit.*, II. 425.
[2] Cooper, *Annals, op. cit.*, I. 211.

PART TWO

BIOGRAPHICAL NOTES ON THE KNIGHTS OF THE SHIRE AND SOME PARLIAMENTARY BURGESSES OF 1422

(alphabetically arranged)

Robert Andrew esquire of Blunsdon St. Andrew, knight of the shire for Wilts in March 1416, 1422, 1426 and 1433, was an influential lawyer with important private connexions but much occupied in the local administrative services of the Crown also. In the Exchequer year 1410–11 he was escheator in Wilts and Hants ; sheriff of Wilts 1416–17, of Oxon and Berks 1418–19, and of Gloucs 1428–9 ; escheator again in Wilts and Hants 1431–2, and in Gloucs 1433–4 (P.R.O., *List of Escheators*, 51, 144, 145 ; *List of Sheriffs*, 50, 108, 153). In the year 1418–19 he was acting as steward of the duchy of Lancaster estates in Oxon and Berks, Hants, Wilts, and Dorset, with a fee of £21 ; how long he had held this office or was to continue holding it is not known (D.L.28, 27, 8). From November 1415 until his death in 1437 Andrew was j.p. in Wilts, except for a short period of 2½ years from January 1417. As early as 1402 he had connexions with the abbey of Malmesbury and in 1425, 1426, and 1432, he acted as proxy in parliament for the abbot (*C.P.R., 1401–5*, 117 ; P.R.O., S.C.10, Nos. 2363, 2376, 2414). By October 1419 he had formed an attachment to Richard Beauchamp Lord Abergavenny, summoned to parliament in May 1421 as earl of Worcester, but the new earl was killed at the siege of Meaux in March 1422. The second marriage of the widowed countess in November 1423 with her late husband's kinsman, Richard Beauchamp, earl of Warwick, resulted in Andrew's employment as a member of the latter's counsel and inclusion among his feoffees (*D.K.R.*, XLI. 803 ; A. Suckling, *History and Antiquities of Suffolk* ; G. G. Francis, *Charters . . . of Neath Abbey* ; *C.P.R., 1422–9*, 195, 277 ; *C.C.R., 1429–35*, 226–7 ; Blomefield, *Norfolk*, VI. 53 ; *Dorset Fines*, 306 ; *Suffolk Fines*, 293, 295 ; *Rot. Parl.*, V. 78). On 6 December 1432 he was appointed one of his executors by Bishop Thomas Polton of Worcester, who died while a member of the royal embassy to the General Council of the Church at Basel in August 1433 (*Chichele Register*, II. 493). Andrew died in the spring of 1437, leaving landed estate, although not in any very considerable amount, in Wilts, Berks, Gloucs, and Worcs.

Sir John Arundell of Lanherne, knight of the shire for Cornwall in January and September 1397, January and October 1404, 1406, 1411, April 1414, March 1416, 1417, May 1421, 1422, and 1423. He was born about 1368, the third son, but became the heir of his father Sir John who died before 1377. He married Eleanor, the daughter of his mother's second husband (Sir William Lambourne) by a former wife and in her right and as heir of his father and mother (Joan, heir of William Lustock of Loddiswell in Devon who died in 1396) he became possessed of very extensive estates in the West Country ; at his death in 1435 he held 24 manors in Cornwall and 10 in Devon besides other more fragmentary rents and properties (Yeatman, *House of Arundell, op. cit.*, 214 ; *Cal. Inq. p.m.*, IV. 162, 209 ; F. C. Hingeston-Randolph, *Register of Bishop Stafford of Exeter*, 6). Although he sat as shire-knight in Richard II's last two parliaments it is only with the revolution of 1399 that Arundell really emerged into political life. He was one of the esquires honoured with knighthood on the eve of Henry IV's coronation (C. L. Kingsford, *Chronicle of London*, 48) and three weeks later was appointed deputy-sheriff of Cornwall (the titular shrievalty was vested in Henry of Monmouth, prince of Wales, as duke of Cornwall) and at the end of November 1399 he became a j.p. in Cornwall, an office he retained until death, except for a few months in 1410 and for three years before his reappointment in February 1422. He was to serve the office of acting sheriff of Cornwall in 1402, 1407-8, and 1418-19, and as sheriff of Devon from May 1414 to December 1415 (*List of Sheriffs*, 21, 35 ; *C.P.R., passim*). On 16 February 1402 the prince of Wales appointed Arundell to be steward of the duchy of Cornwall in the county of Cornwall for life at an annual fee of 40 marks to be taken at the hands of the duchy receiver in the shire ; he continued to hold this office until he resigned it in February 1430, receiving royal letters patent of *inspeximus* and confirmation on 8 October 1413, after Henry V's accession, and on 22 April 1423, after the accession of Henry VI (*C.P.R., 1401-5*, 42 ; *1413-16*, 99 ; *1422-9*, 84 ; *1429-36*, 47). In the meantime from February 1405 to November 1408 Sir John had served as captain of the castle and town of Merk in the march of Calais (the appointment was originally made for life), although he does not seem to have been militarily active except in the summer of 1405 (*C.P.R., 1401-5*, 488 ; *P.P.C.*, I. 250 ; Carte, *Gascon Rolls*, II. 189). A more significant appointment was to come Arundell's way when Henry V's resumption of his war against France in 1417 necessitated effective measures against any attempt to disturb English control of the Channel on the part of France's Castilian allies, and on 14 February 1418 the duke of Exeter (Thomas Beaufort) indentured to maintain 364 men-at-arms and 776 archers who were to serve at sea in 15 vessels under the command of Sir John Arundell during the spring and summer of this year, Arundell acting as Exeter's vice-admiral. Although appointed sheriff in November 1418 and although he was still duchy steward, Arundell continued to act in his maritime command in 1419, now serving under Sir Hugh Courtenay, the son and heir of the earl of Devon, who was the King's Lieutenant at sea from April to November in this year (Newhall, *The Conquest of Normandy*, 197 ; *C.P.R., 1416-22*, 135, 203-4 ; *D.K.R.*, XLIV. 610). At this time Arundell was much involved in executing royal local commissions, especially commissions to ensure the observance of the Statute of Truces, and the prevention of privateering in the Channel, and as time went on he became more and more employed in the raising of Crown loans in the West Country (*C.P.R., passim*). Although he resigned his duchy stewardship in 1430 he continued to act as j.p. in Cornwall until his death on 11 January 1435. He was buried in his chantry chapel at St. Columb Major. The chief of his executors was his bishop, Edmund Lacy of Exeter, and it was he, as ordinary, who granted probate on 7 June 1435 (*C.C.R., 1429-35*, 35, 245 ; *Collectanea Topographica*, III. 392-3 ; Yeatman, *House of Arundell*, 260). (*Note.—* Care has been taken to distinguish this Sir John Arundell from his namesake and neighbour of Trerice and from the Sir John Arundell of Lichet Mautravers [Dorset] who succeeded to the barony of Arundel).

John Arundell esquire of Bideford, knight of the shire for Devon in November 1414, and for Cornwall in 1419, December 1421, and 1422. The eldest son of Sir John Arundell of Lanherne (Cornwall), he married sometime between 1412 and 1417 Margaret the older of the two daughters and coheirs of Sir John Burghersh. The marriage brought manors and lands in Surrey, Hants, Essex, Suffolk, Cambridgeshire, Lincolnshire, Oxfordshire, and Bucks, and kinship with Thomas Chaucer of Ewelme who married Margaret's sister, Maud Burghersh. On Arundell's death on 4 December 1423, Chaucer, with a clerk of the Crown in Chancery (Thomas Haseley, an Oxfordshire neighbour), was granted the wardship of all those of his estates he held by courtesy of England of his wife's inheritance during the minority of his heir, John, who was only three years old at his father's death. In November 1435, after his grandfather's death, Lord Hungerford and others were to pay 1,000 marks to the Crown for this youth's marriage, but his cousin by marriage William earl of Suffolk ultimately got his wardship and married him to a daughter of Thomas Lord Morley (Yeatman, *House of Arundell*, 214 ; *Cal. Inq. p.m.*, IV. 79 ; Napier, *Swyncombe and Ewelme*, 25 ; *C.C.R.*, *1419–22*, 162 ; *C.F.R.*, *1413–22*, 398 ; *1422–30*, 51, 72 ; *C.P.R.*, *1429–36*, 497). John Arundell had been sheriff of Cornwall in 1412–13. His father had been sheriff of Devon when he was first returned to parliament for that county in 1414, and sheriff of Cornwall when next he was elected shire-knight, along with his brother Sir Thomas Arundell, in 1419. He attended the Cornish elections to the parliament of May 1421 when his father was returned. His brother Sir Thomas was sheriff when, in 1422, he and his father were elected (P.R.O., C.219, Bundles 11, 12, and 13).

Sir William Asenhill, knight of the shire for Cambridgeshire in 1406, October 1416, 1422, 1423, 1425, 1426, and 1429. Shortly before November 1404 he married Joan, daughter of Sir John Burgh of Burgh Green (Cambs,) and at this time changed his name from Harpeden to Asenhill. His wife's first husband was Thomas Haselden of Guilden Morden (Cambs) who had died in 1401. Although he had been Edmund of Langley's receiver in Yorkshire, Haselden had been primarily a Lancastrian retainer and, in fact, had been controller of John of Gaunt's Household from *c.* 1369 to *c.* 1386. Asenhill (*sub nomine* Harpeden) had also been attached to Lancaster's clientage and was one of the witnesses of his will (Nicolas, *Testamenta Vetusta*, 144). Like so many members of John of Gaunt's retinue he was engaged for life by Richard II after Gaunt's death (with a fee of £20) and accompanied him to Ireland in the spring of 1399 (*C.P.R.*, *1396–9*, 318, 338). Just when, after the revolution of 1399, Asenhill secured a place in Henry IV's Household is not known, but at the end of 1404, when by reason of their marriage he and his wife were granted an annuity of £40 for life charged on the duchy of Lancaster estates in Norfolk, Suffolk, and Cambridgeshire, he was one of the King's esquires and an usher of the Chamber ; this grant replaced the £20 annuity of April 1399, which Henry IV had since confirmed in February 1400 (*C.P.R.*, *1399–1401*, 206). Asenhill was still usher of the Chamber in May 1408 when a grant of two tuns of wine from the royal prisage at Lynn, made to his wife in her widowhood, was transferred to him (*ibid.*, *1405–8*, 434), and he was retained by Henry V in this capacity. In January 1414, having previously served the office in 1406, he was made j.p. in Cambridgeshire,

L

being at the time royal escheator in Cambridgeshire and Huntingdonshire. He was a member of the royal retinue in Henry V's first expedition to Normandy, but he did not serve in the later campaigns of the reign or afterwards (*D.K.R.*, XLIV. 568). He was sheriff of Cambridge and Huntingdon in 1418–19 and, in July 1420, was re-included in the commission of the peace for the former county and continued to act until his life's end, in the meantime, from the autumn of 1429 until February 1432, serving as j.p. for the borough of Cambridge. By authority of the Great Council his yearly grant of prisage wine at Lynn had been confirmed during Henry VI's first parliament (*C.P.R.*, *1422–9*, 12), and presumably he continued to receive the King's fees, being in 1425 described as ' King's knight ' (*ibid.*, 267). He frequently served on local royal commissions, especially Crown loan-raising commissions (*ibid.*, *passim*). His local connexions were influential : in 1420 he had acted as executor to his brother-in-law, Sir John Ingoldsthorpe of Burgh Green, and two years later, early in 1422, as executor to Sir John's widow along with Sir Walter de la Pole, with whom he was elected to parliament in 1422 and 1423. De la Pole's only daughter, Margaret, had married Asenhill's nephew by marriage, Thomas Ingoldsthorpe (Nicolas, *Testamenta Vetusta, op. cit.*, 203–4 ; Blomefield, *Norfolk*, VII. 126–7 ; *The Genealogist* [N.S.] XVIII. 189). In 1431 Asenhill was made one of his feoffees by John Lord Tiptoft, then steward of the royal Household (*Hist. Mss. Comm. Report, Rutland Mss.*, IV. 86). Still enjoying his annual assignment of two tuns of Gascon wine, although he now took them from the prisage of the port of London, Asenhill died sometime in the spring of 1443.

Thomas Astylle or Astley, m.p. for Ipswich in 1422, was the son of Sir Thomas Astley of Melton Constable (Norfolk) who died in Spain in 1387–8 when serving with John of Gaunt ; he inherited three manors and other estates in Norfolk (Blomefield, *Norfolk*, IV. 349 ; IX. 227, 405, 419, 426 ; X. 257). From 1422 to 1426 he was bailiff of Ipswich (Nicholas Bacon, *Annals of Ipswich*, ed. W. H. Richardson, 92–3). He was feoffee of Edmund Wynter's estates (*C.C.R.*, *1409–13*, 226, 234).

William Balsham m.p. for Melcombe Regis in 1422, 1429, 1432, 1435, 1437 and 1442, and for Lyme in 1431. From March 1410 until his death in 1444 (except from 23 January to 8 December 1412) he was controller of customs and subsidies at Melcombe (the area included Poole and Weymouth, and from January 1434 the administration was regulated from Poole). From October 1415 and April 1421 respectively until February 1423 Balsham was also controller of customs at Exeter and Dartmouth in south Devon and at Bridgwater in north Somerset (*C.P.R.*, *1408–13*, 156, 243, 361, 458 ; *1413–16*, 333 ; *1416–22*, 337, 398 ; *1422–9*, 50 ; *1429–36*, 298, 323 ; *1436–41*, 476). He was present at the shire elections for Somerset to the parliaments of 1417, May 1421, and 1431 (P.R.O., C.219, Bundles 12, 14).

John Barton junior of Thornton (between Buckingham and Stony Stratford), knight of the shire for Buckinghamshire in April 1414, 1417, 1419, 1422, and 1423. He was brother of John Barton senior of Buckingham who was m.p. Bucks January 1397, 1401, January 1404, 1407, and November 1414, and recorder of London 1415–21. Both brothers were members of Lincoln's Inn and closely connected, acting as each other's feoffees and the younger as his brother's executor (*Book of Admissions*, 1 ; Lipscomb, *Bucks*, II. 568, 581). John Barton junior was summoned on 3 February 1412 to assume the degree of serjeant-at-law but successfully resisted although he spent ten days in the Tower for contempt (*C.C.R., 1409–13*, 258, 372). He was again commanded to take the coif on 15 February 1415 and this order, now covering his elder brother also, was repeated on 11 July following, but without success, for on 11 June 1417 Barton junior secured exemption for life from this unwanted promotion (*ibid., 1413–19*, 176, 216 ; *C.P.R., 1416–22*, 108). From February 1412 he served for life as j.p. in Bucks and in Northants too from July 1419 to February 1422. In the Exchequer year 1417–18 he was escheator in Beds and Bucks (*List of Escheators*, 5). He served on very many if more casual royal commissions. He was engaged in an immense amount of private legal business, his legal services being in great demand over a large part of the south midlands. Among the most important of his connexions was that with the abbey of St. Albans which he served as steward for a quarter of a century, for he was occupying that office in 1408, was still acting in 1429, and probably held it down to his death in 1434 (*Gesta Abbatum Mon. Sti. Albani*, ed. T. H. Riley [Rolls Series], III. 518 ; *Annales Mon. Sti. Albani* [Rolls Series], I. 34–5, 124 ; Appendix, 427. There is no mention in these sources of any other steward). Resulting in other important attachments were his activities as feoffee to uses to Richard Beauchamp earl of Warwick from 1417 (*C.F.R., 1413–22*, 207 ; J. H. Jeayes, *Catalogue of Muniments at Berkeley Castle*, 182 ; John Smith of Nibley, *Lives of the Berkeleys*, II. 40–8 ; Wm. Dugdale, *Warwickshire*, 599a), to Joan Dame Abergavenny, eventual coheir to the estates of the Fitz-Alan earls of Arundel and widow of the earl of Warwick's uncle William Beauchamp Lord Abergavenny (*Rot. Parl.*, IV. 410b, 445b).

Sir John Bertram of Bothal castle near Morpeth, knight of the shire for Northumberland in 1413, 1422, 1429, and 1432, was royal escheator in Northumberland in 1410–11 ; sheriff of Northumberland in 1411–12 ; escheator again in 1415–16 ; sheriff in 1416–17, 1422–3, 1430–1, 1434–5, and 1438–9 ; from 20 January 1415 to 1 February 1418 joint-custodian of Roxburgh castle and from 1 February 1418 to 22 March 1421 sole warden ; justice of the peace in Northumberland from January 1418 to July 1423 and reappointed in July 1424. He was the second son of Sir Robert Ogle and his wife Joan, a younger daughter of Sir Alan Heton of Chillingham, but adopted the surname of Sir Robert Bertram of Bothal, his father's maternal grandfather, probably when the castle and manor of Bothal were settled on him in tail male, a settlement licensed by royal patent on 18 May 1403. His father enjoyed a life interest in Bothal in return for estates worth £200 a year until his death on 31 October 1409 (H. A. Ogle, *Ogle and Bothall*, 44 ; *Archaeologia Aeliana*, 4th series, Vol. XI. 45 ; *C.P.R., 1401–5*, 230 ; *1405–8*, 144 ; *1408–13*, 116) when immediately Bertram's elder brother, Sir Robert Ogle, invested Bothal by force of arms and was only ousted as a result of a bill presented by Bertram to the Commons in the parliament of 1410 when the royal Council intervened (*Rot. Parl.*, III. 629–30). Later on the relationship between the two brothers seems to have been one of friendship, although the two branches of the family were to take opposite sides in the Wars of the Roses. Bertram had certainly nothing to gain from prolonging any family feud, for his brother was very influential. Sir Robert's marriage with Maud, sister of the Sir Thomas Grey of Heton who was executed for treasonable complicity in the Southampton plot of 1415, brought aristocratic connexions : Maud's nephews, Thomas and Ralph, married daughters of Richard earl of Cambridge (executed with Maud's brother in 1415) and Henry Lord FitzHugh respectively ; and her brother, William Grey, was consecrated bishop of London in 1426 and promoted to Lincoln in 1431 (E. Bateson, *op. cit.*, II. 244 n. ; XIV. 328). In any case, Sir Robert Ogle was important enough in Northumberland, being justice, steward, sheriff, and escheator for life in the franchisal enclaves of the Durham palatinate in Northumberland, namely, Norhamshire and Elandshire, and was to be the duke of Bedford's lieutenant at Berwick (*D.K.R.*, XXXIII. 99). Bertram, too, seems to have had important, if perhaps solely personal, contacts with the bishop of Durham's ménage : Thomas Holden, steward and executor to Cardinal Langley of Durham, in 1441 left him in his will 50 marks for his daughter's marriage and forgave him a debt of £20 (E. F. Jacob, *Chichele Register*, II. 582). Sir John Bertram's military activities were largely absorbed by developments in the East March towards Scotland where he was for a time custodian of Roxburgh castle and where in 1429 he was a sub-commissioner for the settling of border disputes, where in 1433 he received from the government instructions about its border policy, and where in 1435 he was a commissioner to renew the truce with Scotland which in 1438 he was appointed as a commissioner to conserve (H. A. Ogle, *op. cit.*, 45). He did, however, participate for a short time in the French wars, going abroad for a little while in the summer of 1419, during which he acted as keeper of the castle of Fronsac in the Bordelais (*D.K.R.*, XLIV. 611 ; P.R.O., Exchequer, Issue Roll, 7 Henry V). Bertram did not live to see the older branch of his family ascend into the peerage in 1461 in the person of his nephew, Robert Lord Ogle, who was marked out for Yorkist promotion by his mother's close blood connexion with the family of Richard of Conisburgh. His own son, William, was knighted by the earl of Northumberland at the Lancastrian victory at Wakefield in 1460, but lived through the later Lancastrian disasters to profit by the magnanimity of Edward IV. Sir John Bertram died late in 1449 (*Arch. Aeliana*, 4th series, Vol. XII. 90, 105).

Thomas Blenkinsop, knight of the shire for Westmorland in 1422 and 1426. For at least three generations the family of Blenkinsop had been connected with the lords of Westmorland. In their manor at Helbeck in the parish of Brough they were tenants of the Cliffords by cornage and an annual rent of 6 shillings. Since 1380 the office of constable of the castle of Brough had been hereditary in their family, the grant being made by Roger, fifth Lord Clifford (summoned to parliament from 1356 to 1389) to Thomas Blenkinsop's grandfather, the Thomas Blenkinsop who had sat in the parliament of 1383 as knight of the shire for Cumberland and in the 'merciless' parliament of 1388 for Westmorland. Neither the younger Thomas nor his father, William, who sat for Westmorland in the last parliament of Henry V's reign in December 1421, was ever a j.p., but Thomas had been a collector of a parliamentary subsidy after the sessions of 1406 and 1413. Both Blenkinsops were in 1436 assessed as being worth together no more than £32 a year, Thomas at a small yeoman's income of a bare £6. Thomas was still alive in 1452 when his name appears in a feodary of the freehold tenants of Thomas Lord Clifford (J. Nicolson and R. Burn, *The History and Antiquities of Westmorland and Cumberland*, I. 582–3 ; *Trans. C. and W.A. and A.S.* [N.S.], VIII. 269, 329 ; *C.F.R., 1405–13*, 62 ; *1413–22*, 28).

Sir William Bonville, knight of the shire for Somerset in May 1421 and for Devon in 1422, 1425, and 1427, had been born in the principal manor house of the family at Shute (Devon) on 31 August 1392 the first of the two sons of John Bonville and the grandson and heir of the Sir William Bonville who had sat in a score of parliaments for either Devon or Somerset in the years 1366–1402 and had died in 1408. The wealth and standing of the family can be gauged by the fact that the monetary provisions of the old man's will amounted to some £1,230 (W. H. H. Rogers, *The Strife of the Roses and the Days of the Tudors in the West*, 41 *et seq.* ; *Notes and Queries*, 5th series, VIII. 430 ; F. C. Hingeston-Randolph, *The Register of Bishop Stafford of Exeter* [*1395–1419*], 391), and if the provisions of the will were not sufficient to indicate that the family was thriving, the fact that the wardship of young Bonville was secured by Edward of Norwich, duke of York, would suggest it (*C.P.R., 1405–8*, 393). In November 1413 Bonville offered proof of age and in June 1414 sued out livery of such lands as were not held in dower by his mother (she died later in 1414) and the widow of his grandfather (she was also by the way his maternal grandmother). His landed estates ultimately comprised no fewer than 18 manors mainly concentrated in the south-west (*C.C.R., 1409–13*, 379 ; *1413–19*, 136 ; *C.F.R., 1422–30*, 110, 121). William Bonville's younger brother, Thomas, was by this time already married to a great-granddaughter of Edmund Mortimer, third earl of March, namely, Joan, daughter of Hugh Poynings Lord St. John of Basing, who was a second cousin of Robert Lord Poynings ; and it was probably directly through this Poynings connexion—Robert Lord Poynings married Elizabeth, a daughter of Reginald Lord Grey of Ruthin—that on 12 December 1414 William Bonville contracted to marry another daughter of Lord Grey, Margaret, and to make a suitable settlement of estates in tail in return for a dowry of 800 marks (*C.C.R., 1413–19*, 119). By the time the last instalment of this dowry was due, 26 March 1418, Bonville was either in Normandy on military service as a retainer of the heir presumptive to the throne, the duke of Clarence, or preparing to go there (*D.K.R.*, XLIV. 601), but he must have returned before March 1421 when he was for the first time elected knight of the shire (for Somerset). He may well have returned to France with Henry V, but was back in England to sit for Devon in the first parliament of the next reign. Before Clarence's death at Beaugé in March 1421 Bonville, by this time knighted, had been sufficiently close to the duke to be one of his mortgagees for forty years in certain of his Yorks and Lincs estates, the conveyance by the ducal feoffees being authorised by an act in the King's Council on 13 February 1423 (*P.P.C.*, III. 313). Incidentally, on the following day Bonville was made sheriff of Devon and began his only occupation of the shrievalty in any county. Sometime between April 1426 and his last election to parliament in October 1427 Bonville's first wife, Margaret Grey, died and he married as his second wife a daughter of Edward Courtenay, third earl of Devon : Elizabeth, widow of John Lord Haryngton of Aldingham (in Furness) and Porlock (Somerset) (*Complete Peerage*, II. 218 ; Rogers, *op. cit.*), sister-in-law

of William Lord Haryngton (summoned to parliament 1421–39), and aunt of
Thomas Courtenay, then earl of Devon.   His family ties with the Haryngtons
and Courtenays were to be later strengthened by the marriage of his children
by his first wife, his son to William Lord Haryngton's only daughter and heir,
Elizabeth (*c.* 1440), and his two daughters respectively to William Grenville
(a grandson of Sir Hugh Courtenay of Haccombe) and William, a son of Sir
Philip Courtenay of Powderham and grandson of Walter Lord Hungerford.
Until about 1430 Sir William Bonville, his single tenure of the shrievalty apart,
had been but little employed on local royal commissions, but from this time
forward he was very and ever-increasingly active, being appointed for example
j.p. in Devon in July 1431, in Somerset also in March 1435, and in Cornwall too
in November 1438.   This last commission followed on Bonville's appointment,
in succession to the earl of Devon's brother, as steward of the estates of the duchy
of Cornwall in Cornwall itself with the customary fee of 40 marks a year and
the right to act by deputy.   Sir William held office until the stewardship was
granted to his nephew by marriage, the earl of Devon, on 7 May 1441 (*C.P.R.,*
1436–41, 133 ; *1441–6*, 532).   Bonville disputed the earl's appointment ; in fact,
there was serious danger of a breach of the peace between the two competitors
from November 1440 and this was still the case a year later, when the Council
appointed a committee of lords and judges to settle the contestants' claims (*P.P.C.,*
V. 158, 165, 173).   A way of temporarily allaying the tension was found in
Bonville's appointment in the late autumn of 1442 as seneschal of the duchy of
Aquitaine, a position he held until December 1445 (*C.P.R., 1441–6*, 424).   On
10 March 1449 he was summoned to parliament as a baron and at the end of the
third session of this parliament, in July 1449, he was again appointed seneschal of
Aquitaine, but the situation there as elsewhere in France was becoming increasingly
desperate and it is doubtful whether he proceeded to the duchy ; in any case, a
successor was found in October 1450 in Lord Rivers.   What attitude Bonville
adopted in the parliament of November 1449 when Suffolk was impeached and
ruined is not known, but his son-in-law, William Tailboys, was an adherent of
De la Pole and it is probable that Bonville at this time belonged to the curialist
party.   Certainly the end of the year 1450 brought a resurgence of enmity between
him and the earl of Devon and the latter was for the time being in support of the
duke of York.   The whole of the West Country was disturbed, but William of
Worcester tells us that there was ' maxima perturbatio ' when the earl besieged
Bonville in Taunton castle.   Bonville surrendered to the duke of York who was
sent to appease this region (*Letters and Papers illustrative of the Wars of the English*
in France during the reign of Henry VI [Rolls Series], ed. J. Stevenson, II. 770).
When York's influence deteriorated early in 1452 after the failure of his ' putsch '
at Dartford, Bonville took advantage of the situation to get his original patent
of the duchy of Cornwall stewardship in Cornwall confirmed and in September
following he secured a grant for life, at an annual farm of 100 marks, of the castle,
borough, and manor of Lydford, of the manor of South Teign, and of royal
rights in the forest of Dartmoor ; in April 1453 he further secured a grant for
life of the conservancy of the river Exe (an office formerly held by the earl of
Devon) and of the office of constable of Exeter castle.   Here in Exeter on 30 April
1454 there was a riot, the cause of which was clearly the feud between Bonville
and the earl of Devon.   In the meantime, Bonville had been on 12 September

1453 for a third time appointed seneschal of Aquitaine, but Aquitaine was already lost and Bonville's projected expedition never sailed (*C.P.R., 1452–61*, 18, 91, 166 ; T. Carte, *Catalogue des Rolles Gascons, Normans et François*, I. 238 ; *Wars of the English in France, op. cit.*, II. (2), 492 ; *Reports and Trans. Devon Association*, XLIII. 140 ; XLIV. 254–6). In 1454 the earl of Devon seems to have reconsidered his political position and gone over to the court party of his brother-in-law, the duke of Somerset, and he fought against the Yorkists at St. Albans in 1455. Bonville does not appear clearly to have become disloyal until 1460, but he was engaged in open hostilities with the earl later in 1455 and the Commons petitioned for the imprisonment of both peers and, successfully, for the reappointment of York as Protector to pacify the area of disturbance (*Rot. Parl.*, V. 285, 332). On 15 December 1455 there was a pitched battle between Courtenay and Bonville on Clyst Heath, where Bonville was worsted, so that he 'fled and came to Grenewiche to the kyng and the kynge sent him agayne to the lord protector' (*Devon Association, op. cit.*, XLIV. 257–61 ; *Chronicles of London*, ed. C. L. Kingsford, 165 ; *Six Town Chronicles of England*, ed. R. Flenley, 109). The earl of Devon and his son were committed for a space to the Tower and the suspicion that Bonville had turned over to the Yorkists is further confirmed by the fact of the marriage (in or before 1458) of his grandson, William Bonville, heir of Lord Haryngton of Aldingham, to the fifth daughter of Richard Neville, earl of Salisbury, the sister of the Kingmaker and Bishop Neville of Exeter (*Complete Peerage*, VI. 320). Lord Bonville kept out of the first stirrings of civil war in 1459, and in the Lancastrian parliament of that year swore allegiance to Henry VI and to maintain the succession rights of prince Edward of Lancaster, but he sided positively with the Yorkists at Northampton on 10 July 1460 when they captured the king, who was entrusted to Bonville's charge. Bonville probably owed his election as Knight of the Garter on 8 February 1460 to Yorkist influences in the Order. He saw his son and grandson killed at the Yorkist rout of Wakefield in December 1460 and was himself captured at the next serious Yorkist defeat at St. Albans on 17 February 1461, on the day following which he was executed by Queen Margaret's orders in breach of the king's personal undertaking that his life would be spared. Edward IV's accession followed in three weeks and so Bonville escaped attainder and forfeiture (*Rot. Parl.*, V. 351, 477 ; Anstis, *Register of the Order of the Garter*, 166–7). Bonville was sixty-eight years old at his death.

John Bourton, m.p. Bristol 1417, 1422, 1423, 1427, and 1432, was a merchant with interests in the wine trade and by 1443 in the trade with Iceland (*C.P.R., 1416–22*, 180 ; *D.K.R.*, XLVIII. 361) and a shipowner (*Rot. Parl.*, V. 38a ; *D.K.R., op. cit.*, 365 ; *C.P.R., 1416–22*, 418). As a member of the Common Council he attended all but two or three of the parliamentary elections for Bristol between 1413 and his death in the spring of 1455 (P.R.O., C.219, Bundles 11–15). He was bailiff of Bristol 1416–17, sheriff 1418–19, and mayor in 1423–4, 1429–30, 1448–9 and 1450–1 (W. R. Williams, *Gloucs M.P.s*, 100) and was also mayor of the Bristol staple concurrently in the years 1423–4, 1429–30, 1448–51 (P.R.O., C.67/25). He was father-in-law of William Canynges who rebuilt the church of St. Mary Redcliffe out of the profits of trade with Prussia, Iceland, and Finmark, and also of Thomas Young, recorder of Bristol and exponent

of the Yorkist claims to the royal succession in parliament in 1450 ; Bourton died
a good Lancastrian (witness the provisions for his chantry, *C.P.R., 1452–61*, 342)
but before open hostilities.

William Bowes was m.p. for York in March 1416, May 1421, 1422, 1426,
1431 ; co-sheriff of the city 1401–2 ; mayor of the city 1416–17, 1427–8 (Surtees
Society, XCVI, *Freemen of York*, I. 124, 140) ; he was present at all civic parliamentary elections from 1413 to the time of his death in 1437 (P.R.O., C.219,
Bundles 11–14).

John Bray m.p. Northampton 1422 ; mercer (*C.P.R., 1436–41* 335) ; in
1419–20 he was bailiff of Northampton (C. A. Markham and J. C. Cox, *The
Records of the Borough of Northampton*, II. 557).

William Brocas esquire of Beaurepaire near Basingstoke, knight of the
shire for Hampshire in April 1414, 1415, December 1421, and 1422, came of
a Gascon family, which had crossed to England in Edward II's reign and from
then until the end of the fourteenth century had been attached to the Plantagenet
Court. His grandfather, Sir Bernard, had been master of horse to Edward III,
companion in arms of the Black Prince, chamberlain to Richard II's first queen
Anne of Bohemia, and a friend of Bishop William Wykeham of Winchester
who had made him overseer of parks on the episcopal estates ; at his death (in
1395) he had been buried in the chapel of St. Edmund in the abbey church
at Westminster. William's father, another Bernard, joined the abortive anti-
Lancastrian conspiracy of January 1400 and went to his execution at London on
4 February (*D.N.B.*, VI. 365). The Brocas estates, estimated by the royal
escheators to be worth some 200 marks a year, were forfeited to the Crown but
were restored to the heir, William, by patent of 16 November 1400 (*C.P.R.,
1399–1401*, 386 ; *1401–5*, 474). These were widely scattered in Hampshire,
Surrey, Berkshire, Dorset, and Yorkshire, but the biggest concentration was in
Hampshire. They had been largely acquired by William's grandfather's marriages
into the families of Vavasour of Denton in Wharfedale and Des Roches of Roche
Court near Fareham (Montagu Burrows, *The Family of Brocas of Beaurepaire
and Roche Court*, 132, 151, 444 ; *C.C.R., 1405–9*, 93 ; *1422–9*, 442 ; *Feudal Aids*,
VI. 400, 451, 498, 519 ; R. R. Tighe and J. E. Davis, *Annals of Windsor*, I. 263).
The office of master of the royal buckhounds was held by William Brocas as
tenant in fee tail by grand serjeanty of the Northants manor of Little Weldon
and was worth over £18 a year to him in wages ; the cost of maintaining the
hounds and a staff of three huntsmen secured him also a gross annuity of £50
charged on the issues of Sussex and Surrey. He secured a royal patent embodying
the terms on which he held the office and its customary allowances, and prefer-
ential payment of the annuity, after petitioning parliament in February 1449
(*Rot. Parl.*, V. 167). Brocas had served on one or two commissions of array for
coastal defence in Hampshire in Henry IV's reign, but it was not until Henry V's
reign that he began to be regularly included in county commissions. He sat at
Leicester in April 1414 with his father-in-law, Sir Walter Sandys, in the second
parliament of the reign, and again at Westminster in the following year, at the
close of which session (November 1415) he was appointed sheriff of Hampshire,

an office he was again to hold in 1428–9 and 1435–6. In the meantime he had been much employed on local commissions of array and for raising Crown loans ; from February 1422 until his death on 29 April 1455 he served as a j.p. in Hampshire (*C.P.R.*, *passim*) ; and he was frequently present at the shire elections to parliament. His will, drawn up on 14 March 1455 and proved in the Prerogative Court of Canterbury on 10 May following, provided for his burial in the church of St. Andrew at Sherbourne. Its overseer was Brocas's near-neighbour, William Warbleton of Sherfield, who had been responsible for the capture of the leader of the Lollard revolt at Abingdon in 1431, had been sheriff of Hampshire in 1411–12, of Surrey and Sussex in 1427–8, and of Hampshire again in 1450–1, and had sat for Hampshire in the parliaments of 1425, 1426, 1429, 1445, and 1450, and for Berkshire in 1431. He and Brocas had long been each other's feoffee to uses (Somerset House, *Register Stokton*, fo. 6 ; *C.P.R.*, *1413–16*, 228 ; *1422–9*, 320). Another of Brocas's feoffees had been John Golafre, shire-knight for Berkshire in 1422 and a distant kinsman.

Bartholomew Brokesby esquire of Frisby, knight of the shire for Leicestershire in 1410, 1422, 1425, 1427, 1429, and 1432 ; sheriff of Leicestershire and Warwickshire, 1411–12 and 1419–20 ; j.p. in Leicestershire from February 1413 to February 1415 and from July 1422 until his death in 1449 (*List of Sheriffs*, 145 ; *C.P.R.*, *passim*). From October 1409, at the latest, Brokesby was connected with Archbishop Thomas Arundell and in his personal service, and by the autumn of 1417, perhaps earlier, he was attached to the archbishop's niece, Joan FitzAlan, widow of William Beauchamp Lord Abergavenny, and sister and coheir of Thomas earl of Arundell who died in 1415 ; he acted as her foremost legal agent, as feoffee to uses, and later as executor (*C.F.R.*, *1405–13*, 161 ; Tingey, *Norwich Records*, II. 57 ; *C.P.R.*, *1416–22*, 302, 305–6 ; *C.C.R.*, *1419–22*, 86–90, 167, 176. 183 ; I. H. Jeayes, *Charters, etc., of the Lyttelton family*, 72–3 ; *Wm. Salt Arch. Soc, Trans.* (N.S.), VII, 251 ; *V.C.H.*, *Bucks*, IV. 415 ; S. Shaw, *Staffordshire*, II. 245 ; *Rot. Parl.*, IV. 410, 445 ; *Chichele Register*, II. 538). He was also feoffee to her son-in-law, James Butler, fourth earl of Ormonde, lord-lieutenant of Ireland in Henry VI's reign, and later to her grandson and heir, the earl's eldest son, Sir James Butler, who was created earl of Wiltshire in 1449 (*C.P.R.*, *1429–36*, 27 ; *Hist. MSS. Comm., Mss. of R. R. Hastings*, I. 1, 2). Brokesby died in 1449. A chantry was founded at Saxulby (Gibbons, *Early Lincoln Wills*, 174).

Sir Thomas Brooke of Brook Ilchester (Somerset), Weycroft near Axminster (Devon), and Holditch (Dorset), knight of the shire for Dorset in 1413 and for Somerset in 1417, May 1421, 1422, and 1427, was born in or about 1391, the son and heir of Sir Thomas Brooke, who was knight of the shire for Somerset in at least 13 out of the 21 parliaments which met between 1386 and 1413 and sheriff of Somerset and Dorset in 1390 and of Devon in 1394, and who died seised of extensive estates in all three counties in January 1417. To possession of these properties the marriage of the younger Thomas in 1410 to the daughter of Sir Reginald Braybroke and Joan, granddaughter and heir to John third Lord Cobham, added lands in Wiltshire and Norfolk (Somerset A. and N.H. Society, S. W. Bates Harbin, *Members of Parliament for Somerset* ; Hutchins, *Dorset*, II. 254 ; *Feudal Aids*, I. 497 ; II. 102, 107–8 ; V. 263, 279 ;

F. Blomefield, *Norfolk*, V. 177 ; *C.C.R.*, *1409–13*, 81). Party to the marriage-contract was Sir John Oldcastle, stepfather to Joan Braybroke and jure uxoris summoned to parliament as Lord Cobham from 1410 until his leadership of the Lollard rising of 1414 (after his own conviction for heresy) involved his immediate forfeiture for treason.   In the hopeless Fickett's Field rising of 12 January 1414 young Brooke was clearly implicated, for he was in irons in the Tower four weeks later when his half-brother, Richard Cheddar (m.p. Somerset 1407, 1413, 1417, December 1421, and 1427), and Sir William Palton and two other friends found surety in Chancery in 1,000 marks that he would not attempt to escape ; he was clearly set at large before 24 August 1414.   Oldcastle was in concealment until captured and brought before parliament in 1417 (Brooke and his half-brother then represented Somerset), when he was condemned by the Lords and executed. During the summer of 1417 both Brooke and his half-brother (Cheddar) had been each bound in sureties of £1,000 not to assist or adhere to Oldcastle (*C.C.R.*, *1413–19*, 116, 121, 428).   In the following year Brooke chose a sensible course and began a period of service with Henry V's forces in France—he was at the siege of Rouen in October 1418—probably returning to England for good and all no earlier than February 1421, when the king himself returned for the last time (*D.K.R.*, XLI. 704).   He now began to serve on various local royal commissions : on 12 February 1422 he was appointed j.p. in Somerset and he continued to act until 1433 when his name drops out ; by that date he had already been j.p. in Devon for two years and here he served until his death.   From November 1424 until January 1426 he had been sheriff of Devon.   His neighbour, Bonville of Shute, early in 1427 committed a trespass against him and his men at Axminster in a dispute probably due to rights of way being obstructed by Bonville's recent imparcations, and Brooke's crenellation of his manor of Weycroft in Axminster and emparking of 800 acres there may have been a form of retaliation (*C.P.R.*, *1422–9*, 400, 403).   Brooke's feoffees in Weycroft at this time included the Protector (the duke of Gloucester) and the earls of Suffolk and Salisbury.   Sir Thomas died early in 1439.   His will, drawn up on 12 February 1439, described him as ' lord of Cobham ', a title he seems to have been accorded by courtesy. His eldest son, Edward, one of his executors, who was to represent Somerset in parliament later in that year and again in 1442, was summoned to parliament as Lord Cobham from 1445 until his death in 1461 ; he proved a firm Yorkist, (*Complete Peerage*, III. 345–6 ; E.E.T.S., *Fifty Early English Wills*, ed. F. J. Furnival, 129).   Sir Thomas's will was strikingly like that of his father's in its provision for a niggardly burial ceremonial (three masses of requiem only) and its omission of monastic houses from its beneficiaries : a suggestion perhaps of the persistence in the family of the Lollard infection.

Hugh Burgh esquire of Wattlesborough, was knight of the shire for Shropshire in 1415, March 1416, May 1421, 1422, and 1425.   He was continuously in the service of the Talbot family.   In 1408 he was feoffee to Ankaretta, widow of Richard Lord Talbot (he died in 1396), second wife of Thomas Neville Lord Furnival, brother of the first Neville earl of Westmorland, in certain Talbot estates in Shropshire ; he was also feoffee to Lord Furnival himself in his Nottinghamshire lordship of Worksop ; and in 1411 he acted as attorney in a livery of seisin of certain of the Furnival manors in Yorkshire on behalf of Maud, Lord

Furnival's only daughter and heir by his first marriage, who married Sir John Talbot, dame Ankaretta's eldest surviving son by *her* first marriage to Lord Talbot (H. T. Weyman, *Members of Parliament for Shropshire*, 76 et seq. ; J. B. Blakeway, *Sheriffs of Shropshire*, 66 ; *C.C.R.*, *1413-19*, 24 ; R. White, *The Dukery Records*, 292). Sir John Talbot in right of his wife was summoned to parliament as Lord Furnival from 1410 to May 1421 and from December 1421 in his own right as Baron Strange of Blackmere and Baron Talbot of Hallamshire until 1442, when he was created earl of Shrewsbury. The connexion between John Talbot and Burgh was continuous and close. There can be no doubt that Burgh owed his appointment ' quamdiu placuerit ' as Treasurer of Ireland on 23 February 1414 to the fact that Talbot was then the King's Lieutenant there (*C.P.R.*, *1413-16*, 147). Early in the same year Talbot levied a fine of two parts of his manor of Alberbury to Burgh's use and, in the church there, stood as godfather at the christening of Burgh's first son, John, who was born at Wattlesborough on 12 June 1414 (T. F. Dukes, *The Antiquities of Shropshire*, 107 ; Weyman, *op. cit.*, 86). It was as a member of Talbot's company that on 26 April 1415 he took out royal letters of protection to be operative for one year during his absence in Ireland (*C.P.R.*, *1413-16*, 307). In a petition presented against him to the duke of Gloucester as Protector sometime between 1422 and 1429, regarding his recovery by a supposedly corrupt assize of novel disseisin of certain tenements in Shrewsbury, it was stated that he was ' officer to lord Talbot and other great lords ' and that he had such power at his command from these connexions and from his commission as j.p. in Shropshire (he served as j.p., except for nearly two years in 1419-20, continuously from February 1416 to his death in 1430) that local inquiry or process would be futile (Blakeway, *op. cit.*, 67). Who were the other great lords by whom Burgh was retained is not known, unless John Lord Clifford, who on 8 February 1420 appointed Burgh as one of his attorneys during absence in France, was one (*D.K.R.*, XLII. 341). On 16 November 1429 he was party to a bond for 250 marks on Lord Talbot's behalf (*C.C.R.*, *1422-9*, 207). By the date that the bond fell due Burgh was dead. Appointed for the first time sheriff of Shropshire on 10 February 1430, he died during his term of office on 18 August following. His wife, Elizabeth, who as daughter of John de Mawddwy and granddaughter on her mother's side of Sir Fulk Corbet of Moreton Corbet and Wattlesborough, had brought into Burgh's possession the Corbet and De Mawddwy estates in Shropshire and Montgomeryshire on the death of her brother, Fulk, in 1414, had predeceased her husband on 9 October 1429 (Weyman, *op. cit.* ; *C.C.R.*, *1413-19*, 147 ; *C.F.R.*, *1413-22*, 74 ; *1422-30*, 276, 280). On Burgh's death in August 1430 their son John (later m.p. for Shropshire in 1445 and 1453) was found to be his father's heir and aged sixteen years. Two of Hugh Burgh's fellow-knights of the shire in 1422, Throckmorton and Vampage of Worcestershire, were associated with the widow of Sir William Clopton as John Burgh's guardians by royal grant of 5 December 1430 ; the ward was eventually to marry Clopton's daughter and heir (*C.F.R.*, *1430-7*, 21-2 ; Wedgwood, *History of Parliament, Biographies*, 134).

William Burley of Bromcroft in Corvedale (Salop), knight of the shire for Shropshire in 1417, 1419, May 1421, 1422, 1425, 1427, 1429, 1431, 1432, 1433, 1435, 1437, 1439, 1442, 1445, November 1449, 1450, and 1455. He was feoffee and executor to Thomas Fitz Alan, earl of Arundel (made treasurer of England on Henry V's accession; ob. 13 October 1415) to whom his father, John Burley, had also been feoffee and counsel (*C.P.R., 1413–16*, 336, 344; E. F. Jacob, *Chichele Register*, II. 71, 76). William Burley was in 1435, like his father before him, steward of the former Fitz Alan castle and lordship of Oswestry and other Fitz Alan estates in Shropshire to the former earl's second cousin's son who had been summoned to parliament as earl of Arundel (*C.P.R., 1429–36*, 464). In April 1418 he was attorney to John Talbot Lord Furnival (*ibid., 1416–22*, 153) and feoffee to the Hugh Lord Burnell of Weoley (Herefordshire) and Holgate (Salop), who died in November 1420 (*ibid., 1416–22*, 198, 362, 371, 390). On 20 February 1428, he was appointed deputy-justice in the county palatine of Chester and in North Wales (*D.K.R.*, XXXI. App., 181; XXXVII. App., 673). In 1449–50 he was included among the feoffees of Richard duke of York (E. A. and G. S. Fry, *Feet of Fines for Dorset*, 327–8, 368; Somerset Record Society, XXII. 113, 201) and his political sympathies became definitely Yorkist. Shire-knight for Shropshire in 19 out of the 25 parliaments which met between 1417 and 1455, he was twice Speaker, in 1437 (as a makeshift) and 1445 (*Rot. Parl.*, IV. 502; V. 67), and on three occasions in the second session of the parliament of 1455 he headed an eventually successful deputation of the Commons to the Lords requesting the duke of York's appointment as Protector (*ibid.*, V. 284–6). Burley died on 10 August 1458 (R. W. Eyton, *Antiquities of Shropshire*, V. 43; where there are notes on the marriage of his daughter to the Common Law writer and judge, Thomas Littleton; for Burley's own family background, see *Shropshire A. and N.H. Society Trans.*, 4th series, Vol. VI. 223 *et seq.*).

Edward Burnby, m.p. for Launceston in 1410, 1411, 1413, November 1414, 1417, 1419, and 1422; in October 1423 he was stated to be too sick and aged to exercise the office of coroner in Cornwall. At the time of his probable suicide in 1432 he was retained as legal counsel by the burgesses of Launceston (*C.C.R., 1422–9*, 86; *C.P.R., 1429–36*, 273, 279, 518; R. and O. B. Peter, *History of Launceston and Dunheved*, 124). He attested all shire elections to parliaments between 1419 and 1432, except two (P.R.O., C.219, Bundles 12–14).

John But, m.p. Barnstaple, 1402; Bodmin, 1413, November 1414; Liskeard, 1417; Truro, 1422, 1425. In the years February 1400–5 and February 1407–11 he was 'custos feodorum et libertatum' for the duchy of Lancaster estates in Devon (Duchy of Lancaster, Ministers' Accounts, P.R.O., D.L.28, Bundle 4, Nos. 1–7). In November 1402 he was appointed deputy to the Chief Butler of England in the port of Tawmouth and by 24 May 1413 was deputy-butler there and also at Barnstaple, Plymouth, Fowey, Falmouth, Penzance, and in all other Cornish ports; in November 1418 he was still holding the office at Tawmouth and Barnstaple. He attested the indenture of return at the Cornish elections to the parliaments of May 1413, November 1414, March 1416, 1417, 1422, 1425, 1426 (*C.P.R., 1401–5*, 169; *1413–16*, 10; *1416–22*, 175; P.R.O., C.129, Bundles 11–13).

John Bye, m.p. for Winchester in 1422 only, in 1409 and still in 1413 had been town-clerk of Southampton (A. B. Wallis-Chapman, *The Black Book of*

Southampton, I. 109, 115–16, 118, 139), but by 1416 was town-clerk and later recorder of Winchester, and on 6 November 1422 was appointed by Henry IV's widowed queen, Joan of Navarre, her joint-attorney and receiver in the city and liberty (*Hist. Mss. Comm., 6th Report*, 601–2 ; John Milner, *History of Winchester*, II. 306).

Robert Carlisle junior, m.p. for Carlisle in 1410, 1413, November 1414, 1417, May 1421, and 1422, was probably the son of a Cumberland j.p. of the same name who had been controller of customs at Carlisle in Henry IV's reign. He was in all probability the same as the Carlell who was a member of Lincoln's Inn in 1420 (*Admission Book, op. cit.*, 1). He attested the Cumberland parliamentary elections of May 1421, 1437, 1447, 1453, and 1459 (P.R.O., C.219, Bundles 11–15) and was j.p. Cumberland 1435–71, except in 1461.

Robert Cary esquire, knight of the shire for Devon in 1407, 1410, 1411, 1413, April 1414, March 1416, 1417, 1419, May 1421, 1422, 1425, and 1426, was the eldest son of Sir John Cary of Cockington who was Chief Baron of the Exchequer from November 1386 until his successful impeachment for treason in the Merciless parliament of 1388, when he incurred forfeiture and life-banishment to Ireland. The efforts to secure an interim maintenance and the ultimate recovery of his inheritance bulk large in the recorded activities of Robert Cary during the remainder of Richard II's reign and throughout that of his supplanter, Henry IV. His father had been tenant of John Holland, earl of Huntingdon, in his manors of Cockington and Torrington and by February 1392 Robert Cary was retained in this nobleman's service as esquire. This connexion with the half-brother of Richard II and son-in-law of the duke of Lancaster (John of Gaunt) was evidently useful in alleviating the effects of his father's forfeiture. To the earl escheated Torrington and Cockington, but in July 1388 Cary and his brother got a ten years' lease of their father's other estates in Cornwall, Devon, and Somerset, and, on Sir John Cary's death at Waterford in 1395, Robert got a life-grant of over £15 worth of his property free of rent to the Exchequer, and as executors to Sir John, he and his mother were granted all his personalty and debts not yet seized to the king's use. Early in 1397 Robert petitioned for the recovery of certain entailed parcels of land and he secured various perquisites of royal and comital favour (*C.F.R., 1383–91*, 244 ; *1391–9*, 69 ; *C.P.R., 1391–6*, 46, 261, 613, 657, 696, 208 ; *1396–9*, 100, 102, 191, 212 ; *1446–52*, 212). At Shrewsbury in January 1398 parliament annulled the acts of 1388 and the forfeitures incurred by the victims of the Merciless parliament, and in May 1398 Robert Cary recovered the forfeited estates to the value of £230 a year (*C.C.R., 1396–9*, 266–8). He lost them again, however (not without protest and some resistance), to a member of Henry IV's Household within three weeks of Richard II's deposition, after the parliament of 1399 had re-affirmed the judgements of 1388 (*C.P.R., 1399–1401*, 153, 267, 395). In 1402 Cary approached the king by a petition in parliament in an attempt to get the principal Cary manors of Torrington and Cockington recognised as having been held by his father in fee tail and in consequence as exempt from forfeiture. Over three years passed before Robert secured his writ 'De procedendo' to the Common Bench and Henry IV's grantee, Sir Robert Chalons of Devon, was still in possession of certain at any rate of the Cary estates when

Robert first sat as knight of the shire in 1407 (*Rot. Parl.*, III. 484 ; *C.C.R.*, *1402–5*, 451 ; *C.P.R.*, *1405–8*, 333).   Cary sat in each of the next four parliaments and, in fact, for nearly the next twenty years monopolised one of the Devon seats in the Commons, a sign of a rehabilitation which undoubtedly owed much to his kinship with the Courtenays of Powderham.   For he married Margaret, the daughter of Sir Philip Courtenay ; a granddaughter of Hugh Courtenay second earl of Devon, and Margaret Bohun ; and what was more to the point, sister of her father's heir, Richard Courtenay, the close friend and ally of Prince Henry of Monmouth, chancellor of the university of Oxford at the time of Cary's first election to parliament, and when Henry succeeded to the throne in 1413 promoted to be treasurer of the royal Household and bishop of Norwich.   Cary's relations with Courtenay were very close : he was his tenant for life at Powderham and Chivelstone (*C.C.R.*, *1413–19*, 233) and, after the bishop's death at the siege of Harfleur in September 1415, he came to share Exchequer grants of the wardship of the bishop's estates in Devon and Somerset at farms amounting to nearly £275 a year during the minority of their nephew, the heir (*C.F.R.*, *1413–22*, 104, 115, 124).   The story that Cary won the king's favour by a deed of arms against a knight of Aragon in a Smithfield joust may be apocryphal, but the attribution to Henry V's first regnal year of the recovery of his father's forfeited estates is worth remark and may well be correct (Izacke, *Memorials of Exeter*, 71).   To his connexion with Courtenay he may have owed something for his appointment as j.p. in Devon at the beginning of the reign (he had previously served for a short time under a patent of November 1408) and for his appointment in November 1413 as royal escheator in Devon and Cornwall, an office he was destined to occupy for two whole years, that is, until December 1415.   He did not, of course, serve in the Normandy campaign of 1415 when his brother-in-law died, but he had himself loaned 100 marks towards the expedition as a member of a West-Country syndicate which put forward 860 marks.   Bishop Courtenay as treasurer of the Household and ex officio keeper of the royal jewels was much occupied in the negotiation and ' floating ' of Crown loans and Cary may well have acted as his local agent (*C.P.R.*, *1413–16*, 354).   Cary continued to act as j.p. until dropped in February 1422, but he served and continued to serve on royal local commissions of various kinds, the last in August 1431 probably soon after which he died.   His widow, his second wife, a daughter of Henry IV's chief justice of King's Bench, Sir William Hankford, survived him until 1448.   His son by his first wife, Philip, was knight of the shire in 1433 but died in 1436 (J. J. Alexander, *Devon Members of Parliament*, 50).

Robert Castell esquire of Meriden, knight of the shire for Warwickshire in April 1414 and 1422, as early as November 1400 was an esquire in the personal retinue of Prince Henry of Monmouth, and in June 1401 the prince, as earl of Chester, granted him for life the office of clerk and keeper of the mills and custody of the fishery of Chester.   Castell occupied these offices until his death, but apparently throughout he put in local men to act as managers (*D.K.R.*, XXXVI. 101, 103 ; *C.P.R.*, *1399–1401*, 523 ; *1422–9*, 49 ; *1429–36*, 513 ; John Elton, *History of Corn-Milling*, IV. 76–7).   The same connexion brought him his appointment on 18 September 1403 as steward of the court next to be held at Northwich in the prince's earldom of Chester (*D.K.R.*, XXXVI. 87).   Castell doubtless owed his appointment as sheriff of Warwick and Leicester on November 1410 to this continuing relationship, for the prince was then virtually in control of the government. Henry's accession in 1413 saw Castell installed as a minor account-able official in the royal Household, for at the time of the Agincourt campaign, in which he served as a member of the royal retinue, he was clerk of the Marshalsea of the Household (N. H. Nicolas, *Agincourt*, 377). That he kept up his Warwick-shire connexions is clear from his election to the Leicester parliament of April 1414, at which time he also acted as one of the parliamentary proxies of the prior of Coventry (P.R.O., S.C.10, No. 2204) ; on 4 December 1417 he was made a j.p. in the county and served until after the end of Henry V's reign ; in the Exchequer year 1419–20 he was escheator in Warwickshire and Leicestershire ; and by November 1421 he was steward of the royal Warwickshire manor of Chaylesmore, a position in which he was confirmed, as in his other offices, early in Henry VI's reign and which he retained until November 1434. Apart from the perquisites of these offices, Castell from 15 March 1421 received a life annuity of £40 from the fee-farm of Coventry, and this was confirmed during the first parliamentary session of Henry VI's reign. The original patent of grant described him as ' king's esquire and servitor ' : he may already have been serjeant of the ' avenerie ' of the Household, which he certainly was when Henry V died, and in 1427 he was one of the minor accounting officials of the Household acquitted of account and granted pardon of debts and arrears in accordance with the terms of Henry V's will. Castell died sometime between November 1434 and May 1436 (*C.P.R., 1416–22,* 338, 415, 461 ; *1422–9,* 14, 85 ; *1429–36,* 450, 513 ; *C.C.R., 1419–22,* 141 ; *Rot. Parl.,* IV. 325a).

Thomas Chambre esquire of Spratton, knight of the shire for Northants in 1422, 1431, and 1435, and sheriff of the county in 1426–7, 1432–3, and 1438–9, seems to have lived the life of an obscure country squire with two manors to control, Spratton and Holdenby, until towards the end of Henry V's reign he entered on a military career in France. He may have been the Thomas de la Chambre ordered in March 1420 to array the garrison at Conches, but he was certainly the Thomas Chambre esquire appointed by the Council and approved by Henry V as captain or keeper of the castle of Guines in the march of Picardy, by patent of 22 July 1421. He was reappointed on 1 July 1422 but returned to England in time for Henry VI's first parliament (*P.P.C.,* II. 363 ; *D.K.R.,* XLII. 371 ; XLIV. 630, 632). In May 1423 he was on a commission to take the musters of the retinues of the duke of Exeter, the Earl Marshal, and Lord Willoughby, who were all about to proceed to Picardy ; he too was probably crossing the Channel. Some three years later he again took out letters of pro-tection, dated 7 July 1426, as a member of the retinue of Richard Bokeland, treasurer and victualler of Calais since 1421 ; but he could not have stayed long across the Channel because on 12 December 1426 he began his first term as sheriff of Northants. On 5 May 1428 he once more took out letters of protection as a member of Bokeland's retinue and probably proceeded overseas after assisting at the musters of the earl of Salisbury at the end of June (*C.P.R., 1422–9,* 121, 466 ; *D.K.R.,* XLVIII. 241, 257 ; *List of Sheriffs,* 93). In view of the fact that it was by the hands of Chambre that an advance of £40 was made by assignment at the Exchequer to the (then late) earl of Salisbury on 30 November 1431 (towards the expenses of Charles of Artois, count of Eu, a royal prisoner put into the earl's custody by the royal Council), it seems likely that Chambre had some connexion with Salisbury at that time (Exchequer, Issue Roll, Michs., 10 Hen. VI., P.R.O., E.403/700, Mem. 6). To Bokeland and his heirs, Chambre and his second wife, Eleanor, in 1428 conveyed by final concord, with warranty against her heirs, the Warwickshire manor of Napton and other estates in Leicester-shire and Buckinghamshire (*Miscell. Gen. et Herald.*, 5th series, Vol. IV. 105–6). It was with Bokeland that Chambre was elected to the parliament of 1431. Chambre's first wife is not known, but this second match had brought other estates than these (namely, the manors of Wilby, Northants, and Shankton, Leics) and some influential family connexions. For Eleanor was the daughter and heir of Sir Thomas Drakelow of Wilby and widow of William Vaux, the Northampton lawyer, who had died in 1405 (J. Bridges, *History and Antiquities of Northants*, Oxford 1791, I. 464, 529 ; II. 155 ; G. Baker, *History and Antiquities of Northants*, London, 1822–30, I. 67 ; *Miscell. Gen. et Herald.*, *loc. cit.* ; *Feudal Aids*, III. 123 ; IV. 37, 50). William Vaux of Harrowden, sheriff of Northants in 1436–7, 1449–50, and 1453–4, and of Cambridge and Huntingdon in 1457, and knight of the shire for Northants in 1442 when Chambre attested the election, was Chambre's stepson ; the important lawyer, William Tresham, who was Speaker in 1439, 1442, 1447 and November 1449 and chancellor of the duchy of Lancaster from November 1447 to the time of his murder as a supporter of the duke of York in 1450, was the husband of Chambre's stepdaughter, Isabel Vaux. Chambre had been sheriff when Tresham was elected for Northants to the parliaments of 1427, 1433, and 1439 and he had attested his return in 1432, 1442 (with Vaux), and 1447. Chambre's own last election to parliament (in 1435) was in company with Tresham (P.R.O., C.219, Bundles 14 and 15) and Vaux attended the election. Chambre died some time between 1447 and 1458 when his son, William, presented to the family living of Holdenby.

Sir Thomas Charleton of Edmonton and of Old Fold in South Mimms, knight of the shire for Middlesex in November 1414, May 1421, 1422, 1425, 1427, and 1431, and j.p. in Middlesex between November 1418 and February 1433, was in 1436 with estates worth £100 a year the largest non-baronial proprietor resident in the county (*E.H.R.*, XLIX. 638). Some of these came to him through his marriage with Elizabeth, one of the two daughters and coheirs of Sir Adam Fraunceys, and she also brought him interesting kinships : her sister, Agnes, was wife of Sir William Porter, who had been esquire of the body to Henry V before his accession and was to be one of his executors ; Thomas Montague, earl of Salisbury, was their first cousin (F. C. Cass, *History of South Mimms*, 81). His marriage confirmed Sir Thomas's own links with the city of London, for his wife's grandfather had been lord mayor in 1352–4. He himself was closely akin to the well-established civic family of Frowyke : his mother's sons by a former marriage were Thomas Frowyke esquire and Henry Frowyke, the London mercer (Cass, *op. cit.*, pedigree opposite p. 70).

Charleton was present at the Middlesex elections to almost all parliaments between 1411 and 1435 (P.R.O., C.219, Bundles 10–14), one of the very few from which he was absent being that of 14 November 1420 when he was evidently overseas in France, having joined the duke of Bedford's retinue in the previous

April (*D.K.R.*, XLIV. 617). At this time as an earnest of his military venture Charleton made a settlement of his Middlesex manors, his feoffees including his half-brothers (the Frowykes), John Fray (a Herts lawyer who later became Chief Baron of the Exchequer), and a Kingston-on-Thames lawyer, Robert Skerne (J. E. Cussans, *Hertfordshire*, III. 273). Charleton probably returned to England with Henry V early in 1421, having been knighted in the meantime. Apparently he saw no further military service abroad but seemingly crossed to France in 1430 when Henry VI went there to be crowned (*D.K.R.*, XLVIII. 267). He died on 21 February 1448 and was buried at Edmonton. His son, Thomas, knight of the shire for Middlesex in 1442, 1447, 1453–4, 1459, and 1460, was Speaker for the Commons for the later sessions of the 1453–4 parliament.

Thomas Chaucer esquire of Ewelme, knight of the shire for Oxfordshire in 1401, 1402, 1406, 1407 (Speaker), 1410 (Speaker), 1411 (Speaker), 1413, November 1414 (Speaker), May 1421 (Speaker), 1422, 1426, 1427, 1429, and 1431. He was the son of Geoffrey Chaucer the poet by Philippa Roet, the sister of Catherine Swinford (née Roet), who was the mistress and the mother of John of Gaunt's later legitimated children, the Beauforts, and then the duke's third wife. For the last ten years of the duke's life Thomas was his retainer, with a fee of £10 a year from 1389 until 1394 when this allowance was doubled ; and when Lancaster died in February 1399 Chaucer was constable of the duchy castle of Knaresborough and chief forester in the lordship. He was deprived of these offices when Richard II sequestrated the Lancastrian inheritance but was compensated by a grant of 20 marks a year from the fee-farm of Wallingford (J. H. Wylie, *The reign of Henry IV*, IV. 313 ; *C.P.R.*, *1396–9*, 490, 494 ; H. A. Napier, *Historical Notices of Swyncombe and Ewelme*). On 16 October 1399 he was appointed as constable of Wallingford castle for life and on 26 October as steward for life of the honours of Wallingford and St. Valery and the four and a half hundreds of Chiltern with a fee of £40 (duchy of Cornwall estates settled on Henry, prince of Wales, on 15 October). His former annuities totalling 50 marks were confirmed (*C.P.R.*, *1399–1401*, 15, 33, 34 ; *1413–16*, 157 ; P.R.O., D.L.28, IV. 3 ; *Rot. Parl.*, III. 667). His administration of these offices was facilitated by the fact that the nucleus of his own estates was in the middle Thames valley and that he had made Ewelme (Oxon) his main seat after his marriage to Maud the younger of the two daughters and coheirs of John Burghersh, which not only brought kinship with Philippa later duchess of York (wife of Edward of Norwich), to whom he was later to act as executor, but also estates in Hampshire and Norfolk and elsewhere, apart from those in Oxfordshire at Ewelme and in adjacent vills. His Oxfordshire estates he augmented by purchase and he paid Henry IV's queen nearly £130 a year for leases of royal manors in north Oxon, the most important being Woodstock. He also enjoyed the wardship of the Stonore property from 1403 to 1415 (*Feudal Aids*, II. 214, 357, 370 ; III. 575 ; IV. 187 ; VI. 456, 490 ; Blomefield, *Norfolk*, VIII. 127 ; *C.C.R.*, *1429–35*, 335–9 ; *C.P.R.*, *1408–13*, 283, 298 ; *1413–16*, 7). On 5 November 1402 he was appointed for life to the important royal Household office of Chief Butler of England at a fee of 20 marks and with the right to appoint deputies in the ports to exercise the royal rights of prisage of wines. Except for a short period of seven or eight months in 1407, when his fortunes were under a cloud, and another from March 1418 to May 1421,

M

when he was constantly out of the country, Chaucer exercised the office continuously until his death in 1434, although his renewed occupation of the office from December 1407 down to December 1422 was 'during pleasure' only (*C.P.R., 1401–5*, 170 ; *1405–8*, 327, 380 ; *1413–16*, 1 ; *1416–22*, 60 ; *1422–9*, 7 ; *Rot. Parl.*, IV. 178 b.). The first overt consequence for Chaucer of his kinship (through his mother) with the Beauforts came in June 1406 when his cousin, Henry bishop of Winchester, made him constable of Taunton castle and overseer of the Somerset estates of his see at a very handsome fee of £40 a year, although the relationship may have already procured him the right to farm, in November 1405, the forestership of the Mortimer forests of Neroche, Exmoor, and Mendip, and the parkership of Petherton in Somerset, during the wardship of the young earl of March, for whom he was later to act as feoffee (*C.P.R., 1405–8*, 406 ; *C.F.R., 1405–13*, 21 ; *Dorset Fines*, 274). Chaucer's Speakerships in 1407, 1410, and 1411, must have been very helpful to the Beauforts and their political ally, the young prince of Wales, to whom he was also particularly attached by his Wallingford offices ; they were certainly of considerable embarrassment to Henry IV who complained of Chaucer's prolocutorial 'novelties' on the last of these occasions. The triumph of the political bloc to which Chaucer belonged was assured when Henry V succeeded to the throne in March 1413. He was confirmed in all his offices and in September got the custody of the east Hampshire forests of Woolmer and Aliceholt—Beaufort as Chancellor sealed the patent at Chaucer's own manor of Worldham—and in November he was made sheriff of Hampshire ; he had already occupied the shrievalty of Oxon and Berks in 1400–1 and 1403–4 and the escheatorship in these counties in 1406–7, and had been j.p. in Oxfordshire since 1403, an office he was to hold till death except when prevented by absence abroad (*C.P.R., 1413–16*, 102 ; *List of Sheriffs*, 55 ; *List of Escheators*, 119). During the next few years he saw a considerable amount of diplomatic and military service overseas. On 4 June 1414 he was appointed a member of an embassy to treat with France for the king's marriage with Charles VI's daughter, Catherine of Valois, and for an alliance with John duke of Burgundy (T. Carte, *Catalogue des rolles Gascons*, II. 214). The embassy, which was away from the end of June until late in October, also treated with the duke of Holland (Issue Roll, 2HV, Easter, P.R.O., E.403, No. 617, Mem. 6). In the following summer he served with a retinue of 11 men-at-arms and 36 archers in the Harfleur-Agincourt campaign, his indenture of service being dated 29 April 1415 (Foreign Accounts, E.101, XLVII. 29). On 4 December 1415 he received an addition to his plurality of Crown offices when appointed havener in Cornwall and at Plymouth at a farm of £80 a year (*C.F.R., 1413–22*, 141). In June 1417 he mustered his military retinue in preparation for Henry V's resumption of hostilities with France and doubtless sailed at the end of July with the royal expedition, for on 1 October and 15 December 1417 he was again on embassies to treat with France (T. D. Hardy, *Rotuli Normannie*, 167, 169, 205), and in the following year he was at the sieges of Louviers and Rouen (*D.K.R.*, XLI. 713, 715, 717–18, 720). From March 1419 to the early summer of 1420 he was seemingly in England, but in July 1420 was on an embassy to Brittany to secure the duke's acceptance of the Treaty of Troyes (1420), which was to be ratified in England in the last parliament Henry V was destined to attend, that of May 1421 in which Chaucer was Speaker (*D.K.R.*, XLI. 776 ; XLIV. 620 ;

XLII. 375, 379). Chaucer's cousin, Bishop Beaufort, had been under a cloud since his acceptance from Pope Martin V of a cardinal's dignity, the exemption of his diocese from the authority of the primate, and a licence to hold his see in commendam, all without royal licence. Henry V made Beaufort resign his red hat. In March 1420 Chaucer had reported on the bishop's reasons for staying away from the king's marriage and done his best to conciliate the king. In this parliament bygones between Henry V and his uncle of Winchester became bygones and the latter responded with his (as yet) largest royal loan (for a discussion of the quarrel between Henry V and Beaufort and Chaucer's difficult part in it, see K. B. McFarlane, 'Henry V, Bishop Beaufort and the Red Hat, 1417–1421', *E.H.R.*, 1945). The difficulties of Henry VI's minority probably brought Chaucer and his cousin Henry Beaufort into closer touch than the latter's machinations had permitted in the previous four or five years. On 5 December 1422 Chaucer got his office of Chief Butler renewed and for life, and if his Crown leases and wardships are anything to go by he prospered. The parliament of October 1423 saw him included among the commoner members of the royal Council and he remained a member of it until his death, although his attendances were very spasmodic (*Rot. Parl.*, IV. 201 ; *P.P.C.*, III. 155, 157, 163, 169, 266 ; IV. 263). He was by this time father-in-law of Thomas earl of Salisbury, after whose death, at the siege of Orleans in 1428, Chaucer's widowed daughter and heir, Alice, married as her third husband William de la Pole, earl of Suffolk. Chaucer died on 18 November 1434 and was buried at Ewelme (Napier, *op. cit.*, 44).

Henry Chippenham, m.p. for Hereford in 1406, 1413, November 1414, March 1416, December 1421, and 1422 ; grocer of Hereford (*C.P.R., 1422–9,* 543). In July 1429 he was appointed overseer of murage accounts at Hereford by royal letter patent for three years ; he was mayor of Hereford 1430–3, 1436–7 and 1443–4 (J. Duncomb, *History and Antiquities of Herefordshire*, 365) ; he attested the parliamentary indentures of election on eighteen occasions between 1407 and 1449 (P.R.O., C.219, Bundles 10–15).

Richard Clitheroe, m.p. for Romney in April 1414, 1415, March 1416, 1419, 1420, May 1421, 1422, 1423, 1429, 1435, 1437, 1442, 1445, and 1447. He was executor to Richard Clitheroe of Goldstanton-in-Ash (Kent), m.p. for Kent in 1406 and 1407 (the testator was probably his uncle) (Somerset House Wills, *Register Marche*, fo. 50). He was bailiff of Romney in 1430–1, 1439–42, 1445–8, 1450–3, and 1462–3 (*Hist. Mss. Comm., 5th Report [accounts of Lydd and New Romney]*, 519, 542–4). On 23 May 1432 he was appointed controller of customs and subsidies at Sandwich (*C.P.R., 1429–36,* 179). In 1435 he acted as principal executor to his brother, Bishop John Clitheroe of Bangor (Jacob, *Chichele Register*, II. 533–4). He died in 1463–4.

Nicholas Clopton, m.p. for Wycombe in 1422, was then 'clerk of the courts' to the college of St. George, Windsor (A. K. B. Roberts, *St. George's College, Windsor Castle, 1346–1416*, 148, 215).

Sir John Cockayne of Ashbourne (Derbyshire) and Pooley (Warwickshire), knight of the shire for Derbyshire in 1395, 1402, October 1404, 1419, May 1421, 1422, 1427, 1431, and 1433, and for Warwickshire in 1420 and December 1421. He came of a family resident since the mid-twelfth century at Ashbourne. The town was parcel of the duchy of Lancaster and Henry IV granted Sir John £60 a year charged on the duchy revenues of the vill and from the hundred of Wirksworth to ensure the support that the family had already afforded him (P.R.O., Duchy of Lancaster Accounts Various, D.L.28, XXVII. 10). For Sir John's father had met his death fighting as a loyalist at Shrewsbury in 1403 and so had Sir Hugh Shirley, the father of Sir John's second wife. The fact that Sir John's monumental effigy over his tomb at Ashbourne bears the S.S. collar of livery is further evidence of this strong Lancastrian attachment. His uncle, moreover, John Cockayne of Bury Hatley (Beds), was Chief Baron of the Exchequer from 1400 to 1413 and from June 1406 to his retirement in 1429 a Justice of the Common Bench ; the two branches of the family were on close terms (A. E. Cockayne, *Cockayne Memoranda*, pedigree 1 ; *ibid.*, 81 ; in *D.N.B.*, IV. 682, Justice Cockayne and his nephew, Sir John, are confused, following Foss, *Judges of England*, IV. 303). During Henry IV's reign Sir John Cockayne served on the commission of the peace for Derbyshire spasmodically and on other local royal commissions, the most important being his tenure of the office of escheator in Notts and Derbyshire in 1405–6. In the political troubles which disturbed the second half of Henry IV's reign and all but resulted in a cleavage in the royal family itself, Sir John seemingly supported the party surrounding the king and his second son Thomas against the Beaufort bloc and Prince Henry of Monmouth. In the spring of 1405 he had contracted to serve with Thomas of Lancaster, then admiral of England (Carte, *op. cit.*, II. 189), and in 1410 and 1411 his participation in riots upsetting the north midlands was probably conditioned by these affiliations : his local opponent, Sir Roger Leche, was steward of Household to Henry of Monmouth ; they were both imprisoned in the Tower for a time in 1411 along with other local notables (*William Salt Society, Trans.*, XVII. 28 ; *C.C.R., 1409–13*, 243–4, 261). In June 1412 he made his will preparatory to accompanying Thomas of Lancaster (now duke of Clarence) on an expedition to France in support of the Orleanist, anti-Burgundian faction there (*A. E. Cockayne, op. cit.*, 84, where the will is wrongly assigned to 13 Henry VI instead of 13 Henry IV ; Dugdale, *Warwickshire*, 809). In 1414 and 1415 he was in trouble and up before the King's Bench for his rioting in 1410 but was able to produce a general pardon procured in January 1414 (*Salt Society, Trans.*, XVII. 25, 28, 51). Sir John saw no military service under Henry V, but his son, John, was in the retinue of Richard Lord Grey of Codnor in the first French expedition (*Derbyshire A. and N.H. Society Journal*, XIV. 25). In December 1417 he was put on the Warwickshire commission of the peace and served until the end of the reign, soon after which he was appointed for the first time as sheriff of Notts and Derbyshire (he served for the financial year 1422–3). He was j.p. in Derbyshire from July 1424 and then in 1428–9 was again sheriff in Notts and Derbyshire. In the meantime his duchy of Lancaster annuity of £60 was confirmed on the day after the dissolution of the parliament of 1422 (Duchy of Lancaster, Ministers' Accounts, P.R.O., D.L.29, 197, 3089). In June 1431 he was again j.p. in Derbyshire and served until his death in the winter of 1438–9. In 1434–5 he was for a third time sheriff of Notts and Derbyshire. He served on local Crown loan raising commissions frequently in his own county and he himself contributed substantially. (For Sir John's landed estate see *E.H.R.*, XLIX. 632 ; *Hist. Mss. Comm. Report, Rutland Mss.*, IV. 53 ; *C.C.R., 1413–19*, 427.)

Sir William Coggeshall, knight of the shire for Essex in 1391, January 1397, 1401, 1402, October 1404, 1411, April 1414, 1420, December 1421, 1422. When his father, Sir Henry Coggeshall, died in 1375, William was still under age, and his wardship and marriage were immediately granted to Edmund of Langley, Edward III's third surviving son, only to be transferred by him to William's uncle, Thomas Coggeshall, in February 1376 (*C.P.R., 1374–7*, 188, 369). When Sir William (he was already a knight) offered proof of age in 1379 he was at Milan in the service of Sir John Hawkwood, the most sought-after of condottieri in Italy and husband of one of the bastard daughters of Bernabo Visconti of Milan, and he had married one of Hawkwood's daughters (Antiocha) by his first wife. It was at Hawkwood's petition that Coggeshall's homage and fealty were respited until his return to England and that livery of seisin was granted on 30 July 1379 (*C.F.R., 1377–81*, 262–3 ; Morant, *Essex*, II. 373). Hawkwood's own family had long been settled at Hedingham Sibil in Essex where the Coggeshall estates were mainly concentrated ; Sir William's property in this county plus lands in Cambridgeshire were worth £126 a year as assessed in 1412 (*Feudal Aids*, VI. 438, 406). Between 1384 and 1394 he and Sir Nicholas Twyford were embroiled with Walter Sibille, a prominent London fishmonger and alderman of Bridge ward who had been accused of treasonably admitting the men of Kent into the city during the Peasants' Revolt and who remained under a heavy cloud until January 1384 (R. Bird, *The Turbulent London of Richard II*, 56–60). The dispute, which was over a suit regarding tenements in Exning (Suffolk) worth no more than 8 shillings a year, might have had important political repercussions, because Sibille, stung by the award by a special assize of £800 damages against him, retaliated by accusing Robert de Vere, earl of Oxford, to the duke of Lancaster of 'maintaining' his opponents' suit. Sibille spent three years in prison for defamation, but Coggeshall certainly had connexions with De Vere who was one of his feoffees (*Rot. Parl.*, III. 186, 398 ; *C.P.R., 1381–5*, 433 ; *C.C.R., 1385–9*, 234 ; *1392–6*, 212). Another of Coggeshall's influential connexions and feoffees after his second marriage in 1388 with Ricarda, the widow of Sir Thomas Fichet, was John Lord Cobham, who was one of the members of the parliamentary commission of 1386–9 so detested by Richard II and who was destined to be adjudged traitor in Richard's last parliament (*C.P.R., 1388–92*, 53, 518 ; *C.C.R., 1392–6*, 440–1, 515). Sir William had returned to England from Italy certainly by the end of 1381, when he served on a succession of royal commissions to suppress the disturbances of the aftermath of the Peasants' Revolt in Essex. He served regularly on a variety of local commissions for the rest of his life, especially commissions of array ; as sheriff of Essex and Hertfordshire in 1391–2, 1404–5, and 1411–12 ; and as j.p. in Essex in the years 1401–7, and from 1417 until his death in the autumn of 1426 when he was aged about sixty-eight (*List of Sheriffs*, 44 ; *C.P.R., passim*). He accompanied Richard II to Ireland in 1399, having connexions with the Ricardian court party as well as with its opponents ; at the time of his return from Ireland, before 5 September 1399, Coggeshall seems to have been a member of the household of John Holand, duke of Exeter, half-brother of Richard II and brother-in-law of Henry of Bolingbroke, who, after being implicated in the rising of January 1400 against the latter, was to be executed by a mob at Pleshy (Essex) (K.R. Mem. Rolls, 1 Hen. IV, P.R.O., E.159/176, Easter term, *Recorda*, Rot. 33). In 1404, however, Coggeshall was particularly active in the suppression of anti-Lancastrian disaffection in Essex even before his appointment as sheriff on 18 October 1404. The dowager countess of Oxford the mother of Robert de Vere, in the autumn of 1403 had caused rumours of Richard II's survival to be spread and in anticipation of his coming distributed replicas of the badge of the white hart ' and drow many hertis to hir conclusion ' (Capgrave, *Chronicle of England* [R.S.], 286). She was abetted by the abbots of Colchester and St. Osyth. The Premonstratensian abbot of Beeleigh by Maldon was also implicated, but Colchester seems to have been the centre of trouble. In April and June 1404 Coggeshall and an associate were ordered to bring some of the chief malcontents before the King and Council. His appointment as sheriff in the following autumn involved him further in this business, especially when fresh treasons after Christmas 1404 on the part of the abbot and some of the monks of Colchester were discovered (Capgrave, *op. cit.*, 262–3 ; *C.P.R.*, *1401–5*, 430–1, 432, 436, 506, 514, 517 ; W. G. Benham, *The Red Paper Book of Colchester*, 35). These phenomena seem to have constituted the high-spot of Coggeshall's career. It is significant that they concerned Essex for, after the obscure and transient Italian phases of his early life, Sir William's interests seem to have been largely confined to this county where lay the bulk of his property. His daughters and coheirs (his son John predeceased him) he married off into other Essex families of more than local notability : the husband of his daughter Blanche, John Doreward, was son of the Speaker of that name of 1399 and 1413 who was a former member of Henry IV's Council (*Essex Archaeol. Soc. Trans.*, III. 102) ; his other daughter, Alice, married a future Speaker in John Tyrell, a connexion of Duke Humphrey of Gloucester, and treasurer of the royal Household and chief steward of the duchy of Lancaster in the last few years of his life (q.v.). Richard Baynard, Coggeshall's fellow shire-knight in the last parliament of Henry V's reign and on that occasion Speaker for the Commons, saw fit to nominate Sir William among his executors.

John Cook, m.p. Exeter 1422. In December 1407 he had been recently appointed deputy-butler at Topsham, Exeter's chief port (*C.P.R.*, *1405–8*, 371). Between March 1413 and February 1414, and in the years November 1416–17, November 1418–19, November 1420–1, he was one of the two constables of the staple at Exeter ; on 26 November 1422, in the middle of the session of Henry VI's first parliament, he was appointed mayor of the Exeter staple and acted until 14 November 1423 (Pat. Rolls Supplementary, P.R.O., C.67/24–5). In Michaelmas 1413–14 he was senior bailiff of Exeter and was mayor of the city in 1417–18, 1421–2, and 1424–5 (J. J. Alexander, *Exeter Members of Parliament*, *Devon Assocn. Trans.*, LX. 205 ; Exchequer, L.T.R., Memoranda Roll, 1 Henry VI, P.R.O., E.368/195).

John Cork, m.p. for Helston in 1419, Liskeard in 1420 and 1422, and Bodmin in 1423 ; was a j.p. in Cornwall 1422–45, and was of the quorum in 1422. He was of the quorum of several other Cornish and Devon commissions.

Sir John Juyn, Chief Baron of the Exchequer and Justice of the Common Bench, appointed him as one of his feoffees (*C.C.R., 1429–35, 56*). Between 1419 and 1435 he attested nine Cornish shire elections.

John Cory, m.p. Launceston 1410, November 1414, 1417, May 1421, 1422 and 1423. He was mayor of Launceston in 1397 and 1405 (R. and O. B. Peter, *History of Launceston and Dunheved*, 400). From 26 April 1419 to 4 November 1423 he was controller of customs and subsidies in and between Plymouth and Fowey; he was appointed joint-collector of customs in the same area on 4 November 1423 and was reappointed on 22 July 1425 (*C.P.R., 1416–22*, 215, 392; *1422–9*, 50; *C.F.R., 1422–30*, 53, 55, 61, 89, 90, 94, 108). He was present at the Cornish elections to the 1422 parliament (P.R.O., C.219, Bundle 13).

Thomas Cricklade, parliamentary burgess for Cricklade in 1413, perhaps in December 1421 (it may have been Robert; the christian name is missing from the return), and 1422, and for Calne in 1426, was ordered to be superseded in the office of coroner on 8 July 1419 and again on 26 April 1421 (*C.C.R., 1419–22*, 2, 141).

Robert Darcy, parliamentary burgess for Newcastle-on-Tyne in 1402, knight of the shire for Essex in March 1416, 1419, May 1421, 1423, 1425, 1426, 1432, 1439, and 1445, and in the meantime as burgess for Maldon (Essex) in 1422. He was Clerk of the Common Bench from 10 April 1410 to 23 March 1413 and from January 1423 to his death on 3 September 1448, holding office from October 1440 in survivorship with his nephew, Henry Filongley (*C.P.R., 1408–13*, 219; *1422–9*, 23; *1429–36*, 101; *1436–41*, 471). At her death on 7 April 1419, Darcy was steward of the estates of the aged dowager countess of Hereford, Joan Bohun, Henry V's grandmother, a purparty of whose estates then descended to the king as one of the coheirs, *jure matris*, Mary Bohun; some of these estates, the formerly Mortimer, latterly Fitz Alan, lordships of Chirk and Chirklands, had already been secured to the King's use on 1 July 1418, the legal title being vested in a group of feoffees comprised of Henry V's duchy of Lancaster feoffees and the countess's representatives, among whom was Darcy; the demise to the Crown was not completed until 1435 (*C.P.R., 1416–22*, 172; *C.F.R., 1413–22*, 136; F. Palgrave, *Ancient Calendars* [etc.] *of the Exchequer*, II. 156, 187–9). Those Bohun estates of Henry V's inheritance, which Henry IV had first held *jure uxoris* and then by courtesy until his death, had been incorporated by act of the parliament of November 1414 in the duchy of Lancaster. After the death of the countess of Hereford in 1419 the work of partitioning her third of the whole inheritance (held in dower) between Henry V and Anne countess of Stafford (the other coheir) was undertaken by the council of the duchy of Lancaster, and Darcy was accordingly early in 1421 co-opted as a member of this body; the parliament of May 1421 ratified the partition, certain difficulties over which came up for discussion in Henry VI's first parliament (Duchy of Lancaster, Accounts Various, P.R.O., D.L.28, 4, 11; *Rot. Parl.*, IV. 46–9, 135–40, 191; *P.P.C.*, II. 294). In the first half of Henry VI's reign Darcy acted as feoffee to Walter Lord Fitz Walter; to Joan Beauchamp Dame Abergavenny, niece of the late countess of Hereford and one of the Fitz Alan coheirs (in 1435 he acted as her executor, receiving 400 marks, etc.) ; to Dame Abergavenny's son-in-law, James, fourth earl of Ormond, and subsequently to his son, the fifth earl (*C.C.R.*, *1422-9*, 145, 150, 260, 263 ; *C.P.R.*, *1422-9*, 211, 486 ; *1429-36*, 208-11, 506, 27 ; Jacob, *Chichele Register*, II. 538 ; *Hist. Mss. Comm.*, *Mss. of R. R. Hastings*, I. 1) ; to Richard Lord Grey of Wilton (and later as his executor) ; to John de Vere earl of Oxford, in 1436 ; to Richard duke of York, from March 1440 ; to Henry Bourchier count of Eu, from May 1441 ; and to certain important commoners, including Richard Baynard of Essex, Speaker in Henry V's last parliament (*C.P.R.*, *1429-36*, 183, 602 ; *1441-6*, 162 ; *1461-7*, 45 ; *1436-41*, 533 ; Jacob, *op. cit.*, II. 628 ; *C.C.R.*, *1419-22*, 223 ; *1435-41*, 376 ; *P.P.C.*, V. 136).   At the time of the death of John duke of Bedford, in 1435, Darcy was steward of his Essex lordship of Bradwell (*C.P.R.*, *1429-36*, 494).   Darcy died on 3 September 1448. He had been j.p. in Essex 16 June 1410 to 16 November 1413, 12 December 1414 to 20 July 1424, and 3 June 1427 to his death (but not always of the quorum as Wedgwood implies) ; sheriff of Essex and Herts, November 1419-20 ; escheator for Essex, November 1414–December 1415, November 1420–May 1422, November 1427-8 (Wedgwood, *op. cit.*, 258).   He had only attested one Essex parliamentary election, in 1433 (P.R.O., C.219. 14. 4).

Sir Walter de la Pole, knight of the shire for Cambridgeshire in 1411, November 1414, 1417, May 1421, 1422, 1423, and 1427, was the son of Sir Edmund de la Pole and nephew of Michael de la Pole, first earl of Suffolk, who suffered impeachment and dismissal from his office as Chancellor in 1386 and forfeiture in the Merciless parliament of 1388.   Walter was sixteen years old at the time and by virtue of his marriage with Elizabeth, daughter and heir of Sir Thomas de Bradestone, had already come into substantial if scattered manors in southern England, and he was in possession of an important collection of manors in Gloucs before November 1410.   It was doubtless his interest in this region which later in 1417 accounted for his being chosen by Thomas Lord Berkeley to be one of his feoffees.   Although he did not get seisin of his own inheritance in Cambridgeshire until the death of his father in 1419 Walter held land worth £73 a year in that county in 1412, Sir Edmund seemingly living mainly on the rents of his Bucks and Oxfordshire estates (Napier, *Swyncombe and Ewelme*, 291 ; *Miscell. Gen. et Herald.*, 2nd series, II. 315 ; *C.F.R.*, *1383-91*, 204 ; *C.P.R.*, *1391-6*, 696-7 ; *C.C.R.*, *1409-13*, 134 ; *Cal. Inq. p.m.*, IV. 124, 154 ; *Feudal Aids*, VI. 406, 452, 518, 538).   Walter's politically active life fell in a fallow period in the rise of the De la Poles.   His cousin Michael, the son of Richard II's fallen minister, was not restored to his father's dignity as earl of Suffolk until 1397, but though this rehabilitation was accepted by the Lancastrians the family's influence received a further setback in the second and third earls' premature deaths in Henry V's 1415 expedition.   With these members of the senior branch of the family Sir Walter (knighted between 1387 and 1389) had had close connexions : both he and his father were executors to Michael the second earl under the terms of his will of 1 July 1415 (Surtees Soc., CXVI., *North Country Wills*, 8) and Sir Walter was feoffee to uses of the third earl's widow, Elizabeth, daughter of Thomas Mowbray, first duke of Norfolk (*C.P.R.*, *1413-16*, 402).   He was also to be a feoffee from 1424 onwards to William, son of his cousin the second earl and inheritor of the title in 1415 on the death of his elder brother at Agincourt

(Suckling, *Suffolk*, II. 139). It was not until after the return of this William, the fourth earl, in 1431 from fourteen years of military service in France that the fortunes of the family began to soar again. Three years later, however, his father's cousin, Sir Walter, was dead. Sir Walter had had much of his own way to make. In 1394 and again in 1399 he had accompanied Richard II to Ireland (*C.P.R.*, *1391–6*, 471, 494 ; *1396–9*, 550, 552). What his reactions to the Lancastrian usurpation were there is no means of knowing, but Sir Walter served on no royal commissions at all in Henry IV's reign although his father was a j.p. in Cambridgeshire throughout its duration. It is quite feasible that he was implicated in the Scrope–Mowbray rising of 1405 ; certainly the substantial recognisances to which he was party in March 1406 make it look suspiciously likely (*C.C.R.*, *1405–9*, 111, 117, 128). As a De la Pole he was related to the Masham branch of the Scrope family and in fact later in 1406 he accompanied Sir Stephen Scrope, then Thomas of Lancaster's deputy-lieutenant in Ireland, on his return there (Wylie, *Henry IV*, III. 162 ; *C.P.R.*, *1405–8*, 248). In a year's time Scrope was back in England and Sir Walter in all probability with him. He was for the first time elected to parliament for Cambridgeshire in 1411 when, during an uncomfortable session, Henry IV, under the influence of Archbishop Arundel and his second son, Thomas of Lancaster, re-asserted himself against the prince of Wales and the Beauforts. Sir Walter probably inclined to the former bloc. His service in Ireland may well have afforded him contacts with its Lieutenant and when in the following summer of 1412 Thomas of Lancaster was created duke of Clarence and led a force into Normandy and Guienne in the Orleanist interest Sir Walter was a member of his retinue (*C.C.R.*, *1409–13*, 287 ; Napier, *op. cit.*, 291). The reign of Henry V saw a much greater use made by the Crown of his abilities in the field of local administration. On 18 May 1414 he was made a j.p. for the borough of Cambridge ; in 1417–18 he acted as sheriff of Cambridgeshire and Huntingdonshire, and in February 1419 he was made a j.p. in the former county and served the commission of the peace there until his death except from July 1423 to February 1425 and from February 1429 to December 1431 ; in the meantime he again acted as sheriff in 1423–4 and in 1428–9. Sir Walter seems to have kept out of Henry V's military enterprises in France (his son, Edmund, then a knight of twenty-four years, fought at Agincourt) but from the spring of 1419 for a period of over seven years he was on and off very much to the front as a member of important diplomatic missions : his first for which arrangements were in train on 11 May 1419 was to negotiate with Wladislas II of Poland and also the High Master of the Order of the Teutonic Knights, probably with a view to stabilising the Baltic situation in order to leave the Emperor Sigismund, who supported the Knights, freer to implement his undertakings to Henry V under the treaty of Canterbury of 1416 (*D.K.R.*, XLIV. 611 ; F. Devon, *Issues*, I. 359). It was again probably to give some substance to the Anglo-imperial alliance as well as to embarrass the Dauphin into acceptance of the treaty of Troyes that, while m.p. for Cambridgeshire in the parliament of May 1421 (the last attended in person by Henry V), Sir Walter was appointed on 17 May as ambassador with John Stokes, LL.D., to the Emperor himself. Specifically the embassy was to discuss the grant to Henry and his heirs, by Sigismund, of Dauphiné and all other lands the latter claimed as Emperor in Languedoc. De la Pole delayed starting so that on 17 July the terms of reference were enlarged by an instruction to reach agreement about certain loans made by Henry V to Sigismund on the security of the duchy of Luxembourg ; whatever was the outcome of the mission was reported to Henry V at Meaux on 29 November following (Rymer, *Foedera*, X. 143–5 ; *P.P.C.*, II. 287–8 ; Wylie and Waugh, *Henry V*, III. 359–60). Another embassy was sent forthwith first to seek military assistance from the Rhenish bishops and the Wittelsbachs and then to request Sigismund to ' come and do the King succorse after his many promesses and often tymes wryting ' and to discuss the place of the next General Council of the Church if this issue were raised. De la Pole eventually was ordered to accompany the embassy. It set out from London on 3 March 1422. When it returned to England on 25 September, nearly a month had elapsed from the date of Henry V's death (Rymer, *op. cit.*, X. 161–70 ; *D.K.R.*, XLIV. 632 ; *P.P.C.*, III. 29 ; Devon, *op. cit.*, I. 372). The Exchequer was in arrears of payments to De la Pole for these undertakings to the extent of over £217 in May 1423 when he complained to the Council (*P.P.C.*, III. 29–30, 97). On 22 February 1423 he had been nominated as a member of the English delegation to the impending General Council of the Church at Pavia but, in the event, the personnel of the embassy was almost completely changed and he did not go (*ibid.*, 42). But in June 1425 he was a member of an embassy to Pope Martin V and may well have undertaken to negotiate on the same voyage for an alliance with Alphonso V of Aragon (Rymer, *op. cit.*, X. 319 ; *D.K.R.*, XLVIII. 237–8 ; *C.C.R.*, *1422–9*, 172). Sir Walter's last diplomatic undertaking was not until 1433 when on 24 March he was appointed one of a commission empowered to treat for peace and a mercantile settlement with an embassy from the duke of Brittany (Rymer, *op. cit.*, X. 546). In April 1434 he was present at a Great Council summoned to hear Gloucester's proposal to take charge of the French war (*P.P.C.*, IV. 212). On 2 July following he died, leaving as his heir his thirteen-years-old grandson, Edmund Ingoldsthorpe, who was already married to Joan the second daughter of John Lord Tiptoft. Sir Walter's first wife had died in January 1428. His second, Margaret, survived him and married John Golafre (knight of the shire for Berks in 1422, etc., q.v.), who had close connexions with William, earl of Suffolk. Sir Walter's half-sister had been Golafre's first wife (*C.F.R.*, *1430–7*, 167, 215–16 ; *C.P.R.*, *1429–36*, 333, 465 ; *C.C.R.*, *1429–35*, 340 ; Napier, *op. cit.*, 291 ; *V.C.H.*, *Berkshire*, IV. 346 ; Lipscomb, *Bucks*, I. 395).

Richard Drax, m.p. for Carlisle in 1422 only, was a member of Lincoln's Inn by 1420 and was one of the four governors in 1441–2, 1446–7, and 1454–5 (*Admission Book, op. cit.*, 1 ; *Black Book, op. cit.*, 7, 11, 13, 17, 20, 24, 30) ; from December 1452 to his death in 1457–8 he was j.p. in Surrey.

Richard Duffield, m.p. for Grimsby in 1413, November 1414, 1420, December 1421, 1422, 1423, 1425, 1426, 1431, 1432, 1433, 1435, and February 1449, parliamentary proxy for the abbot of Bardney in November 1414, October 1416, 1419, 1429, and 1431, on the first and last occasion when he was himself a parliamentary burgess (P.R.O., S.C.10, Nos. 2229, 2256, 2293, 2390/7, 2400). He was occasionally attorney in the Court of Common Pleas (Selden Society, *Year Book 1 Henry VI*, 12), and clerk of the peace in the parts of Lindsey in Lincolnshire certainly between August 1420 and November 1444, and probably for some time before and after those dates (Putnam, *op. cit.*, 25 ; P.R.O., E.101. 569/38 ; 569/41 ; E.137. 19. 3).

Robert Ellis, m.p. Great Yarmouth 1414 (November), 1420, 1421 (May), 1422 ; in 1412/13 he shared in the framing of local ordinances for the herring trade (*Hist.Mss. Comm.*, *9th Report*, 305a) ; he was master of a dogger (*C.C.R.*, *1413–19*, 7) and was one of several royally appointed keepers of the sea to protect fishermen off the East Anglian coast in October 1415 (*C.P.R.*, *1413–16*, 363). He was one of the 4 bailiffs of Great Yarmouth in 1413–14, 1416–17, 1422–3, and one of 2 bailiffs 1426–7, 1429–30, 1432–4, 1437–8, and 1442–3 (Blomefield, *op. cit.*, XI. 324–5) ; he was a j.p. for Great Yarmouth from February 1415 to 1443 (*C.P.R.*, *passim*) ; between February 1416 and February 1419 he was collector of customs and subsidies there (*C.F.R.*, *1413–22*, 113, 130, 191, 242, 246).

Sir William Elmeden of Trillesden (co. Durham) and Embleton (Northumberland), knight of the shire for Northumberland in 1422 and 1427, was born about 1391. In 1416 he succeeded his father, Thomas Elmeden, as tenant of the bishop of Durham in some four manors in the palatinate and he inherited or acquired properties in Newcastle-on-Tyne and elsewhere in Northumberland. He was later to run into trouble with Bishop Neville over certain unlicensed enfeoffments that he made of his Durham manors and over pasture rights in Trillesden, and Trillesden manor was temporarily surrendered (R. Surtees, *Durham*, I. 76–8 ; II. 187 ; III. 55 ; Surtees Society, Vol. IX, App. CCLXIX ; XCIX. 61, 144 ; *D.K.R.*, XXXIII. 112–13 ; XXXIV. 184, 229–30 ; XLV. 190). Elmeden entered into kinship with the great border family of Umfraville by marrying for his first wife Elizabeth, the eldest daughter of Sir Thomas Umfraville, a niece of Sir Robert Umfraville K.G., and sister and eventual coheir of the Sir Gilbert Umfraville, a son-in-law of Ralph Neville, first earl of Westmorland, and a leader of the van of the Agincourt force, who met his death at the English reverse of Beaugé in March 1421. In a petition of 1442 Elmeden was to claim that he had served Henry V in France and Normandy during the whole time of his wars. If this was so it is probable that he owed his introduction to the royal service to his brother-in-law, but in Henry V's second expedition of 1417 he indentured with the king on his own account, was with his retinue at Verneuil late in 1417, and was probably at the siege and fall of Rouen before his appointment for life, by letters dated there on 14 February 1419, as constable of the royal Northumberland stronghold of Bamburgh. The border was still unquiet after the ' Foul Raid ' of 1417 and Elmeden returned to England and undertook major repairs in the castle and strengthened its garrison, unfortunately without realising the need for special warrant of allowance at the Exchequer so that he had to petition parliament in 1427 for special consideration (R. A. Newhall, *The English Conquest of Normandy*, 78 ; *D.K.R.*, XLI. 731 ; *C.P.R.*, *1422–9*, 552 ; P.R.O., Ancient Petitions, S.C.8, File 109, No. 5423). On 15 November 1419 his hand at Bamburgh was strengthened when he was made receiver-general of the castle and lordship, and only eight days later he was appointed sheriff of Northumberland, holding this latter office until November 1420 (*C.P.R.*, *1416–22*, 247 ; *List of Sheriffs*, 98). In June 1421 Elmeden again went overseas and probably served in France until Henry V's death but not afterwards (*D.K.R.*, XLIV, 629). On 7 July 1423 he was appointed j.p. in Northumberland in the first issue of commissions in the new reign and continued as j.p. until 1439 ; on 3 May 1425 he was confirmed in his Bamburgh offices. He seems to have surrendered his receivership-general of Bamburgh in November 1440, but retained the constableship until his death in 1448, jointly with John Heron esquire in survivorship after 7 February 1438 (*C.P.R.*, *1436–41*, 179 ; *1441–6*, 132). In November 1442, in exchange for a pardon of amercements and arrears as receiver-general of Bamburgh, he relinquished a claim to £296-odd owed him in this capacity by the Crown ; his petition pleaded his military exertions in France and the Scottish wars and the fact that he had been laid up for the last six years with ill-health resulting from wounds incurred in the royal service. He had frequently served on casual royal commissions in Northumberland, but ceased to do so in the last ten years of his life, which now became shadowed by unsuccessful litigation with Bishop Neville and the prior of Durham as well as by physical incapacity.

John Enderby of Stratton, knight of the shire for Bedfordshire in November 1414, 1419, 1422, 1423, 1426, 1427, 1429, 1431, 1435, 1442, and 1445, was a lawyer of no very considerable landed estate, and that was restricted to Bedfordshire. He served on many short-term local royal commissions, especially those designed to promote the levying of Crown loans and he served on the *quorum* of the commission of the peace in Bedfordshire from July 1424 to March 1439 and again from June 1448 to June 1455, but he was never sheriff or royal escheator. He was a frequent attender at the Bedfordshire elections to parliament, being between 1417 and 1432 an attestor of the indenture of return on almost every occasion when he was not himself elected ; he was present also at the Huntingdonshire hustings in 1422 and 1429, the latter election being subsequently disputed and quashed because the electors were ' foreigners ' to the shire (P.R.O., C.219, Bundles 12, 13, and 14). His main source of local influence seems to have been derived from his long and close connexion with Reginald Lord Grey of Ruthyn whose main residence was in Bedfordshire, at West Park near Silsoe. As early as 12 March 1413 he was acting as counsel to this peer (*C.C.R.*, *1409–13*, 434) and in the following year, in the course of his first parliament, Enderby was party to the arrangements that were then in train for providing for the dowry of Lord Grey's daughter, Margaret, as part of the contract for her marriage with William Bonville (m.p. for Devon in 1422, etc.) (*ibid.*, *1413–19*, 198–200). On 3 July 1416 Lord Grey appointed Enderby and another of his council to be his attorneys in Ireland for a year, although they themselves might depute others to act for them there (*C.P.R.*, *1416–22*, 37), and on 16 February 1421 Enderby was authorised to act for Grey in the same capacity, this time for two years (*ibid.*, 317). Between 1431 and 1433, when negotiations were proceeding for the transfer from Lord Grey to the abbey of St. Albans of the patronage of the cell of Beaulieu (Beds) in return for the celebration of the anniversary of Grey's obit in the abbey, Enderby was acting as Grey's counsel in the conveyance and received 5 marks and an annuity of £1 from the abbey for his ' bona mediatio ' (*Annales Monasterii S. Albani a Johanne Amundesham scriptae*, ed. H. T. Riley [R.S.], II. 267). As one of Grey's council he got involved in May 1437 in a dispute between John Lord Fanhope and Lord Grey when a royal commission, whose members were mainly attached or otherwise favourable to the former, came to sit in Grey's manor of Silsoe ; which was not to his liking. Enderby openly told the commissioners—so proceedings before the royal Council in June and July disclosed— that their patent was procured to indict the Grey tenantry and warned them that ' thei that beth now in commission an other tyme may be withoute ', and he proposed that after this special commission had sat the sessions of the peace should be held, when he and Lord Grey would be present and ' enquere as wel for the Kyng as thei '. There was grave danger of riot, because Grey had a force behind him of several hundreds, including some from his Northamptonshire lordships, so that Fanhope sent off to his place at Ampthill for his ' harneys ' and reinforcements. But one of the quorum of the peace refused Enderby's suggestion and finally the two lords were induced to submit to arbitration and the sessions of the peace were so adjourned (*P.P.C.*, V. 35-9, 57-9). Less than two years later, on 12 January 1439, there occurred at Bedford something like a repetition of the earlier disturbance at Silsoe, when the two hostile sections of the Bedfordshire commission of the peace came into collision at the sessions house (*pretorium*). Enderby's party later contended before the Council that Fanhope's party came armed and insulted them and prevented any peaceful holding of the sessions, but Fanhope's party also averred that their opponents came with over 800 armed men drawn from Bedfordshire and Northants and uttered ' contumelious words ' in the presence of the justices. Though the certifications of both parties were regarded as malicious, Fanhope and his adherents were pardoned first, and, when the commissions of the peace were reissued on 12 March 1439, Enderby and his supporters were excluded, whereas Fanhope and his were reappointed. Enderby did not receive his general pardon until the end of May (*C.P.R.*, *1436-41*, 246, 282, 578). Lord Grey died in 1440 to be succeeded in his estates and titles by his grandson, Edmund, son of Sir John Grey and Constance Holland, stepdaughter of Lord Fanhope and sister of the earl of Huntingdon. In December 1443 Lord Fanhope followed his rival, leaving no legitimate heir. The old quarrel between the families lay dormant for nearly twenty years until in 1460 at the battle of Northampton Edmund Lord Grey went over to the Yorkist side from his position in the Lancastrian van. Rumour had it that ' in countenance ' he took Henry VI's part, but ' a little afore the field he practised with King Edward ', defamed Lord Fanhope (a bastard son of the earlier Lord Fanhope) to Edward by false accusations, and then acted on the understanding that if Edward won the field he should obtain Fanhope's manor of Ampthill (Dugdale, *Baronage*, II. 717). By that time Enderby was dead. He had made his will in 1450 and he died in 1457, leaving two sons : John, by his first marriage with Alice Furtho, and Richard by his second wife Maud (daughter of John Sewell). She subsequently married Robert Bothe and survived until 1474, founding in the year before her death a chantry at Stratton, where John Enderby was to figure on the bede-roll (*V.C.H.*, *Beds*, II. 204, 211 ; *C.P.R.*, *1467-77*, 400).

Robert Erle, m.p. Bedwin, 1422 ; Marlborough, 1425. He was executor and feoffee to Sir William Sturmy (Somerset House, Luffenham Register, fo. 7 ; *C.P.R.*, *1446-52*, 556 ; *C.C.R.*, *1413-19*, 457). He was present at the Wiltshire elections to the parliaments of 1413, November 1414, 1422, 1432, 1433, and 1435 (P.R.O., C.219, Bundles 11, 13, 14).

Sir William Eure of Witton-le-Wear (Durham) and Old Malton (Yorkshire), born about 1396, knight of the shire for Yorkshire in 1422, 1431, 1442, and in February 1449, belonged to a family that traced its descent directly from a sister of John de Balliol of Barnard Castle, father of Edward I's candidate for the Scottish throne of that name. The Eures still held the former Balliol barony of Stokesley which was to the north of the Cleveland Hills, but the family's chief concentration of territory was in the vale of Pickering, where it came to hold the former Vescy lands, including the manor of Old Malton, as a result of Sir William's father Sir Ralph's second marriage with Catherine, one of the daughters and coheirs of Sir William de Ayton of Malton. In the Durham palatinate the family held manors at Witton-le-Wear and Bradley (castellated by episcopal licence respectively in 1410 and 1431), Langley and Waterfall ; its estates in south Northumberland were held in mesne tenancy of the Percy lordship of Mitford (*V.C.H., Yorks, N. Riding*, I. 533 ; II. 303 ; *Feudal Aids*, IV. 80 ; VI. 308, 311, 313, 316 ; R. Surtees, *Durham, op. cit.*, I. LVII n. ; *D.K.R.*, XXXIV. 168 ; E. Bateson, *History of Northumberland*, XII. 490, 501 ; *C.C.R., 1422–9*, 31). Sir William Eure's father, Sir Ralph, had been uncompromising in his loyalty to the Lancastrian dynasty in the Percy rising of 1403, in May 1405 he was with the earl of Westmorland and the king's second son at Shipton Moor when they received the surrender of Archbishop Scrope and his fellow-rebel, the Earl Marshal, and he also figured on the commission which sentenced them to death as traitors at Bishopthorpe. When the rebellion broke out the earl of Westmorland had actually been staying with him at Witton-le-Wear (J. H. Wylie, *Henry IV*, I. 291 ; II. 178, 221–36). In July 1406 Sir Ralph had been granted custody of the temporalities of the vacant see of Durham to the use of the Bishop-elect, Thomas Langley, and by 1415 he was the bishop's steward at an annual fee of £40. One important economic result of this connexion was the lease, a virtual monopoly in fact it was, of the episcopal coal and iron workings on the south Durham field, which, after his father's death on 10 March 1422, Sir William Eure continued to enjoy for the rest of his own life in spite of quarrels with Bishop Langley in 1434 and 1437 (*C.P.R., 1405–8*, 208 ; Raine, *Auckland Castle*, 46 ; *V.C.H., Durham*, II. 323–4 ; *D.K.R.*, XXXIII. 151, 153, 181 ; XXXIV. 184, 207, 230 ; XXXV. 81, 131). The measure of his father's prestige was Sir William Eure's marriage in 1411 to Maud a daughter of Henry Lord Fitz Hugh of Ravensworth, nephew of the martyred Archbishop Scrope, and it was Lord Fitz Hugh, then King's Chamberlain, whom William accompanied on Henry V's first expedition to Normandy in 1415 (N. H. Nicolas, *Agincourt*, 345). His father-in-law's death so early in his own career (in 1425) was a misfortune, but he maintained his connexion with the Fitz Hughs (he shared an Exchequer grant of the estates held by his mother-in-law after her death in December 1427). He further cultivated the connexion with the Nevilles so carefully fostered by his father : from Michaelmas 1426 for nearly a year he shared the wardship of two-thirds of the late earl of Westmorland's castle and lordship of Braunspeth and he was to be later retained at £20 a year by Bishop Robert Neville of Durham who also appointed Sir William's younger brother, Robert Eure, to be steward in the liberties of the palatinate (*C.F.R., 1422–30*, 241 ; *D.K.R.*, XXXIII. 183) ; the Neville connexion was further strengthened by the marriage of Eure's nephew, the young Lord Fitz Hugh, with a daughter of Richard Neville, earl of Salisbury. Regularly occupied in the palatinate of Durham by commissions of the peace, as justice of gaol delivery, and as justice of assize, Sir William was also frequently busy with various royal commissions in other parts of the north-east, notably serving as i.p. in the North Riding continuously from 8 July 1420 to 1459 ; he was sheriff of Northumberland in 1436–7, was appointed steward of the lordship of Holderness in October 1438, and in 1444–5 was sheriff of Yorkshire. In 1442 he was one of four captains charged with the conduct of a fleet for the defence of the coasts as a result of a petition by the Commons in the parliament of 1442, to which he was returned for Yorkshire (*Rot. Parl.*, V. 59–60 ; *C.P.R., 1441–6*, 106–8 ; *P.P.C.*, V. 190, 193, 196 ; *D.K.R.*, XLVIII. 353). Sir William's eldest son, Ralph, brother-in-law of the lukewarm Lancastrian supporter, Lord Greystoke, perished on the loyalist side at Towton in 1461, and despite his close and long-established connexions with the Nevilles, Sir William himself seems to have been (if hesitantly) Lancastrian in his sympathies. Certainly after this Lancastrian disaster he was fined £2,000 and each of his three surviving sons forfeited similar amounts (*C.P.R., 1461–7*, 39). Nothing further is known of Sir William until the notice of his death some time in the year following September 1464 and apart from the fact of his burial in the church of the Gilbertine priory at Old Malton. His widow, Maud Fitz Hugh, survived until 1467, when she appointed her nephews, ' my especiall good lord ', Lord Greystoke, and his brother-in-law, Lord Fitz Hugh, as overseers of her executors. These Greystoke and Fitz Hugh connexions of Sir William Eure and his old attachment to the Nevilles must have presented him with an acute problem of conflicting loyalties in the closing stages of his life (*D.K.R.*, XXXV. 113 ; Surtees Society, *Test. Ebor.*, I. 284).

John Exton, m.p. Chichester 1422 ; between 17 October 1421 and 26 July 1424 he was joint collector of customs and subsidies, from 8 February 1423 as Bishop Beaufort's nominee, in the port of Chichester where on 8 February 1422 he was also appointed joint-surveyor and controller of tronage (*C.F.R., 1413–22*, 381, 383 ; *1422–30*, 19, 25, 53). He was coroner in Sussex from before October 1423 to beyond November 1427 (*C.C.R., 1422–9*, 85, 355, 424). He was present at the parliamentary elections for Sussex in 1419, 1423, 1425 (P.R.O., C. 219, Bundles 12, 13).

Thomas Fauconer represented London in the parliaments of 1411, March 1416, December 1421, 1422, and 1423. From 1402 to 1415 he was alderman of Coleman Street ward (A. B. Beavan, *Aldermen of London*, I. 108 ; II. lxi) ; from 1415 to his death in 1436/7 he was alderman of Cheap ward (Sharpe, *op. cit., Letter Book K, passim*) ; in 1403–4, he was one of the two sheriffs (Beaven, *op. cit.*, I. 100) and in October 1414–15, as a safe anti-Lollard, he was mayor and took an important part in negotiating the city loans towards Henry V's French expedition (Sharpe, *op. cit., Letter Book I, passim* ; H. T. Riley, *Memorials of London*, 604, 613–18, 630). From 21 March to 28 November 1413 he had been one of the collectors of customs at London (*C.F.R., 1413–22*, 6).

William Fenyngham, m.p. for East Grinstead in 1419, 1422, and 1437, for Midhurst in 1432, and for Arundel in 1435, was acting as an attorney in the

Common Bench in 1422 (Selden Society, *Year Book 1 Henry VI*. 31 ; Common Plea Rolls, Michs, 1 Hen. VI, P.R.O., C.P.40/647, Mems. 53, 122, 141).

John Fitlyng, m.p. Hull 1406, 1407, 1411, 1413, 1419, May 1421, 1422, 1423, 1425, 1427, 1431. A merchant of Hull, from 29 February 1416 to 24 July 1417 he was searcher in that port (*C.F.R., 1413–22*, 117, 206). In the year Michaelmas 1422–23 he was mayor of Hull (L.T.R. Mem. Roll, 1 Henry VI, P.R.O., E.368/195). As a result of a petition presented by the Commons in 1427 both he and Robert Holme were to act as overseers and auditors of receipts of levies on vessels using the Humber, the funds from which were to be used to erect and maintain a beacon at Ravenspur (*Rot. Parl.*, IV. 364).

Roger Flore of Oakham, knight of the shire for Rutland in January 1397, 1399, 1402, October 1404, April and November 1414, 1415, March and October 1416, 1417, 1419, and 1422. Before the end of Richard II's reign he was connected with Edward of Norwich later duke of York (*C.P.R., 1399–1401*, 76) to whom at the time of the duke's death at Agincourt he was feoffee and overseer of his will (*ibid., 1413–16*, 350 ; A. Gibbons, *Early Lincoln Wills*, 146 ; *C.C.R., 1413–19*, 294). Already employed as one of Henry V's trustees in the estates with which the king's foundation of the Bridgetine nunnery at Syon was endowed, Flore clearly emerged as a lawyer, predominantly, but by no means exclusively, in the service of the Crown with his appointment as chief steward of the duchy of Lancaster estates north of Trent on 1 December 1416, a position he held together with an *ex officio* membership of the duchy Council until December 1427 (*C.C.R., 1413–19*, 402 ; *1435–41*, 308 ; *C.P.R., 1422–9*, 205 ; D. of Lancr., Accounts Various, D.L.28, 4, No. 9 ; *C.P.R., 1416–22*, 454–9, 461–3 ; R. Somerville, *Duchy of Lancaster*, vol. 1. 420). This appointment took place about a week after the dissolution of the parliament of October 1416, in which Flore acted as Speaker for the first time. He was separately appointed chief steward for the duchy in Lancashire and Cheshire on 22 February 1417 ; this office he relinquished on 9 July 1425. He was to act as Speaker in the next two parliaments of 1417 and 1419, and again in 1422, four times in all (*Rot. Parl.*, IV. 95, 107, 117, 170). On 23 July 1417, the day of Henry V's departure for his second French expedition, Flore was made one of the 12 nominees of the king upon whom his feoffees (in that part of the duchy of Lancaster appropriated to the administration of his will) were to draw if their own number suffered attenuation (*C.P.R., 1416–22*, 118). In 1422 Flore sat in the Commons for the twelfth (and last) time for Rutland since 1397. He was to be parliamentary proxy for the abbot of Croyland in 1425 and 1426 (P.R.O., S.C.10, Nos. 2383, 2390). He had been present at the Rutlandshire elections to the parliaments of 1407, 1420, May 1421, 1423, 1425, and 1426 (C.219, Bundles 10, 12, 13). He died in 1428.

John Ford m.p. for Melcombe Regis in 1410, for Dorchester in 1417, 1419, 1420, May and December 1421, 1422, and 1423, and for Shaftesbury in 1426, may have been the same as the Ford admitted to Lincoln's Inn at Christmas 1424 (Lincoln's Inn Record Society, V. *Admission Register*) and the same as the John Ford who was of the quorum of the justices of gaol delivery at Ilchester by patent of 8 May 1430 (*C.P.R., 1429–36*, 72).

John Forester or Forster, parliamentary burgess for Appleby in 1422, forester for life in Inglewood forest from 1394 (*C.P.R., 1399–1401*, 262 ; *1413–16*, 25 ; *1429–36*, 442, 448 ; *1436–41*, 135), was a member of Lincoln's Inn in 1420 (*Admission Book, op. cit.*, 2 ; *Black Book, op. cit.*, 1).

John Forthey, who sat for Worcester in the parliaments of 1420, 1421 (May and December), 1422, 1429, and 1431, was appointed clerk of the peace in Worcestershire in January 1419 and was still in office at Michaelmas 1426, being superseded sometime between then and 1439 (Putnam, *op. cit.*, 66 ; Exchequer K.R. Estreats, P.R.O., E.137. 48/1).

Henry Frowyke, mercer of London, younger brother of Thomas Frowyke esquire and half-brother of Sir Thomas Charleton, represented the city in the parliaments of 1422, 1423, 1437, 1447, and 1450. He was master of the Mercers' Company in 1426, 1430, 1435, 1442, and 1449 (A. B. Beaven, *Aldermen of the City of London*, I. 17, 251 ; II. 7). He was one of the auditors of the city from September 1421 to September 1424, and by this latter date was alderman of Bassishaw ward, an office he retained until 1457 (R. R. Sharpe, *Letter-Books of the City of London*, I and K, *passim*). In 1427–8 he was one of the two civic sheriffs and in the period 1429–31 was again one of the auditors. In 1435–6 and, again, in 1444–5 (in spite of royal interference with the election) he was lord mayor (in his official capacity he escorted Margaret of Anjou from Blackheath to the city). In the meantime, from 18 June 1423 until 11 July 1425 he acted as one of the two constables of the Westminster staple (P.R.O., Supplementary Patent Rolls, C.67, 25). In a parliamentary petition of April 1425 the London Hanseatic merchants asked for the appointment of an alderman to act as judge in pleas of debt and suggested Frowyke as a suitable man ; unsuccessful on this occasion he was ultimately appointed to this position in 1442 (*Rot. Parl.*, IV. 303 ; *C.P.R., 1441–6*, 133). Frowyke had often been put on royal commissions authorised to consider appeals to the king's audience against judgements given in mercantile cases in the court of Admiralty, and his knowledge of mercantile law and practice would also stand him in good stead when in 1436–7 he was appointed as one of the royal commissaries authorised to treat with the ambassadors of the High Master of Prussia and the consuls and pro-consuls of the various interested communes of the Hanseatic League (*C.P.R., 1436–41*, 62). From 8 July 1446 to July 1457 continuously he was mayor of the Westminster staple (P.R.O., Supplementary Patent Rolls). By this time he was senior alderman of London. His landed property in the city and outside it in Middlesex was worth £54 a year (*E.H.R.*, XLIX. 638). He died sometime between 8 April 1459, when he made his final will, and 8 March 1460, when probate was granted in the Prerogative Court of Canterbury in Ivy Lane in the city (Wedgwood, *op. cit., Biographies*, 357).

Thomas Frowyke esquire of South Mimms, knight of the shire for Middlesex in 1419, 1422, 1427, 1432, and 1435, came of an old London family that had produced an alderman of Cheap early in Edward I's reign and an important early-fourteenth-century goldsmith. The family had rusticated with Thomas's grandfather, clerk of the market at Barnet, who had acquired land in

N

South Mimms and sat for Middlesex in six parliaments between 1352 and 1369 ; Thomas's father, Henry Frowyke, represented the county in Edward III's last parliament and died in 1386, leaving Thomas heir to property which, added to by Thomas's own marriage, was worth £90 a year in 1436 (*London and Middlesex Arch. Soc. Trans.*, IV. 260 ; F. C. Cass, *op. cit.*, 68 *et seq.* ; *E.H.R.*, XLIX. 638). While his younger brother, Henry, went into business in the city as a mercer, Thomas lived the life of a country landlord ' moribus et natu, gestu, victu moderatus' and addicted to field sports (Cass, *loc. cit.*), and he must have been close on forty years old when he was first elected to parliament for Middlesex in 1419. At that time he had not yet been a year occupying the office of j.p., but he retained the commission until his death in February 1449. He was a frequent attender at the shire elections to parliament and served on a variety of local royal commissions, especially Crown loan-raising commissions, and on the river-conservancy boards for the Colne and Lea. He had connexions, and probably friendly ones, with Abbot Whethamstede of St. Albans (*Chronicon Rerum Gestarum in Mon. Sti. Albani*, ed. T. H. Riley [Rolls Series], II. 279) and with another neighbour, Sir Thomas Lewkenore, whose daughter married his son and heir, Henry. His will was proved in the Court of Arches on 17 March 1449 (Somerset House, *Rous Register*, fo. 101). He was buried at South Mimms.

John Fruysthorp, m.p. Old Sarum, December 1421, 1422 ; on 4 November 1422 he was appointed to the office of troner at Southampton (*C.P.R., 1422–9*, 6).

William Fynderne of Childrey, knight of the shire for Berkshire in May 1421, 1422, 1433, and 1435, was possessed of no more than £20 of landed income in Essex when (probably soon after 1418) he married the daughter and coheir of Thomas Childrey and widow of Sir John Kingston and so came into more property in Berkshire, Wiltshire, Dorset, and Cambridgeshire. A lawyer Fynderne sat on a huge number of local royal commissions of various sorts from 1412 onwards, and as an administrator in the offices of sheriff and escheator he must have been almost unique : from the beginning of 1417 to the close of 1432 he spent nearly half the time in one or the other position and his administrative activities at one time or another covered eight shires ; in 1416–17 he was escheator in Hertfordshire and Essex, in 1417–18 and 1424–5 sheriff of Wiltshire, in 1425–6 escheator in Wiltshire and Hampshire, in 1426–7 sheriff of Somerset and Dorset, in 1429–30 escheator in Oxfordshire and Berkshire, in 1431–2 sheriff of Oxfordshire and Berkshire (*C.F.R., passim*). He had been j.p. and of the quorum in both Oxfordshire and Berkshire from 12 February 1422 until the summer of 1423, and from then in Berkshire alone until his death in 1444. Fynderne was involved in much ' purchasing' of estates either as a directly interested party or as feoffee to uses : one of the most interesting of his memberships of trusts was his association in 1417 with John Leventhorpe and Robert Darcy, both of whom were to sit in the 1422 parliament, as their co-feoffee in the reversion of certain Essex estates, acting on behalf of Henry V's grandmother, Joan Bohun, dowager countess of Hereford ; the Bohun inheritance came up for partition in the parliament of May 1421 and for complete settlement in 1422, on both of which occasions Fynderne was returned as knight of the shire (*Cal. of Ancient Deeds*, III. C.2967,

C.3007). He was feoffee to his nephew-in-law, William Darell (the friend and executor of Bishop Thomas Polton of Hereford ; feoffee to Walter Lord Hungerford and his under-treasurer of England in 1426 ; knight of the shire for Wilts in 1427, 1431, and 1432 ; sheriff of Kent in 1416–17, of Wilts in 1420–3 and 1427–8, and of Oxfordshire and Berkshire in 1432–3 ; and brother of John Darell, steward and nephew-in-law of Archbishop Chichele) (*ibid.*, II. C.2584 ; *Cal. Inq. p.m.*, IV. 107, 323), and he was also the feoffee of John Golafre of Fyfield (Berks) (*V.C.H., Berks*, IV. 308), with whom he had been elected for Berkshire to the parliaments of May 1421 and 1422.

Richard Galon, ' gentleman ' of Essex, formerly of Northumberland, m.p. for Maldon in 1413, 1419, 1420, 1422, 1423, 1425, 1426, 1431, and 1433, may have been the —— Galion admitted to membership of Lincoln's Inn prior to 1420 (*Admission Book, op. cit.*) ; he was feoffee with Robert Darcy of Maldon and other lawyers in an Essex estate of Joan Dame Abergavenny, one of the Fitz Alan coheirs (*C.P.R., 1422–9, 486*).

William Gascoigne, m.p. for Bridgwater in 1406, 1407, 1410, 1413, April and November 1414, 1417, 1419, 1420, May and December 1421, and 1422, acted in 1408 as attorney for a London mercer in the levying of a fine in the Common Bench relating to certain Somerset estates (*Somerset R.S., Trans., op. cit.*, XXII. 31). On 30 September 1422 he acted as an attorney in the Upper Exchequer for the two bailiffs of Bridgwater (Exchequer, L.T.R., Mem. Roll, 1 Hen. VI, P.R.O., E.368/195).

John Gerard esquire of Bryn (Lancs) and Kingsley (Cheshire), knight of the shire for Lancashire in 1422, was the son of a knight of the shire of 1384, 1388, and 1394, Sir Thomas Gerard, who died in 1416 with estates in Lancashire alone worth £150 a year. John was then stated to be thirty years old (*Abstracts of the Inquisitions post mortem for Lancashire, 1297–1637*, Chetham Society, O.S., XCV. 123). He married Alice, daughter of Sir John Botiller of Warrington, who had been knight of the shire in ten parliaments between 1366 and 1398, a retainer of John of Gaunt, and Gerard's superior lord of his manor of Windhill (*D.K.R.*, XXXVII, App. II. 196). Sir William Botiller, his brother-in-law, who had been knight of the shire in 1406 and who was to die at the siege of Harfleur in 1415, made John Gerard one of his feoffees. Botiller's widow married William Lord Ferrers of Groby who was summoned to parliament from 1396 to 1445 (*The Complete Peerage*, ed. V. Gibbs and H. A. Doubleday, V. 354–7). Gerard was made a j.p. in Lancashire in March 1418 (Chetham Library, Piccope Mss., VII. 326), and very occasionally served as a local commissioner of array, but his career was very undistinguished. He died on 6 November 1431, the writs of diem clausit extremum issuing in Cheshire on 10 December 1431 and in Lancashire on 22 January 1432 (*D.K.R.*, XXXIII. 32 ; XXXVII, App. II. 301). His heir, Peter, then aged twenty-four years, was knight of the shire for Lancashire in 1445. (For more about the Gerards of Bryn, see my *Knights of the Shire for the County Palatine of Lancaster (1377–1460)*, Chetham Society, N.S., Vol. 96, 65–70, 155–7, 191–2.)

William Gerard, m.p. for Wareham in November 1414, 1417, 1419, 1420, May and December 1421, 1422, and 1423, and for Melcombe Regis in 1425, was party to several Dorset fines, possibly as a lawyer, between 1435 and 1441 (E. A. and G. S. Fry, *op. cit.,* 345, 354-5, 358). He attested the Dorset elections in 1425 and 1430.

Robert Gilbert, m.p. for Gloucester in 1415, 1419, May and December 1421, 1422, 1425, 1427, and 1432, was for twenty years from 1416 of the quorum of the commission of the peace in Gloucs. He was a member, and in 1424-5 one of the governors, of Lincoln's Inn (*Admission Book of Lincoln's Inn,* 2 ; *Black Book of Lincoln's Inn* [Lincoln's Inn Record Society], 2). He was escheator Gloucs, 1412-13, 1416-17, 1428-30. He was parliamentary proxy to the abbot of Gloucester in 1416 (P.R.O., S.C.10, No. 2253).

John Giles was parliamentary burgess for Old Sarum in 1417, for Calne in 1422 and 1423, for Wilton in 1425, for Devizes in 1431, 1432, and 1435. By 1425 at latest and until sometime between November 1442 and 1446 Giles was clerk of the peace in Wilts (Putnam, *op. cit.,* 25 ; P.R.O., E.101. 594/29).

Thomas Godstone, m.p. for Colchester in 1399, 1402, 1407, 1411, 1413, November 1414, 1417, 1419, 1420, May and December 1421, 1422 and 1427, was a brother of John Godstone, mercer of London, the collector of customs at Ipswich from Henry V's accession until January 1421, and m.p. for Colchester in 1425. Thomas had been appointed for life on 1 February 1397 as high bailiff of Guînes in the march of Picardy, and as victualler of the castle of Guînes, and, although he was superseded in the latter office at the beginning of Henry V's reign, he continued to hold the bailiwick until his death in 1432 (*C.P.R., 1399-1401,* 62 ; *D.K.R.,* XLIV. *App.,* 547, 549 ; XLVII. *App.,* 285). He was one of the two bailiffs of Colchester in 1398-9, 1401-2, 1404-5, 1406-7, 1411-12, 1413-14, 1415-16, 1417-18, 1419-20, 1421-2, 1423-4, 1425-6, and 1429-30 (W. Gurney Benham, *Oath Book of Colchester,* 85-106).

John Golafre of Fyfield, knight of the shire for Oxfordshire in September 1397 ; for Berkshire in 1401, October 1404, 1407, 1410, 1413, April 1414, March 1416, May 1421, 1422, 1426, 1426, 1427, and 1429. The son of Thomas Golafre esquire, John inherited modest estates in mid-Berkshire, but by successive marriages with the widows of Sir Ingelram Bruyn (she was niece of Michael first earl of Suffolk, half-sister of Sir Walter de la Pole, m.p. Cambs in 1422, and sister-in-law to Robert James, m.p. Bucks in 1422), John Englefeld, and Sir Walter de la Pole, he accumulated considerable estates in various counties (Lipscomb, *Bucks,* I. 395). An effectual entrée to the court of Richard II was doubtless secured him by his bastard cousin, Sir John Golafre of Langley (Oxon), knight of the King's Chamber from the beginning of Richard's reign. Sir John died in 1396 (and was buried at the king's instance in the royal chapel in the abbey of Westminster), but on 5 December 1395 John Golafre esquire had already been retained by the king at a fee of 40 marks a year charged on the Exchequer (*C.P.R., 1399-1401,* 42 ; Lipscomb, *loc. cit.* ; Nicolas, *Testamenta Vetusta,* I. 135 ; Oxford Hist. Soc., XVII. 340, 411). His cousin's widow, Philippa, married the son and heir of the duke of York and this connexion probably emphasised Golafre's identification with the Court party. In the autumn of 1397, after the king's acts of revenge against the chief of the Lords Appellant of 1388, he was made sheriff of Oxon and Berks, a post he held until the revolution of 1399, and he was one of the commissioners authorised to exercise parliamentary powers when the first parliament in which he served as knight of the shire was dissolved at Shrewsbury in January 1398 (*Rot. Parl.*, III. 360b, 368b, 383a). In the summer of 1399 he stuck by Richard and was placed in custody, but later he accommodated himself to the accession of Henry IV and was allowed to continue to act as sheriff until a successor could be appointed. On 30 October 1399 his royal annuities were confirmed (as they were to be again on the accessions of Henry V and Henry VI), namely, the fee of 40 marks and an additional fee of £10 from the royal mills at Oxford, enjoyed since April 1398 (*Chronique de la Traison*, App. E.292 ; *C.F.R., 1399–1405*, 1, 2 ; *C.P.R., 1399–1401*, 42). He was dropped from the commission of peace for Oxfordshire but served on other more casual royal commissions, and in 1404 was again j.p., now in Berks, and served again as sheriff of Oxon and Berks in 1404–5. He was to act continuously as j.p. in Berks until his death except, as a result of a short period of service in Normandy, from November 1417 to February 1422. He was again to act as sheriff of Oxon and Berks in 1414–15 and 1424–5, and as escheator in these counties in 1409–10 (*List of Sheriffs*, 108 ; *List of Escheators*, 119 ; *C.P.R., passim*). As early as July 1408 he was connected with Thomas Chaucer (*vide supra*, pp. 165–7), whom he made one of his feoffees (*C.C.R., 1405–9*, 400), and with whom for others (e.g. the Stonores) and for whom himself, he acted as feoffee. Chaucer was farming the royal manor of Woodstock as part of the dower of Henry IV's queen, Joan of Navarre, when on 5 September 1413 Golafre was granted for life the offices of controller and overseer of the manor and park and keeper of the gardens and meadows there (*C.P.R., 1413–16*, 92), in which he was confirmed by the Council in February 1423 (*ibid., 1422–9*, 71). On the eve of Henry V's second landing in Normandy, Golafre became one of the feoffees of Chaucer's son-in-law to be, Thomas Montague, earl of Salisbury, and such he remained until the earl's untimely end at Orleans in 1428 (*ibid., 1416–22*, 140 ; *V.C.H., Berks*, II. 136). He probably crossed the Channel himself with the royal expedition (he had been sheriff during Henry V's first campaign), for on 20 May 1418 he was at Caen when Henry V appointed him receiver-general for the duchy of Normandy and all occupied France to hold office under the president of the Exchequer of Normandy. He was superseded on 21 June 1419 (*D.K.R.*, XLI. 712 ; XLII. 320), remained in France certainly until the autumn, but was back in England by the spring of 1420 when he and Chaucer began to farm the Berkshire manor of Bradfield during the minority of a Crown ward ; they were still enjoying the custody in February 1423 (*C.F.R., 1413–22*, 338 ; Receipt Rolls, Exchequer, P.R.O., E.403, No. 14). In July 1426 Golafre became a feoffee to uses of John Holand earl of Huntingdon with a view to the arrangement of an entail as part of the settlement of the earl's marriage to the dowager countess of March (*C.C.R., 1422–9*, 274), and in these years he was feoffee to many other holders of land of lesser importance, especially in Berkshire. His feoffeeship to Chaucer of Ewelme (ob. 1434) ensured a doubtless profitable connexion with Chaucer's daughter and heir and her third husband William earl of Suffolk, and he was involved in certain of the latter's conveyances.

The attachment could only be intensified by his own third marriage to the widow of Suffolk's cousin, Sir Walter de la Pole, sometime after July 1434 ; the connexion bore fruit in Golafre's association with the earl and countess in the custody of the royal park of Cornbury (Oxon) ' pro deductu suo ' but with 3 pence a day wages and other perquisites (*C.P.R.*, *1436–41*, 309). After his death without issue on 23 February 1442 his feoffees eventually conveyed his manors of Fyfield, East Hanney, and Garford, and Eaton, to the earl and countess (*V.C.H.*, *Berks*, IV. 346). In the last two decades of his life especially, Golafre had served locally in the middle Thames area on a multiplicity of royal commissions, particularly commissions for the raising of Crown loans to which he himself made considerable contributions.

John Gonne, m.p. for Bridgwater in 1422 and 1437, acted from 12 July 1421 until February 1423 as one of the two collectors of customs and subsidies and as joint-controller of tronage and pesage of staple goods at Bridgwater (*C.F.R.*, *1413–22*, 380, 381, 383 ; *C.P.R.*, *1416–22*, 378). He was one of the four making the electoral returns for Bridgwater to the county court of Somerset prior to the parliaments of 1420, 1421, 1426, 1427, 1429, 1431, 1432, and 1435 (P.R.O., C.219, Bundles 12–14). On 20 December 1429 he was appointed a collector in Somerset of a double parliamentary tenth and fifteenth (*C.F.R.*, *1422–30*, 293, 330).

John Green ; parliamentary baron for Sandwich 1422, 1423, 1427, 1432, 1445, 1455 ; shipowner (*C.P.R.*, *1429–36*, 73) ; was mayor of Sandwich 1431–2, 1453–4, 1455–6 (W. Boys, *Sandwich Collections*, 156, 370, 416, 671).

Sir John Gresley of Colton near Rugeley, knight of the shire for Staffordshire in 1422 and 1427, was the eldest son of Sir Thomas Gresley of Drakelow (Derbyshire), knight of the shire four times for Derbyshire and twice for Staffs between 1401 and 1421, at the time of Sir John's first return to parliament in 1422 sheriff of Staffs, and j.p. in Derbyshire and Staffs. The family was of considerable importance, administratively and socially, in the north midlands. Sir John's sister, Joan, married Thomas Astley, a great-grandson of Guy Beauchamp earl of Warwick, ' the black cur of Arden ', and so a kinsman of Richard earl of Warwick, whose position (by Henry V's deathbed appointment) as tutor to Henry VI probably accounts for Joan's employment from January 1424 as the baby king's nurse. Another sister, Margaret, married Sir Thomas Blount, m.p. for Derbyshire in 1420, who followed the duke of Bedford in France and in 1429 was appointed treasurer of Calais. A third sister, Innocence, married John Curzon, m.p. for Derbyshire in 1423, 1429, 1432, and 1435. Their cousin, another Margaret, married William Babthorpe, attorney-general to the Crown from 1419 to 1429. Sir John himself was married in 1410 to Elizabeth, a daughter of Sir Thomas Clarell of Aldwark and Tickhill (Yorks) ; her brother was sheriff of Lincolnshire at the time of Sir John's election to Henry VI's first parliament. His second marriage was with a daughter of a Coventry merchant who had been successively the wife of a son of Sir John Massey of Tatton (Cheshire) and John de Delves, m.p. for Staffs in 1426 (F. Madan, *The Gresleys of Drakelow*, 47, 225, 235, 245 ; S. Shaw, *History and Antiquities of Staffs*, II. 284). An undated petition to the Commons that they should procure his reinstatement to the wardenship of the chace of Duffield Frith, to which he had been appointed for life on 4 August 1420 (this chace was parcel of the Lancastrian honour of Tutbury, in which his father was already bailiff and receiver for the High Peak, and over which Sir John's first wife's uncle, Sir Nicholas Montgomery the younger, was steward), but from which he was ousted early in 1424, pleaded eighteen years' service with Henry V and seven years' war service in France and Normandy, for which he had had no fee or reward other than the master-forestership in question (Ancient Petitions, P.R.O., S.C.8, File 114, No. 5698 ; Ministers' Accounts, Duchy of Lancaster, P.R.O., D.L.29, Bundle 402, No. 6451). If his plea was correct, Sir John must have attached himself to Henry V when he was prince of Wales as early as 1404. Certainly he and his father served in the Agincourt campaign with five lances and fifteen archers and Sir John again crossed the Channel in the second expeditionary force in July 1417 (H. Nicolas, *The Battle of Agincourt*, 380 ; *D.K.R.*, XLIV. 568 ; XLI. 711, 716). He was back in England, probably returning in the king's retinue, in the spring of 1421, when he was present at his father's last election to parliament in the county court at Derby, and again in 1422 when he was himself returned, but he must soon afterwards have gone back to France, where as a knight bachelor he served in the retinue of the Regent, the duke of Bedford. By May 1435 he had risen to the position of lieutenant-general to the vicomte of Rouen (J. Stevenson, *Wars of the English in France* [Rolls Series], II. Part I, 41, 277 ; Part II, 436). Following Bedford's death in September 1435 he seems to have retired completely from military service overseas to a life of comparatively no administrative activity, although he was sheriff of Staffordshire in 1439–40 (*List of Sheriffs*, 127). In 1447, soon after he had succeeded his father at Drakelow, he came to terms with his neighbours in Derbyshire, the Vernons, following a great dispute over pasturage rights (*Hist. Mss. Comm., Rutland Mss.*, IV. 29). Sir John did not long survive his father and died on 17 January 1449. His son and heir, John, m.p. for Staffs in 1450 and 1453 and for Derbyshire in 1460, seems at first to have followed the political line of his influential cousin, Sir Walter Blount K.G., a keen Yorkist partisan who fought at Towton in 1461, was destined to be Lord Treasurer in 1465, and was then raised to the peerage as Lord Mountjoy (he had been one of Sir John Gresley's executors) ; but in 1461, little more than a fortnight after Edward IV's legal recognition, he was helping four Lancastrian retainers to hurry to join Henry VI and his queen in Yorkshire. He had married a daughter of Thomas Stanley of Elford, with whom his father had been returned to Henry VI's first parliament. Another sign of his family's continued social importance had been his daughter Thomasine's marriage to the son of John Darell of Coleshill (Kent), a great-nephew (on his mother's side) of Archbishop Henry Chichele (F. Madan, *op. cit.*, 47, 248 ; *William Salt Society, Trans.*, N.S., III. 217).

John Greville esquire, of Chipping Campden and Sezincote, knight of the shire for Gloucestershire in April 1414, 1419, May 1421, 1422, 1423, 1425, and 1427, was the elder son of William Greville of Chipping Campden, the well-to-do Cotswold wool-merchant, whose brass, in the church he helped to rebuild there, proclaims him to have been ' quondam civis Londonie et flos mercatorum lanarum tocius Anglie '. John seems to have begun his career in his father's calling, perhaps as his partner or agent : in October 1395 both of them, as wool-merchants of Campden, took out royal letters of pardon for all sharp practices in their wool-buying (*C.P.R., 1391–6*, 627 ; *Trans. of the Bristol and Gloucs. Arch. Soc.*, IX. 177). The father had followed a policy of investing surplus profits in land—before his death in October 1401 he had bought up the manors of Milcote (Warwicks) and Meen and Pebworth (Gloucs) as well as 14 messuages and land in Campden, —and John Greville's sister's marriage with the lord of the manor of Campden (Edward Ludlow), to whom Greville was feoffee in 1409, and his own marriage with Sybil, daughter and heir of Sir Robert Corbet of Hadley (Shropshire), were significant of the family's rise into the ranks of the gentry ; John Greville's father-in-law's death in 1417 brought him the manors of King's Bromley (Staffs), Hadley (Shropshire), Ebrington and Farmcote (Gloucs), Denchworth and Tubney (Berks), and Assington (Suffolk). After his first wife's death in 1425 Greville married Joyce, daughter of Sir Walter Cokesay of Witley (Worcs) (W. R. Williams, *Parliamentary History of Gloucs*, 32 ; S. Rudder, *A New History of Gloucs*, 599 ; Index Library, Vol. XLVII, *Gloucs Inquests post mortem*, 229 ; *Feudal Aids*, I. 63 ; *C.C.R., 1413–19*, 401, 403–4 ; J. Edmondson, *The Family of Greville*, 4). From 1403 Greville served on many and increasingly numerous local royal commissions in Gloucs and from 1416 to 1439 acted continuously as j.p. (*C.P.R. passim*) ; he was sheriff of Gloucs in 1404–5 (on 10 February 1406 he was granted 20 marks in consideration of the trouble he had been put to as sheriff in labouring in person with a greater number of people than his estate could maintain, and in arraying at his own costs at different times the fencibles of the shire to go on the king's wars into Wales), in 1415–17, and in 1425–6, and he was escheator in 1406–7, 1408–9, 1413–14, and in 1418–19. Greville had some influential con-nexions : his first return to parliament may well have occurred in 1410, when the bishop of Worcester appointed him to be one of his parliamentary proxies (the Gloucs returns to this parliament have been lost) ; just before his death in 1417 Thomas Lord Berkeley made Greville one of his feoffees, and it is possible that Greville's bond of 20 November 1420 to pay the earl of Warwick 500 marks was to ensure that his intentions were favourable to the Beauchamp interest in the dispute between the earl and Berkeley's nephew and heir male, James, who was summoned to parliament from December 1420 ; in 1440 Greville (or perhaps his son) was receiving from the latter a fee of retainer of 13 marks from the Berkeley manor of Alkington (P.R.O., S.C.10, No. 2162 ; *C.C.R., 1419–22*, 122 ; I. A. Jeayes, *Catalogue of Muniments at Berkeley Castle*, 184 ; John Smyth of Nibley, *Lives of the Berkeleys*, II. 77). But Greville's most important aristo-cratic tie must undoubtedly have been that resulting from his occupation of the office of receiver-general in England to the elder of Henry V's two surviving brothers, John, duke of Bedford. Greville was Bedford's chief financial agent by May 1420 at the latest, and he was still exercising this office in 1426 and had done so in the meantime (Exchequer, Issue Rolls, P.R.O., E.403/645, Mems. 1, 8 ; E.403/646, Mem. 4 ; E.403/649, Mem. 4 ; E.403/655, Mem. 12). How long afterwards he administered this position is not known. He died in 1444.

Robert Halsewell, m.p. for Lyme in 1422 and 1425 ; for Bridgwater in 1433 ; for Taunton in 1437. He was appointed on 12 July 1428 controller of customs and subsidies at Southampton (*C.P.R., 1422–9,* 447) ; he was still acting as receiver of Bishop Sydenham of Chichester, his cousin, at midsummer 1438, shortly after the bishop's death. He was also one of his executors. (E. F. Jacob, *Chichele Register,* II. 559–60 ; *Black Book of Lincoln's Inn,* I. 8.)

John Harpour, m.p. for Stafford in 1419, 1420, May 1421, 1422, 1423, 1425, 1427, and 1429, and knight of the shire for Staffordshire in 1431, was by 1435 feoffee to Humphrey earl of Stafford and acted in that capacity for the rest of his life (*C.P.R., 1429–36,* 466 ; *1436–41,* 527 ; *1441–6,* 133 ; *1446–52,* 78 ; *1461–7,* 91 ; *C.C.R., 1422–9,* 318 ; J. Gage, *History of Thingoe Hundred, Suffolk,* 179) ; by 1437 he was steward of the earl's estates (B.M., Additional Charter, 19859). In 1436 he was retained as counsel by his former ward, William Mutton, one of the Stafford mesne tenants and m.p. Staffs 1447 (*C.C.R., 1435–41,* 130), and by 1444 was acting as steward of the abbot of St. Werburgh of Chester at Weston-on-Trent (Stebbing Shaw, *History and Antiquities of Staffordshire,* II. 63).

John Hasting, m.p. for Great Yarmouth in 1422, was master of a dogger (*C.C.R., 1413–19,* 7 ; *C.P.R., 1416–22,* 89) ; he was one of the 4 bailiffs of Great Yarmouth 1417–18, 1420–1, 1424–5, and a j.p. in the borough, 1433–4 (Blomefield, *op. cit.,* X. 324–5).

Sir Edmund Hastings of Roxby (North Yorks) and Edlingham (Northumberland) knight of the shire for Northumberland and Yorkshire together in 1407, and for Yorkshire in 1413, May 1421, 1422, and 1427, came of a long-established North Riding family and his marriages (first to Elizabeth, daughter and eventually coheir to Sir John de Felton, and secondly, before November 1415, to Agnes, widow of Sir Ralph Bulmer and daughter and coheir of Sir Thomas Sutton) brought important additions of territory in Northumberland, Durham, and in Holderness (*V.C.H., Yorkshire, North Riding,* II. 469, 495 ; E. Bateson, *History of Northumberland,* VII. 120, 127 ; XII. 372 ; R. Surtees, *History and Antiquities of North Durham,* II. 284 ; *C.F.R., 1399–1405,* 213 ; *1430–7,* 299, 323 ; *C.C.R., 1402–5,* 262). He had served on sundry royal commissions in the north-east in the first half of Henry IV's reign, managing to hold aloof from all movements of disaffection disturbing that part of the realm in spite of the fact that his first wife's brother-in-law, Sir Thomas Fauconberg of Skelton in Cleveland, to whom he was feoffee and to whose wife he had acted as executor in 1402, had incurred forfeiture for his activities in the Scrope-Mowbray rising of 1405. While sitting in the Gloucester parliament of 1407 for both Yorkshire and Northumberland he was appointed royal escheator in Cumberland and Westmorland and served for a year. In 1409–10 he was sheriff of Yorkshire. After sitting for Yorkshire in Henry V's first parliament he spent the period 20 November 1413–7 April 1414 in the Tower (*C.C.R., 1413–19,* 42, 122) following complaint by John Neville Lord Latimer of Danby in Cleveland to the Chancellor that after the divorce of his wife (Maud, daughter of Thomas sixth Lord Clifford, who proceeded to marry Richard earl of Cambridge) his feoffees, of whom Hastings had been one since 1406, refused to restore his estates. Lord Latimer was half-brother to Ralph Neville, first earl of Westmorland, but after this trouble Hastings seems to have remained on good terms with the Neville family : in November 1422 he was acting as one of the feoffees for the fulfilment of the will of Elizabeth, wife of the earl's eldest son, Sir John Neville (*P.P.C.*, III. 20). Moreover, he had connexions with the Nevilles through the marriage of his wife's niece, Jane Fauconberg, with the earl's eighth son, William. How long he had been associated with another important north-country baronial family, the Greystokes, is not clear, but he was one of the overseers of the will of John Lord Greystoke who died on 8 August 1436 (Surtees Society, *Wills and Inventories*, 86). That the reasons for his spell of imprisonment in the Tower in the winter of 1413–14 were of a largely private character is clear from his appointment in November 1414 as sheriff of Northumberland, an office he served until 1 December 1415 ; in 1416–17 he was again sheriff of Yorkshire and then, in 1418–19, he was sheriff of Northumberland again. He served at this time as j.p. in the North Riding for a year only, but his reappointment in February 1422 began a ten years' membership of the commission of the peace. He served on numerous royal commissions of a casual nature in Henry V's reign but on few in Henry VI's, although he lived on until 8 August 1448, when he must have been of a good age. His eldest son, John, had predeceased him and his heir was his grandson, Edmund (E. Bateson, *History of Northumberland*, VII. 127 ; *D.K.R.*, XLIV. 409).

John Hawley, m.p. for Dartmouth in 1410, 1411, 1413, November 1414, May 1421, 1422, 1423, 1425, 1427, 1429, 1431 and 1432, was the son and heir of John Hawley, a prosperous West-Country merchant, twelve times mayor of Dartmouth 1376–1400 and deputy-admiral at the end of Richard II's reign, and was grandson of Chief Justice Tresilian, a victim of the Appellants in 1388 (J. Maclean, *History of Trigg Minor*, I. 394 ; G. Worthy, *Devonshire Parishes*, I. 369). In June 1401 he was controller of tunnage and poundage at London (*C.P.R.*, *1399–1401*, 468) ; from 20 February 1403 until his death in May 1437 he was duchy of Cornwall feodar and escheator in Devon and Cornwall (*ibid.*, *1401–5* 213 ; *1413–16*, 256 ; *1422–9*, 285 ; *1436–41*, 56). In the second half of Henry IV's reign, with his father, he was heavily involved in piratical ventures controlled from Dartmouth at the expense of Spanish, Breton, and Flemish shipping, but both were royal commissioners of inquiry into similar depredations (*C.P.R.*, and *C.C.R.*, *passim*). In Michs. 1411–12 he was under-sheriff of Cornwall (*P.R.O.*, Lists and Indexes, IX. 22). From April 1413 to May 1417 and from November 1421 to May 1425 he was collector of customs and subsidies at Dartmouth and Exeter (*C.F.R.*, *1413–22*, 4, 14, 70, 72, 113, 129, 381, 383 ; *1422–30*, 2, 3, 25, 53–4, 60). In May 1419 he was engaged in coastal defence in the Channel (*D.K.R.*, XLIV. 610) and again from April to November 1420 when he indentured to contribute 150 men to a fleet of which he was one of the four leaders (*C.P.R.*, *1416–22*, 319 ; R. A. Newhall, *The English Conquest of Normandy*, *1417–24*, 199). From 12 February 1422 to July 1431 he was j.p. in Cornwall. On 10 December 1422 he was appointed deputy-butler at Dartmouth with royal patent letter of aid (*C.P.R.*, *1422–9*, 8).

John Hipperon, m.p. for Guildford in March 1416 and 1422, was by October 1417, and until at least 1437, clerk of the peace for Surrey (B. H. Putnam, *Early Treatises on the Practice of Justices of the Peace*, 25 ; Exchequer, Sheriffs' Administrative Accounts, P.R.O., E.101. 588/49).

Robert Holme, m.p. for Hull in 1421 (December), 1422, 1423, 1427, 1431, and 1435. From 14 January 1409 to July 1417 he was controller and overseer of the king's searcher in the port of Hull (*C.P.R., 1408–13,* 47 ; *1413–16,* 15) ; he was engaged in the wool trade as a merchant-stapler of the Calais fellowship (*ibid., 1422–9,* 385 ; *C.C.R., 1429–35,* 112).

John Hotoft, esquire, of Knebworth, was knight of the shire for Hertford-shire in 1413, April and November 1414, March 1416, 1417, 1419 and 1422. He was a lawyer and almost certainly the same Hotoft who was a member of Lincoln's Inn (*Admission Book,* 2). By 1411, with £20 a year for life, he was controller of Household to Prince Henry (later Henry V), whose treasurer of Household was rector of Knebworth, the manor and advowson of which Hotoft purchased in this year. Immediately on Henry V's accession on 23 March 1413, Hotoft replaced Robert Darcy (m.p. Maldon, 1422) as clerk of the Court of Common Pleas, with a fee of 10 marks a year (*C.P.R., 1413–16,* 378 ; 1, 54). In January 1414 he became a j.p. in Herts and served for the rest of his life, and on other more casual, especially local Crown-loan, commissions. He was escheator in the year November 1419–20. Early in Henry VI's reign Hotoft resigned his clerkship of the Common Bench when he was appointed on 8 February 1423 as treasurer of the royal Household (*P.P.C.,* III. 25, 286). From November 1428 to February 1430 he acted as sheriff of Essex and Herts. He accompanied Henry VI to France in April 1430 for his coronation at Paris, as treasurer of the Household and occupier of the associated office of treasurer for the war ; he returned to England in October when he was granted an annuity of 100 marks. This he surrendered together with his office as treasurer of the Household when he was appointed on 1 February 1431, during pleasure, to the office of king's chamber-lain of the Exchequer voided by the death of John Wodehouse (m.p. Suffolk, 1422). He was followed as treasurer of the Household by Sir John Tyrell (m.p. Essex 1422). (*List of Sheriffs,* 44 ; *C.P.R., 1422–9,* 543 ; *P.P.C.,* V. 32 ; *ibid.,* 29, 71–2 ; *D.K.R.,* XLVIII. 268). Between 1431 and 1433 he acted as counsel to abbot Whethamstead of St. Albans, to whose confraternity he had been admitted in August 1428 (*Chronicon Rerum Gestarum in Mon. Sti. Albani,* ed. T. H. Riley [Rolls Series], I. 24, 55, 64 ; II. 166–8, 185, 257, 269). On 17 December 1439 his office as chamberlain of the Exchequer was granted him for life (*C.P.R., 1436–41,* 359, 566 ; *1441–6,* 158, 186). Hotoft died in the spring of 1443.

Sir John Howard, knight of the shire for Essex in September 1397, for Cambridgeshire in 1407, and for Suffolk in 1422, grandson of Sir John Howard (admiral in the North, 1335–7), great-great-grandson of Sir William Howard (Justice of Common Pleas in Edward I's reign), succeeded in 1388 on the death of his father (Sir Robert) to considerable estates near Bishop's Lynn and in South Norfolk and elsewhere in East Anglia, and these he proceeded to augment by marrying well : his first wife was Margaret, only daughter and heir to John Baron Plaiz, who brought him property in Essex, Norfolk, Suffolk, and Cam-bridgeshire and died in 1391 ; Howard married for his second wife another East Anglian heiress, Alice, only daughter and heir of Sir William Tendring, and this alliance meant the acquisition of estates in the valley of the Stour, notably Stoke

Nayland (G. Brenan and E. P. Statham, *The House of Howard*, I. 10 *et seq.* ; G. E. Cockayne, *The Complete Peerage*, VI. 253 ; *C.F.R., 1383–91*, 295 ; *1391–9*, 46 ; *C.C.R., 1405–9*, 501 ; *1422–9*, 120, 143, 172 ; Blomefield, *Norfolk*, I. 77, 79–81 ; VIII. 133 ; IX. 87).   Sir John's mother's family connexions probably gave him an easy entry into political life in the last decade of the fourteenth century : the daughter of Robert third Lord Scales, with whose family Sir John maintained a close relationship, she was aunt to Sir Simon Felbrigge K.G., kinsman by marriage with Queen Anne (of Bohemia), knight of the royal Chamber, and standard-bearer to Richard II (*C.C.R., 1405–9*, 501 ; *1422–9*, 120 ; Brenan and Statham, *op. cit.* ; J. H. Wylie, *Henry V*, I. 343 ; Blomefield, *op. cit.*, I. 79 ; VIII. 13, 107). Retained for life at a fee of £40 a year charged on the Exchequer by patent of 10 March 1394, Howard accompanied Richard II on his two Irish expeditions of 1394–5 and 1399.   On 1 December 1396 the joint shrievalty of Essex and Herts was committed to him only to be withdrawn, but in 1397 he was included in the commission of the peace for both Suffolk and Essex.   Although his annuity was discontinued he acted as a j.p. in these counties after the revolution of 1399, in Suffolk until May 1408 and in Essex until December 1414, and he resumed service as j.p. in Suffolk in December 1417 and retained the commission for the rest of his life.   In the meantime he served as sheriff of Essex and Herts in 1400–1, of Cambridgeshire and Huntingdonshire in 1401–3, of Essex and Herts again in 1414–15 and in 1418–19.   In 1399 and 1404 he was steward of the liberty of the great Benedictine abbey of St. Edmund of Bury, but how long he continued to act in this capacity is not known (Blomefield, *op. cit.*, V. 243 n. ; *C.F.R., 1399–1405*, 245).   As his royal commissions show, Sir John kept clear of the seditious activities by which Essex was disturbed in 1403–5, although he was connected with one of the sources of disaffection, the dowager countess of Oxford (the mother of Robert de Vere), who was to appoint Howard as overseer of her will (Lambeth Palace Library, *Arundell Register*, Part II, fo. 161).   In 1410 his eldest son, John, died and Sir John acted with the dowager countess of Hereford, Joan Bohun, mother of Henry IV's first wife, as her fellow-overseer of his son's will.   Young Howard had probably been a member of her household (Somerset House, *Register Marche*, fo. 169ᵛ).   John Howard the younger's only daughter and heir, Sir John Howard's granddaughter, Elizabeth, was to marry shortly before midsummer 1429 John de Vere, earl of Oxford.   Sir John's eldest surviving son by his second marriage, Robert Howard, had already married Margaret, the sister of the then Earl Marshal who was to resume his father's title of duke of Norfolk in 1425 (the marriage probably took place in 1420).   One outcome of this marriage was that the inheritance of the great baronial families of Mowbray and FitzAlan became in part ultimately vested in the Howard family in Sir John's grandson, John Howard, m.p. Norfolk in 1455 and Suffolk in 1467, treasurer of Household to Edward IV from 1468 to 1474, summoned to parliament as Lord Howard in the Readeption parliament of 1470, and created Earl Marshal and duke of Norfolk by Richard III, with whom he died at Bosworth.   On the other side here fought John de Vere, Sir John Howard's great-grandson, whose elder brother and father had both been executed as Lancastrians in 1462.   With the death of the duke of Norfolk ended the feud between Sir John Howard's descendants by his first and second wife respectively, a feud arising out of a disputed settlement of certain of the old Howard estates on the countess of Oxford in Sir John Howard's will of 1435. Sometime in the year after this will was drawn up, Sir John set out at the over-ripe age of about seventy-one years on pilgrimage to the Holy Land and died at Jerusalem on 17 November 1437 (Brenan and Statham, *op. cit.* ; N. H. Nicolas, *Testamenta Vetusta*, I. 211).

Roger Hunt, knight of the shire for Huntingdonshire in 1407, 1413, April 1414, 1417, 1419, May 1421, 1422, 1423, 1425, 1426, 1427, 1429, 1431, 1432, and 1433 (Speaker), and for Bedfordshire in November 1414, March 1416, and 1420 (Speaker), was attached to John Lord Tiptoft during the whole of his political career, but was also connected before Henry V's reign with Reginald Lord Grey of Ruthyn (*C.P.R., 1408–13*, 153), and when, in parliament in May 1425, John Mowbray, the Earl Marshal, entered into a dispute over precedence with the earl of Warwick and Hunt acted as his chief of council and spokesman, on that occasion he stated that ' he hade of long tyme beon of counseill with his seid Lord Erl Mareschall ' (*Rot. Parl.*, IV. 267–75) ; and he later appears as one of the executors, attorneys-general and feoffees of this lord, who was promoted duke of Norfolk in 1425 (F. Blomefield, *Topographical History of Norfolk*, I. 236 ; E. F. Jacob, *Chichele Register*, II. 474). He is probably the Hunt (Christian name not stated) who figures in a list of members of Lincoln's Inn admitted prior to 1420 (*Admission Book of Lincoln's Inn*, 2). Roger Hunt certainly held the post of the King's attorney-general in the court of Common Pleas and other courts from 17 August 1408 until about the end of 1409 (*C.P.R., 1405–8*, 459 ; E. Foss, *The Judges of England*, IV. 138). At the time of his return to parliament in 1422 he was of the quorum for the peace in both Huntingdonshire and Bedfordshire (Patent Roll 9 Hen. V, P.R.O., C.66/404, Mem. 20d). On 5 November 1438, at the instance of Cardinal Beaufort, he was appointed Second Baron of the Exchequer, an office he certainly continued to hold for the next ten years, probably, in fact, until his death, of which the date is unknown (*C.P.R., 1436–41*, 219 ; Exchequer, K.R., Accounts Various, Account-books of the keeper of the Great Wardrobe, P.R.O., E.101/409, 2–18).

Robert James esquire of Wallingford and Boarstall (Bucks), knight of the shire for Berkshire in January 1397, 1399, 1402, and 1410, and for Buckingham-shire in October 1404, May 1421, 1422. He was born in 1366, the son of John James of Wallingford, some time receiver-general to the Sire de Courcy, earl of Bedford, and son-in-law of Edward III, who adhered to his French allegiance in 1377 and resigned his English estates, and m.p. for Wallingford on five occasions (1365–76), knight of the shire for Oxfordshire in January 1377, and for Berkshire in 1380, and sheriff of the two counties in 1373 and 1380. Robert James's estates in Berkshire and Oxfordshire received considerable additions in Oxfordshire and Bucks by his marriage before 1385 with Catherine, daughter of Sir Edmund de la Pole and niece of Michael first earl of Suffolk (*C.P.R., 1374–7*, 237, 477 ; *V.C.H.*, Berks, IV. 548 ; J. K. Hedges, *History of Wallingford*, II. 27 ; Lipscomb, *Bucks*, I. 61 ; *C.C.R., 1419–22*, 20–1 ; Oxford Historical Society, LXXXVIII. 121). His connexions with the De la Poles were strong : from 1391 he acted as feoffee to Sir Michael, the son and heir of the first earl who had incurred for-feiture in 1388 (Sir Michael was restored to the earldom in 1397 and confirmed in this dignity in 1399) (*C.C.R., 1389–92*, 501 ; *ibid., 1391–96*, 111, 130, 150,

357, 359, 502–3), and he was attorney for his brother-in-law, Sir Walter de la Pole (m.p. Cambs 1422), when the latter accompanied Richard II to Ireland in 1394 and 1399 (*C.P.R.*, *1391–6*, 472 ; *ibid.*, *1396–9*, 552). By his first marriage John Golafre of Berks was James's brother-in-law and he made James his feoffee ; James reciprocated this trust (*Ancient Deeds*, III. 565 ; Oxford Historical Society, LXXXVIII. 266, 285). They were both feoffees to Thomas Chaucer of Ewelme who acted in the same capacity for James (*C.P.R.*, *1413–16*, 169 ; *1429–36*, 448, 451 ; *C.C.R.*, *1413–19*, 56). Until his father-in-law Sir Edmund de la Pole's death in 1418 James was his tenant in certain Oxfordshire and Bucks estates, and then after that date he held them *jure uxoris*, and these estates included the royal foresterships in fee of Shotover and Stowood (Oxon) and Bernwood (Bucks). He does not, however, seem to have ever enjoyed any Crown annuities, although he was active enough in its employment, serving as escheator in Oxfordshire in 1400–1, as sheriff of Oxfordshire and Berks in 1402–3, as escheator in Oxfordshire and Berkshire in 1407–8 and 1413–14 and in Bedfordshire and Bucks in 1415–16, and as sheriff again in Oxfordshire and Berks in 1416–17 and once more in 1428–9. From February 1407 he was j.p. in Oxfordshire (never, curiously enough, in Bucks or Berks) until his death on 16 February 1432 (*List of Escheators*, 5, 118–19 ; *List of Sheriffs*, 108 ; *C.P.R.*, *passim*). His will was proved in the Prerogative Court of Canterbury on 22 February 1432 (*Chichele Register*, II. 187).

William Kyrton, m.p. for Southwark in November 1414, 1417, 1420, 1422, and 1425, by June 1423 and at the time of his death in the summer of 1428 was a coroner in Surrey (*C.C.R.*, *1422–9*, 413 ; King's Bench, Ancient Indictments, P.R.O., K.B., 9, 218).

John Lancastre esquire, knight of the shire for Suffolk in 1407, 1410, 1411, and 1413, and for Norfolk in 1419, May and December 1421, and 1422, was closely attached to the old baronial family of Mowbray whose marriage alliance in the middle of the fourteenth century with the daughter of the heiress of Thomas Brotherton, half-brother of Edward II, brought it again into the first rank of the English aristocracy and secured for it the title and estates of the Bigod earls of Norfolk and the hereditary office of Earl Marshal of England. Lancastre's marriage with the daughter and heir of Sir John de Boyland made him a tenant of the Mowbrays in the manor of Boyland Hall in the mid-East Anglian township of Bressingham, but this was probably the result rather than the cause of his connexion with the Mowbrays. He doubtless owed his appointment in October 1393 as captain of the castle of Marck in the Picardy marches to the Earl Marshal, Thomas Mowbray's then occupation of the office of King's lieutenant in Calais, Picardy, Flanders, and Artois. He was still captain of Marck when in September 1397 he was closely involved in the circumstances of the murder of Thomas of Woodstock which took place at Calais with the Earl Marshal's connivance (Blomefield, *Norfolk*, I. 12 ; *Feudal Aids*, III. 560 ; *C.P.R.*, *1391–6*, 318 ; *1396–9*, 381 ; *Rot. Parl.*, III. 378, 431, 453). Almost precisely a year later the Earl Marshal, now duke of Norfolk, was banished for life when prepared to settle an accusation of treason, made against him by the future Henry IV, in the lists at Coventry. Two days before this judgement, Lancastre had been granted by the Duke at Coventry on 14 September 1398 an annuity of 20 marks for life charged on the

Mowbray manor of Willington (Beds). On 3 October he was one of his eight continuous counsellors licensed by royal patent to act as the duke's attorneys-general during his exile, but these letters were revoked on 24 March 1399 after the death of the duchess of Norfolk, the Earl Marshal's grandmother. In the meantime on 6 November 1398 Lancastre and another of the duke's attorneys had tendered to the chancellor in Westminster Hall an indenture attesting the departure of Mowbray from Kirkley Roads (*C.P.R., 1396-9*, 422 ; *Rot. Parl.*, III. 384). Although Thomas Mowbray died just before his rival Bolingbroke secured the throne, John Lancastre continued to identify himself with the Mowbray interest. On 25 May 1400 he secured a royal confirmation of his Willington annuity and in July 1402 and in May 1403 he was one of several men connected with the family who, doubtless acting as the young Earl Marshal's agents during his minority, leased at the Exchequer some of the Mowbray estates (but excluding the dower) at farms amounting to some £224 a year, and Lancastre stood surety for the young earl when he secured the farm of Dunwich (*C.P.R., 1399-1401*, 294 ; *C.F.R., 1399-1405*, 162, 208-9, 212-13). How Lancastre fared in the Earl Marshal's active participation in the revolt of 1405 which cost him his life is not known, but he lost his office of constable of Framlingham castle (now the first Mowbray residence) and the custody of the park there in the subsequent forfeitures, retaining however his Willington annuity. A little later he took out letters of protection as a member of the retinue of John Beaufort earl of Somerset, captain of Calais, whose wife was a Holland and cousin to the recently widowed countess of Norfolk, but these letters were revoked on 22 May 1406 (*C.P.R., 1405-8*, 86, 186). In 1407, 1410, and 1411 he was shire-knight for Suffolk, and attended the elections for Norfolk to this last proper parliament of Henry IV. His Mowbray connexions were still as strong as ever : as counsel to the late Earl Marshal's brother and heir, John, he was party early in 1413 to the marriage of the widowed countess to the son and heir of Lord Grey of Ruthin and sat again for Suffolk in Henry V's first parliament (*C.C.R., 1409-13*, 434), and in the spring of 1415 he was one of the Earl Marshal's feoffees when he began to make preparations for the first of Henry V's French campaigns (*C.P.R., 1413-16*, 319, 333 ; Blomefield, *op. cit.*, V. 198, 328, 449 ; A. Suckling, *Suffolk*, I. 268 ; R. Loder, *The History of Framlingham*, 394). During the earl's absences abroad, he acted as one of his attorneys-general. By 1423 and probably during the greater part of Henry V's reign, Lancastre was steward of the lordship of Framlingham. From time to time his influence was useful to the citizens of Norwich (J. C. Tingey, *Records of the City of Norwich*, II. 58-62 ; Blomefield, *op. cit.*, III. 126). The will of Isabel, widow of William Ufford, second earl of Suffolk, who had died in 1382, appointed him in 1416 her executor ; and in 1417 he was an administrator of the will of Thomas Lord Morley who was at his death captain-general of the forces in France. In April 1421 he was one of Robert Lord Willoughby of Eresby's feoffees (Blomefield, *op. cit.*, II. 470 ; VIII. 58 ; *C.C.R., 1419-22*, 198 ; E. F. Jacob, *Chichele Register*, II. 96, 113). In Henry V's reign he had served on numerous local commissions by royal patent, as sheriff of Norfolk and Suffolk from 1 December 1415 until 20 February 1416 and for the whole financial year 1416-17, and as escheator in Norfolk and Suffolk in 1418-19. From early in 1416 until the end of the reign he was a j.p. in Norfolk and in July 1423 was made a j.p. in Suffolk ; in November following he was appointed sheriff again but rendered no account in the Exchequer. He very probably died in this year, because there is no further notice of him.

John Langley, m.p. for Chippenham in 1422 and knight of the shire for Gloucs in 1429, 1432, 1435, 1437, and 1442, was of the quorum of the peace for Gloucs in 1422-3, and was serving again in 1432-9 and 1441-58. He was counsel to Maurice de la River esq., with an annuity of £1 (*C.C.R., 1435-41*, 130).

Thomas Lavington, m.p. for Reading in March 1416, 1417, 1420, May 1421, 1422, 1423, 1425, 1427, 1429, 1431, 1435, and 1442, j.p. for Berkshire in 1448-9 and in 1452-4, was cousin, 'servant', and executor of Thomas Polton, bishop of Worcester (*Letters of Queen Margaret of Anjou*, etc., ed. C. Munro, Camden Society, 1863, p. 14 ; E. F. Jacob, *Chichele Register*, II. 202 ; *C.P.R., 1436-41*, 321).

Sir Robert de Laybourne of Conswick near Kendal, knight of the shire for Westmorland in October 1404, 1411, and 1422, held lands in that county that were stated in 1436 to be worth only £53 a year, but he stood fourth highest in the list of the commoners of Westmorland assessed (Nicolson and Burn, *History of Westmorland and Cumberland*, I. 144 ; *Cumberland and Westmorland A. and H. Society, Transactions*, N.S., VIII. 329). In 1398 and 1406 he acted as a local collector of parliamentary subsidies, in 1431 as an assessor of rents for tax purposes, and in May 1415, April 1418, March 1427, and October 1429 as a commissioner of array ; in July 1424 he began to serve as a j.p. in Westmorland and from January to December 1426 he was royal escheator in Westmorland and Cumberland (*C.F.R., 1391-9*, 263 ; *1405-13*, 62 ; *List of Escheators*, 23). He was occasionally an attestor of the indenture drawn up at the Westmorland elections to parliament, as in 1407, 1429, and 1435 (P.R.O., C.219, Bundles 10, 14). But otherwise, and apart from his own elections as knight of the shire, he seems to have lived in a state of political seclusion. He apparently had no aristocratic connexions. The immediate reason for his first return to parliament in 1404 seems to have been purely personal : he petitioned the King and Lords regarding the forcible abduction of his nine-year-old step-daughter and ward by the sheriff of the day, Thomas Warcop of Lambertset, who had married her to his son. Laybourne alleged his failure to obtain remedy at Common Law because Warcop had acted under colour of his office, and he asked that writs should require the personal appearance before parliament of those responsible for the abduction, failing which he requested that the Council or the justices of assize might hear the case ; the dispute, however, would seem to have been resolved by arbitration (*Rot. Parl.*, III. 564).

John Leventhorpe esquire was knight of the shire for Hertfordshire in 1413, March 1416, and 1422. Coming originally from Leventhorpe (Yorks, West Riding), by 1391 he was receiver-general in England and Wales to Henry of Bolingbroke (then earl of Derby), and on the death of John of Gaunt he became receiver-general and attorney-general for the duchy of Lancaster first for Richard II and then for Bolingbroke after his accession as Henry IV. He continued to hold these offices until March 1423 and to act as an ex-officio member of the duchy Council. His regular fees were 100 marks a year, but these were supplemented in 1413 by annuities amounting to £44 and when in June 1421 he was appointed steward of the duchy lands and the former Bohun estates in Essex, Herts, Middlesex, Surrey, and London, he secured another £20 a year. When occupied away from the manor of the Savoy he received a half-noble a day as expenses (*D.K.R.*, XXX. 37 ; *C.C.R., 1392–6*, 448 ; Duchy of Lancaster, Accounts Various, P.R.O., D.L.28. 4. 1–11 ; D.L.29. 58. 1095). In the course of his official career he managed to secure many profitable wardships. He possessed or farmed estates on his own account in Essex and Herts worth £53 a year (*Feudal Aids*, VI. 58, 441). For a short time at the beginning of Henry IV's reign he was collector of wool customs in the port of London (*C.P.R., 1399–1401*, 8, 140), but his duchy offices seemingly proved too exacting, resulting as they did in routine progresses through the duchy lordships in England and Wales, some-times alone, sometimes with other members of the duchy Council. Resident at both Ugley (Essex) and Sawbridgeworth (Herts), he became on 3 March 1406 a j.p. in both these counties. Henry IV appointed Leventhorpe as one of his executors (*Rot. Parl.*, IV. 5 ; *Chichele Register*, II. 421 *et seq.*). Soon after his accession, Henry V made drastic changes in the higher administrative staff of the duchy, and Leventhorpe was the only member of the old duchy Council to retain office ; it was in this capacity that in July 1415 Henry V made him one of his feoffees in certain parcels of the duchy estates for the fulfilment of his will and he became one of this king's executors also (*C.P.R., 1413–16*, 356–7 ; Rymer, *Foedera*, IX. 289–93). He was to be particularly involved in the negotiations in 1421–3 for the partition of the lands held by the dowager countess of Hereford (Joan, the King's grandmother) before her death in 1419, between the coheirs of the Bohun inheritance, the king and Anne countess of Stafford (*C.P.R., 1416–22*, 363–4 ; Duchy of Lancaster, Accounts Various, P.R.O., D.L.28. 27. 10 ; D.L.29. 58. 1095 ; *P.P.C.*, II. 294 ; D.L.28. 4. 11 ; *Rot. Parl.*, IV. 176). On 10 March 1423 Leventhorpe resigned his office as receiver-general of the duchy of Lancaster but, as one of Henry V's feoffees and as the only person to be an operative executor of the wills of both Henry IV and Henry V, his counsel was of great importance during the settlement of the problems of the Household finances of these two kings. In any case, he remained keeper of the records of the duchy of Lancaster and was, moreover, appointed surveyor of those duchy estates enfeoffed by Henry V to the fulfilment of his will (at a fee of £100 ♦ year) ; his son, John Leventhorpe junior, acted as receiver-general to the feoffees (D.L.28. 5. 1 ; 4. 11). By 1433 Leventhorpe was the only commoner left among Henry V's feoffees ; he was still their surveyor of estates and custodian of all duchy records. He died on 27 May 1435 and was buried at Sawbridgeworth (Herts). His will was proved in the Prerogative Court of Canterbury on 5 November 1435 (*Chichele Register*, II. 526–30).

Sir Thomas Lewkenore, knight of the shire for Sussex in 1422 and 1425, came of a politically undistinguished family, which from the beginning of the fourteenth century (and perhaps longer) had been tenants of the Bohuns in the manor of South Mimms (Middlesex), but which had also come into the consider-able property of the Tregoz family on the coast and downs of south Sussex. Born about 1390 he first married into a family that had enjoyed great influence

o

in the court of Richard II, his first wife Philippa (he was her second husband) being a daughter of Sir Edward Dalingrigge, the builder of Bodiam castle, ten times knight of the shire for Sussex in as many years in the first half of Richard II's reign, and a member of the King's Council after Richard's assumption of his royal authority in 1389 ; her first husband, Richard Berners of West Horsley (Surrey), was the son of the Sir James Berners who suffered for his devotion to Richard II in the Merciless parliament of 1388, and by him she had had a daughter who became the wife of John Feriby esquire of Surrey who was to act for a short time in 1438 as controller of the royal Household. Lewkenore's second wife, another widow, Elizabeth, daughter and coheir of William Echingham, a member of an old Sussex family, through her first marriage also brought the Lewkenore family into connexion with the Lancastrian court of the period of Henry VI's majority : her stepson, Thomas Hoo, son of her first husband, Sir Thomas Hoo (he died about the same time as Lewkenore's first wife, that is, about October 1420), began his career as an esquire of the Chamber to Thomas Beaufort duke of Exeter (whose will he witnessed), became keeper of the seals in Normandy in 1435, was Chancellor of France from March 1445 until October 1449, and was summoned to parliament as Lord Hoo of Hoo and Hastings from February 1449 until his death early in 1455. Probably a more influential tie than any of these was Lewkenore's kinship with John Kemp, bishop of London in 1422, archbishop of York from 1426 until his translation in 1452 to Canterbury, Chancellor of England from 1426 to 1432 and again from 1450 to his death in 1454 ; the archbishop's mother was a daughter of Sir Thomas Lewkenore, our shire-knight's grandfather (F. C. Cass, *South Mimms*, 37 ; Manning and Bray, *Surrey*, III. 37 ; *Collectanea Topographica et Genealogica*, VIII. 110 ; *Complete Peerage*, ed. Vicary Gibbs, VI. 566–7 ; *Sussex Arch. Soc., Trans.*, VIII. 110 ; Hasted, *History of Canterbury*, II. 424 n. ; J. Dallaway, *The Rape of Arundel*, ed. E. Cartwright, II. 38 ; *C.C.R., 1419–22*, 240 ; *1422–9*, 88). Sir Thomas Lewkenore's political attachments are, however, open to conjecture only, because, apart from the numerous local royal commissions he served, there is not a great deal of information about him. He served in the first French expedition of Henry V in 1415 not unnaturally as a retainer of his Sussex neighbour, the earl of Arundel, then treasurer of England, but the earl was invalided home after the surrender of Harfleur, and whether Lewkenore stayed on for the campaign of Agincourt is not known (*D.K.R.*, XLIV. 569, 571). He does not appear to have taken part in the later cross-Channel expeditions. On 12 February 1422 he began a thirty-year-long occupation of the position of j.p. in Sussex. In the first and last years of his cousin Archbishop Kemp's first tenure of the great seal, in 1426 and again in 1431–2, he was sheriff of Surrey and Sussex. On 7 August 1448 he was appointed j.p. in Surrey, but the commission was cancelled two days later. He continued to serve the commission in Sussex, however, until his death in 1452. He seems to have been friendly with the powerful Pelham family of Pevensey, and he acted as feoffee to the Poynings family as well as to his stepson Thomas Lord Hoo (*C.C.R., 1422–9*, 388 ; *Collectanea Topographica et Genealogica*, III. 259 ; VIII. 122). In London he seems to have had a powerful friend in Sir William Estfeld, the great mercer and stapler, who left him in his will in 1445 a silver-gilt goblet (Lambeth Palace Library, *Stafford Register*, fo. 139). Far more politically active than Sir Thomas were his four sons who together between 1449 and 1478 represented Sussex and each of its five parliamentary boroughs at one time or another in parliament (Wedgwood, *History of Parliament, Biographies*, 540–2). They all seem to have been pro-Lancastrian in varying degrees of loyalty ; John, a younger son, died a Lancastrian at Tewkesbury Field and Sir Thomas's grandson, Thomas, the son of his heir (Sir Roger), was a leader in Buckingham's revolt against Richard III and incurred forfeiture, the attainder being posthumously reversed in 1485 (*ibid.*).

John Lisle of Wootton, in the isle of Wight, knight of the shire for Hampshire in 1417 and 1422, was descended from ancestors who had been summoned by individual writ to parliament between 1299 and 1314. And his father, Sir John Lisle (knighted on the eve of Henry IV's coronation), had been of some significance under the first Lancastrian king : from November 1400 in receipt of a Crown annuity of £40 for good service to Henry IV and his father, John of Gaunt, he had been j.p. in Hampshire, knight of the shire in 1401 and January 1404, sheriff of Wiltshire in 1404–5, and in the course of the same year had been appointed governor of Guernsey. The family had property in the isle of Wight, Hampshire, Wiltshire, Dorset, and Berkshire which must have yielded something like £200 a year, and John Lisle secured possession in March 1408 of all but his mother's dower-estates, soon after his father's death. Apart from a year of service as sheriff of Hampshire in 1412–13, as occasional commissioner of array, and as knight of the shire, Lisle led a singularly inactive life ; he never once was appointed j.p. in Hampshire or the isle of Wight and seems to have completely held aloof from the military activities attending Henry V's resumption of the French war. He did, however, attend the Hampshire parliamentary elections in 1419, 1423, 1426, and 1427 (*Complete Peerage*, VIII. 39–44 ; C. L. Kingsford, *Chronicles of London*, 48 ; *P.P.C.*, I. 261, 276 ; II. 106 ; *C.C.R.*, *1402–5*, 49 ; *1405–9*, 320 ; *1409–13*, 7, 354 ; *C.F.R.*, *1405–13*, 104, 119 ; P.R.O., C.219, Bundles 12 and 13). In 1412 he had been proceeded against by Humphrey later duke of Gloucester, who successfully disputed his right to a lease of his father's (which he had renewed) of a 600-acre pasture in the forests of Savernake and Chute (Wilts). Sir William Sturmy, who was to be shire-knight for Wilts in 1422, procured an assize of novel disseisin against him for dispossession of the same herbage. These incidents alone appear to have ruffled the serenity of Lisle's career (*C.P.R.*, *1401–5*, 161 ; *1408–13*, 415 ; *C.C.R.*, *1409–13*, 380). He died at London on 17 February 1429, providing for his burial at Chute. He left six sons and five daughters. His will was proved in the Prerogative Court of Canterbury on 10 March 1429, his eldest son John sharing with his mother the burdens of administration. He was already of age and married to a niece of William Lord Botreaux ; he was later m.p. for Hampshire in 1433 and February 1449, sheriff of Hampshire in 1438–9 and for Wilts (contrary to the statute of 1371) in the following year (*C.F.R.*, *1422–30*, 268 ; Somerset House Wills, *Register Luffenham*, fo. 10 ; J. C. Wedgwood, *History of Parliament, Biographies*, 546).

Robert Lovell esquire of Rampisham (Dorset) and Clarendon (Wilts), knight of the shire for Dorset in May 1421 and 1422, was the second son of John Lord Lovel of Titchmarsh (summoned to parliament between 1375 and 1407)

by Maud, granddaughter of Robert second Lord Holland (she was a second
cousin of Thomas Holland, the nephew of Richard II, who was created duke
of Surrey in 1397 and beheaded by the Cirencester mob in January 1400). Robert
Lovell's father in 1387 was expelled from Richard II's court by the party of the
Lords Appellant as an undesirable influence, but in 1399 was one of those who
came over to Henry of Lancaster's side, and he was later a member of the royal
Council approved by parliament in 1404 and 1406. So far Robert's career had
hardly begun. He had been to Ireland in the royal expedition of 1394, and in
1397 he was a member of the retinue of the King's Lieutenant of Ireland, Roger
earl of March (*C.P.R., 1391–6*, 447, 482 ; *1396–9*, 145). By 1406 he was serving
with Henry of Monmouth against Welsh rebels (*ibid., 1405–8*, 159, 260). He
probably owed this attachment to his kinship with the friend of the heir apparent,
Henry Lord Scrope of Masham ; Lord Scrope and Lovell married two sisters,
Philippa (the elder) and Elizabeth, the granddaughters and coheirs of Guy Lord
Briene (summoned to parliament 1350–89). Robert had married Elizabeth about
1390 when she was a royal ward (*The Complete Peerage*, ed. Vicary Gibbs, II.
361–2 ; VIII. 219–21), and, though her sister died in 1406, the connexion
between Lord Scrope and Lovell seems to have been maintained (as his second
wife Scrope married Lovell's mother's second cousin, Joan Holland). A useful
connexion this proved to be when Prince Henry secured control of the government early in 1410 and Lord Scrope became treasurer of England. To the new
régime Lovell doubtless owed his appointment on 24 May 1410 as deputy-clerk of
the works in the royal manor and park of Clarendon (*C.P.R., 1408–13*, 204),
and it was probably his intimacy with the Treasurer which accounted for the
fact that ten weeks later a meeting of the Council attended by the prince, Bishop
Beaufort, Lord Scrope and others, was held in Lovell's London inn in Old Fish
Street (*P.P.C.*, I. 350–1). It is to this period or shortly afterwards that the
beginnings of Lovell's later financial troubles must be assigned : the substance
of a petition he was to present in 1427 (P.R.O., Ancient Petitions, File 121,
No. 6016) suggests that, as an official of Prince Henry's household in the latter half
of Henry IV's reign, Lovell was involved in debts contracted on the Prince's behalf
against which the latter failed to indemnify him ; these amounted in all to the
neighbourhood of £2,330. After Henry V's accession when Master Richard
Courtenay was made treasurer of the royal Household but before September
1413 when he was preferred to the see of Norwich, the latter's ' ontrewe ymagina-
cion and besy labour ' resulted in Lovell's accounts being embezzled and ' he y
put under warde and y kept there unto the tyme he had be cohercion aliened
his castel of Werdour [Wardour, Wilts] with the membres ', plus rents worth
200 marks a year, to his brother, Lord Lovell, in return for £1,000 which
Courtenay took to the king's use. Whether or not Lovell's petition of 1427
was successful in securing an appropriation on the estates enfeoffed to the fulfilment of Henry V's will and the repayment of his debts is not known, but the
petition itself was superscribed to the effect that it was presented to the King
and Lords by the duke of Gloucester himself. Despite the fact that Lovell's
landed estate, not counting seven manors in Somerset held *jure uxoris*, was worth
about £150 a year (*C.C.R., 1399–1402*, 77, 86 ; *C.F.R., 1399–1405*, 60–1 ;
Collinson, *Somerset*, 111, 185 ; *Feudal Aids*, VI. 419, 426, 428, 477, 508), the
reverses he suffered early in Henry V's reign resulted in continuous financial

embarrassment. Probably to the parliament of 1414 must be assigned a petition he made to the king, in which he complained that he could not be expected to pay the debts he owed the Crown unless his own debtors paid him first, and he instanced in particular John Wyse, a Pembrokeshire esquire who was then captain of Carmarthen castle, but Wyse counter-petitioned in March 1415 (Ancient Petitions, File 188, No. 9374 ; *P.P.C.*, II. 149). In February 1417 Lovell raised a mortgage of 1,000 marks on five Briene manors in Somerset and Dorset ; in October 1417, and in 1419, 1420, and 1426, he was successively pardoned outlawry for divers debts amounting to over £1,800 (E. A. and G. S. Fry, *Feet of Fines for Dorset*, 278 ; *C.C.R.*, *1413–19*, 453 ; *C.P.R.*, *1416–22*, 229, 233) ; one of the pleas for which he was in exigent in 1419 was for a debt of 100 marks to the duke of Gloucester and for failure to render account as his receiver, perhaps in Wilts where the duke was keeper of Clarendon forest. He seems to have kept clear of trouble in one important respect, for he was not involved in the treason of his kinsman by marriage, Lord Scrope of Masham, on the eve of the royal expedition to Normandy of 1415, which Lovell joined with a retinue of two men-at-arms and six archers (*D.K.R.*, XLIV. 563 ; Nicolas, *Agincourt*, 381). Service abroad and the comfort of letters of protection must have been a Godsend to Lovell in these years of foreign conquest and personal penury. In the spring of 1420 he was in France with the duke of Bedford, but early in the following year he returned, probably in the king's company, and sat in his first parliament (*D.K.R.*, XLII. 389 ; *C.P.R.*, *1416–22*, 319). He went abroad again in 1423 (*D.K.R.*, XLVIII. 226) or else merely sheltered behind letters of protection, but his general credit was now so improved that from February 1422 he was appointed to all commissions of the peace for Dorset down to his death in 1428 although, as his petition of 1427 suggests, he was still making heavy weather financially. Another sign of recovered prestige was the second marriage (some time before April 1428) of his daughter and heir, Maud, widow of Sir Richard Stafford, to John Lord Arundell, who was to recover the earldom of Arundel in 1433 ; her daughter, Avice, by her first marriage, was destined to become countess of Wiltshire, marrying James Butler, son of the earl of Ormond, before 1441 (*Complete Peerage*, ed. V. Gibbs, *op. cit.*, I. 248 ; II. 361–2 ; *Complete Peerage*, ed. G. E. Cockayne, VI. 141 ; *C.P.R.*, *1436–41*, 500).

Geoffrey Lowther esquire, knight of the shire for Kent in 1422, 1426, and 1432, was a member of the influential Cumberland family of the Lowthers of Lowther castle near Penrith, being a younger son of Hugh Lowther, m.p. for Westmorland 1371–3 ; his eldest brother, John, had been m.p. for Westmorland in 1377 and appears to have been tutor to Thomas Lord Clifford in 1378–80, and another brother, William, had been m.p. for Cumberland in 1393 and 1404 and sheriff in 1400 and 1406 ; a nephew, Sir Robert Lowther, the son-in-law of Bishop Strickland of Carlisle (1400–19), had been seven times m.p. for Cumberland between 1391 and 1417 ; another nephew, William, was parliamentary burgess for Appleby in 1420 ; and yet another nephew, Hugh, was to be m.p. for Cumberland in 1426, 1431, and January 1449. Through his mother, who was a Tilliol of Scaleby, Geoffrey was related to Sir Peter Tilliol, who was thirteen times m.p. for Cumberland between 1378 and 1426 and represented the county in 1422 when Geoffrey was first returned for Kent (*D.N.B.*, LV. 56; *Transactions of the Cumberland and Westmorland A. and A.S.* [N.S.], XVI. 129; amended *ibid.*, XLVIII 120–1). A lawyer by profession, it is quite possible that Geoffrey was the Lowther who figures in the list of surnames of members of Lincoln's Inn admitted before, and still surviving in, 1420 (*Lincoln's Inn, Register of Admissions*, 2), but his earliest associations were with Cumberland. From 1395 he shared with a member of his mother's family a grant in survivorship of a royal ferry across the Solway, and for a short time at the beginning of Henry IV's reign he occupied the forestership of the royal forest of Inglewood, within the metes of which were his family's most important holdings (*C.P.R., 1391–6*, 596; *1399–1401*, 174, 452; *C.F.R., 1405–13*, 31, 56). By this time Geoffrey seems to have attached himself to the service of a younger brother of the earl of Westmorland, Thomas Neville, who was in right of his wife Lord Furnival. He very probably owed his annuity of 19 marks, charged on the lordship of Edwinstowe (Notts) and granted to him for life as an esquire in the king's fee, to this connexion, for Lord Furnival was at the time of the grant Treasurer of the Exchequer. The association of the Lowthers with the great northern baronial house of Neville seems to have been a close one in this period, for Geoffrey's nephew, Sir Robert Lowther, was to act in 1425 as one of the earl of Westmorland's executors. Geoffrey's connexion with Lord Furnival, however, terminated with the latter's early death in 1407, which was a misfortune because by that time Lowther was sufficiently close to him to have been appointed as one of his executors and as one of his feoffees in certain of his Shropshire estates, which then descended to the Talbots (*C.P.R., 1405–8*, 45; Surtees Society, II (*Wills and Inventories*), 73; *ibid., Testamenta Eboracensia*, III. 40; *ibid.*, CXVI (*North Country Wills*), 28; *C.F.R., 1399–1405*, 120; *C.C.R., 1413–19*, 24). Soon after Henry V's accession Lowther secured confirmation of his royal annuity and also petitioned, although with what result is not known, for ratification of his estate in the office of bailiff of the West Riding wapentake of Staincliffe, parcel of the duchy of Lancaster (Ancient Petitions, P.R.O., S.C.8, File 184, No. 9188; File 188, No. 9392; *C.P.R., 1413–16*, 31). When began his attachment to the youngest but longest surviving brother of Henry V, Duke Humphrey of Gloucester, is not clear, but both he and his nephew served in Gloucester's retinue in the Agincourt campaign of 1415, by which time he was one of the ducal feoffees. In November 1415 the duke was appointed warden of the Cinque Ports and constable of Dover castle and by November 1417, if not earlier, Geoffrey Lowther was his deputy in both of these posts, was still acting as lieutenant-warden in 1443, and probably continued to act until the duke's death in 1447 (N. H. Nicolas, *Agincourt, op. cit.*, 333; *C.P.R., 1413–16*, 338; *1429–36*, 503–6; *1416–22*, 129; *C.C.R., 1413–19*, 511; P.R.O., C.219, XII. 2). His office automatically involved him for at least a quarter of a century in functioning as returning officer of all elections to parliament for the Cinque Ports, in numerous Kentish commissions especially for the holding of military arrays and musters of troops embarking from Dover or neighbouring ports and later for the raising of Crown loans, and from July 1420 until 1446 he served on the commission of the peace for Kent (*C.P.R., passim*). It was as vice-constable of Dover that in 1427 Lowther was indirectly involved in the dispute between Archbishop Chichele and Pope Martin V when the latter suspended

the primate from his office as ' legatus natus ' ; it was Lowther who was responsible for the papal collector's surrender of the bull of suspension. The archbishop
was in sympathy with Gloucester's hostile attitude to Cardinal Beaufort, at any
rate so far as the Cardinal's legatine authority was concerned. This accord was
reflected in the friendship of their subordinates : in 1427, for example, Lowther
was associated with John Darell, the archbishop's steward and nephew-in-law,
in an Exchequer lease, and he had been the first to attest the indenture of election
when Darell was returned for Kent to the parliament of 1425 (*D.N.B.*, X. 229 ;
C.F.R., 1422–30, 160, 173 ; P.R.O., C.219, XIII. 3). In the meantime it was
doubtless Lowther's attachment to the duke of Gloucester, now appointed
Protector of England, that was responsible for his promotion, in succession to
John Leventhorpe, to the offices of receiver- and attorney-general for those
portions of the duchy of Lancaster estates not enfeoffed by Henry V for the
administration of his will. His appointment, which carried with it membership
of the duchy council, had been made some time between Henry VI's accession
and 6 March 1423, and he held the office concurrently with his lieutenant-
wardenship of the Cinque Ports until February 1438 (Duchy of Lancaster,
Accounts Various, P.R.O., D.L.28, IV. 12 ; V. 2). How long Lowther survived
his patron, Gloucester, is not known, but he was still alive, and he must then
have been an old man of over seventy years, when on 17 January 1451 he was
present in the chapter-house of the abbey of St. Albans at the election as abbot,
for the second time, of Gloucester's personal friend, John Whethamstead.
Gloucester, of course, was buried there. If a pedigree drawn up at Shap at
the end of the century is to be trusted, Lowther died without issue and was
buried at Sebergham (Peter Newcombe, *History of the Abbey of St. Albans*, 345,
Hist. Mss. Comm, 10th Report, VI. 97–8).

John Ludwell, m.p. for Old Sarum in May and December 1421, for
Chippenham in 1422, and for Cricklade in 1423, was in Michaelmas term 1422
acting as attorney in the King's Bench (Placita Coram Rege, P.R.O., K.B.27/646,
Mem. 86).

Thomas Marlborough, m.p. for Southampton in 1395, 1402, 1411, April
and November 1414, 1415, May 1421, 1422, 1423, and 1426, and town-clerk in
1422, was one of three lawyers appointed by Henry IV's Queen, Joan of Navarre,
on 6 November 1422 to act as her attorneys in the royal courts, and to collect all
her revenues (Queen Joan enjoyed the greater part of the fee-farm of Southampton) (*The Steward's Book of Southampton* ; H. W. Gidden, *The Sign Manuals
and Letters Patent of Southampton to 1422*, I. 88, 90).

John Michell, m.p. for London in 1411, 1420, 1422, 1426, 1427, and 1435.
A ship of his was at Newcastle-on-Tyne in November 1415 (*C.C.R., 1413–19*,
236). In December 1403 he was a grocer and was still a member of that company
when auditor in 1413–14 and when appointed one of two sheriffs of London
and Middlesex for the year 1414–15, but during this year of office after one and
a half years as alderman of Baynard Castle ward (since February 1414) he became
alderman of Bridge ward (he so acted until 1444) and more or less simultaneously
became a member of the fishmongers' company which had its hall in that ward

(Beaven, *op. cit.*, I. 97, 343 ; II. 4, 9 ; Sharpe, *Letter-Book I*, 95, 117, 127 ; *C.C.R.*, *1402–5*, 223 ; *1413–19*, 236) ; he was also a member of the brewers' company (*C.C.R.*, *1405–9*, 149 ; W. Herbert, *History of the Twelve Great Livery Companies of London*, I. 57). Between March 1416 and June 1418 he was engaged in diplomatic work over truces with Flanders and Burgundy (*D.K.R.*, XLIV. 577, 582, 594, 600, 606). In the civic years October 1424–5 and October 1436–7 he was mayor of London (Beaven, *op. cit.*, II. 4). From July 1425 to 1430 he was mayor of the staple at Westminster (P.R.O., C.67/25). He died early in 1445 (Somerset House, *Register Luffenham*, fo. 29).

Sir William Montfort of Coleshill in Arden, knight of the shire for Warwickshire in 1422, 1423, 1427, 1429, 1437, 1445, and 1450. As the eldest surviving son and heir of Sir Baldwin Montfort, who died in 1386 when in Spain with John of Gaunt's forces, and as a result of his marriage with Margaret, daughter and heir of Sir John Peche of Hampton-in-Arden, Montfort came into possession of considerable estates primarily in Warwickshire, and a second marriage brought the Staffordshire manor of Aldridge, so that by 1436 he was the wealthiest non-baronial landowner in Warwickshire with £281 income a year, £23 of this total being already settled on his eldest son, Baldwin. Montfort's father had married well and his son Sir William's career was to a large extent predetermined by his mother's family connexions. She was a daughter of John Lord Clinton of Maxstoke, a peer of the realm. Her maternal great-grandfather was Guy de Beauchamp, earl of Warwick, one of the Lords Ordainer of 1311 ; Richard Beauchamp, earl of Warwick from 1401 to 1439, was thus her second cousin, and it was with him that her son, William, took service (Dugdale, *Warwickshire*, 405, 730 ; *C.C.R.*, *1409–13*, 382–4 ; Stebbing Shaw, *History of Staffordshire*, II. 99 ; *E.H.R.*, XLIX. 639). How long he had occupied this position in the Beauchamp household is not known, but by 1417 Montfort was acting as the earl's steward and chief of his council with an annual fee of 40 marks. From this time forward to his appointment as j.p. in Warwickshire in February 1422 (he was to serve in this office down to his death in 1452 except for a period of five years following the earl's death in 1439), Montfort was with the earl's retinue on military service in France, apparently returning to England in the meantime only when Warwick himself returned to deputise for the duke of Clarence at the coronation of Catherine of Valois in 1421 (Dugdale, *op. cit.*, 730 ; *D.K.R.*, XLIV (*French Rolls*). 591, 629 ; *C.P.R.*, *1416–22*, 461). Montfort's connexion with the earl remained close : he apparently went in his suite to France when in 1437 the earl was appointed lieutenant of France and Normandy ; he was one of the earl's feoffees to uses and after the earl's death in 1439 he was one of the ' patentarii ' or feoffees for the fulfilment of the will of the dowager countess, Isabel ; they also purchased the wardship of the heir, the young Earl Henry, and acted until his death in 1445. Montfort also acted as the countess's executor (*C.P.R.*, *1436–41*, 359–60 ; *1446–52*, 22, 268, 375 ; *C.C.R.*, *1422–9*, 127 ; *Dorset Fines*, 306 ; *Rot. Parl.*, V. 77 ; *V.C.H.*, *Bedfordshire*, III. 403 ; *D.K.R.*, XLVIII. 319 ; *C.F.R.*, *1437–45*, 122 ; Somerset House, Registers of Wills, *Luffenham*, fo. 27). What were Montfort's relations with the new earl of Warwick, Richard Neville, the later king-maker, who had married Richard Beauchamp's daughter Anne, who succeeded to the bulk of the Beauchamp heritage on the death of her niece in January 1449, and by whom Montfort's grandson Simon was to be retained as counsel in 1457, is not known, but at his death Sir William was closely connected with the great Lancastrian, Humphrey duke of Buckingham, a distant kinsman, who was his feoffee. Sir William's son by his second wife, Sir Edmund Montfort, ' Counsellor and Kerver ' to Henry VI, was so staunch a Lancastrian that he accompanied Margaret of Anjou into exile, only returning permanently to England with Henry Tudor in 1485 (*C.P.R., 1452-61*, 58 ; Dugdale, *op. cit.*, 730 ; J. C. Wedgwood, *History of Parliament [Biographies]*, 602-4). In the course of his life, Montfort had served Warwickshire seven times as knight of the shire and had acted as a justice of the peace there, in all for a quarter of a century He had also served the office of deputy-sheriff of Worcestershire (the shrievalty was held in fee by the earls of Warwick) in 1423-4, as sheriff of Leicestershire and Warwickshire in 1431-2, as deputy-sheriff of Worcestershire in 1440-1, and as sheriff of Leicestershire and Warwickshire again in 1441-2 and 1450-1. He served on many other more casual local royal commissions, especially for the raising of Crown loans (*List of Sheriffs*, 145, 158 ; *C.P.R., passim*). He died on 6 December 1452, having in his will in September 1451 provided for a chantry at Coleshill. Probate was allowed in the Prerogative Court of Canterbury on 16 May 1453 (Lambeth Palace Library, Kemp Register, fo. 302).

Sir Robert Moton of Peckleton, knight of the shire for Leicestershire in 1422 only, was the great-grandson on his father's side of Ralph Lord Basset of Sapcote, who died in 1378 when the barony fell into abeyance. Both the moiety of the manor of Sapcote which he inherited with other Leicestershire estates through the Basset relationship and the ancestral Moton manor of Peckleton were mesne tenancies of the duchy of Lancaster, and Robert Moton's wardship and marriage soon after his father's death in 1391 (he was then aged seventeen) were granted to Sir Walter Blount, John of Gaunt's retainer and subsequently one of the duke's executors. Moton's first marriage was clearly influenced, however, by the Basset relationship, for he married Margaret, a daughter of his near neighbour Sir Anketill Malory of Kirkby Malory and his wife, the widow of Ralph Lord Basset (she was stepmother to Robert's grandmother). The most important connexion Moton's first marriage brought him was with Richard Lord Grey of Codnor (a peer of parliament from 1393 to 1417), husband of Moton's wife's uterine sister, Lord Basset's second coheir, Elizabeth (John Nicholls, *History and Antiquities of Leicestershire*, Vol. IV, Part II, 869, 870, 893 ; *Complete Peerage*, II. 8 ; *C.C.R., 1392-6*, 201 ; *C.P.R., 1391-6*, 98 ; A. Gibbons, *Early Lincoln Wills*, 110). Lord Grey of Codnor was in 1400 appointed by Henry IV as admiral of the royal fleet from the Thames northwards and by the spring of 1402 at latest Moton had joined his brother-in-law's company at sea (*C.P.R., 1401-5*, 175). In November 1412 the two brothers-in-law arranged a partition of the Basset estates held in dower by their mother-in-law in Lincoln-shire, Leicestershire, Northants, and Staffs, all seemingly with complete amity (*C.F.R., 1405-13*, 254-5), because it was as a member of Lord Grey's retinue that Moton proceeded in Henry V's first expedition to Normandy in 1415 (*Derbyshire A. and N.H. Society Journal*, Vol. 14, 25). Lord Grey died in August 1419 after service in France. Whether Moton had been abroad in his retinue continuously or not in the intervening years, he served on no commissions in the midland shires during this time. But he served, in fact, on very few royal commissions at any time and never on the commission of the peace and had to wait until 8 November 1451 before he was appointed sheriff of Leicestershire and Warwickshire, by which time he was about seventy-six years old. He had, however, been present at the Leicestershire parliamentary elections in 1414, 1423, 1425, 1427, 1431, 1432, and 1433 (P.R.O., C.219, Bundles 11, 13, 14), and that he was held in respect is clear from the way in which he was called in to attest several important charters of notable folk, for instance, Lord Lovell's settlement of his estates in 1430 (*C.C.R.*, *1429–35*, 58), a deed appointing in 1436 attorneys to convey the manor of Ashby (Leics) from the feoffees of Joan Beauchamp, Dame Abergavenny, to Humphrey, duke of Gloucester, and in 1449 a charter by which her grandson and heir, Sir James Butler, the heir of the earl of Ormond, enfeoffed his Leics and Derbyshire property (*Hist. Mss. Comm.*, *Mss. of R. R. Hastings*, Vol. I, pp. 1, 2). What was the relationship between Dame Beauchamp of Abergavenny and the Motons I have not discovered, but in 1434 her will left 100 marks to Sir Robert's eldest son, Reynold (he predeceased his father in 1444), and another 100 marks towards the marriage of Isabel Moton, probably Reynold's daughter (Jacob, *Chichele Register*, II. 537). The connexion is particularly interesting because it had been with Bartholomew Brokesby, Dame Abergavenny's agent, that Sir Robert Moton had been elected to the parliament of 1422. The link with the Butlers would suggest that Moton was biased towards the anti-Yorkist bloc and his appointment as sheriff in November 1451 would tend to confirm this suspicion. But he had his connexions with the other side, having married as his second wife Elizabeth, daughter of Sir Edmund Mulsho, a close adherent of the duke of York ; she was the widow of Baldwin Bugge of Thurlestone, father-in-law of Moton's son Reynold (Nicholls, *op. cit.*). The ties with the Greys of Codnor had, meanwhile, been maintained : in 1442 Sir Robert appears as joint-creditor with Elizabeth Dame Grey of Codnor, his sister-in-law, and by 1459 one of his granddaughters by his first marriage had married Dame Grey's grandson, Henry seventh Lord Grey of Codnor (*C.P.R.*, *1441–6*, 119, 121 ; *Hist. Mss. Comm. Report*, Mss. of Lord de l'Isle and Dudley, Vol. 1, p. 192). Sir Robert Moton died in 1456, the last few years of his life having been rendered difficult by his attempts to change the entail of his family estates in an effort to benefit William, his son by his second marriage, to the detriment of the daughters and coheirs of his deceased son and heir, Reynold (Nicholls, *op. cit.*, 869).

Henry Mulsho esquire of Geddington, knight of the shire for Northants in 1422, belonged to a family closely linked with Edmund of Langley's eldest son, Edward of Norwich, earl of Rutland from 1390, duke of Aumâle for the last two years of Richard II's reign only, and then on his father's death in 1402 his successor in the title of duke of York. Mulsho probably owed to this connexion his office as royal escheator in Northants and Rutland from November 1395 to February 1397 and as alnager of cloth in Northants from 18 May 1398 until his displacement at the revolution of 1399 (*C.F.R.*, *1391–9*, 239, 271 ; P.R.O., *List of Escheators*, 95). What part Mulsho played in the uncertainties of his patron's career in the first half of Henry IV's reign is not known, but the Yorkist attachment was clearly maintained : he was in 1408 one of the lessees (for ten years) of all the dower estates of York's sister, Elizabeth widow of Edward

Lord Despenser, in Glamorgan and Morgannwg ; to this period (*c.* 1405–9) must be assigned his occupation of the position of lieutenant to the duke in Jersey, where he himself acquired some property ; and for some time before August 1411, when with the duke's permission he sold the office, Mulsho was York's lieutenant-constable of the Tower. On 12 January 1412 he took out letters of protection as retained by Henry IV's second son, Thomas of Lancaster ; but this connexion was probably a byproduct of the Yorkist attachment, for York joined Clarence in the pro-Orleanist expedition to France later in that same year (*C.C.R., 1405–9*, 366–7, 524 ; *C.P.R., 1408–13*, 303 ; *1413–16*, 315 ; Carte, *Catalogue des Rolles*, II. 204). In Henry V's reign next to nothing is known of Mulsho (York was killed at Agincourt in 1415) until we find him in April 1419 acting as a member of a commission of array at Harfleur where three years later he was acting as king's lieutenant. He was back in England in the spring of 1422, when he undertook to keep the peace towards a servant of the then lieutenant-constable of the Tower, Robert Scot, and appeared in Chancery (where he was dismissed), but on 25 July 1422 he took out letters of protection as being about to return to France as a royal retainer and he may have crossed the Channel only to return with Henry V's funeral equipage (*D.K.R.*, XLII. 426–7 ; XLIV. 638 ; *C.P.R., 1416–22*, 444 ; *C.C.R., 1419–22*, 259). He sat in Henry VI's first parliament and was in England for the next two years, during which time he had relations with William Lord Lovell. His main connexion at this time was, however, with Humphrey, duke of Gloucester, Henry VI's younger uncle, protector of England and chief councillor. Probably by 2 July, certainly by 12 October 1423, Mulsho was the duke's treasurer of household, an office which suggests an attachment of some duration and intimacy. He was still occupying this position in May 1424 (Exchequer, Issue Rolls, Easter, 1 Hen. VI, P.R.O., E.403/660, Mem. 10 ; *ibid.*, Michs., 2 Hen. VI, E.403/663, Mem. 1). Later in that year, on 4 November 1424, he took out letters of protection as about to cross to Hainault to join the duke of Gloucester's retinue there in his private war with John of Brabant which threatened the Anglo-Burgundian alliance. Whether Mulsho was invalided home or returned with the duke on 12 April 1425 is not known, but on 1 June he drew up his last will and it was proved, *Sede episcopali Lincolniensi tunc vacante*, by Archbishop Chichele's chancellor at Higham Ferrers on 31 August following. Mulsho had died, however, before 14 June when the sheriff of Northants was ordered to arrange for the election of his successor as verderer in the royal forest of Rockingham. It is probable that his tenure of this minor office went back to the time of his former patron, Edward of Norwich, who in 1397 had been made warden of all the royal forests below Trent (*C.C.R., 1422–9*, 75, 174 ; *D.K.R.*, XLVIII. 233 ; Jacob, *Chichele Register*, II. 371–2). It was perhaps not long before his death that Mulsho was superseded in his treasurership of the ducal household by William Bothe clerk, who, until then Gloucester's receiver-general, does not appear as his household treasurer and, as such, receiving monies at the royal Exchequer on his master's behalf before 21 May 1425.

Sir William Palton, knight of the shire for Somerset in 1422. Born about 1380 Palton came of an old but politically inactive Somerset family, the Paltons of Croscombe near Wells, who possessed considerable estates in the south and west of England, in Wilts, Oxfordshire, Hampshire, and Somerset. Sir William also enjoyed, certainly from 1405, possession of six Somerset and eight Devon manors, and properties in Gloucs and Cornwall, in right of his wife, who died in 1413, and after that date by courtesy down to his own death in 1449. She was Elizabeth, daughter and heir of Sir John Wrothe of Brompton Ralph (Somerset) and Enfield (Middlesex), and cousin of Sir John Tiptoft, who was Treasurer of England from July 1408 to December 1409 and in 1422 was appointed a member of the royal Council (*C.C.R., 1399–1402*, 458–9 ; *1402–5* 486, 522 ; *C.F.R., 1422–30*, 37 ; Devon and Cornwall Record Society, XXXI, *Feet of Fines for Cornwall*, 120 ; Somerset Record Society, XXII, *Feet of Fines Henry IV–VI*, 174 ; Collinson, *History of Somerset*, II. 152 ; *Feudal Aids*, I. 232, 488, 490, 496 ; IV. 367, 379, 385, 391–2, 420 ; V. 255, 273 ; VI. 510, 535). Palton was, however, himself well connected. His mother was a sister of the first Lord Botreaux (summoned to parliament 1368–90) and he was cousin german to the William Lord Botreaux summoned as a peer to parliament from 1413 to 1461. The association between the two families was always close : Lord Botreaux was among Palton's feoffees and Palton was feoffee to Lord Botreaux's mother, and they were connected in other ways (*Somerset Archaelogical and Natural History Society Proceedings*, XXXIV. 68 ; *C.P.R., 1381–5*, 542 ; *1416–22*, 69 ; *1422–9*, 190, 257, 462 ; Collinson, *op. cit.*, III. 354). By a second marriage with Anne Courtenay, Palton was to ally himself with the family of the Courtenay earls of Devon. Despite these influential attachments he did not deviate from the Palton tradition of comparative political inactivity and he served in few local offices and on few royal commissions, important exceptions being his soon-vacated appointment on 6 November 1414 as sheriff of the Welsh counties of Glamorgan and Morgannwg, his commissions as j.p. in Devon in October 1415 for three years and as j.p. in Somerset for a year and a half from February 1422 ; and his tenure of the shrievalty of Devon from 15 January to 12 December 1426 (*C.F.R., 1413–22*, 79 ; *C.P.R., 1413–16*, 418 ; *1416–22*, 459 ; *List of Sheriffs*, 35). Perhaps he was felt in official circles at times to be unsound, for some of his associations were with dubious characters. He was one of four who on 8 February 1414 went surety in 1,000 marks for Thomas Brooke (his fellow-m.p. in 1422), the stepson-in-law of the leader of the recent Lollard rising, Sir John Oldcastle ; Brooke had seemingly been involved in the recent conspiracy and had been imprisoned in the Tower. Four years later, on 14 February 1418, Palton joined with another son-in-law of Oldcastle, Richard Clitheroe esquire, in standing surety for a cousin of the earl of March, Sir John Mortimer of Hatfield (Herts), who was then a cause of much uneasiness on the part of the Council governing with the duke of Bedford in Henry V's absence in France. Three years later Mortimer was imprisoned in the Tower on suspicion of treason, escaped in 1422, was recaptured in 1424 and executed for treason. (*C.C.R., 1413–19*, 116, 456). In the meantime Palton had taken out letters of protection on 13 April 1418 as being about to go overseas in the retinue of Thomas duke of Exeter, and these were renewed on 2 March 1419 ; how long he remained overseas or where he served is not known, but he was seemingly back in England early in 1422, when he was appointed j.p. in Somerset (*D.K.R.*, XLIV. 604, 610).

Sir John Pelham, knight of the shire for Sussex in 1399, 1401, January and October 1404, 1406, 1407, 1422, and 1427. Born about 1355, the son of a coroner in Sussex, Pelham owed his rise to his service under the Lancastrians. By his marriage (before 1391) with Joan, widow of Sir Hugh Zouche, Pelham acquired estates in Cambridgeshire and Suffolk, but his appointment in 1393 by John of Gaunt as constable of Pevensey castle for life and his appointment in March 1394 by Archbishop Courtenay to be his forester and master of hunting in Sussex, also for life, transferred his main interests to Sussex. In 1403 his revenues were calculated to be £870 ; his rent-roll at Michaelmas 1404 showed a yield of some £670 from the rape of Pevensey and his Sussex estates alone ; at the end of Henry IV's reign he was assessed for taxation at £540 and this sum did not include annuities or the whole of the duchy of Lancaster revenues which he enjoyed from the rape of Pevensey and the Lancastrian honour of the Eagle, these latter alone in 1418–19 amounting to nearly £270 (M. A. Lower, *Historical and Genealogical Notices of the Pelham Family*, 8–14 ; T. W. Horsfield, *History of Sussex*, I. 315 ; *Feudal Aids*, VI. 410, 457, 504, 521 ; *Sussex Archaeological Society Trans.*, LXIX, 63 ; *C.P.R.*, *1389–92*, 150 ; *1396–9*, 249). John of Gaunt's retainer, Pelham was also a member of the suite of Henry of Bolingbroke (then earl of Derby) as early as 1389, and this connexion predetermined his part in the events of 1399. If he did not actually land with Bolingbroke at Ravenspur he had joined his forces by the time Henry reached Pontefract a few days later ; his wife was besieged at Pevensey by loyalist forces from Sussex, Surrey, and Kent. Pelham had earned his knighthood and the signal honour of being one of the esquires dubbed in the Tower on the eve of Henry IV's coronation by the new king himself, and twelve days later he was granted for life the privilege of bearing the royal sword in the king's presence. Probably already, as he certainly was by September 1402, Pelham was one of the twelve knights of the Chamber. The author of the French *Chronique de la Traison et Mort de Richart Deux* describes him as responsible for the conduct of Richard II from the Tower to Leeds castle (in Kent) (Horsfield, *op. cit.* ; Lower, *op. cit.* ; *D.N.B.*, LXIV. 248–50 ; Exchequer, K.R., Wardrobe Accounts, P.R.O., E.101. 404, 21 ; C. L. Kingsford, *The Chronicles of London*, 48). In February 1400 he was put on the commission of the peace for Sussex and served as j.p. in that county until his death ; he also served for a short time in 1406 in Hampshire and for ten years from that date in Surrey (*C.P.R.*, *passim*). In the meantime in 1401–2 he was sheriff for Sussex and Surrey (*List of Sheriffs*, 136). In these years he held several profitable custodies and wardships and marriages, not the least important of which was the custody of the temporalities of the diocese of Winchester after the death of Bishop Wykeham in 1404, at first a sole custody and then shared with Thomas Chaucer, the cousin of Wykeham's successor, Henry Beaufort (*C.P.R.*, *1401–5*, 451, 458). A few weeks later on in the Coventry parliament, on 11 November 1404, he was appointed to act with the then Treasurer, Thomas Neville Lord Furnival, as associate-Treasurer for the King's Wars for the next three years, being required to render account to the next parliament in which, on 19 June 1406, he and Lord Furnival successfully procured their discharge ; at the end of this long parliament of 1406 he was one of the twelve shire-knights who were members of a committee charged to attest the engrossment of the parliament-roll (*Rot. Parl.*, III. 546, 577, 584). In the meantime, in March 1405, he had been entrusted with the custody of Edward of Norwich, duke of York, who was suspected of being party to a plot to get young Edmund Mortimer, earl of March, and his brother Roger spirited away from Windsor castle to the Welsh marches, and immediately afterwards, by patent of 5 March 1405, Pelham was granted for life the keepership of the New Forest, which York had held along with his wardenship of the royal forests south of Trent. York was in Pelham's custody until October 1405 (*C.C.R.*, *1405–9*, 2 ; *C.P.R.*, *1401–5*, 497) and from 3 February 1406 the Mortimer boys were in his custody, at Pevensey also, for three whole years, Pelham being allowed 500 marks a year for their maintenance from their own family estates (*C.P.R.*, *1405–8*, 276 ; J. H. Wylie, *The Reign of Henry IV*, II. 42). He was to keep up his connexion with the young earl of March, in the summer of 1408 procuring a lease of some of his estates during his minority and seven years later he was among his feoffees to uses and he was also a feoffee of Edward of Norwich (*C.F.R.*, *1405–13*, 114 ; *Somerset Fines*, *op. cit.*, 177 ; *C.P.R.*, *1408–13*, 399, 401, 406, 410). Before the end of the long parliament of 1406 Pelham was appointed to administer the office of chief steward of the duchy of Lancaster south of Trent which entitled him to an *ex officio* seat on the council of the duchy and a fee of £100 a year. He held the post until after Henry V's accession and right through the troublesome years of the rest of Henry IV's reign, during which time he quite clearly adhered to the king and the party of Archbishop Arundel rather than to the Beaufort bloc which supported the claims of Henry of Monmouth to rule instead of his decrepit and rapidly-failing father ; when late in 1411 the prince of Wales was compelled to retire from the control of the government it was to Pelham that the Exchequer was entrusted. The great seal had been accepted by Archbishop Arundel on the previous day (Wylie, *op. cit.*, IV. 51). Only a week before, the Chancellor had founded a chantry in his cathedral nave and Pelham and his wife figured on his bede-roll (*Literae Cantuarienses*, ed. J. B. Sheppard [Rolls Series], III. 123). On the death of Henry IV, to whom Pelham was to act for the rest of his own life as executor, he was immediately replaced in the treasurership of the Exchequer by Thomas earl of Arundel, and Bishop Beaufort superseded the archbishop at the Chancery ; not long afterwards Pelham's duchy of Lancaster stewardship fell to Sir Walter Hungerford (*Rot. Parl.*, IV. 5 ; *C.P.R.*, *1413–16*, 54 ; Duchy of Lancaster, Accounts Various, P.R.O., D.L.28, IV. 5). Pelham comfortably accommodated himself to the new state of affairs, especially after Archbishop Arundel's death in February 1414 removed an important reminder of the late reign, and in May 1414 Pelham was included in an unfruitful embassy from Henry V which offered an alliance to Charles VI of France in return for a restoration of his French heritage (Wylie, *The Reign of Henry V*, I. 404). Preparation for war was decided on in the November 1414 parliament. In the following February Pevensey castle was chosen as the place of ward for the now all-important state-prisoner, James I of Scotland, and he remained in Pelham's keeping until late in January 1416, Pelham receiving an allowance of £700 a year (*C.P.R.*, *1413–16*, 286). Pelham served on none of Henry V's campaigns, being sixty years of age by the time of the first expedition, but he acted on loan-raising commissions and at musters of retinues, and his son, John, who later became chamberlain of Household to Queen Catherine of Valois, served on the second campaign which began in the summer of 1417. Sir John was, moreover, a member of the Council left behind by Henry V to govern England in his absence, and Thomas, duke of Clarence, the heir presumptive, made him one of his executors on 10 July 1417. In the spring of 1419 Henry IV's widow, Joan of Navarre, when accused of plotting the king's death by necromancy, was placed by the Council into Pelham's custody at Pevensey (*P.P.C.*, II. 218, 219, 239 ; R. A. Newhall, *The English Conquest of Normandy*, 240 ; Devon, *Issues of the Exchequer*, 362 ; *C.P.R.*, *1416–22*, 75, 85, 148, 197, 199, 201, 210, 270, 417 ; *C.C.R.*, *1413–19*, 435). Along with Queen Joan at Pevensey were her second son by her first marriage, Arthur of Brittany, and the bastard of Bourbon, both taken prisoner at Agincourt, and after May 1422 Pelham had in custody the uncle of the young earl of March, Sir John Mortimer of Bishop's Hatfield (Herts), who had threatened to raise an insurrection in his nephew's interest or else join Charles VII of France. Mortimer was to be at Pevensey until June 1423 ; his escape from the Tower, where he was transferred, while under suspicion of treason, was to result in his execution later in the same year (*Wars of the English in France*, ed. J. Stevenson [Rolls Series], I. 397–8 ; Devon, *op. cit.*, 384 ; *P.P.C.*, II. 332 ; III. 11). In the summer of 1428 Pelham acted as principal executor to Sir Thomas Erpingham, like himself one of Henry of Bolingbroke's stalwarts in 1399, a great Lancastrian commoner. On 8 February 1429 he himself made his will, providing for his burial in the Cistercian abbey of Robertsbridge and he died on 12 February (*Chichele Register*, II. 408–9 ; *C.C.R.*, *1422–9*, 388, 435 ; *C.F.R.*, *1422–30*, 236).

Sir Henry Plesyngton of Burley, knight of the shire for Rutland in 1420, 1422, and 1425, j.p. in Rutland from February 1422 continuously until his death in 1452, and sheriff of Rutland in 1426–7, 1431–2, and 1440–1, was next younger brother and heir to Robert Plesyngton, who died some time before 1409 while still in ward to Joan of Navarre, Henry IV's queen. They were the sons of Sir Robert Plesyngton (ob. 1405) who at Henry IV's accession had recovered the estates of his father, Sir Robert Plesyngton, a former Chief Baron of the Exchequer (1380–6), who (in 1399) had posthumously incurred forfeiture for treason for his support of the Lords Appellant of 1388. The family estates, of which Sir Henry secured livery of seisin in February 1420, included the manor of Healaugh and half of Reeth in upper Swaledale, the manors of Ilkley (West Riding, Yorks), Toynton (Lincs), and Burley (purchased by his grandfather from Bishop Despenser of Norwich), and there was property in Southampton (worth £20 a year) and in London (*D.N.B.*, XLV. 423 ; *C.F.R.*, *1405–13*, 159, 204 ; *C.C.R.*, *1419–22*, 33 ; *Feudal Aids*, III. 297, 350 ; IV. 49, 213 ; VI. 456 ; *V.C.H.*, *Yorkshire, North Riding*, I. 240 ; *H.M.C.*, *11th Report, Mss. of Southampton*, 3). Sir Henry (he may well have been knighted during the last year of Henry V's reign when he accompanied the King to France [*D.K.R.*, XLIV. 628]) married Roger Flore's daughter, Agnes, for his first wife (*V.C.H.*, *Rutland*, II. 246), and Flore appointed him the overseer of his will on 15 April 1424, describing him as ' his son ' (Somerset House, *Luffenham Register*, fo. 9). By 1 March 1425, however, Agnes Flore was dead and Sir Henry had married, as his second wife, Isabel, daughter and heir of Aubrey Wittlebury (*V.C.H.*, *Rutland, op. cit.*). She outlived him by over eight years after his death in September 1452. In his will he arranged to be buried in the church of the hospital of St. Mary outside Bishopsgate, London, and provided for the sale of his Yorkshire estates at Radcliffe and Ilkley to endow a pilgrimage by four mass-priests to Jerusalem, Rome, and Compostella (Somerset House,

. *Register Rous*, fo. 17). The marriage and wardship of his heir, William, was thought worth the getting by Edmund Beaufort, duke of Somerset (*C.P.R., 1452-61*, 30).

Thomas Poge, m.p. for Nottingham in 1420, December 1421, 1422, 1423, and 1427, was mayor from Michaelmas to Michaelmas, 1421-2, and 1423-4 (Stevenson, *Records of Nottingham*, II. 428 ; *C.P.R., 1422-9*, 193). For some of his activities as a merchant stapler of Calais using the port of Hull, see *C.P.R., op. cit.*, 348.

Walter Portman, m.p. for Taunton in 1417, 1419, May and December 1421, 1422, 1425, 1426, 1427, 1431, and 1435, was sometime counsel to the Luttrells of Dunster (H. C. Maxwell Lyte, *Dunster and its Lords*, 131-3). He was of the quorum as a justice of gaol delivery in Somerset (*C.P.R., 1429-36*, 469). Walter was the father of John Portman, a member of the Middle Temple Inn, and grandfather of William Portman, the Marian Chief Justice (J. Hutchins, *History and Antiquities of Dorset*, I. 262).

Reginald Pympe esquire, knight of the shire for Kent in 1411 and 1422. The son and heir of William Pympe, sheriff of Kent in 1363, 1371, and 1374, and knight of the shire in 1372, Reginald succeeded his father in 1376, when he was still a minor, in property that was assessed at 100 marks a year in 1412. His chief estates were the manor of Pympe's Court in Loose near Maidstone and the nearby manor of Nettlestead on the Medway, where he built a new manor house which he made his usual residence. This manor, held by the family formerly of the Clares and later of their descendants and successors, the earls of Stafford, had remained in the wardship of the superior lord during Pympe's minority and the reality of the Stafford tie is otherwise vouched for in the heraldic devices in the windows of the church there. Pympe, moreover, married into a neighbouring family also connected with the Staffords, his wife being a daughter of Sir Ralph Frenyngham ; his brother-in-law, John Frenyngham, to whom he was feoffee, founded a chantry at East Farleigh at the time of Pympe's first return to parliament in 1411 and made provision for inclusion in the bede-roll of Hugh and Thomas, the second and third earls of Stafford, and of Ralph, the latter's brother, who had been murdered at York by Sir John Holand, Richard II's half-brother, in 1385. Two of Reginald Pympe's descendants, John and another Reginald, were to join the unsuccessful rebellion of Henry Stafford, second duke of Buckingham, against Richard III in 1483, their lands being then forfeited but restored by Henry VII (Hasted, *History of Kent,* II. 146, 286 ; *Archaeologia Cantiana*, XXI. 219, 241 ; XXVIII. 165 ; *Kent Records*, VII. 74 ; XII. 125-6). Reginald Pympe's active life fell in the period of the minority of Humphrey Stafford, first duke of Buckingham, and there is no evidence of any clearly discernible political attachment on his part, although his eldest son, John, who predeceased his father in December 1421, had been a member of the retinue of Duke Humphrey of Gloucester since 1415 and had accompanied him to France in the spring of 1421, the year of his death (Nicolas, *Agincourt, op. cit.*, 334 ; *D.K.R.*, XLIV. 569, 625-6). Reginald seems to have suffered from financial embarrassments at times, but he was sufficiently influential to serve on occasional royal commissions of array and subsidy-assessment in Kent ; in 1409–10 he was sheriff of Kent, in 1411–12 escheator in Kent and Middlesex (*List of Sheriffs*, 68 ; *List of Escheators*, 66), and from March 1418 to July 1420 he served as j.p. in Kent (*C.P.R.*, *1416–22*, 454). He died in the summer of 1426, the writ of *Diem clausit extremum* being issued on 28 August. Eleven years later died his grandson and heir, Reginald, the son and heir of his eldest son, John.

Walter Reson, m.p. for Wareham in March 1416, 1420, May 1421, 1422, 1423, 1425, 1427, 1431, and 1432, and for Melcombe Regis in 1419 ; from 10 October 1415 until 18 July 1417 he was controller of customs and subsidies at Melcombe ; from 18 July 1417 until November 1427 he was collector of customs and subsidies in that port area, from 25 July 1421 being also one of the three overseers and controllers of tronage and pesage there. From 22 November 1418 (reappointed by 4 February 1424) he was deputy-butler at Melcombe (*C.P.R.*, *1413–16*, 333 ; *1416–22*, 12, 175, 392 ; *1422–9*, 65, 177 ; *C.F.R.*, *1413–22*, 203, 291, 292, 294 ; *1422–30*, 20, 24–5, 108, 152, 196). In 1422–3 he was mayor of Wareham (J. Hutchins, *History and Antiquities of Dorset*, I. 82). He attested almost all parliamentary elections for Wareham, when he was not himself returned, between 1414 and 1437, and was present at the Dorset elections in 1417, May 1421, and 1425 (P.R.O., C.219, Bundles 11–15).

Sir Robert Roos of Gedney (Lincs) and Hunmanby (East Riding, Yorks), knight of the shire for Lincolnshire in 1422, is not to be confused with the younger son of William Lord Roos of Hamlake of the same name, who was one of the royal Carvers to Henry VI from 1432 to his death in the winter of 1448–9 and who figured as ambassador in most of the important diplomatic missions to France between 1441 and 1448. The Lincolnshire knight of the shire was dead by September 1441. He was the son and heir of Sir James Roos and had livery of his Lincs and Yorks estates in November 1411 after proof of age, and about the same time he married Joan, one of the three daughters and coheirs of Sir John Rochford of Boston, steward of the bishop of Ely, m.p. for Lincs in 1377, 1390, 1394, 1397, and 1399 and for Cambs in 1407. In 1436 his landed property in Lincs, Yorks, Staffs, Norfolk, and Suffolk, made him the second largest non-baronial landowner in Lincs (his nephew by marriage, Philip Tilney of Boston, being the first) with an annual income of £165 (*C.C.R.*, *1409–13*, 252, 276 ; Blomefield, *Norfolk*, IX. 108 ; *E.H.R.*, XLIX. 635 ; *Feudal Aids*, III. 268, 291, 336, 362 ; VI. 268). He was made j.p. for the parts of Holland in Lincs in July 1420, and was reappointed in July 1423 and served until his death ; between November 1420 and May 1422 he was sheriff of Lincs and he was again sheriff in 1431–2 and 1435–6. These appointments coincide with the periods of Duke Humphrey of Gloucester's greatest political influence, but there are safer indications of Roos's connexions with the duke ; he served in his retinue in the 1415 expedition to France ; from July 1424 until 1431 he was Gloucester's co-feoffee to Sir John Keighley in his Lincolnshire manors ; in January 1432 when the duke shared a grant of the wardship of the Fitz Walter estates Roos was one of his mainpernors, and he was again his surety when Gloucester secured the wardship of the property of the late duke of Norfolk (N. H. Nicolas, *Agincourt*, 333 ; *C.C.R.*, *1422–9*, 267, 329 ; *1429–35*, 110 ; *C.F.R.*, *1430–7*, 81, 143). Roos was

P

also connected with Robert Lord Willoughby of Eresby ; they served each other as feoffee (*C.C.R.*, *1419–22*, 194, 198 ; *1422–9*, 379). Roos does not appear to have been present at any of the Lincolnshire elections to parliament except in his capacity as sheriff, but from October 1414 onwards his attorney was consistently present at the Yorkshire elections along with the other attorneys of the lords of the franchises, Roos being described in the indentures of election as of Gedney or Hunmanby (P.R.O., C.219, Bundles 11–14).

John Russell, apprentice-at-law, was knight of the shire for Herefordshire in April 1414, 1417, 1419, 1420 (when he was an unsuccessful candidate for the Speakership), May and December 1421, 1422, 1423 (Speaker), 1426, 1429, 1431, 1432 (Speaker), and 1433. He was four times escheator of his shire and the attached area of the Welsh march, in 1410–11, 1415–16, 1419–20, and 1432–3, and was once sheriff, in 1417–18 ; he was a j.p. in Herefordshire from February 1407 for the last thirty years of his life (except for the short time when he was omitted from the commission from December 1427 to March 1428), and he also served the commission of the peace in the neighbouring county of Gloucestershire from the beginning of Henry V's reign in March 1413 to November 1416. A pleader in the central royal courts, he was engaged as counsel to the duchy of Lancaster year by year from 1403 to 1421 (E. Foss, *The Judges of England*, IV. 140 ; Duchy of Lancaster, Accounts Various, P.R.O., D.L.28, Bundle 4. 3–11 ; Duchy of Lancaster, Miscellaneous Accounts, P.R.O., D.L.41, Bundle 4. 23). He was parliamentary proxy for the abbot of Gloucester in 1410, 1411, and 1417 (P.R.O., S.C.10, Nos. 2153, 2175, 2268). On 17 August 1415 he was appointed an overseer of the will of Edward duke of York (killed at Agincourt) ; he was already one of the duke's feoffees in an important group of his estates and remained one of the committee from 1415 until 1433, when, following a petition in parliament in the previous year, Richard, the duke's nephew and heir, secured livery of seisin of his inheritance (*C.P.R.*, *1413–16*, 350 ; *C.C.R.*, *1413–19*, 294 ; *1429–35*, 134, 214, 260 ; A. Gibbons, *Early Lincoln Wills*, 146). He was executor to John Lord Haryngton of Aldingham (the main family seat was by this time at Porlock, Somerset), who was son-in-law of the third earl of Devon, and who died on 11 February 1418, probably on military service in France (C. E. H. Chadwyck Healey, *History of West Somerset*, 256). Already Russell was the feoffee of Joan widow of William Beauchamp of Abergavenny (*C.P.R.*, *1416–22*, 302, 305–6 ; S. Shaw, *History of Staffordshire*, II. 245 ; *V.C.H.*, *Buckinghamshire*, IV. 415 ; *C.C.R.*, *1419–22*, 86–90) ; and in 1426, probably as a result of his Yorkist connexion, he also began to act as a feoffee for the marriage settlement of John Holand, earl of Huntingdon, and his wife, Anne, dowager countess of March (*C.C.R.*, *1422–9*, 274 ; *C.P.R.*, *1429–36*, 4, 114).

Russell died in the spring of 1437, the writ of *diem clausit extremum* being issued on 20 June to the escheator in Herefordshire alone, which suggests that he held no land outside that county (*C.F.R.*, *1430–7*, 300). (The *D.N.B.* article on John Russell [*op. cit., sub eo nomine*] is incorrect in identifying Russell with the knight of the shire for Wilts in 1450, the Herefordshire lawyer having then been dead for thirteen years. As Round pointed out in his *Family Origins*, there is no basis for supposing the Speaker to have been of West-Country origin or an ancestor of the first earl of Bedford. W. R. Williams, in his *Herefordshire*

Members of Parliament, makes the error of identifying him with the John Russell who sat for Weymouth in 1450 and, moreover, confuses him with John, son of Sir John Russell of Worcester, to whom the Speaker acted as executor.)

John Seymour, m.p. for Ludgershall in 1422 and for Wiltshire in 1435, 1439, and 1445 ; he was sheriff of Hants, 1430–1, 1436–7, 1453–4 ; of Wilts, 1431–2, 1450–1 ; of Somerset and Dorset, 1433–4 ; of Herefordshire, 1457–8. From March 1438 until July 1461 (except from 29 August to 8 December 1459) he was j.p. in Wilts.

John Shelley, m.p. for Rye in 1410, 1417, 1420, December 1421, and 1422, and for Sandwich in 1426, 1429, and 1435, was sometime counsel to the burgesses of Lydd, a member of the Cinque Port of Rye.

Sir John Skelton, knight of the shire for Cumberland in 1402, 1406, and 1422, came of a good Cumberland family with substantial estates in the west of the county. Lessee for life of the purpresture of Armathwaite in the royal forest of Inglewood from 1387, Skelton secured in January 1399 what proved at first to be only a temporary prospective lease of several closes in the forest, but in 1407 these were granted him for life. The first grant came as a direct result of his attachment to the eldest son of the duke of York, Edward of Norwich, then duke of Aumâle (Nicolson and Burn, II. 340 ; *C.C.R., 1396–9*, 500 ; *C.P.R., 1396–9*, 556, 562 ; *1399–1401*, 52 ; *1405–8*, 294 ; *1429–36*, 271 ; *C.F.R., 1430–37*, 263). Skelton was acting as lieutenant-warden in November 1398 to Aumâle who was Warden of the West March towards Scotland at that time, and when the duke accompanied Richard II to Ireland in 1399 Skelton was made one of his attorneys (*Cal. Documents re Scotland*, IV. 108 ; *Rot. Scot.*, II. 146). His grant of the office of controller of the castle of Bordeaux for life in 1399 probably came by this channel of patronage ; Skelton was still holding the office in July 1401 and may have gone overseas when Edward of Norwich, now reduced in dignity to his former title of earl of Rutland, was appointed lieutenant of Aquitaine (*C.P.R., 1399–1401*, 161), but he was present at the rout of the Scots at Homildon Hill on 14 September 1402, where he took prisoner the son of the Regent of Scotland, Murdoch earl of Fife, along with William Lord Graham. Skelton was knight of the shire in the next parliament and again four years later when the Commons petitioned on his behalf for compensation for his inability to ransom Murdoch Stewart. At Michaelmas 1404 Skelton had been granted a royal annuity of 40 marks and in 1404–5 had served as sheriff of Cumberland ; the outcome of the parliamentary petition of 1406 was a further annuity of 100 marks which he later, in December 1412, changed for one of £51 13s. 4d. charged on the issues of the alnage of cloth in Somerset and Dorset (*C.P.R., 1401–5*, 411 ; *1405–8*, 69, 336, 340 ; *1408–13*, 455 ; *Rot. Parl.*, III. 597 ; *List of Sheriffs*, 27 ; *Cal. of Docs. re Scotland*, IV. 148). He was again sheriff of Cumberland in 1408–9. His annuities were renewed by Henry V and he served on a number of local commissions and during the vacancy of the see of Carlisle in 1419–20 farmed the temporalities (*C.P.R., 1413–16*, 229, 373 ; *C.F.R., 1413–22*, 289). But he was not appointed to the commission of the peace for Cumberland until 3 December 1420 during the duke of Gloucester's ' custody ' of the realm (he served continuously until 1437), and his third appointment to the shrievalty of Cumberland, for which he had to wait until November 1431, also coincided with Gloucester's determined effort at that time to make himself paramount. Skelton served as escheator for Cumberland and Westmorland in 1433-4. His son John, who had seen much military service in France and had been granted lands in the ' bailliages ' of Caen and the Côtentin and also property in Harfleur, had been granted an annuity for life of £20 as his personal retainer by Duke Humphrey in September 1423 and twelve years later on still had close connexions with him (*D.K.R.*, XLI. 707, 766 ; XLII. 395 ; XLIV. 627 ; *C. and W.A. and A.S. Tract Series*, Vol. 2, 177 ; *C.C.R.*, *1429–35*, 445). Skelton's other son, Richard, had been a member of Gloucester's retinue in Normandy as early as 1417 (*D.K.R.*, XLIV. 597, 608). In 1437 and 1439 Sir John secured a grant in survivorship of the Inglewood forest leases to him and his son John, and also of his royal annuity of 40 marks (enjoyed since 1404), and he must have died soon after.

Robert Skerne of Kingston-on-Thames, knight of the shire for Surrey in 1420 and 1422. In 1412 he held land in Surrey worth £20 a year, but in right of his wife, Joan the daughter and heir of Sir William de Windsor and his wife, Alice Perrers, Edward III's mistress, Skerne also held a manor in the Vale of White Horse (Berks) and several properties in Oxford (*Feudal Aids*, I. 60 ; VI. 518 ; *V.C.H., Berks*, IV. 288 ; *Oxford Historical Society Trans.*, LXXXIX [*Oseney Cartulary*], II. 398–9 ; III. 234 ; Manning and Bray, *Surrey*, III. 83). On 28 October 1417 Skerne was included in the quorum of the Surrey commission of the peace and served as j.p. until December 1431. He was a commissioner for sewers between Bermondsey and Deptford Strand, but served on very few other local royal commissions apart from that of the peace. He was sworn to the peace with other Surrey notables in May 1434. He had connexions with Sir Thomas Charleton, for whom he acted as feoffee to uses in estates in Middlesex and Buckinghamshire (Cussans, *Hertfordshire*, III. 273 ; *C.C.R.*, *1429–35*, 124). Skerne died on 4 April 1437 and was buried in All Saints' church, Kingston. His brass described him as ' validus, fidus, discretus lege peritus ' and told how ' regalis juris vivens promovit honores ' (*Surrey Arch. Collections*, VIII. 61 ; XXIX. 103). In 1459 his nephew founded a chantry at Kingston for members of the Skerne family including Robert (*C.P.R.*, *1452–61*, 499).

Robert Squibbe, m.p. for Shaftesbury in 1419, 1420, May and December 1421, 1422 ,and 1423, was acting in November 1422 as attorney in an Exchequer plea (Exchequer, L.T.R. Memoranda Roll, 1 Hen. VI. P.R.O., E/368/195 sub *Recorda*). He was connected with John Hody, later Chief Justice, as a co-feoffee (E. A. and G. S. Fry, *op. cit.*, 312 ; *Somerset Record Society, Transactions*, XXII. 68, 192).

Sir Humphrey Stafford, knight of the shire for Staffordshire in 1406 and for Dorset in April and November 1414, 1417, 1419, 1420, May 1421, 1422, 1426, 1427, and 1432 ; sheriff of Staffordshire in 1403-4, and of Dorset and Somerset in 1415-16 and 1423-4. He had inherited and married into large landed possessions in the west midlands and in the south-west of England ; his father had been one of the wealthiest commoners in England with £570 a year. The Staffords were, of course, well connected : Sir Humphrey's grandmother was a daughter of Ralph first earl of Stafford and so Sir Humphrey was second cousin to Humphrey the sixth earl and first duke of Buckingham ; he himself married the daughter of his stepmother by a former marriage, Elizabeth Maltravers ; one of his daughters married James, the nephew of Thomas Lord Berkeley—in the contract of marriage drawn up on 25 July 1414 Lord Berkeley declared his nephew to be his heir male to the entailed Berkeley estates—and in the subsequent dispute between James and his cousin, the countess of Warwick, and her husband Richard Beauchamp earl of Warwick, who seized Berkeley castle immediately after Lord Thomas's death in 1417, Sir Humphrey Stafford was indirectly involved (his temporary ejection from his Staffs manor of Perton by John Throckmorton (*q.v*), Warwick chamberlain of the Exchequer, and one of the earl's clerks, John Baysham, was probably incidental to the major dispute) (John Smyth of Nibley, *The Lives of the Berkeleys*, ed. J. Maclean, II, 40–8 ; *C.C.R.*, *1413–19*, 469 ; *1419–22*, 28) ; Sir Humphrey's second son, John, on 16 March 1426 was contracted in marriage with a daughter of William Lord Botreaux (*Collectanea Topogr. et Geneal.*, IV. 249 *et seq.*) ; his eldest son Richard had married Maud, who later became countess of Arundel, the daughter of Robert Lovell esquire, Sir Humphrey's fellow-knight of the shire in May 1421 and 1422 (W. H. H. Rogers, *The Strife of the Roses and the Days of the Tudors in the West*, 139 *et seq.* ; E. F. Jacob, *Chichele Register*, II. 249) ; his third and only surviving son, William, married Katherine, daughter of Sir John Chidiock, by whom he had a son Humphrey who was later Lord Stafford of Southwick and (shortly before his execution for treason in 1469) earl of Devon (W. H. H. Rogers, *loc. cit.*) ; Alice, another daughter of Sir Humphrey, married first Sir Edmund Cheney of Broke (Wilts), knight of the shire for Wiltshire in 1429, and then after his death in the following year, Walter Tailboys, cousin and heir of the half blood of Gilbert de Umfraville, earl of Angus (Rogers, *loc. cit.* ; J. Hodgson, *History of Northumberland*, Part II, Vol. I, 6). Sir Humphrey died at the age of about sixty-three on 27 May 1442 and was buried in the chapel of St. Anne, founded by him in the Benedictine abbey church of Abbotsbury. His half-brother, John Stafford, then (since 1425) bishop of Bath and Wells, whom he did not live to see succeed Chichele as archbishop of Canterbury in the following year, was his principal executor (Jacob, *Chichele Register*, II. 620–4). The two brothers were always on intimate terms and Sir Humphrey's connexion with John, who was appointed dean of the Court of Arches and archdeacon of Salisbury in 1419 and chancellor of the diocese early in 1421, was appointed keeper of the Privy Seal in May of the same year, served in that office until 16 December 1422 when he was promoted treasurer of England (a position he held until the crisis of March 1426), and was later from 4 March 1432 until January 1450 Chancellor of England, must have predetermined his political attitudes in the later stages of his own rather undistinguished career. One of the most interesting results of their relationship was the foundation of a chantry at Abbotsbury, after a petition to amortise property therefor which the Lords allowed to pass with the duke of Gloucester's concurrence in the parliament of 1429 ; on the bede-roll, along with founders' kin and the three Lancastrian kings, was Gloucester's own name (*C.P.R.*, *1429–36*, 63). But this was only one sign of the closeness of the connexion between Sir Humphrey and his ecclesiastical kinsman ; there were many others (e.g. *C.F.R., 1430–37* ; 19, 42, 92 ; *C.C.R., 1419–22*, 132).

Sir Richard Stanhope of Rampton, knight of the shire for Nottinghamshire in 1402, January and October 1404, 1406, December 1421, 1422, 1429, 1431, and 1433, came of a family of merchants of Newcastle-on-Tyne interested in the Flanders wool-trade. His grandfather, Richard, had been collector of customs between Berwick-on-Tweed and Scarborough in 1364, and mayor of Newcastle in 1364–5 and again (at the time of Sir Richard's birth) when he was parliamentary burgess for Newcastle in Richard II's first two parliaments. Sir Richard's father, John, had been mayor of Newcastle in 1366–7, but his marriage with Elizabeth, daughter and heir of Stephen Maulovel of Rampton (Sir Richard's mother), necessitated the transference of his interests into the midlands. Richard Stanhope was of age when, at the end of Richard II's reign, he succeeded to the manor of Rampton and, as heir-general to Sir John Longviliers, his mother's great-uncle, to other property in Notts ; and in due course he acquired estates in Warwickshire, Derbyshire, and Lincolnshire (S. Glover, *Derbyshire*, II. 164 ; Thoroton, *Nottinghamshire* [ed. J. Throsby], III. 243 ; *C.C.R., 1413–19*, 62 ; *Feudal Aids*, III. 264 ; IV. 126 ; VI. 415). On the eve of Henry IV's coronation he was one of forty-six esquires knighted in honour of the occasion (C. L. Kingsford, *Chronicles of London*, 48). If this were not enough to bring him into active support of the new dynasty his attitude might well have been conditioned by his first marriage with Elizabeth (or Joan), the sister of Sir Ralph Staveley, who was a retainer of John of Gaunt, steward of Household to Henry of Bolingbroke when he was still only earl of Derby, by the middle of Henry's reign constable of the castle of the High Peak and master-forester, steward and bailiff of that lordship of the duchy of Lancaster, knight of the shire for Lancashire in October 1404 and 1407, and sheriff of the county palatine in 1411–13 (for Staveley, see my *Knights of the Shire for Lancashire, 1377–1460* [Chetham Society, N.S., 96], 107–11). In any case Stanhope took the king's fee of 40 marks as a royal retainer on 18 March 1400 and enjoyed it until December 1406. He fought on the king's side in the battle of Shrewsbury and in the course of the Coventry parliament of October 1404 was appointed sheriff of Notts and Derbyshire and j.p. in the former county. In the course of his shrievalty he served with the king in Wales and in the north and helped in the suppression of the northern rising of 1405, receiving compensatory grants of 100 marks and £40 (*C.P.R., 1405–8*, 53, 84, 102). Probably because he was not in sympathy with the prince of Wales's political aims he was dropped from the commission of the peace in February 1407 and the same reason is possibly behind his imprisonment in the Tower with other midland notables for a month in the autumn of 1411 ; on 7 May 1412 he saw fit to secure a royal pardon for treasons and other offences (*C.C.R., 1409–13*, 243–4, 261 ; *C.P.R., 1408–13*, 398). He was thrice petitioned against in the Leicester parliament of April 1414 on the score of oppressive behaviour, in one case for forcible enclosure of common pasture, and on another charge was arrested although he subsequently counter-petitioned in the next parliament for damages (*Rot. Parl.*, IV. 29, 55). In November 1417, after a lapse of ten years, he was reincluded in the Notts commission of the peace and now he began again to serve frequently on local royal commissions. Probably his second marriage as far back as 1411 with Maud, only sister and eventual heir of Sir Ralph (later Lord) Cromwell of Tattershall, had something to do with this ultimate recovery of Stanhope's influence with the government. His connexions with his wife's family were close (*C.C.R.*, *1422–9*, 135 ; Surtees Society, *Test. Ebor.*, II. 40) ; for instance, he acted in 1434 as one of the two executors of his mother-in-law, Joan Dame Cromwell, her son, then treasurer of England (1433–43), being overseer. Sir Richard died on 9 April 1436, his heir, John, being his grandson by his first marriage (grandson on his mother's side of John Markham, Justice of Common Pleas) and (another reminder of the original Staveley family link) husband of Elizabeth, daughter of Sir Thomas Talbot of Bashall in Bowland (Lancs) and stepdaughter of Sir John de Assheton of Ashton-under-Lyne (Lancs) who had married Stanhope's first wife's sister. Sir Richard's other children by his first marriage had married into local families of note in the midlands, the Bassets and the Strelleys, but his two daughters by his second marriage with Maud Cromwell had been even better provided for : Joan was to marry a younger son of Henry Bourchier, earl of Essex, and Maud was contracted with Robert Lord Willoughby of Eresby and later with a younger brother of Warwick the Kingmaker, Sir Thomas Neville (Glover, *op. cit.*).

Thomas Stanley esquire of Elford, knight of the shire for Staffordshire in 1422, was the third son of Sir John Stanley K.G. of Knowsley and Lathom (Lancs) who had been first of all deputy-lieutenant and then lieutenant of Ireland from 1386–1391, from December 1399 to June 1402, and then again for the last seven months of his life in 1413–14, who had been steward of Household to Henry of Monmouth (then prince of Wales) in the early part of Henry IV's reign, and who later, from 1405 until the king's death in 1413, was steward of the royal Household itself (see my *Knights of the Shire for the County Palatine of Lancaster, 1377–1460*, Chetham Society, N.S., Vol. 96, 123). Thomas's marriage with a Cheshire heiress, Maud, daughter of Sir John Arderne, brought him tenure of estates in Cheshire estimated at his death to be worth £110 a year and manors in Staffs also, as well as kinship with Sir Robert Babthorpe, controller of the royal Household to Henry V and one of his executors (Babthorpe was his mother-in-law's second husband) (*Feudal Aids*, V. 23 ; *D.K.R.*, XXXVII. [*Recognisance Rolls of Chester*], 668, 678 ; Stebbing Shaw, *op. cit.*, I. 353). He was implicated in 1409 in certain disorders in the north midlands which were the subject of a parliamentary petition in 1410, but after appearance in the Court of King's Bench in Hilary term 1411 he procured a pardon. In May 1414 he was again indicted Coram Rege of having infringed the statute of Liveries, but two years later procured a pardon *ad hoc*, having pleaded that he had given liveries merely to secure a retinue for service in the suite of the earl of Warwick after the latter's appointment in February 1414 as captain of Calais and governor of the marches of Picardy (*Rot. Parl.*, III. 630–2 ; *William Salt Archaeological Society Trans.*, XVI. 86 *et seq.* ; XVII. 19 ; *C.P.R.*, *1413–16*, 403). He did not serve abroad, so far as is known, in Henry V's wars, participated in little local administrative work for the Crown, and he sat as knight of the shire in parliament only once. He was, however, Master of the Gild of the city of Lichfield, and was present at the parliamentary elections for Staffs in 1423, 1425, and 1429, in the interim occupying the office of sheriff of Warwickshire and Leicestershire in 1427-8 ; in 1433-4 and in 1438-9 he was sheriff of Staffordshire (Thomas Harwood, *History of Lichfield*, III. 399 ; P.R.O., C.219, XIII. 2, 3 ; XIV, 1 ; *List of Sheriffs*, 127, 145). In his later life he served on royal loan-raising commissions—on occasion he himself contributed—and on sundry local commissions. He got entangled in the Gresley-Vernon feuds in 1441—his daughter Anne had married the eldest son of Sir John Gresley, his fellow shire-knight of 1422—and at the same time ran foul of the men of Lichfield, for what reason is not known (*C.C.R., 1436–41*, 422 ; *Salt Society Trans.*, XVII. 160 ; F. Madan, *The Gresleys of Drakelow*, 281). With his nephew, Sir Thomas Stanley, controller of the royal Household to Henry VI at this time, he was in 1447 one of a committee of feoffees to uses in the Derbyshire and Leicestershire estates of Sir James Butler, the eldest son of the earl of Ormond, who was himself created earl of Wiltshire in 1449 and became one of the bulwarks of the later Lancastrian party. With such connexions it is amazing that Stanley of Elford kept out of the troubles that followed the turn of the century. Not so his son and heir, John, who fought as a Lancastrian at Bloreheath in 1459 and as a Yorkist at Tewkesbury, where he was made a knight banneret, in 1471. Thomas Stanley died on 13 May 1463 and was buried at Elford (*Hist. Mss. Comm., Hastings Mss.*, I. 1 ; Wedgwood, *History of Parliament, Biographies, op. cit.*, 799 ; D.K.R., XXXVII. 678).

Nicholas Stanshawe of Gloucs, m.p. for Appleby (Cumberland) in 1420, May and December 1421, and 1422, was a member of Lincoln's Inn in 1420 (*Admission Book, op. cit.*, 3, 8), and so was his son after him.

Robert Stanshawe of Stanshawe Court (near Chipping Sodbury), knight of the shire for Gloucestershire in 1422, 1423, 1426, and 1433. Himself a second son, he and his younger brother Nicholas entered the legal profession and the two brothers were doubtless the Stanshawe senior and junior who were already members of Lincoln's Inn in 1420 (*Admission Book*, 3). Robert's son was to go there in 1433, the fourth member of the family on the extant registers of the Inn (*ibid.*, 9). None of them rose very high in the profession, but Robert served as j.p. in Gloucs from 1423 till his death in 1447, except for a spell from 1426 to 1432. From 27 March 1423 onwards he enjoyed an annuity of £10 from the earl of Warwick, charged on his manor of Cherhill, near Calne (Wilts), being retained by the earl for life, doubtless as legal counsel (*C.P.R., 1446–52*, 22). From 1429 onwards he acted as one of the earl's feoffees to uses (*Feet of Fines, Dorset*, 306). He attended the Gloucs elections of knights of the shire to the parliaments of 1429, 1432, and 1435 (P.R.O., C.219. 14. 3–5). He died in 1447, his will (dated 18 March 1447) being proved by the Prerogative Court of Canterbury (Lambeth Palace Library, *Stafford Register*, fo. 159). If the will was adhered to, he was buried at Yate.

Thomas Stevens, m.p. for Gloucester in 1420, 1422, 1423, 1427, 1431, 1432, and 1442, was on 17 July 1421 appointed by the Exchequer to investigate the evasion of customs on exported staple merchandise along the Essex bank of the Thames and in East Anglia. Some five months later he was pardoned outlawry for debt, being described in the patent as mercer of London, *alias* gentilman of Gloucester. On 10 May 1434 he was appointed controller of customs at Bristol and was confirmed in office on 21 February 1441 after trouble with the deputy water-bailiff at Bristol in November 1439 (*C.P.R., 1416-22*, 356, 391 ; *1429-36*, 323 ; *1436-41*, 268, 414, 476, 478).

John Sturmy, m.p. for Ludgershall in 1422 ; for Marlborough in 1423 ; for Bedwin in 1431. He was the natural son and an executor of Sir William Sturmy and was present at his death (Somerset House, *Register Luffenham*, fo. 7 ; he is described in the will as Sir William's son, but the Sturmy estates were shared between John Seymour, son of Sir William's daughter Maud, and her sister Agnes).

Sir William Sturmy of Wolfhall near Bedwin was knight of the shire for Hampshire in 1384 ; for Wiltshire, in January 1390 ; for Hampshire again in November 1390 ; for Devon, in November 1391 ; for Wiltshire, again, in 1393, 1399, and 1401 ; for Devon again in October 1404 (when Speaker) ; yet again for Wiltshire in 1413, November 1414, 1417, and 1422. He was the heir of his uncle, Henry Sturmy, on the latter's death in 1381 and was then already of age (*Wilts Arch. and Nat. Hist. Magazine*, Vol. LI, 329) and capable of coming into possession of inherited estates in north Hants and east Wilts worth (in 1412) nearly £130 a year, in addition to which and about the same time he came into property in Devon *jure uxoris* worth another £40 a year (*Feudal Aids*, VI. 416, 450, 530). Sturmy appears in the accounts of the treasurer of the royal Household as early as December 1383 as the recipient of monies, and he may well already have been a member of it (P.R.O., E.101/401/2). Certainly one or two royal commissions on which he served in 1386 and 1387 suggest that he was in sympathy with Richard II's actions, and his returns to parliament (successively for three counties) in the period of Richard's recovery of power from the Lords Appellant (1390-3) suggest considerable local influence. He was retained by Richard II as a Household knight in October 1392 at a fee of 40 marks a year (*C.P.R., 1399-1401*, 453), went on Richard's first Irish expedition of 1394-5 with an esquire and six mounted archers (P.R.O., E.101/402/20), and from 11 April to 8 November 1397 was a member of a royal diplomatic mission which proceeded by way of Paris to Avignon and Rome to both Boniface IX and Benedict XIII 'in quibusdam arduis negociis et negociis statum pacis et tranquillitatis universalis sacrosancte ecclesie tangentibus contra scismam in dicta sacrosancta ecclesia pendentem' (Enrolled Foreign Accounts, Exchequer, L.T.R., 3.H IV, E.364/36, Mem. A). He soon accommodated himself to the revolution of 1399, sat in the first and second parliaments of the new reign, had his Crown annuity confirmed, and became for the first time a j.p. in Wiltshire. Two days after the end of the parliament of January–March 1401 he became a member of the royal Council itself with an annuity of 100 marks a year, and he continued to act (and be paid) in that capacity until July 1402 (*ibid.*), although for the greater part of this time he was absent in Germany on diplomatic missions that were part of a continental drive to secure recognition for the house of Lancaster : first, between 12 May and 9 August 1401, to the duke of Guelders to receive his homage and perhaps to forward his recognition of the anti-Kaiser, Rupert III of Bavaria, to whose eldest son Lewis, count palatine of the Rhine and duke of Bavaria, Henry IV was to marry his eldest daughter, Blanche, in the following year; Sturmy proceeded on a second mission to Germany which took him out of England from 12 September to 5 December 1401 (Exchequer, Accounts Various, K.R., P.R.O., E.101/318/16). From 16 February to 23 July 1402 he was again in Germany ' pro certis negociis maritagium Blanchie filie Regis tangentibus ' and to make arrangements for the safe-conducts and transport of the princess's entourage, and he only returned to England with Blanche's escort after her marriage at Heidelberg; until this event took place Sturmy was her steward of Household (Enrolled Foreign Accounts, Exchequer, L.T.R., P.R.O., E.364/36, Mem. A; Accounts Various, E.101/404/11). Earlier in the year in which he was to act as Speaker for the Commons at Coventry (6 October–14 November 1404), in a session which yielded the largest parliamentary subsidy of the reign, Sturmy had been in Rotterdam trying to iron out difficulties over claims and counter-claims for compensation for acts of piracy by Flemish and English merchantmen in the Narrow Seas (*Literae Cantuarienses*, ed. J. B. Sheppard [Rolls Series], III. 78). By the advice of the Coventry parliament, Sturmy was made a member of a small mission to the High Master of the Order of Teutonic Knights, charged with the business of easing the tension that had arisen as a result of the attempts to exclude English cloth importers made by the Prussian and Baltic towns of the Hanseatic League. He left England for Prussia on 31 May 1405 and did not return, by way of Lübeck, Hamburg, Bremen, and Dordrecht, until 18 February 1406. The mission was successful in suspending the embargo on trade imposed by the Hansards and in negotiating a truce, but the settlement of damages made a final treaty difficult to achieve and Sturmy spent almost the whole of 1407 at Marienburg, Middelburg, and The Hague trying to arrange (or perhaps postpone) a final settlement which was still unattained in 1415; in these negotiations Sturmy seems to have taken no part after 1407 (Wylie, *Henry IV*, II. 71–8; IV. 1–7; *Historical Letters of Henry IV*, ed. F. C. Hingeston [Rolls Series], II. lii; *Literae Cantuarienses*, op. cit., III. 90, 94, 101, 104; *Rot. Parl.*, III. 568, 574; Ancient Petitions, P.R.O., S.C.8, File 109, No. 5406; *Hist. Mss. Comm.*, *5th Report, Mss. of Dean and Chapter of Canterbury*, 443a). Sturmy's next diplomatic employ-ment did not come about until 3 March 1418, when he was appointed one of the two ambassadors charged to treat for the marriage of Henry V's brother, John duke of Bedford, to Jacqueline of Hainault, the daughter and heiress of the late count of Holland, who was eventually to marry the youngest of the sons of Henry IV, Humphrey duke of Gloucester. Nothing, of course, came of the proposal, but the ambassadors did make the passage to Holland (*P.P.C.*, II. 241, 343; *D.K.R.*, XLIV. 599). In the meanwhile, Sturmy had from some time before the summer of 1412 served Henry IV's queen, Joan of Navarre, as the chief steward of her estates and he was probably still occupying this position at the time of her disgrace in 1419 when she was imprisoned on charges of necromancy, for he received at the Exchequer the custody of a parcel of her Wiltshire dower-estates, including the manor of Ludgershall (*Kingsthorpiana*, ed. J. H. Glover, 15; *C.P.R.*, *1408–13*, 373; *C.F.R.*, *1413–22*, 321–2). His stepson-in-law, Sir Hugh Luttrell of Dunster, was Queen Joan's steward of Household. Sturmy was in favour with Henry V who confirmed his 1392 annuity of 40 marks on 5 November 1413; the king kept in touch with him after his second French invasion of 1417 (Wylie, *Henry V*, I. 468 n.). He was absent from the Wilts commission of the peace between November 1415 and February 1422, but he served as sheriff in 1418–19. Sturmy's position as hereditary steward and chief forester of the royal forest of Savernake (Wilts) brought him in 1417 into conflict with Humphrey duke of Gloucester who, acting presumably in his capacity as warden of the royal forests south of Trent and on the strength of a grant by Henry IV of the revenues of Savernake forest, dispossessed him of his stewardship and confined his interest to the occupation of three out of the five bailiwicks of the forest, where he was to act merely as any other forest bailiff. Sturmy petitioned Henry V against Gloucester's action and eventually, in October 1420, he was restored to his wardenship by the duke's letter patent (*Wilts. Arch. and N.H. Magazine, op. cit.,* LI. 271 *et seq.,* where ' Savernake archives ' are cited). At Henry VI's accession Sturmy's thirty-year-old royal annuity was renewed ; he continued to act as j.p. until July 1425, but he was otherwise inactive down to his death, which took place in his manor of Elvetham (Hants) on 22 March 1427. He was buried in the church of the Trinitarian priory of Easton in the forest of Savernake, of which he was patron and to which he bequeathed *inter alia* a volume of Decretals and two volumes of Ranulf Higden's *Polychronicon.* His feoffees included his wife's son-in-law, Sir Hugh Luttrell, seneschal of Normandy during the last two years of Henry V's reign, Bishop John Stafford of Bath and Wells, and Bishop Thomas Polton of Worcester who was also overseer of Sturmy's will. Probate was granted in the Prerogative Court of Canterbury on Lady Day, 1427, (Somerset House, *Register Luffenham,* fo. 7 ; *C.P.R., 1422–9,* 35, 449–50, 571. For the circumstances of Sturmy's death and an allegedly feigned, death-bed enfeoffment to exclude the coheirs, see a petition in Chancery brought by John Seymour, Sturmy's grandson, in 1451 [*ibid., 1446–52, 555–6*]). Sturmy's heirs were his daughter Agnes, wife of John Holcombe, and this John Seymour, the son of his eldest daughter Maud, wife of Roger Seymour of Hache Beauchamp, and ancestor of Henry VIII's third queen, Jane Seymour, and her brother, Protector Somerset (*Wilts Arch. and N.H. Magazine, op. cit.,* LI. 271 *et seq.,* 500 *et seq.*). For the Sturmy group in the Commons in the 1422 parliament, see p. 84.

John Sumpter, m.p. for Colchester in March 1416, 1419, 1422, 1423, and 1427. In May 1404, with his father, he had been involved in treasonable movements in Essex, fomented by Robert de Vere's mother, the dowager countess of Oxford, and encouraged by the abbots of Colchester and St. Osyth (*C.P.R., 1401–5,* 432). He was bailiff of Colchester in 1422–3 and 1424–5 (W. Gurney Benham, *Colchester Oath Book,* 84, 102–3). He was feoffee to uses of several East Anglian landholders including Robert Teye esquire, m.p. for Essex in 1397 and 1401, and Sir William Coggeshall, m.p. for Essex ten times between 1391 and 1422 (*C.C.R., 1422–9,* 290, 293, 408 ; *C.P.R., 1422–9,* 4, 391 ; *C.P.R., 1452–61,* 503). A connexion with John Leventhorpe, receiver-general of the duchy of Lancaster and m.p. for Herts in 1422 (*C.F.R., 1413–22,* 304) must have been created by the grant in the winter of 1419 to Leventhorpe of the wardship of that purparty of Sumpter's mother-in-law's estates in Essex which was the inheritance of his son then under age (the estates were held in mesne tenure of the earldom of Hereford then in process of division between the Bohun coheirs, Henry V himself and the dowager countess of Stafford ; the king's share was incorporated in the duchy of Lancaster).

Hamond Sutton, m.p. for Lincoln in March 1416, 1420, May 1421, 1422, 1423, 1425, and 1426, and knight of the shire for Lincolnshire in 1431, 1435, and 1439, escheator for Lincolnshire November 1423-4, and sheriff November 1428-9, j.p. in Lindsey August 1433–December 1434 and October 1436–November 1458. By May 1433 he was mayor of the Calais staple and in that year was mainly, as two years later when he was no longer mayor he was partly, responsible in negotiating corporate loan₃ by the Staplers to the Crown totalling in all some £8241-odd. By May 1443 and until the spring of 1447 he was again mayor of the Calais fellowship (*D.K.R.*, XLVIII. 293, 357 ; *Rot. Parl.*, IV. 474b, 484b ; *P.P.C.*, V. 278 ; *C.P.R.*, *1446–52*, 53). In 1436 he had already been the fifth non-baronial landowner in Lincs with lands there and in Notts worth £105 a year (*E.H.R.*, XLIX. 635). He died shortly before February 1462 when about seventy years old (*C.F.R.*, *1413–22*, 73 ; Wedgwood, *op. cit.*, 828-9).

John Tamworth, parliamentary baron for Winchelsea in 1419, 1422, 1427, and for Hastings in 1435 and 1445 ; shipowner (*C.P.R.*, *1413–16*, 421 ; Exchequer Issue Rolls, Easter and Trinity 10 Henry V, P.R.O., E.403, 655, Mems. 3, 8, 18 ; Exchequer Receipt Roll, Michs., 1 Henry VI, P.R.O., E.403, 703, Mems. 6, 7). From 8 February 1422 until February 1426 he was collector of customs and overseer of tronage at Chichester (*C.F.R.*, *1413–22*, 381, 383 ; *1422–30*, 20, 53, 108) ; from 28 January 1423 until June 1429 he was deputy-butler at Winchelsea (*C.P.R.*, *1422–9*, 8). In 1422-3 he was mayor of Winchelsea and in 1445-6 bailiff of Hastings (*Sussex Arch. Collections*, VIII. 234).

John Throckmorton, knight of the shire for Worcestershire in November 1414, 1420, 1422, 1432, 1433, and 1439, had followed his father in the enjoyment of the ' good lordship ' of the Beauchamps, earls of Warwick (W. Dugdale, *History of Warwickshire*, 558–9) : from October 1416 he had an annuity of 11½ marks from Earl Richard, augmented by 1431 when he was being allowed an additional 20 marks a year (Dugdale, *loc. cit.*). Throckmorton had served with Warwick in Normandy in 1417–18, being then in his second year as under-sheriff of Worcestershire, which position he occupied in 1416–18 and later in 1419–20 and 1430–1 (*List of Sheriffs*, 158 ; the office of sheriff was vested in fee in the earls of Warwick). He acted as a member of the quorum of the commission of the peace in Worcestershire from January 1414 to his death on 12 April 1445, and from October 1433 to December 1439 he was also a j.p. in Warwickshire. On 13 January 1419 he began what proved to be a tenure for life of the Beauchamp chamberlainship of the royal Exchequer (Exchequer, Issue Roll, Easter 7 Hen. V., P.R.O., E.403, 640, Mem. 10 ; Wedgwood in *History of Parliament, Biographies*, 851–2, is in error in putting Throckmorton's appointment as chamberlain in 1438, and is apparently unaware of the history of the two chamberlainships so that he does not point out the additional evidence for the strength of Throckmorton's attachment to the Beauchamp interest which this appointment afforded). In the last decade of Earl Richard's life, Throckmorton had acted as his feoffee and attorney and after the earl's death (in April 1439) as his executor (Blomefield, *Norfolk, op. cit.*, VI. 53, 111 ; E. A. and G. S. Fry, *Feet of Fines for Dorset*, 306 ; *C.F.R.*, *1430–7*, 314 ; N. H. Nicolas, *Testamenta Vetusta*, 233).

By this time, in fact, since Michaelmas 1433, concurrently with his chamberlainship of the Exchequer, Throckmorton held office as under-treasurer of England (*alias* clerk to the Treasurer). He retained the chamberlainship until his death in 1445 but relinquished the under-treasurership at Michaelmas 1443 (P.R.O., *List of Officials* [typescript] ; Wedgwood, *op. cit.*, 851 ; F. Palgrave, *Ancient Calendars and Inventories of the Treasury of the Exchequer*, II. 158 ; *P.P.C.*, V. 81). He had represented Worcs in the parliaments of November 1414, 1420, 1422, 1432, 1433, and 1439 ; in 1435, 1439, and in 1442 he had acted as parliamentary proxy for the abbot of Evesham (P.R.O., S.C.10, Nos. 2427, 2432, 2460) ; and he had been present at the Worcs elections to parliament in 1413, May 1421, 1427, 1431, and 1435 (P.R.O., C.219, 11–14).

Sir Peter Tilliol of Scaleby, knight of the shire for Cumberland in 1378, November 1380, 1385, 1391, September 1397, 1410, 1413, 1417, 1420, December 1421, 1422, 1425, and 1426. A minor at the time of his father Sir Robert Tilliol's death in 1367, Peter's wardship and marriage were eventually granted in February 1370 to Alice Perrers, Edward III's mistress. The Tilliols held lands in west Cumberland and Peter came into property in the bishopric of Durham and in the East Riding of Yorkshire, but the main centre of their territorial interest lay between Carlisle and the Border where they held considerable estates in the vicinity of their castle of Scaleby, held by them of the Crown by cornage since Henry I's reign (*C.F.R.*, *1356–68*, 347, 349 ; *C.P.R.*, *1367–70*, 376 ; *C. and W.A. and A.S.*, *Tract Series*, No. 2, 154 ; Nicolson and Burn, *Westmorland and Cumberland*, II. 121 ; *Cal. Inq. p.m.*, IV. 159 ; R. Surtees, *North Durham*, I. 28, 215 ; Surtees Society, *Feodarium Prioratus Dunelmensis*, 112 n. ; *Feudal Aids*, IV. 84 ; VI. 548). To his income from family property Tilliol was able to add by securing suitable farms of royal estate (at annual rents) in and around Carlisle and in Inglewood forest and in other parts of Cumberland where the Crown retained certain demesne lands. By 14 October 1377 Peter had offered proof of age and a year later sat in his first parliament at Gloucester, the beginning of a parliamentary career due to last for nearly half a century (*Rot. Scot.*, II. 3). On 7 December 1379 he was one of a committee temporarily charged with the custody of the West March towards Scotland (*ibid.*, 19) and on 26 May 1380 he was made a j.p. in Cumberland, an office he was to hold more or less continuously down to 1401, but then not again until 1423. Perhaps it was in 1384 that he was taken prisoner by the Scots (*ibid.*, 72), for early in the following year he was arranging for his ransom, being then at large. In 1386–7 he was royal escheator in Northumberland, Cumberland, and Westmorland (an office he was again to hold in 1391–2) and in the following financial year, 1387–8 (the year of the Appellants' tenure of power), he was sheriff of Cumberland. He was again sheriff in 1394–5. In June 1399 he took all steps necessary for his joining Richard II's second expedition to Ireland and probably went there. He was at the time of Henry of Bolingbroke's return to England farming the temporalities of the see of Carlisle, then occupied by one of Richard's warmest supporters (Bishop Merke) (*C.P.R.*, *1396–9*, 555, 573 ; *C.C.R.*, *1396–9*, 508). Tilliol was dropped from the Cumberland commission of the peace in 1401, but he served on other royal commissions in the county and in 1403–4 was sheriff. His connexion with the Nevilles, of whom he held the manor of Torpenhow (over which he had a successful suit with the young earl of Northumberland in 1423 [Selden Society, *Year Book I*

Henry VI, 95]), kept him out of the troubles which afflicted the north in the unquiet time of Henry IV. That this Neville attachment was close is evident from the earl of Westmorland's choice of him in October 1424 to be one of his executors (Surtees Society, Vol. 2, *Wills and Inventories*, 73). The earl died on 21 October 1425. In the following February, Tilliol served in his last and thirteenth parliament at the age of about seventy. He survived until the winter of 1434–5. His son and heir, Robert, an imbecile, outlived him by only a year and then the estates of the family were inherited by Sir Peter's daughters, Isabel (widow of Sir John Colville, grandson of the Sir John Colville executed at Durham for complicity in the Scrope-Mowbray rising of 1405 and on his mother's side of the Sir William Fulthorpe who had presided on the tribunal which condemned to death Archbishop Scrope of York), and Margaret, wife of Sir Christopher Moresby of Moresby in west Cumberland and of Windermere (*C.F.R., 1430–7*, 216, 231, 277).

Robert Treage, m.p. for Bodmin in 1413 and 1420 ; for Helston in March 1416 and 1419 ; for Liskeard in 1417 ; for Lostwithiel in May 1421 and 1422 ; for Truro in December 1421 and 1425. From July 1414 to November 1423 he was joint-collector of customs and subsidies in and between Plymouth and Fowey. In February 1426 he was appointed havener in Cornwall and at Plymouth (*C.F.R., 1413–22*, 69, 71, 204–5 ; *1422–30*, 125). In October 1413 was Exchequer co-lessee of the alien priory of Modbury (Devon), the lease being confirmed in June 1421 ; in February 1424 he was Exchequer co-lessee of the manor and borough of Helston, the lease being terminated by private parliamentary petition in 1432 (*C.F.R., 1413–22*, 39 ; *1422–30*, 72 ; *C.P.R., 1416–22*, 378 ; *1429–36*, 107, 133, 275 ; *Rot. Parl.*, IV. 384a, 396b). He was present at the Cornish elections to the parliaments of 1425 and 1429 (C.219, Bundles 13, 14).

John Trewint, m.p. for Liskeard in 1416 and 1435, for Truro in 1419, and for Lostwithiel in 1420, December 1421, 1422, 1423, and 1425, was ordered to be removed from the office of coroner in Cornwall on 6 July 1421 (*C.C.R., 1419–22*, 168).

John Tyrell of Herons in East Horndon (Essex), knight of the shire for Essex in 1411, 1413, March 1416, 1417, 1419, May 1421, 1422, 1425, 1429, 1431 (Speaker), 1433 and 1437 (Speaker), and, in the meantime, for Herts in 1427 (Speaker), came of a well-established Essex family. He himself had secured a good match when he married Alice, a daughter and coheir of the Sir William Coggeshall who was to be his fellow-knight of the shire in 1411 and 1422. She brought him the manor of North Benfleet and the estate of Jervais in South Benfleet (Essex). Within a year of Alice Coggeshall's death in 1422 he married Catherine, widow of John Spenser, keeper of the Great Wardrobe, and she brought him the manor of Banham (Suffolk). By 1428 he had acquired lands at Northavon and Middleton (Hants), at Hunsdon, Bradfield, and Standon (Herts), and at Wendy (Cambs) as well (*Essex Arch. Soc. Trans.*, N.S., VII ; III. 79 ; Morant, *Essex*, I. 261 ; *Feudal Aids*, I. 190 ; II. 216, 350, 373, 451 ; III. 588 ; VI. 445, 523). He was in great demand as a member of committees of feoffees to uses and at one time and another acted in this way for Richard duke of York, John de Vere earl of Oxford, Lord Fitzwalter, Sir Thomas Erpingham, John Doreward (Speaker in 1399 and 1413), Richard Baynard (Speaker in 1420), John Harpour (m.p. Stafford in 1422 and at other times) and others. It was as a retainer of Sir Walter Hungerford, steward of the duchy of Lancaster south of Trent and soon to become steward of Henry V's Household as well, that Tyrell took out letters of protection for himself as being about to proceed on military service in Henry V's first expedition to France in 1415 (*D.K.R.*, XLIV. 573), but in fact he and his son William served with Humphrey, duke of Gloucester (P.R.O., E.101. 45. 13), and it was with Gloucester that John Tyrell was permanently to be connected in an attachment that was to determine the main courses of his political career. Certainly in 1416 Tyrell was acting as the duke's steward in Essex (W. G. Benham, *The Oath Book of Colchester*, 24), and by July 1418 he was one of the ducal mortgagees (*C.P.R., 1416–22*, 129). When in 1421 James Lord Berkeley sued out livery of the estates of his uncle, whose heir in the barony he was, it was only after a dispute with the heir-general, the countess of Warwick, and her husband, Richard Beauchamp, which had prompted him to seek and procure the aid of Duke Humphrey ; it was to Tyrell and a clerk in the duke's employment, Walter Sheryngton, that on 1 November 1420 Berkeley bound himself in a recognisance for 10,000 marks, undertaking to pay them (in the duke's interest) 1,000 marks within eighteen months of his having sued out livery of his castle and lordship of Berkeley and to grant to the duke the reversion of all his lands in Wales and elsewhere to the annual value of 400 marks, saving his own estate therein for life after their recovery. With the powerful support of the duke, who was then *custos Anglie*, this act of champerty was eventually successful (John Smyth of Nibley, *The Lives of the Berkeleys*, II, 40 *et seq.*). In the meantime Tyrell had served as sheriff of Essex and Herts in 1413–14 and in April 1419 had been appointed to the commission of the peace in Essex (*List of Sheriffs*, 44). He again served as sheriff in the same double bailiwick in 1422–3. Before the end of this year of office he had married (for his second wife) the widow and executrix of the late keeper of the Great Wardrobe, and together they petitioned the Council for payment of Henry V's debts to the late keeper which amounted to £2,700, and sought to be regarded as creditors with preference ; arrangements were made no earlier than December 1424 for the payment of no more than 1,000 marks owed to the late king by the earl of Northumberland, and the payment of even this quarter of the debt was to be spaced over the next five years, failing which Tyrell was to have recourse again to the Council and Henry V's executors (*P.P.C.*, III. 131 ; *C.P.R., 1422–9*, 267). He was still closely attached to Gloucester and was sheriff of Norfolk and Suffolk in 1426–7. In February 1427 he was made steward of the honours of Clare (Suffolk) and Thaxsted (Essex), at first during royal pleasure and then, on 1 June, until the duke of York, the heir of his uncle Edmund, late earl of March, should come of age. Tyrell's engagement had probably been secured by Duke Humphrey, who had been granted the wardship of the largest share of the Mortimer estates (*ibid.*, 353, 395, 401). Before the termination of his year of office as sheriff in East Anglia, Tyrell was irregularly elected knight of the shire for Herts to the parliament which sat from 13 October to 8 December 1427 and from 20 January to 25 March 1428 and in which he was Speaker. During the recess (on 19 December 1427) he was appointed chief steward of those estates of the duchy of Lancaster not enfeoffed to help fulfil the will of Henry V ; this office and an *ex officio* place on the duchy council he was to occupy nearly until his death in 1437 (W. R. Williams, *Lancaster Official Lists*, 19 ; *C.P.R.*, *1422-9*, *560* ; *1429-36*, *613-28* ; *1436-41*, *578-94*). It is difficult not to see Gloucester's influence in this appointment. Tyrell was so very much his man. In the previous April he and the Dean of the Arches, Dr. William Lyndwood, had been about to proceed to Holland (*D.K.R.*, XLVIII. 249) and there can be little doubt that the purpose of their visit was diplomatic work on behalf of the Protector, who had taken advantage of the recent return of his brother of Bedford to France to renew his interest in the affairs of his wife Jacqueline of Hainault. She was pestering him and the Council throughout the spring of 1427 for material help and in July, probably acting on the report of his agents, Gloucester got a grant of 5,000 marks from the Council to raise troops for the garrisoning of his wife's castles and towns in Holland ; he was forbidden to undertake a policy of aggression against the duke of Burgundy, however, without parliamentary consent. From 21 April 1430 until Henry VI's return from France in February 1432 Gloucester was *custos Anglie*. Tyrell was again Speaker in the only parliament which met in the interim, that is, in January 1431. On its last day Tyrell was granted £100 by warrant of the Council ; perhaps by way of reward, for Dr. Lyndwood, now Secondary in the Office of Privy Seal, who was *persona grata* to Gloucester, and, probably for this reason, had supplied the place of the Chancellor (Archbishop Kemp) at the opening of parliament when he delivered the customary sermon, was to receive the same gratuity. The grants may, however, have been advances of cash for their future service, for both men were to proceed to France and act for the next six months as members of the Council that was to attend on the king's person there (*P.P.C.*, IV. 82, 84, 109). Tyrell went abroad with a retinue of two men-at-arms and nine archers. Their muster was ordered on 4 May 1431. Three weeks later Tyrell was appointed treasurer of the royal Household with 100 marks a year and he continued to hold the office, and the co-ordinate position of treasurer of the King's Wars, after his return to England with the Court in February 1432 (in July 1434 Tyrell was involved before the Council in an unexplained leakage, over two years before, of 500 marks paid to him as treasurer of the Household by an Exchequer assignment on the London customs, which the collectors alleged was paid and of which he and the cofferer of the Household denied that they had ever received payment [*P.P.C.*, IV. 266]). About the time of his appointment to the treasurership of the royal Household, Tyrell was knighted. Tyrell's third occupation of the Speakership was not completed. Returned as knight of the shire to his thirteenth parliament in January 1437, he was elected to and served the Speaker's office until (what proved to be) within a week or so of the end of the parliament when he was superseded, allegedly in virtue of his failing health. This may well have been so, for he immediately afterwards resigned (or was displaced from) both his stewardship of the duchy of Lancaster and his treasurership of the Household and died before the summer had spent itself, his inquest post mortem being taken on 1 September 1437. At the time of his last Speakership he had been in receipt of the largest non-baronial income of anyone in Essex— £394 a year (*E.H.R.*, XLIX. 633 ; *D.N.B.*, LVII. 443). He was buried with his second wife in the church of the Austin friary in London (Stow).

Regarding Sir John's long attachment to the duke of Gloucester it is worth noting that his eldest son, Thomas, identified his interests with those of William Bothe, who had been treasurer of household to Gloucester early in Henry VI's reign and who became bishop of Coventry and Lichfield in 1447 and succeeded Kemp at York in 1452. Thomas was to be knight of the shire for Essex in 1442, 1445, 1447, February 1449, and 1459. His younger brother, William the elder, who married a daughter of Robert Darcy (m.p. Maldon in 1442) was knight of the shire for Suffolk in 1447 and 1459. Sir John Tyrell's fifth son, William the younger, was burgess of parliament for Weymouth in February 1449 and knight of the shire for Essex in November 1449, 1450, and 1455 (Wedgwood, *op. cit., Biographies*, 891–4). These sons were all Lancastrians and fought as such in the civil wars, William the elder being executed in 1462 for anti-Yorkist plotting.

Richard Tyrell (or Terell) esquire of Stoke Dabernon, knight of the shire for Surrey in 1422 and 1429, was brother of Sir John Tyrell of Heron in East Thorndon (Essex) and also of Edward Tyrell who sat for Essex in the parliaments of 1427, 1432, and 1435. All his estates seem to have been in Surrey, but he was buried in the church of the nunnery at Sopwell near St. Albans (Jacob, *Chichele Register*, II. 631 ; *Feudal Aids*, V. 121, 123, 125). Little is known of Richard Tyrell. He may have had some connexion with Calais in Henry IV's reign, because in March 1405 he was executor to Nicholas Usk, late treasurer of Calais, and he was later feoffee to John Norbury, who had been treasurer of England at the beginning of the reign and was later captain of Guînes (*C.P.R., 1405–8, 6 ; 1408–13, 65 ; C.C.R., 1413–19, 178–9*). Like his brother John, Richard was a friend of the great London stapler, Sir William Estfeld, who left £40 for distribution for Richard's soul's health, £20 among the latter's tenants in Surrey when next a parliamentary fifteenth should be levied (Lambeth Library, *Stafford Register*, fo. 139 *et seq.*). Richard had other London connexions, for he and his wife in 1417 are known to have paid quarterage as members of the Brewers' Company (W. Herbert, *Twelve Great Livery Companies of London*, I. 63 n.). Tyrell may have been a lawyer ; he was certainly literate, for he drew up his will at Stoke Dabernon on 26 May 1431 in his own hand ; he appointed as its overseer one of the barons of the Exchequer, Nicholas Dixon, who as rector of Cheshunt (Herts) had close connexions with the Norbury family, who were patrons of the living. Tyrell died some time between 26 May and 10 July 1431, when probate was allowed in the Prerogative Court of Canterbury (Somerset House, *Luffenham Register*, fo. 14).

William Ufford m.p. for Oxford in 1420, 1421 (December), 1422 and 1426 ; he was one of the two bailiffs of Oxford in 1404–5, 1410–11, and 1414–15 ; in 1419 he was made alderman ; and he was mayor in 1424–5 and 1426–7. (Oxford Hist. Soc., XLIV. 150, 212, 268 ; XXXVII. 19–22 ; LXXIII. 269.)

David Urban, m.p. for Bodmin in May 1421 and for Helston in 1422, 1423, and 1427, was of Penryn near Falmouth. In October 1418 he was lieutenant to Sir John Arundell, steward of the duchy of Cornwall in Cornwall, in his capacity as vice-admiral to the duke of Exeter (*C.P.R., 1416–22*, 204). On 26 January 1421 he went surety for John Hals, a justice of assize on the western circuit, when the latter was granted the wardship and marriage of the heir of a John Urban of Southflett (Kent), who was perhaps David's brother (*C.F.R., 1413-22,* 371). He was present at the Cornish elections to the parliaments of 1427 and 1429 P.R.O., C.219, Bundles 13, 14). On 1 February 1434 he was appointed a collector of a parliamentary tenth and fifteenth in Cornwall (*C.F.R., 1430-7* 192). He died before June 1442.

Thomas Urswyk esquire, knight of the shire for Lancashire in May 1421 and 1422, was the younger son of Sir Robert Urswyk who had been a member of Edward III's and his son Edmund of Langley's households and later on a retainer of John of Gaunt (for Sir Robert Urswyk's career see my *The Knights of the Shire for the County Palatine of Lancaster, 1377-1460,* Chetham Society, New Series, Vol. 96, pp. 42-7). Thomas's elder brother, another Sir Robert, who succeeded to the family estates on their father's death in 1402 and who, on his own death in 1420, was followed in their possession by Thomas as his brother and heir, was sheriff of Lancaster from 1415 to 1419. By March 1419 Thomas Urswyk was filling the position of receiver for the duchy of Lancaster properties in Lancashire and Cheshire, but he had more probably taken over this office in 1417, for in March 1442 it was stated in a grant to him of an annuity of £10 for life that he had held the receivership for twenty-five years (*D.K.R.,* XXXIII. 16 ; XL. 536). The fee for the office was the modest allowance of 10 marks a year, but through its occupation the way lay open to other offices in the local duchy administrative services in Lancashire, such as the master forestership of Quernmore which he was holding in 1441 (*V.C.H., Lancashire,* VIII. 75), and to profitable duchy leases. When sitting in his first parliament in May 1421, Thomas secured the transference to himself of his lately-deceased brother's lease of herbage and pasturage rights in Lancashire north of Ribble in the woods of Myerscough and Fulwood and a score of cattle-farms or vaccaries in the duchy forests of Wyresdale and Bleasdale at a yearly rent (now increased by 20 marks) of £84 15s. ; the lease was renewed for twenty years in 1442 (Chetham's Library, Manchester, Piccope Mss., VII. 329). On 24 February 1423 Urswyk's office as duchy receiver was renewed by Henry V's feoffees in the estates under their control (Duchy of Lancaster, Ministers' Accounts, P.R.O., D.L. 29/89/1631) ; in the meantime, while Henry VI's first parliament was still in session, Urswyk was appointed on 10 December 1422 by Thomas Chaucer, Chief Butler of England, to be his deputy-butler at Liverpool, and in May 1429 the area of this commission was extended to include Lancaster and all other ports in Lancashire (*C.P.R., 1422-9,* 8, 537). He served on many royal local commissions and was a j.p. in Lancashire from 1418 onwards. Early in 1443 Sir Thomas (later the first Baron) Stanley succeeded him as duchy receiver in Lancashire and Cheshire ; Urswyk probably died soon after this, for nothing further is known about him (for a fuller account of Urswyk's life see my *Knights of the Shire for Lancashire, op. cit.,* 147-51).

John Vampage esquire, of Pershore and Ruyhall in Ripple, apprentice-at-law, knight of the shire for Worcestershire in 1422, 1426, and 1427. At the time of his first election to parliament in 1422, when his father-in-law (William Wollashull) conducted the hustings as deputy-sheriff, Vampage was escheator in Worcs (he held office, 22 May 1422-1 November 1423) and, by patent of

12 February 1422, he was a justice of the peace and a member of the quorum (W. R. Williams, *Worcs. M.P.s*, 27 ; *W. Salt Arch. Soc. Trans.* [N.S.], VII. 251 ; *C.P.R., 1416-22*, 462 ; Patent Roll, 9 Henry V, P.R.O., C.66, 404, Mem. 19ᵈ ; *List of Escheators* [P.R.O.], 178-9). By 1427 he was connected with Richard Beauchamp earl of Warwick, for whom in that year he acted as attorney and feoffee to uses. He is not to be found in 1439 among the earl's executors, but was a member of a committee of 'patentarii' or feoffees in the Beauchamp estates to the use of the dowager countess and the late earl's executors during the minority of the heir. To this Beauchamp attachment must be ascribed his tenure of the office of deputy-sheriff (the earl of Warwick held the shrievalty in fee) in Worcs for the Exchequer year dating from Michaelmas 1428 (*C.C.R., 1429-35*, 226-7 ; *C.P.R., 1436-41*, 279, 360 ; *1446-52*, 268, 375 ; *List of Sheriffs*, 158). On 15 October 1429 'in pleno parliamento' he was appointed by the King's Council as Attorney-general to the Crown in the Court of Common Pleas and elsewhere, 'quamdiu placuerit'. He sued out his patent on 28 October and administered the office at the customary annual fee of £12 until his death in 1452, in January 1448 being granted the position for life. He chose to remain an apprentice-at-law and secured in February 1442 a patent of exemption for life from being made a serjeant-at-law. After 1445 he was among the 'legis periti' summoned to parliament by individual writs of assistance (*P.P.C.*, IV. 4 ; *C.P.R., 1429-36*, 24 ; *1441-6*, 95 ; *1446-52*, 131 ; Prynne, *Brief Register*, 411). His position as a Crown lawyer will account for his inclusion from November 1443 among Henry VI's feoffees in those parcels of the duchy of Lancaster assigned for the fulfilment of his will, an arrangement ratified in parliament on 6 April 1446 (at this time Vampage was one of eight apprentices-at-law retained as legal counsel by the duchy administration at an annual fee of £2) (*Rot. Parl.*, V. 70, 165 ; *D.L.28. 5. 2*). He was in great demand as a feoffee to uses and sometimes found municipal employment as legal counsel. His son was escheator for Worcs in 1440-1 and three years later he was himself under-sheriff. He died at the end of June 1452, his will being proved in the Prerogative Court of Canterbury on 22 September (Somerset House, *Register Rous*, fo. 17). He had provided for his burial in the Benedictine abbey of Pershore, but in fact he was buried at Minster Lovell (Oxon).

Sir Richard Vernon, knight of the shire for Staffordshire in 1419 and for Derbyshire in 1422, 1426 (Speaker), and 1433, was born in 1390, the son of Sir Richard Vernon and Joan, daughter of Rees ap Griffith of Wichnor. The family resided at their manors of Haddon (Derbyshire) and Harleston (Staffs), but held other estates of the duchy of Lancaster. The wardship of these duchy estates and the manors of Marple and Wibersley and the forestership of Maccles-field (Cheshire), together with Richard's marriage, fell to an important Lancastrian supporter after his father Sir Richard Vernon's death in 1401, namely, to Roger Leche esquire, who soon after Henry V's accession was to become chief steward of the duchy estates north of Trent and by May 1416 chamberlain of the duchy. By the death in 1409 of his great-uncle, Sir Fulk de Pembridge, young Vernon became heir to estates in Tong (Shropshire) and Sheriff Hales and Kibbleston (Staffs), and in 1411 he came of age and sued out livery of his inheritances. He married Benedicta, daughter of Sir John de Ludlow of Stokesay and Hodnet (Shropshire) (*Feudal Aids*, VI. 592-4 ; *Hist. Mss. Comm., Report, Rutland Mss.*,

IV. 28 ; *William Salt Arch. Soc. Procs., Parliamentary History of Staffordshire*, I. 191 ; J. P. Earwaker, *East Cheshire*, II. 50–1 ; Duchy of Lancaster, Accounts Various, P.R.O., D.L.28/4/2). On 1 July 1416 Vernon took out letters of protection as retained by the king to serve overseas, but, if indeed he proceeded, he was soon back, for in November 1416 he was appointed sheriff of Staffordshire. At the end of his year of office he became a j.p. in the same county and served until February 1422 (*D.K.R.*, XLIV. 581 ; *List of Sheriffs*, 127 ; *C.P.R., 1416–22*, 459). He was to be first appointed to the commission of the peace in Derbyshire on 7 July 1423 and was to be j.p. there, apart from a gap between 1432 and 1437, until his death in 1451 ; he was again j.p. in Staffordshire from March 1430 until 1432. He was to be sheriff of Nottinghamshire and Derbyshire in 1424–5 and of Staffordshire again in 1427–8, and all his life he was active as a member of royal commissions of shorter duration in the shires where lay the bulk of his estates (*C.P.R., passim*). On the third occasion of his election to parliament, at Leicester in February 1426, Vernon was chosen Speaker for the Commons. The quarrel between the Protector, the duke of Gloucester, and his uncle the Chancellor, Bishop Beaufort of Winchester, was at its most critical stage, and during the first of the two sessions Beaufort resigned the great seal. The widow of Vernon's great-uncle, Sir Fulk de Pembridge, in 1410 had founded a chantry at Tong in which prayers were to be said for the good estate of (among others) Thomas Beaufort later duke of Exeter and in June 1414, by which time the patronage of the college had been conveyed to Vernon, the bishop of Winchester's name had been added to the list of beneficiaries (Dugdale, *Monasticon*, Vol. VI ; Part III, p. 1402 ; *C.P.R., 1408–13*, 280). Whether Vernon kept up with any intimacy this Beaufort connexion is not known, but that he was likely to have been at variance with Gloucester's interests it seems reasonable to assume from the fact that he was dropped from the commission of the peace in Derbyshire and Staffordshire in 1432 when Gloucester temporarily seized control of government. But Vernon's aristocratic connexions had in the course of time multiplied. From, at the latest, April 1430 he was in close touch with Humphrey earl of Stafford who made him one of his feoffees, and his appointment a year later as a royal justice in South Wales (Vernon was lord of the manor of Stackpole Elidor near Pembroke) during the absence from England of James Lord Dudley, chief justice in South Wales but a Staffordshire magnate, was doubtless due to some existing tie between the two men (*C.C.R., 1429–35*, 357 ; *C.P.R., 1429–36*, 116). In December 1439 he was appointed steward of the duke of Norfolk's Derbyshire estates, and sometime before November 1448 this connexion secured him a three years' occupation of the office of steward of the Earl Marshal's Court of Chivalry (*Hist. Mss. Comm. Report, Rutland Mss.*, IV. 29 ; F. Devon, *Issues of the Exchequer*, 463). In the meantime, he had engrossed some duchy of Lancaster local administrative offices in the neighbourhood of his Derbyshire estates, the stewardship of the lordship of the Peak and the farm of the forest of Champayn ; he was holding the bailiwick of the Peak in 1438 and his extortions were the subject of complaint to the duchy council about the year 1440 (*Rutland Mss., op. cit.*, I. 1 ; Duchy of Lancaster, Accounts Various, P.R.O., D.L.28/5/2). His appointment in May 1445 as treasurer of Calais and in September 1446 as joint-warden of the Calais mint, Vernon probably owed to Humphrey Stafford, recently created duke of Buckingham, who was captain of the town and lieutenant of the march of Calais (*D.K.R.*, XLVIII. 365–6, 371, 381 ; *C.P.R.*, *1446–52*, 4, 411, 460).

He seems to have given his Calais offices some personal if intermittent attention, but he certainly found his letters of protection useful in these years, especially when he became heavily involved in litigation over the Pembridge estates with Sir William Trussell from June 1448 onwards (*William Salt Society Transactions*, N.S., III. 188 *et seq.*, 200). Vernon did not long survive his resignation of the treasurership of Calais in May 1451 (his son William succeeded him), because a month later a younger son, John, was granted the offices in South Wales which his father had been granted for life by patent of 2 June 1450 : the sheriffdom of Pembrokeshire, the constableship of the castles of Pembroke and Tenby, the master-forestership of Coydrath, and the stewardship of certain royal lordships (*C.P.R.*, *1446–52*, 337, 460). The Derbyshire alabaster effigy over Vernon's tomb in the collegiate church of Tong bears the S.S. collar of the Lancastrian livery (*Shropshire A. and N.H. Soc. Transactions*, V. 329). (For Sir Richard Vernon's sons : William, knight of the shire for Derbyshire in 1442, November 1449, 1450, and 1467, and for Staffordshire in 1455 ; and Fulk, knight of the shire for Derbyshire in 1439 ; see Wedgwood, *History of Parliament, Biographies*, 907–8. His eldest son, Richard, who predeceased his father, had sat for Derbyshire in 1432.)

Robert Vessy, m.p. for Exeter in March 1416, and 1422 (*C.P.R.*, *1408–13*, 438 ; *1416–22*, 300 ; *1429–36*, 478). In 1415–16 and 1418–19 he was one of the four bailiffs of Exeter ; in 1421–2, senior bailiff ; in 1425–6, mayor (R. and S. Izacke, *Remarkable Antiquities of the city of Exeter* [1724], 70, 73–4 ; *Devon Association Trans.*, LX. 205). He was one of the two constables of the Exeter staple November 1419–20, 1 December 1421–26 November 1422, and November 1423–4, and was mayor of the Exeter staple December 1426–November 1427 and November 1429–October 1430 (*Supplementary Patent Rolls*, P.R.O., C.67. 24–5). From 14 November 1423 he was joint-collector of customs and subsidies at Exeter and Dartmouth (*C.F.R.*, *1422–30*, 53, 54, 60, 90, 91, 95, 108, 152, 196–8, 200). He was dead by November 1435.

Robert Walsh, ' gentleman ' of Lincoln, m.p. for Lincoln in 1417, December 1421, 1422, 1425, 1426, 1427, 1429, 1431, 1433, and 1435, may have been the —— Walsh senior admitted to Lincoln's Inn prior to 1420 (*Admission Book, op. cit.*). In 1427 he was appointed keeper of the lesser piece of the royal seal for the statutory recognisances of debts at Lincoln, a Council appointment (*C.P.R.*, *1422–9*, 444), and in 1435–6 he was a j.p. in the parts of Kesteven (*ibid.*, *1429–36*, 620). He had attested the shire elections in 1425 and 1426 (P.R.O., C.219/13).

John Warfeld, m.p. for Wallingford in December 1421, 1422, 1427, 1429, 1431, 1432, 1433, 1435, and 1437, was receiver and steward of the estates of Thomas Stonore and later of his feoffees, of whom he was one, between 1415 and 1443 (*Stonore Letters*, Camden Series, XXIX. 29, 31, 36, xxii ; XXX. 179–80). He was present expressly as coroner in Berks at the shire elections to the parliaments of 1432, 1433, and 1435 (P.R.O., C.219, Bundle 14. 3, 4, 5).

Sir Thomas Waweton, knight of the shire for Huntingdonshire in

January and September 1397, 1401, 1402, November 1414, 1420, and 1422 ; and for Bedfordshire in 1413, April 1414, 1419, 1425 (Speaker), and 1432. He was the son of John Waweton of Great Staughton (Huntingdonshire) who served as knight of the shire in eleven parliaments between 1365 and 1395. As a result of the re-marriage (in 1369) of his grandmother to John Baron Tiptoft, by whom she had issue, Sir Thomas Waweton enjoyed the kinship of Sir John (later Lord) Tiptoft who was treasurer of Henry IV's Household, and then Treasurer of England (1408–9), who became steward of Aquitaine and later president of the Exchequer of Normandy as well in Henry V's reign, and was a member of the royal Council and steward of the Household to Henry VI. There are numerous signs that Waweton's career was influenced by that of his distinguished cousin (*D.N.B.*, *sub.* Sir John Tiptoft). He was one of his feoffees to uses in some of Tiptoft's Cambridgeshire estates (*C.C.R.*, *1422–29*, 70–1 ; *Feudal Aids*, I. 178) and the Commons may well have been influenced in their choice of Waweton in 1425 as their Speaker by his connexion with Tiptoft and his attachment to Edmund the late earl of March, who had died in Ireland in the same year. This latter attachment may have been brought about through Tiptoft who was the late earl's brother-in-law and had recently been granted the chief stewardship of all the Mortimer· estates in Wales and the Marches that were then in the king's hands by reason of the minority of Richard duke of York, the Mortimer heir. How long Waweton had been retained by the late earl is not known, nor in what capacity, but at the earl's death he enjoyed an annuity for life of 40 marks charged on the Mortimer manor of Ryhall (Rutland), which passed into the possession of the dowager countess, who re-married herself to John earl of Huntingdon, Tiptoft's cousin by marriage, and which, on her death in 1432, reverted to Tiptoft and his wife (*Rot. Parl.*, V. 399b ; *C.C.R.*, *1422–9*, 222 ; *V.C.H.*, *Rutland*, II. 270). The Commons of 1425 successfully petitioned on behalf of the dowager countess of March to secure favourable terms for her in the settlement of her dower. Waweton's election as Speaker took place in his eleventh parliament. He had previously served various offices in the counties from which he had been returned : from 3 December 1395 to 17 February 1397 he had acted as royal alnager of cloth in Beds ; for two years from February 1405 he was a member of the commission of the peace in Hunts ; in 1415–16 he was Sheriff of Beds and Bucks and again in 1422–3, at which time he was also a j.p. in Beds, his first appointment dating from February 1422. He was dropped from the commission of the peace early in Henry VI's reign and not reappointed until January 1435, but in the meantime had again served as sheriff of Beds and Bucks in 1428–9, a year in which there were disturbances in both counties. Waweton himself contributed to disaffection in Bucks by his irregular acts at the elections for this shire to the parliament of 1429 (he was also party to the disputed election in Huntingdonshire ; *vide supra*, pp. 17–20). He was again sheriff in 1432–3 (*C.F.R.*, *1391–9*, 166, 193 ; *C.P.R.*, *1401–5*, 517 ; *1405–8*, 492 ; *1416–22*, 449 ; *1429–36*, 39, 41, 578 ; *P.R.O.*, *C.219*. XIV. 1 ; *List of Sheriffs*, 2). He had frequently contravened the electoral statute of 1413 providing for the residence of knights of the shire and their electors by being elected in one shire and acting as an elector in another, or by conducting elections as sheriff in the shires of his bailiwick and assisting at elections outside it (*vide supra*, p. 21). As j.p., Waweton was closely involved in the riots at the sessions of the peace in Beds, in the early summer of

1437 and again in January 1439, between the factions of Reginald Lord Grey of Ruthin and John Lord Fanhope, Waweton actively adhering to the former ; on the second occasion he was suspended from the commission of the peace and not restored until November 1443, after which he continued to serve down to June 1448 (*P.P.C.*, IV. 35, 58 ; *C.P.R.*, *1436–41*, 246, 282). He died some time after 1450, his second wife Alana, daughter of Sir Simon Felbrigge K.G. and widow of Sir William Tyndale of Dean (Northants), whom he had probably married in 1427, surviving him until 1458 (Bridges, *History of Northants*, II. 338). His first wife, Maud (parentage unknown), was still alive in September 1422 when they were granted a papal indult to have a portable altar (*Cal. of Papal Registers, Papal Letters*, VII. 324).

Sir Thomas Wenlock, knight of the shire for Bedfordshire in 1422, 1423, 1425, and 1426, as a member of the retinue of Sir John Cornwall served in the first expedition of Henry V to Normandy in 1415 and fought at Agincourt where he took four prisoners. He seems to have been engaged in military service in France for the greater part of the rest of the reign, returning to England in February 1421 with Cornwall when the latter accompanied Henry V on his last visit to England, but going back to France, again with Cornwall, later in the spring of the same year (N. H. Nicolas, *Agincourt*, 361 ; App., 61 ; *D.K.R.*, XLIV. 385, 615, 628), only to return and apparently for good immediately after Henry V's death in 1422. It is clear that Wenlock's attachment to Cornwall, who was a remote kinsman of the ducal house of Brittany but closely related to the Lancastrian royal house by his marriage to Henry IV's sister, Elizabeth, dowager countess of Huntingdon, went back in time beyond his participation in these military enterprises and was due to other than a purely military contract between them : on 16 July 1413, while still an esquire, he had mainperned Cornwall and his wife, the dowager countess, in an Exchequer grant of royal revenues from certain alien priory estates ; when in England in 1421 he stood surety for Cornwall in a grant of the wardship of certain of the Fitz Alan estates during the minority of the heir of John Lord Arundel, and again in December 1423 when the death of one of the sisters and coheirs of Thomas earl of Arundel brought more Fitz Alan property into Crown control by royal rights of wardship (*C.P.R.*, *1413–16*, 101 ; *C.F.R.*, *1413–22*, 420 ; *1422–30*, 63). The first to attest the indenture of return at Wenlock's election for Beds to Henry VI's first parliament was Sir John Cornwall ; three feoffees of Cornwall also sealed the indenture (P.R.O., C.219. 13. 1). In spite of the Cornwall connexion, Wenlock served on no royal commissions and next to nothing is known of his activities in Henry VI's reign beyond the facts of his return to parliament as knight of the shire and the approximate date of his death shortly before 20 June 1429, when the writ of *diem clausit extremum* was issued to the royal escheator in Bedfordshire (*C.F.R.*, *1422–30*, 237).

Robert de Whelpyngton, m.p. for Newcastle-on-Tyne in 1413, November 1414, 1422, and 1423, was employed as legal counsel by that borough (R. Welford, *Newcastle and Gateshead in the 14th and 15th centuries*, 246 ; *Archaeologia Aeliana*, III. 32), and he was sheriff of Newcastle in 1420–1 and mayor in 1435–6 and 1438–9 (J. Brand, *History and Antiquities of Newcastle-on-Tyne* [1789], II. 424).

On 10 November 1418 he had been appointed by the Crown as controller of customs and subsidies at Newcastle (*C.P.R., 1416–22,* 174). He was a j.p. in Northumberland from July 1424 to 1447 and from September 1431 onwards was a j.p. and justice of gaol delivery in the Durham palatine franchises of Norham-shire and Islandshire in Northumberland. Between 1426 and 1434 he was steward of the liberty of the priory of Tynemouth, a cell of the abbey of St. Albans (E. Bateson, *History of Northumberland,* VIII. 215).

Robert Whitgreve, m.p. for Stafford in 1411, March 1416, 1420, May and December 1421, 1422, 1423, 1425, 1426, 1427, 1429, 1431, 1432, 1433, 1435, 1437, and 1442, and knight of the shire in 1445 and November 1449, was feoffee to uses by 1426, and otherwise closely attached, to Humphrey earl of Stafford, who came of age in 1424 and then became a member of the royal Council, and who was created duke of Buckingham in 1444 (Wedgwood, *History of Parliament, Biographies, sub nomine* ; *C.P.R., 1446–52,* 78 ; *Hist. Mss. Comm., 4th Report,* 328b ; *C.C.R., 1422–9,* 318, 326). On 18 July 1415 (not in 1428, as Wedgwood) Whitgreve was appointed one of the four tellers of the Exchequer of Receipt, being confirmed for life by patent on 24 November 1445 ; in this capacity he had been at times one of the principal Exchequer agents in transporting cash to Normandy and France to Henry V's Keeper of the Wardrobe, *ex officio* Treasurer of the Wars, or to the King's Chamber, in 1418, 1419, 1422, and again occasionally in Henry VI's reign (*P.P.C.,* IV. 112, 266 ; *C.P.R., 1441–6,* 335, 415 ; Exchequer, Issue Rolls, P.R.O., E.403. 622 [Michs., 3. HV] Mem. 7 ; *ibid.,* 636 [Trinity 6. HV], Mem. 15 ; *ibid.,* 655 [Easter 10. HV], Mems. 1, 2, 7, 13, 15 ; *ibid.,* 658 [Michs., 1. HVI], Mem. 5).

John Whithorne, m.p. for Wilton in November 1414, 1415, 1417, 1419, 1420, May and December 1421, 1422, 1423, 1425, and 1433, was on 20 February 1424 ordered to be replaced as coroner in Wilts as insufficiently qualified but was still in office four years later when the order was repeated (*C.C.R., 1422–9,* 96, 362). At the time of the death of John, duke of Bedford, in 1435, Whithorne was his receiver of rents in Wilts, Hants, Somerset and Dorset, and was retained by the Exchequer in that office (*C.P.R., 1429–36,* 507). Later he fell foul of Humphrey, duke of Gloucester, who claimed him as his villein and imprisoned him at Pembroke for seven years until the duke's death in 1447 (*Rot. Parl.,* V. 448a).

Sir Robert Whitney of Whitney, knight of the shire for Herefordshire in March 1416 and 1422, was the son of Sir Robert Whitney, knight of the shire in 1377, 1379, January 1380, and 1391, sheriff of the county in 1377–8, a retainer of Richard II from 1393 with a fee of 40 marks, and herberger to the royal House-hold during Richard's Irish expeditions of 1394–5 and 1399 (*C.P.R., 1391–6,* 320, 450–1 ; *1396–9,* 480–1 ; *1399–1401,* 54). The father's annuity was confirmed by Henry IV within a month of his accession and he and his brother and others of their kin fell fighting in the Lancastrian service at Pilleth in Radnorshire on 22 June 1402, when Sir Edmund Mortimer, uncle of Edmund the young earl of March, fell into the hands of Owen Glendower. Robert Whitney the son, in consideration of his family's losses and the wasting of his estates by the Welsh rebels, was granted on 14 February 1404 the nearby Mortimer castle and lordship of Clifford and the lordship of Glasbury, nominally worth 100 marks a year, with the right to all the escheated lands of rebels there ; the grant was made as from 15 October 1403 and was to hold good until the heir, the earl of March, came of age ; surplus profits were to be accounted for at the Exchequer (*ibid.*, *1401-5*, 354). What aristocratic connexions Whitney formed and cultivated are not clearly discernible, but immediately after his first appointment as sheriff of Herefordshire in November 1413 he was one of those who found surety that John Talbot Lord Furnival would keep the peace following his open quarrel with Thomas, earl of Arundel, then Treasurer, over certain rights of common in Shropshire (*C.C.R.*, *1413-19*, 97-9). Whitney was again to be sheriff in 1427-8, 1432-3, and 1436-7 ; he was also royal escheator in Herefordshire and the appurtenant march in 1430-1 ; and from July 1423 to October 1432 he was a j.p. in the county. That Whitney himself kept clear of the Lollard infection to which his county and immediate neighbourhood were early in the century especially subject (Sir John Oldcastle was a near-neighbour to Whitney at Almeley) seems fairly certain, but he had connexions with those who actively sympathised with the new doctrines ; with John ap Harry, for instance, knight of the shire for Herefordshire from 1406 to 1410, for whom he was mainpernor in July 1417 that he would lend no support to Oldcastle (*ibid.*, 434). In the early part of his life Whitney may well have seen much military service on the Welsh border in the course of the suppression of Glendower's rising, but his participation in the revived French war under Henry V was very short-lived. As late as October 1419 he had not served in Normandy ; in 1420 he did, however, apparently spend some time across the Channel and on 6 December 1420 was appointed captain of Vire in the Côtentin ; he must have returned with Henry V in February 1421, for he was present at the coronation of Catherine of Valois, receiving a livery from the royal Wardrobe for the ceremony (*D.K.R.*, XLII. 382 ; Wardrobe Accounts, 8 Henry V). He remained in England. He was not again elected to parliament after 1422, but he was the first to seal the indenture of return at the Herefordshire elections of 1425, 1426, 1427, and 1431, and, as sheriff, he of course conducted the elections of 1433 and 1437 (P.R.O., C.219, Bundles 12, 13).

Edmund Winter esquire, knight of the shire for Norfolk in 1420, December 1421, 1422, 1427, 1429, and 1437, was the son of John Winter, some time steward of the duchy of Cornwall estates in Cornwall (superseded in February 1402) and later duchy of Lancaster steward in Norfolk, deputy-butler at Yarmouth and Cromer, j.p. in Norfolk, and knight of the shire for Norfolk in 1401, January 1404, 1407, 1410, and 1411. Edmund at the time of his father's last return to parliament was royal escheator in Norfolk and Suffolk, holding office from November 1410 to December 1411 ; he again served this office in 1417-18, and in the following year, 1418-19, was sheriff of the joint bailiwick of the two counties. He served on numerous casual royal commissions in East Anglia but was not made j.p. in even his own county of Norfolk until 1 March 1422 and then served only until the summer of 1423. At the time of his election to parliament in 1422 he was for a third term occupying the escheatorship of Norfolk and Suffolk, acting from May 1422 to November 1423 (P.R.O., *List of Escheators*, 16 ; *List of Sheriffs*, 87). Winter was well-connected by marriage and in other ways. His first marriage with Olive, daughter and coheir of Sir William

Hampton, brought him property in Herefordshire and Norfolk and kinship with Robert Scot, lieutenant-constable of the Tower to the earl of Huntingdon, m.p. for Huntingdonshire in 1401, 1402, 1404, 1411, 1419, and 1425, and for Bedfordshire in 1420, sheriff of Cambridgeshire and Huntingdonshire in 1405–6, 1411–12, 1416–17, and 1420–3 (May), and escheator in these counties in 1404–5 and 1409–10 (Scot married Winter's wife's sister). Winter's second wife Alice (née Furneux) was the widow of John Wodehouse of Kimberley (Norfolk), a former chancellor of the duchy of Lancaster, executor to Henry V and, down to his death in January 1431, royal chamberlain of the Exchequer. One of Winter's daughters by his first marriage married John Heydon, apprentice-at-law and counsel to the duchy of Lancaster, and later deputy-steward of the Lancastrian estates north of Trent, and some time recorder of Norwich. Winter's brother-in-law, Ralph Lampet of Stody (Norfolk), became the earl of Huntingdon's lieutenant-admiral in 1429 and in 1436 his lieutenant-constable of the Tower (Blomefield, *op. cit.*, VI. 505 ; VIII. 98 ; IX. 368 ; J. C. Wedgwood, *History of Parliament, Biographies*, 524). The two latter were among Winter's executors when he made his will on 20 February 1449. He died before 2 March when probate was granted (Blomefield, *op. cit.*, VIII. 98). Almost twenty years before, on 12 May 1429, Winter had been himself appointed to occupy a similar position of trust when the duke of Norfolk drew up his last testament (Jacob, *Chichele Register*, II. 474). How long this Mowbray connexion had been then in being is not known, but it must be remembered that the Winter family were mesne tenants of the Mowbrays in the old Bigod manor of Town Barningham Winter, their principal manor (Blomefield, *op. cit.*, VIII. 97–8). This was not Winter's sole aristocratic attachment : he was one of the feoffees of Thomas Lord Morley (ob. Sept. 1416), whose grandson and heir married a daughter of Michael de la Pole, second earl of Suffolk (*C.P.R., 1416–22*, 53, 265 ; *C.C.R., 1422–9*, 289 ; *1435–41*, 435).

John Wodehouse esquire was knight of the shire for Norfolk in 1410, November 1414, March 1416, 1417, and May 1421 ; and for Suffolk in 1422. Early in the reign of Henry IV, Wodehouse was attached to the service of Prince Henry of Monmouth (later Henry V) as constable of his castle of Rising (near Bishop's Lynn) and keeper of the chace there (a patent for life of 26 August 1402 allowed him 5 pence a day). In February 1403 he was made steward of the lordship of Rising, also for life, and his fees were increased by £12. (In April 1403 he received a grant of 20 marks a year in lieu.) He seems to have been of the prince of Wales's immediate personal entourage but was also already interested in the administration of the duchy of Lancaster, enjoying in 1399 an annuity of 2 marks, increased in 1405 by another 20 marks charged on the Lancastrian honour of Pontefract (Duchy of Lancaster, Accounts Various, P.R.O., D.L.28, 4, Nos. 1–4 ; *C.P.R., 1422–9*, 15, 68 ; *1429–36*, 121 ; *P.P.C.*, I. 207). On 4 April 1413 he was appointed chancellor of the duchy of Lancaster ; by 1414 he was duchy steward in Norfolk and Cambridgeshire ; by Michaelmas 1418 he held this office in Norfolk and Suffolk, but whether still in Cambs I do not know (W. R. Williams, *Duchy of Lancaster Official Lists*, 2 ; D.L.28, 4, No. 8 ; *ibid.*, 27, No. 8). In July 1413 he purchased the estates of the alien priory of Panfield (Essex), a daughter house of the Norman abbey of St. Stephen of Caen, including its cell at Well Hall near Lynn. From December 1414 to November 1423, and from July 1424 to his death, he was a j.p. in Norfolk. On 6 July 1415 he was appointed king's chamberlain in the Exchequer for life at 8 pence a day (*C.P.R., 1413–16, 52, 57, 301, 336, 340, 365, 421*). In July 1415 he was made one of the feoffees of a parcel of the duchy of Lancaster estates for the fulfilment of Henry V's will, of which he was an executor (*ibid., 1413–16, 356–7, 408 ; 1416–22, 172*). He served on Crown loan-raising commissions and commissions of array, etc., in East Anglia in these years. By 1422 he was occupying the office of steward of the liberty of the abbey of St. Edmund of Bury (P.R.O., L.T.R., Memoranda Roll, 1 Henry VI, P.R.O., E.368/195). Between December 1422 and February 1423 he was acting as executor to William Kynwolmersh, late Treasurer of England (Jacob, *Chichele Register*, II. 236). In October 1423 he acted as parliamentary proxy of the abbot of Bury St. Edmunds (P.R.O., S.C.10, No. 2347). In June 1424 he resigned the chancellorship of the duchy of Lancaster but retained his other offices, including that of chamberlain of the Exchequer, until his death which occurred on 27 January 1431 at his manor of Roydon. He was buried in the under-chapel of the cathedral church of Norwich where he had founded a chantry in which prayers were to be said for Henry V and Queen Catherine of Valois to whom Wodehouse had acted as chancellor (just when and for how long is not known). The cantarist was endowed with the rectory of Gayton, formerly parcel of the alien priory of Panfield ; the patronage was to be vested in the royal chamberlain of the Exchequer, with devolution to the Treasurer (*C.P.R., 1416–22, 376* ; P.R.O., D.L.28/5/8). Wodehouse had come to possess twelve manors in Norfolk, four in Suffolk, two in Cambridgeshire. His will shows a great interest in wool growing, for he possessed at his death 2,000 ewes alone. Sir William Estfeld, London merchant-stapler, was one of his friends and executors. The will was proved at Lambeth in the Prerogative Court of Canterbury on 2 March 1431 ; the overseers appointed by Wodehouse were Bishop Alnwick of Norwich (keeper of the Privy Seal), the Lords Hungerford and Cromwell, Nicholas Dixon (under-treasurer and puisne baron of the Exchequer), John Dalton (former deputy-keeper of the Great Wardrobe) and Wodehouse's wife.

William Wood, m.p. for Winchester in 1413, November 1414, 1420, May 1421, 1422, and 1423, was from 1415 to his death in 1431 joint-farmer of the alnage of cloth in Hants (*C.F.R., 1413–22, 110* ; *1422–30, 16*). He had been recorder of Winchester in 1408 (R. R. Sharpe, *Letter Books of the city of London, Letter Book*, I. 70).

Nicholas Wotton of Ramsbury, parliamentary burgess for Marlborough in 1422 only, was parliamentary proxy for the abbot of Malmesbury in December 1421, 1423, 1425, and 1432, as well as in 1422 (*Lincoln's Inn Admission Book*, 3 ; Selden Society, *Year Book 1 Henry VI*, 58–60 ; Placita Coram Rege, Michs., 1 Hen. VI, P.R.O., K.B.27. 646. 86 ; P.R.O., S.C.10, Nos. 2332, 2337, 2355, 2363, 2414).

Sir Thomas Wykeham of Broughton near Banbury, knight of the shire for Oxfordshire in 1402, March 1416, 1422, and 1425, was the great-nephew and heir of Bishop William Wykeham of Winchester, being the eldest of the sons of

William Perrot by the daughter of the bishop's only sister, Agnes (W. H. Williams *Oxfordshire Members of Parliament*, 29 ; Nicholls, *Leicestershire*, IV. 805 ; *Collectanea Topogr. et Geneal.*, II. 225 *et seq.*). The bishop must have taken a special interest in his prospective heir and the office which Thomas held as early as 1383 in Richard II's Household as a servitor of the pantry was doubtless secured by his influence. Both Thomas and his younger brother, William, were ' servientes regis ' in September 1397 (*C.P.R., 1396–9*, 193 ; *1452–61*, 514). The bishop may well have had much to do with Thomas's marriage with Margaret, daughter and coheir of William Willicotes of Chastleton and North Leigh (Oxon), eight times knight of the shire for Oxfordshire between 1385 and 1410, who was at the time of Queen Anne of Bohemia's death, and even at the end of Richard II's reign, the chief steward of her manors and lands (*ibid., 1396–9*, 593). Bishop Wykeham died on 27 September 1404 and as his heir Thomas succeeded to estates said to have been worth £400 a year. These included the north Oxfordshire manor of Broughton, which he proceeded to crenellate by royal licence of 19 March 1406, and ultimately in 1418, when the remainder fell in, the manors of Burnham and Brean on Bridgwater Bay in north Somerset, and probably his Hampshire manors of Deane, Ash, Quidhampton, Church Oakley, and Otterbourne near Winchester. He himself acquired the north Berkshire manor of Appleton, and in 1418 increased his Oxfordshire holding in the Banbury district by purchasing from the widow of Amery Lord St. Amand the manors of Bloxham and Alkerton, a third of Adderbury, and the hundred and frankpledge view of Bloxham (*D.N.B.*, XLIII. 230 ; *C.P.R., 1405–8*, 161 ; *1416–22*, 175 ; *C.C.R., 1413–19*, 272, 422, 508, 510 ; *1435–41*, 175, 375, 450 ; *Feudal Aids*, II. 346 ; IV. 185–6). The administration of Bishop Wykeham's will, with its bequests amounting to between six and seven thousand pounds, along with negotiations for the recovery of the bishop's loans to the Crown—Thomas was one of his executors as well as his heir—must have kept him busy for some time and his new territorial position in north Oxfordshire was, moreover, acknowledged when on 27 January 1405 he was appointed for the first time a j.p. in the county. He was to serve the commission of the peace until March 1410, from February 1412 until November 1413, and then from April 1418 until his death in 1443 (*C.P.R., passim*). As to what were Wykeham's most influential connexions it is only possible to offer conjectures, but he may well have been attached to Henry Beaufort, his great-uncle's successor in the see of Winchester : on 15 October 1408, as being about to proceed overseas, he took out royal letters authorising his appointment of general attorneys, his intention probably being to accompany the royal embassy charged with conveying to Pope Gregory XII the news that if he did not sincerely promote the settlement of the papal schism the payment of papal dues from England would be suspended (Beaufort was the leader of the delegation) ; in 1427 Wykeham's eldest son, William, was in the retinue of Beaufort's nephew, Edmund, and in October 1430 was in the cardinal's own retinue (*Carte, Catalogue des Rolles*, II. 196 ; *D.K.R.*, XLVIII. 248, 279). Whatever his connexions Wykeham lacked nothing in influence in the shires where he held the bulk of his property : he was sheriff of Oxfordshire and Berkshire in 1413–14, in 1416–17 of Hampshire, in 1417–18 of Oxfordshire and Berkshire again and also in 1426–7 and 1430–1, and he served on many local royal commissions, apart from that of the peace, especially those appointed for the purpose of raising Crown loans

(*C.P.R., passim*). He died sometime in 1443, probate of his will being granted in the Lincoln consistory court on 9 January 1444 (H. Gibbons, *Early Lincoln Wills*, 173).

Richard Wynnesley (or Winslow) of Winslow, m.p. for Leominster in 1422, 1427, 1432, and 1442, was by December 1420 bailiff of the abbot of Reading's liberty of Leominster and, as such, was thenceforward returning officer for the borough until 1442 (P.R.O., C.219, Bundles 12–15). In May 1421 he had been under-sheriff of Herefordshire (*ibid.*, 12, No. 5). He was almost certainly the Wynslowe in the list of members of Lincoln's Inn in 1420 (*Admission Book, op. cit.*, 2).

Sir John Zouche of Kirklington, knight of the shire for Nottinghamshire in 1407, 1413, 1419, 1422, and 1442, was the second son of William third Baron Zouche of Haringworth who died in 1396, and brother of the William Lord Zouche who was summoned to parliament from 1396 to his death in 1415. He was granted possession of certain family estates in Hampshire, Wiltshire, and Derbyshire worth £58 a year, but his Nottinghamshire holdings, including a knight's fee at Kirklington, came to him through his marriage with Margaret, daughter and coheir of Sir John Burgh of Kirklington and Burgh Green (Cambs), widow of Sir John Lowdham of Lowdham (Notts) (*C.C.R., 1396–9, 404 ; 1402–5, 435 ; C.P.R., 1391–6, 2 ; Feudal Aids, IV. 127, 192 ; VI. 415, 455, 535 ; Blomefield, Norfolk, VII. 126–7 ; Collectanea Topogr. et Geneal., I. 344*). Despite the fact that he had been involved in disorders in the Midlands in 1411 and was with other notables imprisoned for a short time in the Tower (*C.C.R., 1409–13, 243–4, 261*), he was thereafter very frequently employed on many royal commissions of various sorts in Notts and Derbyshire, especially on Crown loan-raising commissions. Although he never served as justice of the peace in either county he was sheriff in both in 1426. He was friendly with Sir Thomas Chaworth (m.p. for Notts in 1406, 1417, 1420, May 1421, 1433, 1437, and 1445, sheriff of Notts and Derby in 1403–4, 1417–18, and 1423–4, and of Lincolnshire in 1408–9 and 1418–19) who was in the Tower early in 1414 seemingly on suspicion of Lollardy, but Zouche himself was doctrinally sound and served on the Lollardy inquiry of 1414 in Notts and Derbyshire after Oldcastle's rebellion. He married his two daughters, Elizabeth and Margaret, into Chaworth's family. At the time of the death of Henry Bowet, archbishop of York, in October 1423, Zouche was his biggest debtor, owing him £266 13s. 4d., according to an inventory drawn up shortly afterwards. When and why this debt was incurred is not known, nor whether Zouche had other relations with this northern primate (*Historians of the Church of York*, ed. J. Raine [Rolls Series], III. 322). In 1423 he had important connexions with William Lord Lovell of Titchmarsh, supporting him in recognisances for 1700 marks, when he used out livery of his estates (*C.C.R., 1422–9, 72, 75*), along with two other fellow-knights of the shire in Henry VI's first parliament (Robert Lovell of Dorset and Henry Mulsho of Northants). How came about this connexion with the young Lord Lovell is not known. Zouche made a first will in October 1433 but amplified its provisions with a later instrument drawn up on 9 September 1445. His bequests included one of a missal and breviary given him by his nephew, Lord Zouche. Sir John died soon after and was buried in Southwell Minster, where his widow was later buried with him (*Hist. Mss. Comm. Report, Mss. of Lord Middleton at Wollaton Hall, Notts*, 112 ; Surtees Soc., Vol. 30, *Test. Ebor.*, II. 153). (Care has been taken not to confuse Sir John Zouche with his nephew's second son, the Sir John Zouche who married Elizabeth, daughter of Richard Lord Grey of Codnor [A. W. Gibbons, *Early Lincoln Wills*, 168 ; Nicholls, *Leicestershire*, II. 372].)

APPENDIX

TABLE OF *PERCENTAGES* ILLUSTRATING CHANGES IN THE CHARACTER OF BOROUGH REPRESENTATION IN THE PERIOD 1422–78

Dates of parliaments examined, for which full lists of burgesses are available.	Percentage of parliamentary burgesses resident in the boroughs returning them.	Percentage of boroughs returning two residents.	Percentage of boroughs returning two ' outsiders '.	Percentage of boroughs returning one ' outsider ' only.	Percentage of boroughs returning at least one resident.	Percentage of boroughs returning one or two outsiders.
1422	77	64	15	21	85	36
1442	58	39	23	39	77	61
1447	53	38	34	29	66	62
Feb. 1449	48	30	36	33	64	70
Nov. 1449	51	40	39	21	61	60
1450	53	36	32	31	68	64
1453	47	35	41	24	59	65
1467	45	32	45	23	55	68
1472	50	40	42	18	58	60
1478	43	30	44	27	56	70

GENERAL INDEX

(The italicised names are those of knights of the shire and parliamentary burgesses of whom there are biographical notes in Part II, and the italicised page references are to these notes.)